Computers
and
Programming

Computers and Programming

A NEOCLASSICAL APPROACH

Peter Olivieri, Ph.D.
Michael W. Rubin, Ph.D.

School of Management
Boston College

McGraw-Hill Book Company

New York   St. Louis   San Francisco   Auckland   Düsseldorf   Johannesburg
Kuala Lumpur   London   Mexico   Montreal   New Delhi   Panama   Paris   São Paulo
Singapore   Sydney   Tokyo   Toronto

Computers and Programming
A NEOCLASSICAL APPROACH

1234567890SGDO798765

Library of Congress Cataloging in Publication Data

Olivieri, Peter.
    Computers and programming.

    1. Electronic digital computers—Programming.
I. Rubin, Michael W., date   II. Title.
QA76.6.043   001.6'42   74-19139
ISBN 0-07-047692-6

This book was set in Caledonia by Black Dot, Inc.
The editors were Kenneth J. Bowman and Matthew Cahill;
the designer was Pencils Portfolio, Inc.;
the production supervisor was Sam Ratkewitch.
The drawings were done by ECL Art Associates, Inc.
The printer was Segerdahl Corporation;
the binder, R. R. Donnelley & Sons Company.

To Amy and Rita

Contents

Preface

PHILOSOPHY

We feel that two of the purposes of education are

1. To improve the thinking processes
2. To provide the tools with which people can be creative and constructive

Being optimists, we think that people want to improve their reasoning abilities, work toward the solutions of meaningful problems, and enjoy life while they are working. Furthermore, we are confident that all of these goals are attainable.

THE APPROACH OF THIS BOOK

This textbook is designed as an introductory text on computers. Frequently in computer courses, the students feel that the text is dry and impersonal. Because of this, we have made an effort to make this particular computer text both interesting and informative. Our approach has been to add a few characters and, hopefully, a bit of humor to a traditionally difficult-to-read subject. With no sacrifice to rigorous treatment of the material, this approach should make learning a more enjoyable and lasting experience for the reader. Do not misunderstand us. We think that using the computer is, in itself, interesting, challenging, and rewarding. With the computer, a person can solve difficult problems, gain insight into complex situations, and expedite many projects. You might ask, "Then why the characters and the informality of the approach?" We feel that serious education and an informal approach are not incompatible; on the contrary, they are supportive. We enjoyed writing this book, and we hope readers will enjoy it also.

COVERAGE AND EMPHASIS

The contents of the book are designed to present methods of problem solving, languages for communicating with the computers, and information on how computers operate. The approach in each of these topical areas has been to present ideas and tools that can be used to solve problems and design systems.

The text begins with an introduction to computers using "a visit to the computer center" as a vehicle for getting the student involved almost immediately. In Chapter 2, sections are devoted to algorithms and their design, that is, how one approaches and sets up a problem for solution. The concepts presented here are general and can be applied to problem solving even beyond their direct application in computers. Following this presentation, formal languages are presented in the next two chapters. Chapter 3 is a FORTRAN manual complete with most of the advanced topics in FORTRAN. Chapter 4 uses the computer in the time sharing mode and provides a thorough manual for the BASIC programming language. These languages, FORTRAN and BASIC, are the languages most widely used in academia.

Chapter 5 follows with a discussion of the internal organization of the computer. A machine language and an assembly language are introduced to illustrate how the machine actually deals with information. The discussion then relates these languages to the internal representation of data in computers.

File preparation and maintenance, a topic of critical importance in advanced computer applications, is treated in Chapter 6. Tape systems and disk systems are compared and contrasted.

The philosophy of the book has been maintained in Chapter 7, a presentation of several representative computer applications. Here the emphasis is, as always, on understanding the system so that the ideas may be adapted for use in systems the reader may design.

The implications of computer technology in the future, a topic that is important to each of us, is discussed by the characters of the book in Chapter 8. How they had so much information "at their fingertips" during an impromptu discussion is still a mystery to us.

The appendixes provide auxiliary material. They include sections on using the keypunch and a section on the history of computers, a topic frequently encountered in Chapter 1 of many textbooks. Because this section, while interesting, is not used in problem solving, it is not included as a chapter in this book.

A NOTE TO THE STUDENT

Despite the informal presentation, you will be exposed to both subtle and direct learning experiences that will provide the knowledge and skills necessary to use computers successfully. The exercises at the end of a section have been carefully designed to be both challenging and entertaining. The material in this book is likely to be new to you, possibly quite different from your previous courses. It is important that you not be like the butcher who backed into a meat grinder. Don't get behind in your work.

If you haven't covered all chapters of the book by the time your course is over, you can probably finish the text on your own (if only to pick up some new material for parties).

A NOTE TO THE TEACHER

The chapters of this book have been written to allow you flexibility in the scheduling of your course. Chapters 1 and 2 are preparatory and should be covered first. Then, however, you may choose any of the next three chapters to cover next. Furthermore, the book has been designed so that you may cover either or both of the higher-level languages, FORTRAN and BASIC. The chapter on tapes, disks, and files is for more advanced programming. The material in Chapter 7 is illustrative, and Chapter 8 usually provides excellent class discussion.

ACKNOWLEDGMENTS

There is an old saying about those many individuals who give of their time and effort to help in the preparation of a text such as this one. But it is so old that we've forgotten it.

Anyway, we'd like to thank our editor, Ken Bowman, for his support and confidence in this new venture.

Our thanks to Joanne McNally, Denise O'Hare, Anne O'Reilly, and Stephanie O'Leary for their help in typing and proofreading the manuscript. Kevin O'Connor, Tony Sukiennik, and Dee Laputka spent many hours verifying computer programs for us and we are grateful for their efforts.

We would like to thank IBM, Honeywell, and Digital Equipment Corporation for their generous supply of excellent photographs.

We are grateful for the critiques of both Jack and Jane Neuhauser during the preparation of the text and to our wonderful families for the encouragement and support they provided during our endless work schedules.

Certainly, most importantly, we would like to give our accolades and very sincere thanks to our departmental administrative assistant, Linda Gray, who worked hard and long typing and retyping the manuscript. Without her pleasant, cheerful, and skillful talents, we'd still be getting there.

Peter Olivieri
Michael W. Rubin

Computers
and
Programming

chapter
1

Introduction
to
the
computer
facility

In this chapter the main character of the text enrolls in a computer course and takes a tour of a typical computer center. Here, he becomes familiar with the different machines that are found there and begins to acquaint himself with the terminology that is part of the computer world. The last section presents the concept of communication with computers through programming languages.

1.1 HOW WE GETTING THERE?

Picture, if you will, one of the characters of our little novel. He is 18 years of age, with brown hair, brown eyes, and a 160-pound frame towering 5 feet $10\frac{1}{4}$ inches into the air. Our hero has the label Howard Gettindere (Howie to his friends—both of them). Howie attends the University of Greater Haste (UGH) and is a freshman again. His philosophy is somewhere to the left of whoopee!

On one particularly pleasant Tuesday sometime ago, Howie arose and called to find out what the weather for the day was to be. While trying to edge a proposition into the recorded announcement, Howie suddenly realized how strange it was to use one machine to call another machine. Upon reflection, he began to realize the subtle influence that machines have upon his everyday life.

He has often used the telephone directory (organized and printed by computer) to find the telephone numbers for college tutors. He has dated girls selected for him by computer (these were obviously "first-generation" computers with some minor bugs). He has driven his car on (and off) highways designed by computer, received a computer-processed paycheck, phone bill, electric bill, and pill bill! He has flown home to Feeling, Ill., to visit the folks after being scheduled on an airline by computer. Some of his textbooks (he thinks) have indexes prepared by computer. He is scheduled into classes by machine. (Sure, he remembers quite well the time the biology class met in the girls' gym! Computers aren't all bad.)

After much reflection, Howie said to himself, "Self! It probably is a good idea to get to know a little bit more about these here machines. First, they exist and certainly have an effect on me; second, maybe I can use them in my work; and third, I have always wanted to find out if folding, spindling, and mutilating really works."

This realization was a tremendous breakthrough for Howie, since the last quantitative course he took was English literature. (Howie considered that to be quantitative because he had to keep track of the page numbers.) Howie had such a mental block against numbers that he had to have his dormitory room number sewn on the inside of his coat!

The point was made. Howie decided to get himself enrolled in a computer course. His first step was to visit the offices of the computer science department at UGH and inquire about the introductory courses they offered. He soon discovered that there were a variety of courses available and that he should enroll in one that would give him an appreciation of what the computer can and cannot do, as well as a skill in a programming language. He signed up for the appropriate course and decided to wander over to the computer center and "make like a computer science major."

1.2 THE COMPUTER ROOM

While Howie was wandering around the lobby immediately adjacent to the computer room, he couldn't help but wonder at the machines behind those plate-glass windows. In fact, the windows reminded him of a maternity ward and he wondered if machines could ever reproduce themselves.

"Yes Sir," the doctor would say, "you're the proud father of a 50-pound minicomputer. Yes, he has his mother's tapes but that is clearly his father's line printer!" Ugh!

Howie chuckled. It sure was busy in a computer center. He knew that the students who were running around with decks of computer cards called themselves programmers because programming was what you did when you wanted to get the computer to do something for you.

Anyway, these "programmers" would come in with a couple of sheets of paper containing a variety of henscratchings and sit down at a machine that was much like a typewriter and type what was on their scratch sheets. The typewriter, Howie would later discover, was really a keypunch machine and punched holes in cards rather than letters on paper.

When typing was finished, the programmer would have a deck of computer cards ready to be loaded into the computer. The next step would be to fill out a card which evidently told the computer operator something and then hand the completed deck through a window to a person in the machine room. You would then be told to return at such-and-such a time and the "output" would be ready.

"Sure looks simple up to now!" Howie thought. "What the heck? Why not try it?" He went over to the keypunch machine and found it to be much like a typewriter, and, after a little experimenting, even he could use it. (If Howie could read, he could have used Appendix A.)

But, what to type? He clearly didn't know any programming, so he did the next best thing. He reached into the nearest wastebasket to get any old piece of paper, just to try something. Unfortunately on his first attempt he met with a cup of yesterday's coffee! "Some dry run," he thought. He moved to the next wastebasket and there, right on top, was a sheet clearly labeled FORTRAN PROGRAM. Howie didn't have to use his immense knowledge of logic and set theory to know that he had struck paydirt!

Excited, he began to type, one line to a card:

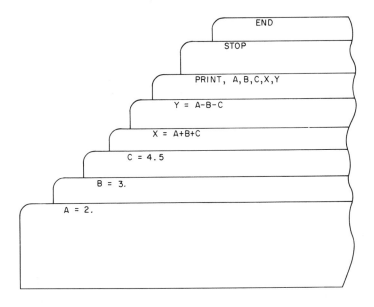

Howie got a boot out of the last two cards. Dumb machine! You have to tell it when to *stop* and *end*. Well, Howie had a program. He didn't know what it did, but it sure was exciting . . . sort of like being on a mystery ride and trying to figure out where you are going.

Now for the next step. What other cards did he need to get this program into the computer? "Play dumb," Howie thought. "Get their sympathy." He wandered over to the window where the programs were handed in and put on his "Lassie-just-found-out-about-the-leash-law" look.

"I guess I let this job get out of control . . ." he started to say.

"Oh! The job control cards are out? Okay. Here is a set. Give me your program," the attendant said. "There. Come back in an hour for your output."

"Right!" Howie firmly replied. "Wow!" he thought, "I pulled that one off. That was the best snow job I've given since I got out of the midterm by telling my instructor about my having to attend the funeral of my great aunt who had gone down with the Titanic and whose body was recently recovered when a foot patrol from an icebreaker in the North Atlantic noticed a foot protruding from the peak of a massive iceberg."

Ask your instructor about the *job control cards* needed at your computer center and type up the same program as Howie did. Use Appendix A to help you become familiar with a keypunch. Hold on to your output; you may want to refer to it later.

If your instructor informs you that BASIC is the language to be taught in your course, obtain the proper procedures for using a terminal and type the following:

```
10   A = 2.0
20   B = 3.0
30   C = 4.5
40   X = A + B + C
50   Y = A − B − C
60   PRINT A, B, C, X, Y
70   END
run
```

This program is the same as Howie's except that his uses punched cards as input (batch processing) and the one above uses a typewriter for input (time sharing).

Howie walked back to his seat to wait for his output and was surprised to see a large group of people entering the room. One of them, apparently the spokesperson, went directly to the desk and announced, "Hello. We are from NOSE. (N. Olfactory System Engineers) and are here for our scheduled tour of the computer facility."

"Where does your group work?" asked the receptionist.

"We work in a smelting plant," the spokesperson replied.

Figure 1.1 The computer room.

"Okay, please go right in. By the way, what does the 'N' stand for?" queried the receptionist.

"Nothing," came the reply.

"Aha," thought Howie, "another big break; I'll just sneak in with this illustrious group and get my first introduction to a computer center."

The data-processing manager arrived, introduced himself as A. Bacus, and graciously led the group into the mystical machine room. As his speech began, it became clear that this fellow had done this quite often as he went from machine to machine with enough polish to keep up the entire boot supply of the Russian Infantry. He really shined in his work!

"There are five basic parts to a computer system," Mr. Bacus be-

Computer console

Figure 1.2 The computer console.

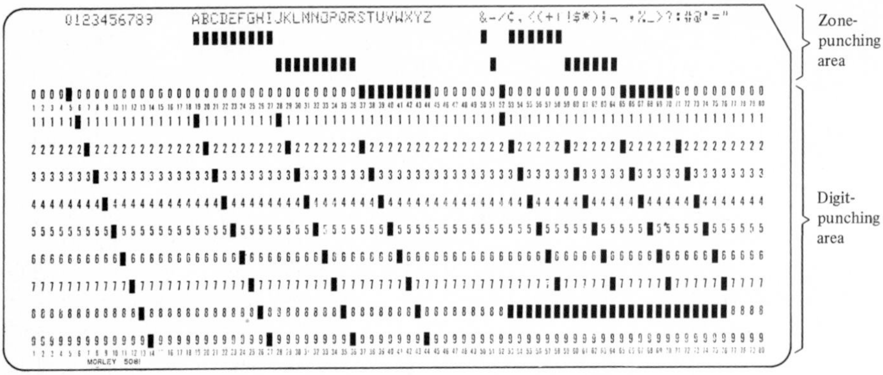

Figure 1.3 A punched card.

gan. "There are *input* units, *output* units, *central processing* units (CPU), *memory* units, and *auxiliary storage* units. All of these units are referred to as *hardware* since they are physical pieces of equipment. *Software* refers to computer programs or instructions that inform the computer what is to be done."

Howie began to fidget! Hardware, software, what about "somewhere," which is where Howie felt he should be—somewhere else!

"The primary input units are the *card reader* and the *console*. The input units put in information for the computer to process."

Figure 1.4 The card reader.

"The console is just like a typewriter and allows the operator to key in instructions directly to the computer. For our general users, however, it would be impractical for us to have them file into the machine room one at a time to type in their programs. Instead, we have them type their program onto cards and then we put them directly into the card reader. This machine automatically feeds the cards in one end, sends to the computer the information on the cards, and then returns the cards out the other end of the reader. It 'reads' the cards by sending an impulse through the punched holes where they appear, and thus it can distinguish between a punch and no punch and the location of that punch."

One of the members from NOSE sneezed. Undaunted, A. Bacus continued. "Well, I mentioned that the card reader sent the information on the cards to the computer. The computer puts the data into its memory. Memory is quite an appropriate term. A tape recorder, in a sense, 'remembers' what you have spoken. In a similar fashion, the memory of the computer remembers what has been sent to it by one of the input devices. Quite briefly, in many computers the information is recorded on what is called a *core* (another word for memory is core) by magnetizing it. If you magnetize or demagnetize a series of these cores, it becomes possible to code a tremendous variety of information. Other types of main storage devices are currently being developed and used in different computers. One of these newer developments is a semiconductor or solid state memory which consists of small silicon chips. These chips are currently being used in the IBM-370 computer series."

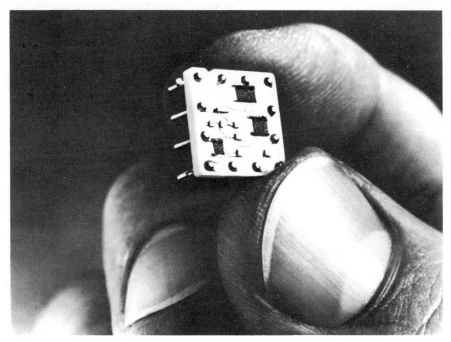

Figure 1.5 A printed circuit with chip transistors used in memory.

Figure 1.6 A second-generation transistor, 50,000 third-generation transistors, and a thimble.

"What if there isn't enough room in the memory?" asked Howie.

"A good question," responded Bacus, and Howie had the strange feeling that he was "set up."

"I mentioned earlier that there were five main components of a computer system. One of the things I mentioned was auxiliary storage. Over here we have our two main auxiliary storage devices. On the left is a *disk unit*. A disk is similar to a record and stores information instead of songs. When we stack a bunch of these 'records' together we have a *disk pack*. When we don't have enough room in the computer memory, we can put our data or information onto the disk. It stores up to 10 million characters."

Howie wondered what would happen if he put one of those disks on his record player. It would probably render an updated version of "I'm Dancing with Tears in my Eyes Cause the Girl in my Arms Bit my Nose."

Figure 1.7 A magnetic disk unit.

Figure 1.8 A disk pack.

"In addition to being able to store extra information on the disk pack, one can also use a *magnetic tape*. This tape is very much like tape

Figure 1.9 The tape drive.

recorder tape, only larger. A typical reel holds 2400 feet of half-inch-wide tape and can store up to 7 million characters of data."

Howie had about 7 million characters worth of questions, but he knew that this was only a tour and he would be covering much of the material in future classes. "Let the fellow continue," Howie thought.

One of the NOSEs asked, "Do you use auxiliary storage when your CUP runneth over?"

"I'm sorry," A. Bacus apologized. "I don't quite understand what you mean."

"Well," he continued, "in the beginning you talked about the five basic parts of a computer system. You mentioned the input units, output units, memory, auxiliary storage, and the CUP . . ."

"No," Bacus interrupted, "that's the CPU, the *central processing unit*. This part of the computer does the processing. It is here that the additions, multiplications, complex mathematics, and such are performed. Why, the machines today operate so fast that they can, in fractions of a second, perform tasks that would have taken humans several lifetimes to perform. In fact, create a visual picture, if you will, of someone knocking over your cup of morning coffee. Before the first drop hit the floor, a fairly large computer could charge 2000 checks to 300 different bank accounts *and* score 150,000 answers on 3000 examinations *and* figure the payroll for a company with 1000 employees *and* examine the electro-cardiograms of 100 patients and alert a physician if needed *and have some time left over.* All that before the first drop of the spilled coffee hit the floor!"

"Egad!" thought Howie, "even Al Geebra, Public School 35's addition, subtraction, multiplication (up to sevens table), and division champion couldn't do it that fast."

Bacus continued, "Computers have been instrumental in the development of new time units. Operations like addition can be done in a nanosecond, or one thousandth of a millionth of a second. The newer computers operate in trillionths of a second—picoseconds. That's pretty fast."

Howie remembered that he had, long ago, invented a new time unit, "justa," which lasted over an hour. He can remember responding to his folks' request for chores to be done . . . "justasecond."

"Finally, we have here on your left, the output units. Naturally, after the computer gets the information on the input side and does the processing, it must have someplace to display the results. The primary output unit is the line printer. It's kind of like an automatic typewriter except that some line printers can print up to 3000 lines in a minute. Of course, there are other ways in which the results might be displayed. Answers might be punched onto cards, written onto magnetic tape or disk, typed at the console typewriter, or even displayed on a CRT (a cathode-ray

Figure 1.10 The line printer.

tube similar to the one in a TV set). There are many different ways. Well, ladies and gentlemen, I hope you have enjoyed your tour. If there are any questions, I'd be glad to answer them now."

A short, white-haired lady up front asked, "What makes a computer so powerful; I mean what are its major powers so to speak?"

"Well, as we have seen, one of them is speed. It is also reliable and accurate and has an immense capacity for memory."

"It must have some limitations?" another person asked.

"Of course!" said Bacus. "Among the foremost are its complexity and cost. A small-sized card processing system leases for several thousand dollars a month. Also, a computer is limited by what man can tell it to do. It's like a player piano that plays up to several tunes at a time but follows the music instructions of each exactly."

When Howie heard the mention of music, he remembered back to his childhood days when he studied violin under Prof. Clef. The Prof used to say, "Look at it this way, Howie. The more you fiddle, the stronger your pitching arm will get." Howie was disappointed with violin lessons; he had only learned one song real well, "I'm So Miserable Without You, It's Like Having You Around." Another guest had asked what the CPU actually did. A. Bacus was answering.

"It is here that the machine performs mathematical operations and makes logical decisions. There are three parts to the central processing unit: the *memory* (which we discussed), the *arithmetic unit*, and the *control unit*. The control unit controls the overall operation of the computer and coordinates its parts. Those parts, card readers, line printers, disks, consoles, and so forth, are often called *peripheral equipment*. The CPU is sometimes called the *mainframe*.

"Are there any more questions?" asked A. Bacus. Since no questions were forthcoming, he continued, "I hope you enjoyed your tour."

1.3 COMPUTER LANGUAGES

While waiting for his first output, Howie decided to see if he could enlist the aid of some knowledgeable person in the room in finding out more about computers and things. After much looking around, he finally spotted Bea Keeper who he knew was a computer science major. He looked around and couldn't see anyone else he knew, but he wasn't sure if he should approach her. "To Bea or not to Bea, that was the question."

Beatrice took an immediate liking to Howie. He had that certain air about him . . . and she liked him in spite of it. Howie was clearly a challenge. If she could teach him to understand what computers were all about, she probably would be awarded a scholarship from AID for grad school to continue her research on "A Programmed Instruction Approach to Brainsurgery in the Home."

"Well, waddaya think, Bea, can you give me some of your wisdom while I'm waiting for my output?" asked Howie.

"I guess so," Beatrice smiled.

Howie felt that romantic twinge and snuggled a little closer to Bea. Bea got the idea. "You remind me of Don Juan," she said.

"Tell me just how," asked Howie, elated.

"Well, for one thing, he's been dead for years!"

"Okay, Bea, okay, business only. Will you help me get a head start in computer science?"

"Sure, Howie." Bea was in control. "Let me talk awhile about computers and things. It really isn't that hard to learn about computers and programming. Sure, it's new and as such is a challenge, but conceptually it is very much like math and a language—for example, algebra and French. To converse with a computer you must be able to speak its language."

"You mean the machine has a language of its own?" interrupted Howie.

"That's right. In fact, it's called machine language. The language itself is all numbers. For example, a message to add two numbers together might look like this: 10100101101011101001101."

Howie wondered if he could still beat the deadline for withdrawal from Computer Science I.

"But," Bea continued, "someone with a good deal of foresight recognized that it would be difficult for people to converse with computers if they had to do it completely with numbers. So, they developed a language that was fairly understandable and decided to let the computer translate it into numbers."

"The machine became its own interpreter," exclaimed Howie.

"Yes, in a sense that's true."

"What language was used? Was it English? French? Pig Latin?" questioned Howie.

"Well, there are many languages that are used," Bea continued. "The most common are FORTRAN (for FORmula TRANslation), BASIC (for Beginners All-purpose Symbolic Instruction Code), COBOL (for COmmon Business Oriented Language), PL/1 (for Programming Language 1), and, more recently, APL (for A Programming Language)."

"Wait a minute," interrupted Howie, "I didn't know I was going to have to become a linguistic connoisseur. I done just got English down pat."

Bea began to wonder if this job was going to make a lunar landing look simple. "Learning the different languages is usually not the problem," she said. "The rules and regulations (punctuation, etc.) are strict but fairly few in number. In programming, it is the process that is most important. Once you understand the logic of a problem, translating it into one of these higher-level languages is pretty straightforward. At some point you will be exposed to flowcharting, which is a technique for representing a program that will help you a great deal in getting skilled with the logic part of programs."

"Fine," replied Howie. "I just submitted something called a FORTRAN program. How does the machine know how to translate it?"

"You may not believe this, Howie," Bea began, "but there is a special computer program already in the machine that does the translating. There is one for each higher-level language that the particular machine uses. That program is really called a *compiler*. It not only does the translating, but it checks for errors in the program."

"Wait a minute," cried disbelieving Howie. "You mean to tell me that the computer checks to see if I have made mistakes?"

'Yes, in a sense, that's true," replied Bea. "Of course, it cannot find errors that you made in your logic; it identifies those that are syntax errors."

"Syntax? Is that a government levy against bad behavior?" asked Howie.

"No, a syntax error occurs when you spell something wrong, leave out a period, or violate one of the rules of the language itself. When you do this, the compiler identifies the type of error and where it is in your program. Your output will include a list of any errors."

"Hey, that's pretty nifty," Howie commented. "I suppose that then I have to correct the errors?"

"Yes, when you 'get the bugs out' you are *debugging* your program. Say, Howie, have you had lunch?"

"No, in fact, I haven't had breakfast," said Howie. "Let's go down to Al Casseltza's place for a sandwich." He took Bea's hand.

"Howie Gettindere!" she exclaimed.

"I dunno. Let's take your car!" replied Howie.

TOPIC SUMMARY FOR CHAPTER ONE

Input	Software
Output	Hardware
Disk pack	Core
Tape	Picosecond
Arithmetic unit	Mainframe
STOP	END
Compiler	COBOL
APL	PL/1
CPU	Card reader
Memory	Console
Disk	Auxiliary storage
Nanosecond	Line printer
Control unit	Peripheral equipment
Keypunch	FORTRAN
BASIC	Machine language
Syntax	Debugging

chapter 2

Fundamental programming concepts

In order for a computer to be used efficiently, the problems to be solved must be well organized and carefully prepared. This will involve the problem formulation—a precise statement of both the objectives and the constraints to be imposed on the solution. After the problem has been well formulated, an explicit methodology for solving the problem must be prescribed. This chapter presents some general concepts useful in obtaining such a methodology. These concepts include the logic of solution techniques and the organization of procedures through flowcharting. In addition, some mathematical notation is introduced because of its wide applicability in computer problems. The concepts presented in this chapter form the background for the development of specific programming languages.

2.1 ALGORITHMS AND FLOWCHARTS

Howie Gettindere had finished his homework for the week and decided to take his first college date to the movies Friday night. He knew that he had a lot to do on Friday and, since he didn't want to make any mistakes, he made a list of things to do before and during his date. He jotted them down on index cards for convenience. Unfortunately for Howie, while he was sleeping in the library, one of UGHs faculty members knocked Howie's cards off the table onto the floor. The resounding crash awakened Howie, and he quickly picked them up. The shuffled deck looked like this:

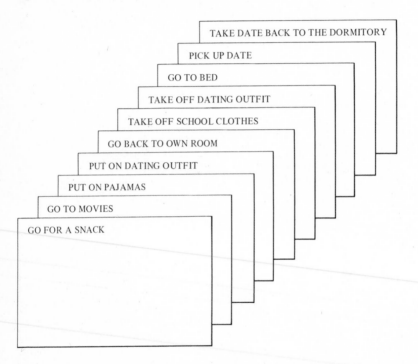

Now, Howie was no dummy! He knew right away that the new order was incorrect because he clearly wouldn't put on his pajamas before he put on his dating outfit (unless he wore his pajamas underneath his dating outfit). Since he hadn't yet memorized the card order, he had three alternatives:

1. Cancel the date.
2. Reshuffle them and hope for the best.
3. Try to put them in the correct order.

He decided to let one flip of a coin decide which of the three approaches to adopt, and number 3 won. Maybe you can help Howie out. Try to arrange the cards in the correct order. The solution is given in Figure 2.1, but don't peek, since anyone who prematurely gazes upon Figure 2.1 without first contemplating the solution is subject to several sleepless nights of anguish over whether or not they have contracted the dreaded "foot-in-mouth" disease and three Fs for the term.

The preceding example illustrates the importance of performing ordered tasks in the correct sequence. We all have learned how to sequence tasks involved in our daily lives, and consequently, we perform these tasks without consciously giving any regard to the ordering process. When more involved tasks are to be performed, we sometimes use a formal ordering process to accomplish our objectives (e.g., we may write down a schedule of the courses we would like to take for the next few semesters to make sure that we have taken all the prerequisites in the proper order).

When we use the computer to help us with problem solving, we must be very careful to tell the computer in exactly what order it should perform our tasks. This is because the computer does not think, but only executes our instructions. It does this in exactly the way we tell it to (which, unfortunately, may not be the way we intended to tell the computer to execute our instructions). To be sure that we tell the computer the correct order for performing our tasks, we may want to write down a carefully ordered plan which we would like the computer to follow. This carefully ordered plan is called a *flowchart*.

We have already seen a flowchart. Figure 2.2 is a flowchart for Howie so that he can plan a successful date for Friday.

Howie got the cards in order and his date turned out so successfully that Friday that he decided to call the same girl, Isabella Ringing, and ask her for a date for next Friday.

"This certainly is another opportunity for me to demonstrate my

Not now, try it yourself first.
The real solution is in
Fig. 2.2

Figure 2.1 Not the correct answer.

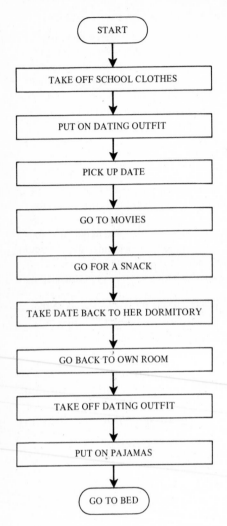

Figure 2.2 A flowchart for Howie's index cards.

expertise in flowcharting," Howie thought, and he asked his roommates to watch him.

"Now here is the problem, Rudy." (Howie had two roommates, Rudy Mentry who was a transfer student from the prep school, and Cole Shoulder, who was a shy, quiet soul from the eastern front of Siberia.)

"What I want to do is call Isabella and ask her for a date. I learned this new technique called flowcharting that kind of draws a picture of what you are trying to do. I can make it as detailed or as general as I like. For example, it may look like this." Howie began writing on the room memo board.

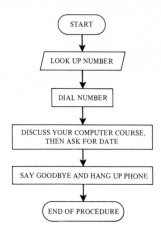

Neither Rudy nor Cole knew anything about computer programming, but they suspected that Howie didn't know anything either.

"Hey, Howie," Rudy interrupted, "what if Isabella is not the one who answers the phone, or what if the phone is busy?"

"Geez! Always a wise guy!" Howie muttered. "Okay," he began to erase the old chart, "how about this one?" Howie expanded his first flowchart to read as follows:

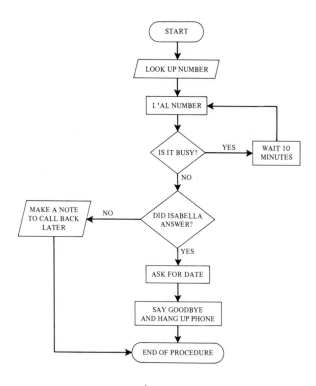

"Well, that's better, but what if her roommate answers or she doesn't accept the date?" asked Cole.

"Wow, you're sure making this difficult," complained Howie. "I'll make one more flowchart."

The final flowchart that Howie made was as follows:

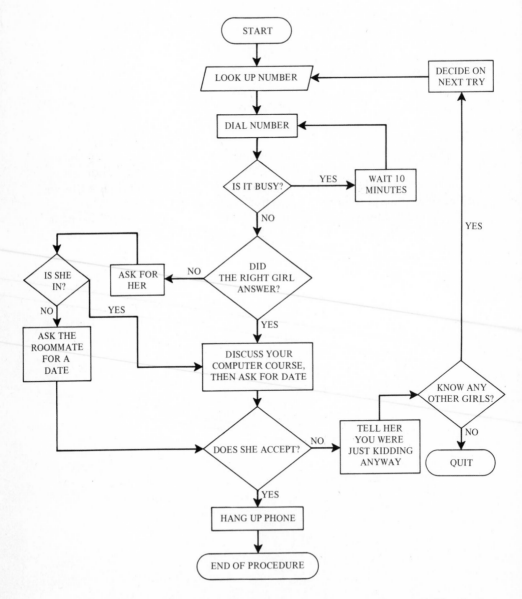

"Do those shapes that you are using have any significance?" asked Cole.

"Sure they do," recounted Howie, recalling the last computer course lecture he attended. "In order to maintain some consistency, all programmers use the same set of symbols with each symbol meaning the same thing. That way, they can read each other's flowcharts and, in any case, have a common basis from which to begin to write programs themselves.

"For example, the symbol for reading or inputting is kind of shaped like a computer card and is used to represent card input; some of the more common symbols are:

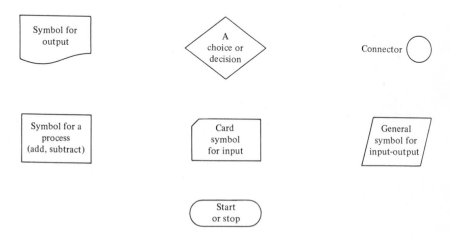

"What do you call those steps you have in that program?" asked Cole.

"A flowchart," was Howie's quick response.

"NO, NO, NO! I mean the process. You know, the logic of the whole thing. It must have a name."

"It's called an *algorithm*," stated Rudy.

Howie believed him. It does have a kind of rhythm associated with it.

In order to test their algorithm, the group decided to call in a stranger and have him place the call to Isabella using the flowchart. Cole went out into the corridor to seek out a likely victim for the experiment. Lo and behold! Who should be stomping down the stairs but Mammoth Harry, who got his name from his brawn, not his brains. If brains were water, Harry wouldn't have enough to give a flea a foot bath.

"Hey, Mam," called Cole. "Come in here for a sec. Will you help us with an experiment? Here is a chart of instructions for placing a call for us. Will you just do what it says? We want to test something."

Mammoth nodded in affirmation. You could tell that he meant yes because when he shook his head from right to left, the rattle sounded much different from when he shook it up and down. When he got to the part 'Ask for Isabella' it became clear that Harry had dialed the wrong number. But he always followed instructions, this guy, and before you knew it he had obtained a date with one of the waitresses at Frequently Fried Chicken. Some chick!

Mammoth, in his own way, is much like a computer. A computer only performs precisely according to the instructions you give it. It cannot take into consideration any deviation from those instructions. If an error occurs, it is the fault of the person who prepared the logic or the instructions.

A more detailed flowchart could, of course, have been written. It could have included the precise instructions on how to dial a call (i.e., pick up receiver, listen for dial tone, place finger in hole corresponding to first number, etc.). This kind of flowchart would be referred to as a *detailed systems* flowchart as opposed to Howie's, which was more of a *general systems* flowchart. In practice, it is usually advisable to begin with detailed flowcharts and then, after some experience has been gained, to rely on more general flowcharts.

Howie explained to his contemporaries that he would, of course, have included all the necessary detail.

"What would you do with the flowchart?" asked Cole.

"Now," Howie said with authority, "once a flowchart is written, it is then translated into a language that the computer can understand. This process of setting up the logic is called *algorithm design,* while the translation process is referred to as *coding.* There are rules in any computer language for changing a 'box' on the flowchart to a computer instruction."

"But how can you get the computer to dial a phone?" protested Cole.

"Well, in this case, you really wouldn't," Howie admitted. "The flowchart we've been looking at was only an illustration of the kind of logic needed to put together a series of instructions. In practice, the flowcharts would represent a more quantitative-type problem.

"Like what?" insisted Cole.

"Hey, you know that beer can we keep over on the shelf? You know, the one that we all have to put money in every time one of us tells a terrible joke. Well, we can construct an algorithm and flowchart to describe the process of counting up the money. It would look something like the illustration on page 23.

"Now this one," Howie proudly exclaimed, "could be easily translated into instructions for the computer. For example, once the individual totals were done you would get the grand total (last box) by 'coding' the equation like this (using an * to signify multiplication):

$$T = P + 5 * N + 10 * D + 25 * Q + 50 * H + 100 * C + 200 * B + 500 * F$$

"In fact, many times, one box on the flowchart represents one statement in the computer program. When you have prepared all the statements you have your completed computer program ready for solution by the computer. Any questions?"

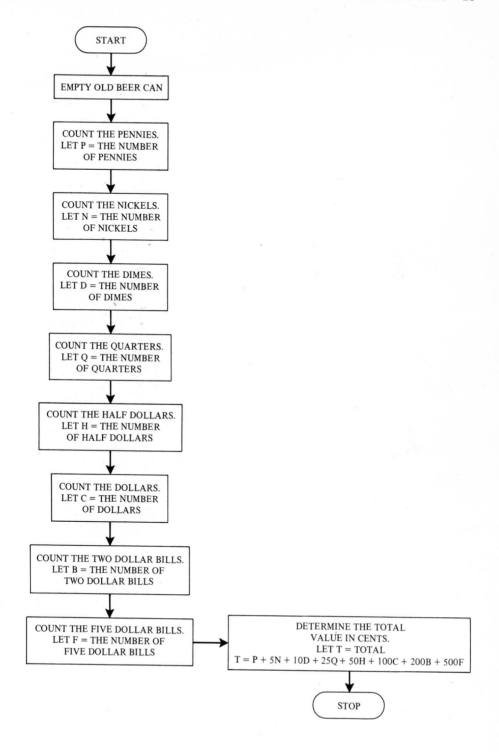

Cole had fallen asleep on the couch and Rudy was busy reading *MAD* magazine. Howie put a dollar in the beer can.

While the room was quiet, Howie began to think about the problem of raising money for the upcoming dormitory dance. The dance committee had proposed that a car be raffled and had asked Howie to find a desirable new automobile at a good price and also decide on a pricing policy for the raffle tickets. Earlier that day a salesman had told Howie that he would sell him a new car for only $3000 because he liked Howie.

Now, Howie wanted to decide on a ticket pricing policy that would encourage people to buy tickets, not just one ticket, but several. Howie decided that only 3500 tickets would be sold; this would make people feel they had a chance of winning. The pricing policy would be:

> 1st ticket cost: $1.00
> 2d through 5th, each cost: $.90
> After the 5th, each cost: $.80

Howie felt he could impress the dance committee if he flowcharted an algorithm showing how much to charge a ticket purchaser who wanted to buy some number $(N > 0)$ of tickets. He drew a flowchart (see page 25) with C being the amount to charge and N being the number of tickets requested.

The next day Howie presented his flowchart to the committee, and they were duly impressed. However, there were some questions. One committeeperson said, "I see that if a person buys one ticket you go from step 1 to step 2 to step 3 to step 4 to step 5 and charge the person $1. What about someone who wants to buy three tickets?"

"In that case," Howie commented, "you go to 1 and set $C = 0$. Then, at step 2 the answer is 'no' so you proceed to step 6. At that point you increase C by 1 so C is now equal to 1 (you have charged for the first ticket). Then you go to step 7 where the answer is 'yes.' You go to step 8 and increase C by $(N - 1) \times 0.90$ which is $(3 - 1) \times 0.90$ which is 1.80. So C is now $2.80 and that is what you charge."

"Okay, but what about the person who wants seven tickets?" asked another committeeperson.

"In that case you would go from step 1 to 2 where the answer is 'no,' proceed to 6 where C becomes 1, then to 7 where the answer is 'no.' Move on to 11 where C becomes 4.60 ($1.00 for ticket number 1 and a sum of 3.60 for tickets 2, 3, 4, and 5), and, finally, to 12 where C is increased by 2×0.80 and becomes $6.20, which is what you charge the customer."

Howie was so convincing that the committee approved of the pricing policy.

A week later, Howie went to buy the car. He paid the car dealer $3000 and was about to leave when he decided to try to sell the salesman a raffle ticket. He noticed the salesman's nametag read "Bill Eumore."

"By the way, Mr. Eumore, would you like to be my first raffle ticket

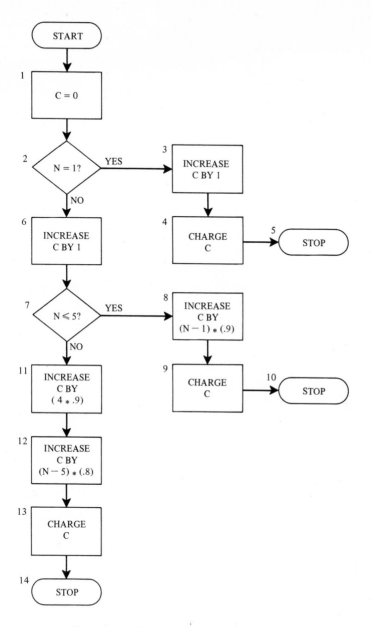

customer? Only $1 for a ticket, and we will only sell 3500 tickets so you have a good chance of winning your car back."

"Okay, Howie," Bill reluctantly replied, "I'll buy a ticket." He reached for his wallet.

"Thanks," smiled Howie. "By the way, we have a discount policy, if you would like to buy more than one ticket. I thought of the policy myself and, in fact, happen to have a flowchart right here . . ."

When Howie finished explaining the flowchart, Mr. Eumore looked at Howie and then announced: "I'd like to buy all the tickets." Howie was elated! Mr. Eumore handed Howie $2800.60, and said, "Since I'm going to win, you won't even have to take the car."

Use Howie's flowchart to check on Mr. Eumore's calculation. Was $2800.60 the correct amount?

Howie left with the $2800.60 and no car; he felt a little strange. Then he remembered that the only other thing he had to do today was to go pay the printer $20 for the raffle tickets. Howie headed for the print shop.

TOPIC SUMMARY FOR SECTION 2.1

Ordered tasks
Flowchart
Flowchart symbols
   Input
   Output
   Process
   Choice
   Connector
   Start/Stop
Algorithm
Logic error
Detailed systems flowchart
General systems flowchart
Coding

Problems for Sec. 2.1

1. A novice electrician rewired the elevator in an apartment with four floors, and the floor buttons are not wired correctly. Thus, when you push a button, you don't know what floor the elevator will go to. Since you often visit your friends in this building, you decide to be a nice guy and relabel the buttons. Draw a flowchart to discover which buttons correspond to which floors.

2. At a party you are attending, the host introduces a new game. One of the guests is to be selected at random and blindfolded. Since you suspect that the game is an offshoot of spin the bottle, you volunteer. To your dismay, you discover that you must correctly identify a banana, an apple, and an orange from a bowl of fruit. Before you begin, you

decide to write up a flowchart of your particular algorithm. What would that flowchart look like?

Would your algorithm work for a 200-pound, 8-foot banana? Should it? What if a baseball were substituted for the apple?

3. Draw a flowchart to describe the process of barbecuing a hamburger under the following constraints:

(a) The hamburger should be on the rare side, and currently is.

(b) The roll is to be toasted and currently isn't.

(c) You have only one spatula.

(d) There is room for only one hamburger and one roll on the grill.

(e) You are so hungry you could eat a horse (and maybe you will).

(f) The fire is going out.

4. Draw a flowchart for feeding a frisky dog outside on a rainy day when you are wearing white pants.

5. Construct a flowchart that describes how you study a particular subject of your choice.

6. Construct a flowchart that describes how you get dressed in the morning after partying a little too much the night before.

7. A classmate of yours bought a watch for $103, including the tax. He paid for it in eight bills, but they were not five twenties and three ones; there were no one-dollar bills among the eight and he received no change. Can you discover how he paid for the watch?

8. A devious medieval king has told you, the Duke of Data Processing, that because of the apparent fiefdom you are building, he has tentatively decided to execute you. To make up his mind he is going to allow you to select from a hat a piece of paper which has written on it either the word "guilty" or the words "not guilty." There are only these two pieces of paper in the hat. If you pick the paper with the word "guilty" on it, you lose (probably your head).

You suspect that the devious king has written "guilty" on both sheets. He then asks you to make your selection. You don't have to draw a flowchart for this one; just figure out what to do.

2.2 ROUND AND ROUND SHE GOES, WHERE SHE STOPS, NOBODY KNOWS

Howie's professor, Phil Ovitt, had a part-time job to supplement his meager salary. His job is building chimneys in a housing development, for which he would get paid $175 every time he finished six chimneys. Since each house looked similar, it was hard for Phil to figure out when he had finished six chimneys, so he developed a system for counting. Every time he started a chimney he put a brick in his left overall pocket and upon completion of the chimney he counted the bricks in his left pocket. If there were six bricks in his left pocket, he would go to the developer, get paid

$175, and go off to plan his class lessons. (Phil never did figure out why he was dragging around on Friday and Saturday.)

A flowchart for this counting method is as follows:

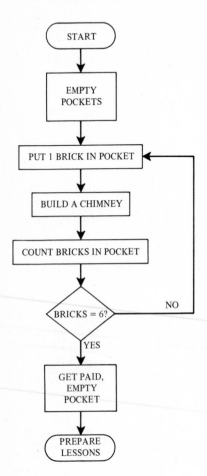

Since computers frequently have to do repetitive tasks, the people who designed them built them with bricks and pockets. You may not recognize these objects when you look at the machine, but rest assured that they're in the little gray box kept out of sight. They only use the sharp-looking, expensive cabinets to make the computer look fancy. How much would *anyone* pay for a brick and a pocket?

"Hey, Professor!" Howie yelled. "Feel like you're going around in circles? Put a brick in the pocket; count the bricks; put a brick in the pocket; count . . . ."

"Yes, Howie, it is repetitive. It's like going around in a circle. If a computer were instructed to do the counting, it would also have to repeat

"There must be a fireplace somewhere in this room."

the test over and over. We refer to that process as *performing a loop*," commented Prof. Ovitt.

While they were talking, Prof. Ovitt's part-time boss, the developer of the homes, drove up.

"Hello, Mr. Derr," Phil exclaimed.

"Just call me Bill," he said. "Say, Phil, for someone who teaches quantitative stuff, you're not very consistent. Take a look at those last six chimneys. They are all different heights. From now on, keep them at 880 bricks each, okay?"

"Sure enough," said Phil.

Howie had a suggestion. "Say, Professor, I have a good algorithm for you to use to keep track of how many bricks you've used so far."

"Yes, what would that be, Howie?" asked Phil.

"Well, for each brick you lay, put one in your pocket. After you finish cementing that brick, count those in your pocket. If you have 880, then stop cementing. Pretty good, huh?" said Howie.

"I'll tell you, Howie," mused Phil, "it is a little ridiculous to talk about having 880 bricks in my pocket at the top of a chimney. For crying out loud, I don't have enough bricks for that.

"However," the professor proudly exclaimed. "I do have plenty of nails. Every time I start to lay a brick I'll put a nail in my right pocket. After laying the brick, I'll take the nails out of my pocket and count them to see if I have finished. If I have less than 880 nails, I'll put them back into my pocket and continue building. If I have 880, I will get down and count the bricks in my left pocket to see if I have finished my sixth chimney. If so, I'll go get paid. If not, I'll put the bricks back into my pocket and start a new chimney."

"It sure is easy to see how you got to be a professor, Professor."

"Thank you, Howie, and now see if you can sketch a flowchart of the algorithm I just gave you," asked the professor.

Howie began by drawing on a large plank that was lying on the ground.

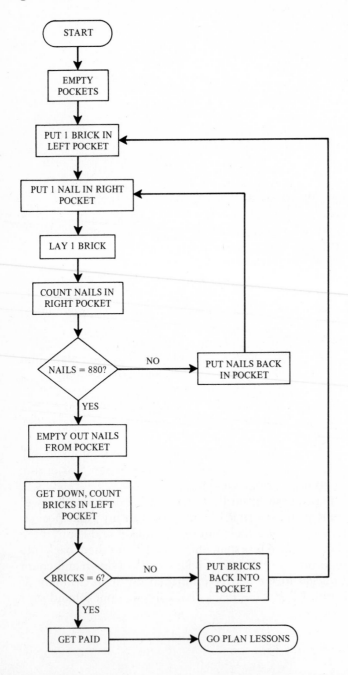

"Wow," exclaimed Howie, "we've got two loops here. I'll bet in computer jargon this is called a cloverleaf."

"Not quite, Howie," chuckled Phil, "when one or more loops are combined as in your flowchart, they are commonly referred to as *nested loops*. There is a kind of nesting arrangement, one within another."

"Are we gonna cover this stuff in class at all?" queried Howie.

"Sure we are. We'll be talking about it in much more detail later on."

"Whew!" sighed Howie.

REVIEW EXERCISES

1. A friend of Howie's, Phyllis In, is taking a course in algorithm construction. Her professor, Phil Ovitt, assigned them the following problem:

    You have three billiard balls—a green one, a red one, and a yellow one—and a balance scale. You are told that one ball is either slightly heavier or slightly lighter than the other two balls, but you aren't told whether it is heavier or lighter. Determine the odd ball.

    Can you do this problem for Phyllis, and how few weighings does it take?

    Solution: See page 32.

2. A king has asked you, the wise mathematician, to design a bridge over the moat containing horrible monsters. You performed this task admirably, and consequently the king asked how you would like to be paid for this. After negotiating, you agreed to receive your payments over 30 days at the rate of $.01 the first day, $.02 the second day, $.04 the third day, etc., doubling the previous day's pay each day. Let's look at a flowchart that would help in figuring your pay each day and the sum of payments through that day.

    The flowchart would look like Solution 2 on page 33.

3. Prof. Ovitt has instructed his class to write a flowchart for an algorithm to help the registrar compute the grade-point average for each student for last semester. Each course has assigned to each student a number grade (like 88), and the algorithm is to add a student's grades together, divide the total by the number of courses for which the student had grades, and print the student's name and average. Try to draw the flowchart.

    A solution to the problem, in which every student had the same number (say, five) of courses last semester, would be as shown in Solution 3, page 33. In this flowchart, N represents the number of grades a student has beside his name (in this case, five).

    Note that the inside loop is similar to the inside loop in the flow-

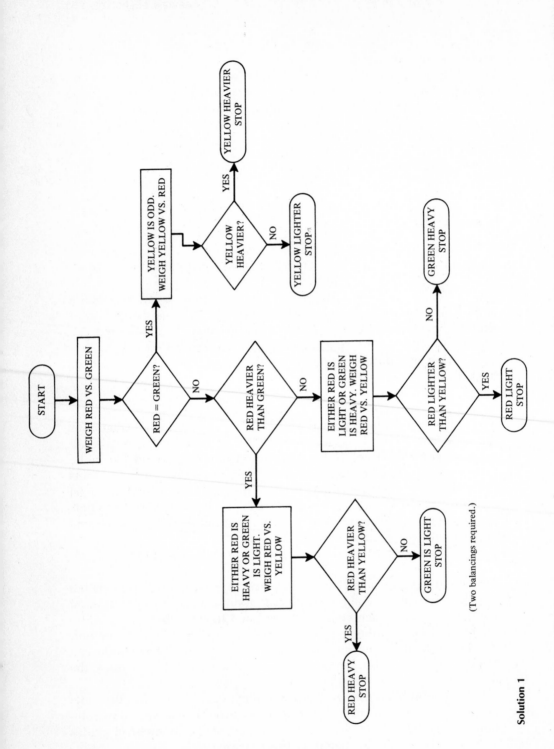

START

WEIGH RED VS. GREEN

RED = GREEN?

YES → YELLOW IS ODD. WEIGH YELLOW VS. RED

YELLOW HEAVIER?

YES → YELLOW HEAVIER STOP

NO → YELLOW LIGHTER STOP

NO

RED HEAVIER THAN GREEN?

YES → EITHER RED IS HEAVY OR GREEN IS LIGHT. WEIGH RED VS. YELLOW

RED HEAVIER THAN YELLOW?

YES → RED HEAVY STOP

NO → GREEN IS LIGHT STOP

NO → EITHER RED IS LIGHT OR GREEN IS HEAVY. WEIGH RED VS. YELLOW

RED LIGHTER THAN YELLOW?

NO → GREEN HEAVY STOP

YES → RED LIGHT STOP

(Two balancings required.)

Solution 1

32

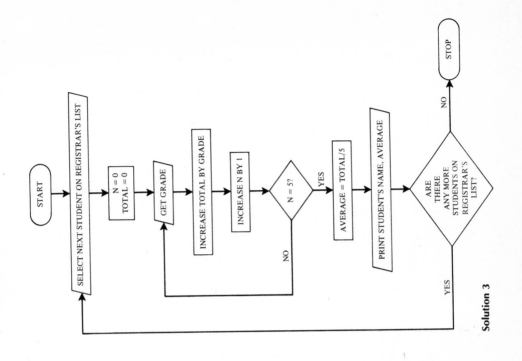

Solution 3

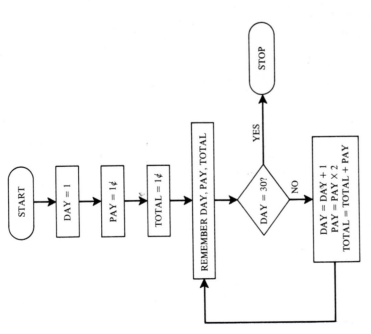

Solution 2

33

chart for Prof. Ovitt's algorithm for building chimneys. Also note the nested loop structure of the flowchart. However, the outer loop now will be performed as many times as is necessary to obtain all the students' averages; we have not specified the number of students in advance.

Suppose the registrar said that not all students had five courses last semester. Revise the flowchart to take into consideration that slight change. Assume that if a name appears on the registrar's list, that student has taken at least one course.

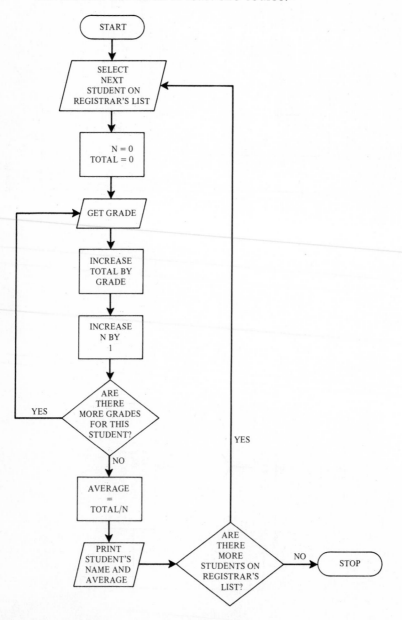

Howie's flowchart was the following one. Can you find the error in it?

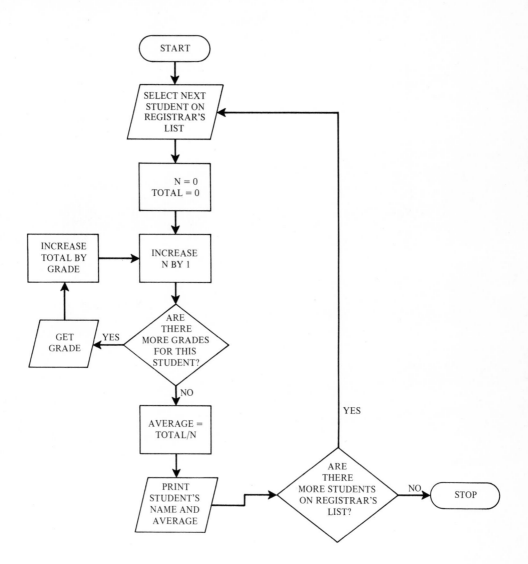

Problems for Sec. 2.2

1. A test is given to the students in your class who wear shoes. There are four questions, and it would be quite a feat to answer all correctly. For each correct answer a score of 25 points is given. There are 50 people in your class and 15 of them do not wear shoes. Construct a flowchart that will display the grade for each individual who takes the test. Assume there are no loafers.

COMPUTER CROSSWORD

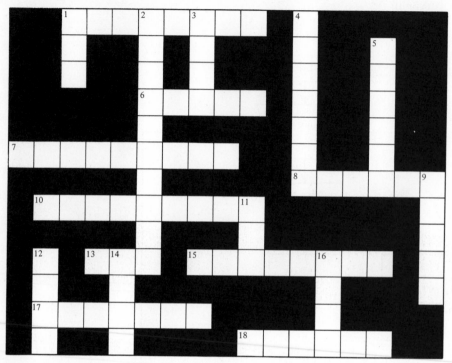

Across

1. The translator that converts a higher-level language into machine language.
6. An example of this type of device is the card reader.
7. A graphical description of a problem solution.
8. When a bird has finished building his nest, it might be said that he has _____.
10. A prescribed set of well-defined rules for the solution of a problem.
13. Common abbreviation for the control cards needed to process a program.
15. Used to prepare cards for processing.
17. Tapes and disks are examples of auxiliary _____.
18. Another name for core.

Down

1. Abbreviation for central processing unit.
2. Equipment used with the computer for outside communication.
3. Loop.
4. A higher-level language.
5. Input.
9. Get the errors out of the program.
11. In the game "giant step," you must go all the way back to the beginning if you forget to say _____ I.
12. A recordlike device used to store data.
14. Another term for memory.
16. One thousandth of a millionth of a second is called a _____ second.

2. Your roommate suggests the following game:
   (*a*) Only two players at a time. Call them player A and player B.
   (*b*) Player A mentions any number that is not greater than 10. Player B mentions any number that is not greater than 10 and this is added to A's number. This process continues until 100 is reached, each player adding to the growing total.
   (*c*) Whoever is the first to reach 100 is the winner.
   (*d*) Zero and negative numbers are not permitted.
   Draw a flowchart that will guarantee you a win every time your opponent begins the game.

3. (*a*) The population of the Republic of Uwait is currently about equal to the population of the United States, which is approximately equal to the number 200 million. The population is growing at the rate of 3 percent per year. This does not mean that the heights of the populace are increasing at 3 percent, although they certainly are increasing, but rather that the total number of people in the Republic is on the rise. As that country's Minister of Flowcharts, you decide to draw one to calculate what the population will be in 100 years.
   (*b*) An associate of yours, Manny Hares, is raising rabbits. His current kennel has 100 million rabbits and they are increasing their numbers at the rate of 6 percent per year. He has applied for a government grant to do a research project to determine how many years it will be before there are more bunnies than people. Lettuce draw a flowchart that will illustrate this.

4. Construct a flowchart that will convert any Roman numeral from 1 to 50 to its arabic number (the numbers we use) equivalent.

5. | *English system* | *Metric system* |
   | --- | --- |
   | 1 foot = 12 inches | 100 centimeters = 1 meter |
   | 3 feet = 1 yard | 10 millimeters = 1 centimeter |

   2.54 centimeters = 1 inch

   (*a*) Draw a flowchart for an algorithm which will convert a measurement of x yards, y feet, and z inches into meters (e.g., convert measurements like 1 yard, 2 feet, 5 inches into meters).
   (*b*) Draw a flowchart for an algorithm which will convert a measurement (x, y, z) where x is yards, y is feet, and z is inches into a measurement (a, b) where a is an integer number of meters, b is the remainder in millimeters.
   (*c*) Draw a flowchart for an algorithm to convert a measurement of m meters (m may be a decimal number) into the equivalent measurement (x, y, z) where x is in yards, y is in feet, z is in inches (e.g., 2.5 meters = 2 yards, 2 feet, 2.425 inches).

6. See Review Exercise 1. You have 12 billiard balls numbered 1 to 12 and a balance scale. You are told that one ball is either slightly heavier or slightly lighter than the other 11 balls, but you aren't told whether

it is heavier or lighter. Draw a flowchart for determining the odd ball and whether it is heavier or lighter in *three* uses of the balance scale.

2.3 ARITHMETIC EXPRESSIONS

Howie's roommate, Cole Shoulder, knew that Howie was a computer novice, so he suggested that Howie write a program to determine how they should share the room and board expenses.

"Since there are three of us, we'll each pay one-third," commented Cole.

"That's easy," Howie beamed, "we'll just add the room and board up and divide by 3. Here's what I write in my program:

$$Myshare = room + board/3$$

Cole, remembering how long it took Howie to get his last program to run, interjected, "That sure looks good to me. I wonder if we could do the calculations now and settle up instead of waiting for the computer run. Since room expenses are \$1200 for the term, and board expenses are \$900 for the term, let's just see what the answer should be."

"Okay," replied Howie.

$$Myshare = room + board/3$$

Then

$$Myshare = 1200 + 900/3$$

Now, 900/3 is 300, so

$$Myshare = 1200 + 300 = \$1500$$

Cole thought for a minute, then replied, "Okay, you give me a check for \$1500; I'll get some money from Rudy and go pay the bursar for the room and board."

Howie suddenly felt like he did when Bill Eumore bought all of his raffle tickets last week—sort of like a Hawaiian who just bought a snowblower—so he went to see his computer professor to discuss the high cost of higher education.

At Prof. Ovitt's office, Howie recounted the division of the room and board bills. "I'm afraid that you may have paid more than your share, Howie," he said. "The problem is with your expression

$$Room + board/3$$

You probably meant to write

$$(Room + board)/3$$

which would have left you with a bill of

$$(1200 + 900)/3 = 2100/3 = \$700$$

We call expressions for which we can obtain numerical values *arithmetic expressions*. When you are working with arithmetic expressions, it is important to evaluate the operations in the correct order. As you know from class, the symbols and the operations we use in arithmetic expressions are as follows:

** Exponentiation
* Multiplication
/ Division
+ Addition
− Subtraction

"In evaluating an expression, you first do all the exponentiation, moving through the exponentiation from right to left. Then you do all the multiplication and division, moving from left to right. Finally, the addition and subtraction is performed by moving through the expression from left to right. This is called the *hierarchy* of operations in an arithmetic expression.[1] For example, to evaluate $4^2/2 + 2^3 - 2 \times 5$, you might write that expression for a computer as

$$4 ** 2/2 + 2 ** 3 - 2 * 5$$

The computer then evaluates first the exponentiation to get

$$16/2 + 8 - 2 * 5$$

since $4^2 = 16$ and $2^3 = 8$. Then it performs multiplication and division to get

$$8 + 8 - 10$$

Finally, addition and subtraction are performed to get 6 as the answer."

Howie began to understand his mistake and went back to his room where he met Cole again. "Cole, I'd like my check back! I made a mistake and you know it!" he snapped at Cole.

Cole replied, "Okay, don't get sore. We'll refigure your share. The total bill is $2100. You and Rudy pay two-thirds since we have only three roommates. Furthermore you pay half of that bill, so let's figure it out."

$$\$2100 \times 2/3 \times 1/2$$

"I know how to do that," interjected Howie importantly. "First you write it computer style as

$$\$2100 * 2/3 * 1/2$$

Then you do exponentiation first, multiplication and division next, and finally addition and subtraction. Now let me see."

"There's no exponentiation!" said Cole, annoyed.

---

[1]The hierarchy of operations may be different for some compilers from the rules mentioned here.

"I know! We go right to multiplication and division," Howie replied. "Let's see . . .

$$\$2100 * 2/3 * 1/2$$

Since 1/2 is 0.5, we have

$$\$2100 * 2/3 * 0.5$$

and 3 * 0.5 is 1.5, so

$$\$2100 * 2/1.5$$

or

$$\$2100 * 1.33333 . . .$$

which gives

$$\$2800$$

which is my share!" This revelation sent Howie running back to the professor.

"Well, Howie," said the professor after hearing the latest episode, "you should try using parentheses to keep the operations you wish to perform in the proper order. For example, you could have written your arithmetic expression as

$$\$2100 * (2/3) * (1/2)$$

When the expression has parentheses they are reduced first, and in this case you have:

$$\$2100 * (0.666666 . . .) * (0.5000) = \$700$$

for your share, which is what we figured before.

"For longer expressions, it may be useful to have sets of parentheses inside of sets of parentheses. In that case you reduce the expression in the innermost parentheses first, then the second set of parentheses, etc., until your entire expression is reduced. For example a complicated expression like

$$4^2/2 + 2^3 - 2 \times 5$$

would be written as

$$4 ** 2/2 + 2 ** 3 - 2 * 5$$

But it may look less confusing as

$$((4 ** 2)/2) + (2 ** 3) - (2 * 5)$$

This would be evaluated as

$$(16/2) + 8 - 10$$

then

$$8 + 8 - 10$$

and finally

$$6$$

One final note: If you have two sets of parentheses they must be separated by an operator. That is, if you want to write 5 times 2 for a computer, you can write

$$5 * 2$$

or

$$(5) * (2)$$

but not

$$(5)(2)$$

"Gee, Professor, how did you learn all that in only about 50 years?" Howie queried.

The professor must have seen his good friend, Prof. O'Silver, at that point, because he walked away quickly and as he left Howie heard him in the distance saying, "Hi, O'Silver!"

TOPIC SUMMARY FOR SECTION 2.3

Evaluating expressions	Division
Arithmetic expressions	Addition
Exponentiation	Subtraction
Multiplication	Hierarchy of operations
Using parentheses	

2.4 INTEGER AND REAL NUMBERS

The next day a strange thing happened to Howie in his computer class. In the middle of class the kid sitting directly behind Howie, Scott Free, fell asleep. Scott's head fell down to his desk, and the pencil Scott had on his ear went flying, point first, into Howie's back. Naturally, this awakened Howie, who, startled, shouted, "OH!"

"That's right, Howie," replied the professor. "That arithmetic expression, when properly evaluated, is zero. You've learned that material well." The professor continued, "Now I want to summarize today's lesson. In some computer languages it is useful to differentiate between whole numbers or integer numbers, and numbers with decimal parts. Examples of integer numbers are 1, 10, 12, 295 and are sometimes called *fixed-point numbers*. Examples of decimal numbers are 0.83, 2.4, 1000.0, 99.99 and are sometimes called *floating-point numbers* or *real numbers*. Both integer numbers and decimal numbers are called constants. The reason that they are classified into two types of numbers is that the computer may handle these different types of numbers in different ways. We'll be more specific about this in later classes."

At this point the pain in Howie's back had subsided, and he fell asleep again. When he awoke, he noticed Prof. Ovitt over in the corner of the room explaining some concepts to Seymour Movies, one of the slower kids in the class. It wasn't that Seymour Movies was dumb, it's just that he was faithful in his attempt to live up to his good name, and this sometimes interfered with his time for studying.

Howie approached and listened.

"All right, Seymour," said Prof. Ovitt, "now tell me what we mean by a constant."

"An integer constant is any number written without a decimal point, and a real constant is any number written with a decimal point," recounted Seymour.

"Can you give me some examples?" asked Phil.

Seymour began to fidget. As he looked over Phil Ovitt's shoulder, he noticed Howie waving frantically and pointing to a large cue card he was holding in his other hand. It read:

Seymour smiled and read aloud: "The integer constants might be 50, 0, −5, or +3. Examples of real constants are 50 point 0, zero point zero, −5 point zero, plus 3 point zero, and one divided by two."

Seymour blew it! He had read the last number from Howie's sweatshirt. Prof. Ovitt turned around and caught Howie in the act. "Mr. Gettindere," he called. "Come over here, will you."

"Mr. Gettindere," commented Prof. Ovitt, "how about explaining the difference between constants such as those you just displayed and variables."

Howie clutched his throat and made motions like he was trying to speak but could not. It was the old "laryngitis in a pinch" trick. The last time Howie used this ploy was in his senior year in high school during the final match of the debating team. Oddly enough, Howie still won by default, when the opponent collapsed in laughter.

"Okay, Howard, I understand," said Prof. Ovitt. "Forget it!"

Seymour had spent this time sneaking a look at the textbook pages covering variables. So, when Prof. Ovitt turned to him, he was ready.

"That's okay, Professor," he said. "I know what variables are. I had them in algebra last year. Variables are like X, or TOTAL when X or TOTAL may take on different values. That is, their values vary. We've seen variables a lot so far in your class. They just weren't labeled yet. For example, when you gave us Review Exercise 2.2, the variables DAY, PAY, and TOTAL were used in the flowchart. Their values changed all through the program."

"Very good," commented Ovitt. Phil turned and began writing on a blackboard. "There is even more to be learned from that exercise. The statement DAY = 1.0 is called an ASSIGNMENT statement because it assigns to the variable named DAY the value of 1.0. Please don't consider the = sign as the usual equals sign. If you did, one of the statements in the same program would not make any sense. That one is

$$DAY = DAY + 1.0$$

These values are not equal in the traditional sense. Rather, we are saying take the old value for DAY, add one to it, and assign this new total to a variable called DAY. Kind of an update routine."

When Phil turned around, Seymour was gone. Phil thought to himself the probability of that young man's majoring in computer science is about equal to the probability that a cannibal would complain because too many cooks spoiled the broth.

Phil left.

TOPIC SUMMARY FOR SECTION 2.4

Integer numbers	Real numbers
Fixed-point numbers	Floating-point numbers
FORTRAN integer constant	FORTRAN real constant
Variables	Equals sign denotes assignment

2.5 SUBSCRIPTS

Prof. Ovitt was busily preparing his computer science lecture for the following day. He had, of course, given the "subscripts" lecture before, but he was always looking for a new and more interesting way to present the material. It was late in the day and most of the other faculty members had gone home. The only exception was Prof. I. M. Whittier who, unfortunately, fancied himself as the resident humorist.

"Hi Phil," bellowed Ivan, "working late tonight?"

"Yes, I . . . ." Before he could answer, Ivan interrupted.

"Got a great joke for you, Phil. Use it in your class to keep 'em awake."

Phil tried to think of something funny, for Ivan had tenure and Phil would be well advised to laugh. Tenure for Ivan, that was pretty funny in itself.

Ivan was going full tilt.

"There were these 10 prisoners in one of the cell blocks at the state prison. The prisoners wiled away the hours by telling one of the stock 20 jokes they had exchanged over the years. Although they had all heard the jokes before, they enjoyed their retelling during the week.

"After a while, the warden—who was a blood relative of Captain Bluebeard—decided that the inmates were enjoying themselves far too much, and he ordered that the joke-telling sessions cease.

"Well, as you might imagine, the inmates didn't take this too lightly. In their clever manner they devised a new system for telling the same old jokes. Instead of telling the jokes in the old narrative format, the teller would simply call out a number, say, 12, and the cell block would erupt in riotous laughter as the inmates recalled the contents of joke 12.

"One day, a new inmate was brought to the block. During his first evening, one of the other inmates quite suddenly yelled out '19,' at which time the walls reverberated with laughter. This went on for several days, and the new inmate couldn't figure out what was going on. Finally, in desperation, he decided to try it himself. Early the next evening he yelled out '16.'

"Silence.

"Stunned, he yelled once again, 'Hey guys, 16!'

"Again, nothing.

"Completely baffled, he turned to one of his cellmates and said 'Hey, every night someone yells out a number and everyone breaks up. Tonight, I give a try with 16 and nothing happens. How come?'

"'Well,' came the sympathetic reply, 'some people can tell a joke and some people can't!'"

Phil had to admit that it was a funny story, but he didn't get the chance as Prof. Whittier was leaving—holding his side in sheer pain from his own laughter.

Phil chuckled aloud—more from what he had discovered than from the joke itself. Here, unbelievably, was a great example of subscripts. The customary way to refer to a single item in a list is with a subscript. Thus a joke might be more easily referenced by referring to its position in the list.

	JOKE LIST
Joke 1	Traveling salesman story
Joke 2	Farmer's son tale
Joke 3	Three little bears story
Joke 4	The knock, knock joke

Thus, Joke 3 refers to the third item in the list. The number 3 is the subscript. It is a kind of pointer, pointing to the particular joke desired.

Phil was getting warmed up. He began writing his notes feverishly.

"Another name for a list is an *array*. Thus, in the above example, Joke is the name of an array containing four items. A particular item can be referenced by referring to its subscript. The name and subscript are labels that we use as a convenience in looking up an item. The item can be jokes, as above, or numbers or messages or whatever. Our subscripts are merely pointers in a list.

"We are, of course, not limited to using a single subscript. We can use as many subscripts as we need pointers.

"For example, suppose that we have four prisoners in our cell block and each has responsibility for five jokes. We could identify which prisoner was telling which joke by using two pointers (or subscripts) and deciding which pointer refers to a prisoner number and which pointer refers to a particular joke.

"Picture our joke array (on paper) as looking somewhat like the following:

JOKE NUMBER

		1	2	3	4	5
	1					
PRISONER	2					
NUMBER	3					
	4					

"At the position of row 1 and column 1 in this table would be prisoner number 1's first joke. Here we have an example of an array with really more than one list. We have a prisoner list and a joke list. To refer to any item in this array we need two pointers.

"If we call our array Joke, then we can locate a particular joke by using our first subscript to indicate which prisoner will speak and the second subscript to denote which joke he will tell.

"Thus, Joke 3,4 would represent the third prisoner's fourth joke. For our own convenience, it will be useful in programming to write these subscripts a little differently. Therefore, we will write Joke(3,4) instead of Joke 3,4. With our new notation, the parentheses contain the two subscripts separated by a comma. The name of our array is placed before the parentheses.

"When we deal with these kinds of tables, it sometimes helps to think of the subscripts in parentheses as row and column pointers. The first subscript points to a particular row and the second to a particular column . . . ."

The class was going well the next day, and Prof. Ovitt had just completed his example of an array with two subscripts.

"Mr. Gettindere," the professor asked, "could you give us another example of such an array?"

Howie didn't like to be called on in class because it interfered with his daydreaming.

"Well, I'm glad you asked me that . . ." began Howie.

Clara Fy saw that Howie was in trouble and interjected: "Maybe a real example I ran across Saturday while I was working at the clothing store 'Suit Yourself' would be helpful. To keep the records straight, the store uses an array for sales figures for each day. The regular salespersons are Max E. Mum, Terry Cloth, and Minnie Mum.[1] There are five types of suits that the store sells. The array for Saturday's sales looked like this." Clara went to the chalkboard and drew the following figure.

		SUIT TYPE			
SALESPERSON ↓	1	2	3	4	5
Max E. Mum	10	8	7	5	9
Terry Cloth	1	17	3	9	11
Minnie Mum	0	0	−2	1	0

Clara continued: "If we let Max be salesperson 1, Terry be salesperson 2, and Minnie be salesperson 3, we could call the entries in the array Sales(I,J) where I refers to the salesperson number and J refers to the suit type. For example Sales(1,3) is 7, and this says that sales for person 1 of type 3 suit is 7. Sales(3,1) = 0. Any questions?"

"Yeah," queried Brandon Cattle, the kid from Texas, "how can Sales(3,3) be −2?"

"Unfortunately, Minnie had to accept two returns of type 3 suits she had sold previously. The store is considering putting all this informa-

[1]No relation to Max.

tion on a computer disk when it automates its inventory system. Then it will want to keep many day's sales records on disk, so it will expand the sales array to three dimensions. The entries will be Sales(I,J,K) where I will be the salesperson number, J will be the suit type, and K will be the day. If we consider that Saturday was the first day of the records, then Sales(1,3,1) would be the sales made by Max of suite type 3 on day 1, and has the value of 7. If Max sells 6 of type 3 suit on the second day, then Sales(1,3,2) = 6. Another name for an array is a *matrix,* and while we're on the subject, I'd like to talk about the eigenvalues of matrices."

Just then the bell rang and the class cleared out of the room faster than the hole of a doughnut gets lost when you eat the last bite of the doughnut.

TOPIC SUMMARY FOR SECTION 2.5

Single subscript	Pointers
Double subscripts	Arrays
Three dimensions	

Problems for Sec. 2.5

In order to raise money to make up for the deficit from the car raffle (see example, Section 2.1), the dance committee has decided to sell magazine subscriptions. The magazines and their subscription prices are the following:

1. *True Concessions, The Magazine of the Vending Industry,* $9.95
2. *Don't Litter, A Birth Control Magazine for Animals,* $.72
3. *Hard to Digest,* $4.95
4. The everpopular *Reader's Disgust,* $3.00

The students selling the magazines are these:

1. Rudy Mentry
2. Howie Gettindere
3. Seymour Movies

When the magazine sales drive was over, the record of magazine sales was displayed in a matrix called SALES with SALES(I,J) being the sales by person I of magazine J. The magazine prices could be put in a list PRICE with PRICE(J) being the price of magazine J.

1. What is the PRICE list?
2. Draw a flowchart for an algorithm that sums the total amount of money collected. *Hint:* Use a nested loop configuration, summing the number of magazines of a particular type sold by all persons with the inner loop, and summing over the magazine types in the outer loop.

COMPUTER RIDDLES

Evaluate the following expressions in the blanks provided. Then substitute a letter for each number using the following substitution rule: 0 = blank, 1 = A, 2 = B, 3 = C, 4 = D, 5 = E, 6 = F, etc. When you have finished you can read down the page to answer the question: "Why isn't 10 cents worth now what it was worth in 1960?" Note the first expression has been done for you.

		Answer	Letter equivalent
1. $-20 + (6 ** 2)/9 + 20$	=	4	D
2. $3 * (6/2)$	= _____		
3. $3 * (4/2) ** 3 - 11$	= _____		
4. $20 * 20 - 395$	= _____		
5. $2 + 2 * 6 - (-5)$	= _____		
6. $8 ** 2 - 6 * 3 ** 2 - 10$	= _____		
7. (Number of days in September) $- 22$	= _____		
8. $(-1) ** 6$	= _____		
9. The number 22	= _____		
10. $2 ** (1 * 3) - 3$	= _____		
11. In Clara Fy's example Sales(3,1)	= _____		
12. Sales(1,4) + Sales(3,3)	= _____		
13. $8 *$ Sales(2,1)	= _____		
14. Sales(1,5)/Sales(2,4)	= _____		
15. Sales(1,1) + [Sales(3,3)] $** 2$	= _____		
16. Number of small associates of Snow White	= _____		
17. Number of nickels equal to a quarter	= _____		
18. Number of musicians in a quartet	= _____		

2.6 DEBUGGING PROGRAMS

"Before you begin writing programs," started Prof. Ovitt, "you should be aware of some techniques that are available for helping you detect any errors in your program. We all make mistakes, particularly in programming. But don't be discouraged, making errors can be a very worthwhile learning experience. In fact, many times we can use the computer to find the errors for us."

"What kind of mistakes are you referring to?" asked Rudy.

"There are three major types of errors that occur," Phil answered. "Let me list them on the board."

1. Compilation errors
2. Execution errors
3. Logic errors

"You know what compilation errors are, don't you, Seymour?" asked Prof. Ovitt.

"No, sir," he replied. "But I know what an execution error is!"

"Never mind!" said Ovitt. "I know just what you're going to say. Forget it! A compilation error occurs when the computer is reading your program and translating it into machine language. If you have violated any of the rules of the particular programming language you are using, a *translation* (or *compilation*) *error* occurs."

"Does the computer just stop when it finds an error?" asked Clara.

"Of course not," said Howie, "it whistles for you and tells you what mistake you've made!"

"I know you're joking, Howard," commented Prof. Ovitt, "but you're not far from right. While the computer doesn't whistle, it does give you a listing of the errors that you made in your program.

"If you use a statement that violates a rule of the programming language, the type of error and where it is will be printed for your benefit. This is usually done on the line following the statement with the error. Some systems even print an arrow pointing to the character where the error was detected.

"The other kinds of compilation time error messages you may get are summary messages. These appear at the end of the printed program and identify those errors that cannot be associated with a particular statement. For example, if you instructed the computer to find a statement that was numbered 5 and there was no such statement in your program, this error would be listed as a summary message."

"Would you give us an example of a compilation error?" asked Seymour.

Prof. Ovitt spoke as he began to write.

"I'm sure that all of you will become quite familiar with compilation error messages once you begin writing programs, but I can give you some brief examples to illustrate these types of errors using punched-card processing:

1. Punching commands in the wrong card columns
2. Putting periods or commas in the wrong place
3. Spelling keywords wrong
4. Using the wrong symbols

"When you get these kinds of errors, you will have to correct them before submitting your program again."

"And then it will run fine, right?" asked Clara.

"Well, if you've been careful in making your corrections, it should compile properly. However, there is then a possibility of an *execution error*. An execution error will occur if, as the computer begins executing the commands, it encounters a condition that prevents further processing.

"For example, if your commands have instructed the computer to read several cards of data and these are not enough data cards for the program, then the following message might be printed.

PROGRAM TERMINATED
EXECUTION ERROR OCCURRED IN LINE 50

where line 50 has the READ command mentioned above.

"An execution error would also occur if you were attempting to divide something by zero. While there are many more ways in which execution may be terminated, these are common ones."

"Those also seem pretty easy to correct," suggested Howie. "Just like with compilation errors, all that is needed is to make the obvious correction and resubmit the program."

"That's right, Howard," replied Prof. Ovitt. "It is not that difficult to correct compilation and execution errors, particularly since the computer has identified the error and its location.

"You won't be as fortunate if you have the third type of error in your program," said Prof. Ovitt.

"You mean logic errors?" asked Howie.

"Yes, that's right," responded Phil. "After your program has been debugged of all compilation errors and execution errors, it can be executed and produce some output. If the output isn't what you expected it to be, you've probably made a logic error."

"Sounds logical," affirmed Howie.

Rudy was wondering how you would know if your output isn't correct, so he asked Prof. Ovitt. "Prof. Ovitt, how would you know if your output isn't correct?"

"Take my advice," responded Phil, "when you write a program, no matter how large or small, always use test data for which you know the answer to verify the logic of your program. Simply because your program causes answers to be printed doesn't mean that they are the right answers."

"What kinds of errors are most common?" asked Clara.

"Well, I have quite often seen beginning programmers type a 1 where they meant to type an I or perhaps an O when they meant a zero. These are usually quite hard to find, unless you're looking for them. Other common errors are incorrect loops or incorrect decision branches.

"If you get what appears to be a logic error in your program, I would recommend your following these steps." Prof. Ovitt erased the board and began to write.

1. Check the input data to see if it contains incomplete or erroneous data.
2. Check for mistypings.
3. Check the sequence of the statements in the program for correctness of the order.
4. Check to see if some statements may have been inadvertently added or omitted.

5. Work through the program by hand to determine how the results that were printed were obtained.
6. Liberally place PRINT commands in your program to display results all along the way. Make sure you label what gets printed to aid your deciphering.
7. Run a TRACE on the program as it executes.

"As you can see, detecting logic errors can be quite involved, and thus time spent carefully preparing a program before processing is time well spent."

"What's a TRACE?" asked Seymour.

"A TRACE is a procedure for having the computer follow the execution of a program and print what it is doing as it goes along.

"Don't be discouraged," said Prof. Ovitt. "If you are aware of the kinds of errors that may occur, you will be less likely to make them. Besides, the computer will find most of the errors for you. You will learn a great deal about computers and programming from the errors you make. Let the machine be a teacher also. Now, if there are any more questions I'll handle them after class."

As Howie and Rudy were walking out, Howie turned to his friend. "When I write my first program and get an error, it won't be my first error today," he said.

"What do you mean?" asked Rudy.

"Well, when I got up this morning, I put my socks on the wrong feet!" replied Howie.

"Don't be silly, Howie," said Rudy, "how can you put your socks on the wrong feet?"

"I put them on Cole's!" Howie replied.

chapter 3

Fortran programming

One of the most widely accepted methods of utilizing the computer is through programming in the FORTRAN language and executing those programs by batch processing. The purpose of this chapter is to present FORTRAN and simultaneously extend the level of sophistication of the algorithmic processes that were introduced in Chapter 2.

By quickly introducing complete programs, Section 3.1 provides a preview of many statements in the FORTRAN language. These statements presented in Section 3.1 will be covered in greater detail in subsequent sections.

The early sections of this chapter use unformatted input and output statements associated with the WATFOR and WATFIV FORTRAN compilers. If you are not using one of these FORTRAN compilers, it will be necessary to skip to Section 3.12 to cover FORMATTED INPUT and OUTPUT after Section 3.2, then return to the normal sequence starting with Section 3.3.

3.1 AN INTRODUCTION

While leaving class one Tuesday, Howie overheard two of his classmates talking. Their conversation was as follows:

Clara Fy was speaking. "Did you finish the computer assignment for Thursday?"

"Sure did," replied Neva Dunn. "It was a snap. I'll bet everyone has finished that one." Neva had reason to claim it was easy. It was his second time through the course. He took computer science his first siesta here.

"Not everyone," thought Howie silently. "In fact, I better go ask Rudy Mentry for some help. He always makes things seem so clear when he explains them."

"Hey, Rudy! Got a minute?" asked Howie.

"Sure, Howie," replied Rudy, knowing what he was in for, yet feeling a sense of compassion for a fellow student in need.

"You know the computer assignment for Thursday?" Howie asked. "I could use a little help on it. Here's a copy of the problem."

ASSIGNMENT 5

Write a FORTRAN program that calculates a value for the expression A + B + C and a value for the expression A − B − C with the values A = 2.0, B = 3.0, and C = 4.5. Have the program print out the values of A, B, C, and the two answers it calculates. Punch the program on cards and run the program through the computer.

"The problem, Rudy, is that I just don't know how to get started," lamented Howie.

Rudy began, "Well, first let's let X and Y be the quantities we want to calculate. Then the problem is solved with these statements

```
A = 2.0
B = 3.0
C = 4.5
X = A + B + C
Y = A − B − C
PRINT, A, B, C, X, Y
STOP
END
```

Rudy continued, "Statements like A = 2.0 and X = A + B + C are ASSIGN-MENT statements, as mentioned in Chapter 2. When a program is read into the computer, the cards are read in the order they are stacked in the card deck. At execution time (the time when the computer performs the calculations), the instructions are executed in the same order as they were read, unless a CONTROL statement alters that order of execution. By the way, a CONTROL statement is very different from the job control cards required by the computer center. If we had left out the statement A = 2.0 and tried to run the program, the computer would not have been able to calculate A + B + C because it would not have had a value for A. Hence the computer would stop and print an error message. Before a variable can be on the right-hand side of an [=] sign at execution time, it must have been given a value previously in the program. The STOP statement tells the computer to stop executing the statements of the program. The END statement must be the last statement of the FORTRAN program. This tells the computer that the last card of the program has been read in and the computer can begin execution of the program. The PRINT[1] statement is an output statement and tells the computer to print the values of the variables or expressions that follow it."

Howie suddenly realized that the program that had been assigned for homework was the same program he had found in the wastebasket at the computer center. He was just going to tell Rudy this, but Rudy started talking first.

"Glad to be able to help you Howie. I'm sure you'll have no trouble now. It would take a pretty slow person to forget an easy program like this, once they've seen how it goes."

Howie decided to say "Thanks" and let it go at that. When he went to run the program, he recalled that he no longer had that deck of cards that he had already prepared at the computer center. He had used the eight cards to send postcards to all his friends. Even though he still had six left over he had already put stamps on them, so they could not be reused. Now he was faced with the problem of determining how to punch up the cards. So he decided to go to his best source.

When Howie arrived at the computer center, the wastebasket was still in the same place. "Now, if the maintenance people have not emptied the contents of the basket," thought Howie, "I will use them."

The first card that he withdrew had no resemblance to the material that Rudy had gone over. It read:

---

[1]Your computer installation may use a different output statement, depending on the particular version of FORTRAN being used.

Howie threw a quarter (exact change) in the basket and tried again. This time he found one that seemed more appropriate. He looked closely at the columns on the card in an effort to determine where things should be typed.

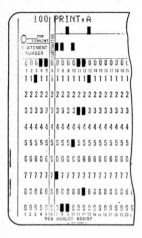

One card wasn't enough to make a decision, so Howie reached in for a handful. Now, he had a set like the following:

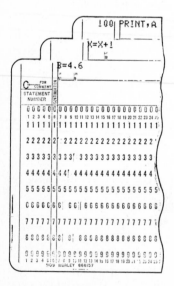

Howie saw a clear and distinct pattern. Every time a statement number was used it appeared in columns 1 to 5. Column 6 was always empty and the FORTRAN statement always started in column 7. With an air of triumph, Howie turned and saw Rudy coming into the center.

"Hey Rudy!" he exclaimed. "Came over to punch up your program, huh!"

Before Rudy could respond, Howie volunteered to help.

"When you're punching the FORTRAN statement, you punch beginning in column 7."

Rudy, sensing that Howie was a trifle overconfident, replied "How many columns can you use for a FORTRAN statement?"

"Why, all of them, of course—up to column 80."

"Sorry pal," said Rudy. "FORTRAN statements can only be punched between columns 7 and 72 of the card. The remaining columns, 73 to 80, are ignored by the machine."

"Wait a minute, Mr. Wizard," cried a surprised Howie. "What if my FORTRAN statement is too long to fit between columns 7 and 72?" Howie doubted that he would ever create a statement that long, but he was wondering what Rudy's response would be.

"In that case you continue it on the next card. To tell the computer that you are continuing, you punch a 1 in column 6 of that second card. Anytime the machine detects a punch in column 6, it knows that the FORTRAN statement has been continued from the previous card." Howie had been wondering what column 6 was going to be used for.

"I have another question," said Howie. "If the computer ignores columns 73 to 80, why don't they just have a card with 72 columns?"

Rudy answered, "Well, one use for these columns is for card numbers. If you type card numbers on each card in columns 73 to 80 and you drop your deck or accidentally mix the cards up, you will be able to put them back in order."

"Makes sense," Howie replied. "Are there any other columns that are used for something?"

"Well, if you type the letter C in column 1 that card will not be treated like a FORTRAN statement. It is called a *comment card,* and you can type anything you want on this card. Programmers usually put a reminder in here about what a particular program segment is doing. Although the computer isn't going to 'do what the card says,' when the program gets printed out on your output sheet, the comment cards will appear in the listing. It can be a handy reference point. Well, I've got to get going . . . see you later, Howie."

Howie recalled what happened to Hannibal when he crossed the Alps with an elephant. He got a mountain that never forgets. So that he wouldn't forget, Howie decided to write on a 3×5 card the rules for punching cards in FORTRAN. (See the boxed comment at the top of page 58.)

Howie recalled that computer center control cards had to be inserted in the program deck and that his instructor had given him these cards.

After he had submitted his deck for the homework problem, Howie decided to try some other programs for fun while he was waiting

Columns	Contents
1 to 5	Statement numbers (if needed)
6	Continuation indicator (if needed)
7 to 72	FORTRAN statement
73 to 80	Individual card numbers (if desired)

A C in column 1 identifies a COMMENT card.

for his output. In his remedial math course he had an assignment to calculate the values of 2 raised to the powers of 1 through 15. Howie thought he would write a program to do this, so he could check his math. First, he drew a flowchart.

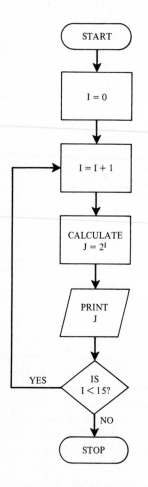

Then, he wrote the program

```
         I = 0
    6    I = I + 1
         J = 2 ** I
         PRINT, I, J
         IF (I .LT. 15) GO TO 6
         STOP
         END
```

Quite frankly, Howie was amazed! He thought to himself, "This program has a lot to it. For example, a new statement being used is that IF statement. That was a CONTROL statement. With it, you could control the order in which statements are executed." Howie had recalled that the general form of the IF statement was

Evaluate
this
↓

IF (   ) STATEMENT X
NEXT STATEMENT

The expression in the parentheses will be evaluated as either true or false. If it is true, STATEMENT X will be executed. If it is false, STATEMENT X will not be executed; execution will continue with NEXT STATEMENT. STATEMENT X in Howie's program is GO TO 6, which when executed causes the computer to go to the statement numbered 6. Inside the parentheses in the IF statement there is a comparison. We compare two things by using what is called a *relational operator*. Howie recalled that he had a relation that was an operator for New England Telephone Company. The operators that can be used in this IF statement are:

.LT.   Less than
.GT.   Greater than
.LE.   Less than or equal to
.GE.   Greater than or equal to
.NE.   Not equal to
.EQ.   Equal to

Howie pinched himself to see if he was awake. It didn't seem possible that he was remembering all this, even including the periods on either side of an operator.

Work through Howie's program and see if it will, in fact, print out the first 15 powers of 2.

Now, Howie was really feeling at home with the computer. He decided to try to program a problem he had read somewhere else. In fact, it was Review Exercise 2.2 that appears in this book. Howie redrew the flowchart for computer solution.

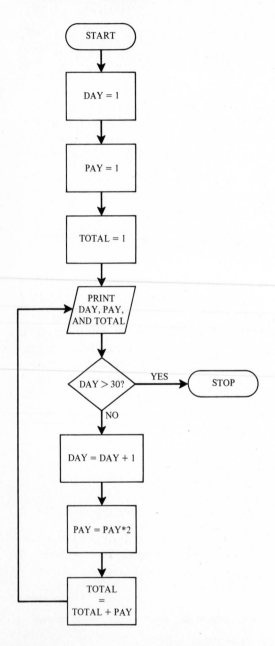

Howie then wrote the FORTRAN statements for this problem.

```
                  Program for a Wise Mathematician

                        DAY = 1.0
                        PAY = 1.0
                        TOTAL = 1.0
                  11    PRINT, DAY, PAY, TOTAL
                        IF (DAY .GE. 30.0) STOP
                   9    DAY = DAY + 1.0
                        PAY = PAY * 2.0
                        TOTAL = TOTAL + PAY
                  12    GO TO 11
                        END
```

This program is different from previous ones in several ways.

1. More than one statement has a number, and statement 11 appears before statement 9. That's okay, the statements are executed in order of
   appearance, not in order of statement number.
2. The STOP statement is in the middle of the program. This does not
   prevent the second half of the program from being executed, however.
   The IF statement will cause the program to ignore the STOP statement
   many times.
3. Statement 12 is a GO TO statement. That statement will cause the execution of the program to go to statement 11 whenever statement 12 is
   executed.
4. Statement numbers are only needed when you reference a particular
   statement. Thus, statement numbers 9 and 12 are really not necessary.
   They are used for explanatory purposes only.

   Howie wondered if there was an easy way to check on whether or
not a program was correct before submitting it to the computer. If there
was some kind of shortcut, it would not only help him to understand more,
but also save time. Oddly enough, as he looked across the room Howie saw
Manny Tricks, who was known all over campus as the resident expert on
shortcuts. For example, Manny only took three courses a semester, figuring that when he was a senior they'd have to let him graduate 'cuz he was
a senior. He also saved time in class by not taking any notes. If there were
anyone who would know a shortcut for testing a program, he certainly
would. Howie approached.

   "Hi Man!" called Howie. "Say, do you know of any ways to look
at a computer program before you hand it in to the machine and tell
whether or not it works?"

   Manny cleared his throat. "Well, Howie," he began, "there is one
method that I use and I'd be glad to show it to you." Manny always liked
to show off and quite willingly began.

"When you look at a program, I'd recommend doing the following. First, list across the top of a blank piece of paper all of the names used in your program. This should not include FORTRAN words like PRINT, STOP, GO TO, etc., but only those names that you make up. Do you have a program handy?"

Howie brought out the program for the wise mathematician.

"Now, to start off, we would write the variable names at the top of a page. In this case,

DAY   PAY   TOTAL

The rest is rather simple. You merely go through the program as if you were the computer. Whenever you give a value to one of the names above, you put it in the proper column. This goes for value changes also. Here, I'll work this one out and make notes over on the right. Any time something gets printed out, I'll draw a square around it.

TRACING THE PROGRAM

DAY	PAY	TOTAL	Comment
1			First statement, DAY = 1.0
1	1		Second statement, PAY = 1.0
1	1	1	Third statement, TOTAL = 1.0
[1	1	1]	Fourth statement, PRINT, DAY, PAY, TOTAL
	DAY is *not* greater than 30		Fifth statement, don't STOP
2	1	1	Statement labeled 9, DAY = DAY + 1.0
2	2	1	The following statement, PAY = PAY * 2.0
2	2	3	The next statement, TOTAL = TOTAL + PAY
	Go to statement 11		Statement labeled 12, GO TO 11
[3	2	3]	Statement 12, PRINT, DAY, PAY, TOTAL
3	4	3	The IF statement, don't STOP
3	4	7	DAY = DAY + 1.0
3	8	7	PAY = PAY * 2.0
3	8	15	TOTAL = TOTAL + PAY
	Go to statement 11		Same transfer as before
[3	8	15]	PRINT, DAY, PAY, TOTAL
. . .			. . .

"Now," Manny interrupted, "this should be enough to determine whether or not the FORTRAN statements are working. You see, you are kind of being the computer and working through the problem. In this case, something called PAY is being doubled each DAY for 30 days. The TOTAL amount collected is also being calculated. Was that the problem?"

Howie was impressed. "Yes, that was the problem. It is also a nice way to check the program. Many thanks, Manny."

TOPIC SUMMARY FOR SECTION 3.1

ASSIGNMENT statements
CONTROL statements
STOP statements
END statements
PRINT statements
Card columns
    Statement numbers
    FORTRAN statements
    Continuation indicator

COMMENT card
Control cards
IF statement
Relational operators
Order of EXECUTION
GO TO statement
Program tracing

CROSSWORD PUZZLE

Across

1. The statement that tells the computer to halt processing.
5. The real meaning of an equal sign in a computer language.
8. A rope is often tied in a _____.
9. Al Gorithm's first name.
11. If arrested while reading this book, you would say, NO _____!
11. A statement used to place messages in a program.
13. A nifty IF statement.

Down

·2. Statement used to display results.

3. Statements that affect the sequence in which commands are executed.

4. Signifies the conclusion of your particular program.

6. The card column where FORTRAN statements may start.

7. The unconditional transfer of control statement is _____ TO.

9. Shortened form of your uncle's wife.

10. One of the relational operators.

12. You!

Problems for Sec. 3.1

1. Punch on cards and run Howie's Assignment 5. Add some COMMENT cards to the card deck.
2. Which of the following types of statements are executable FORTRAN statements? (You are allowed to look other places besides Section 3.1 of this book to obtain an answer.)
   (*a*) ASSIGNMENT
   (*b*) CONTROL
   (*c*) STOP
   (*d*) END
   (*e*) PRINT
   (*f*) COMMENT
   (*g*) GO TO
   (*h*) IF
3. What is the difference between an END statement and a STOP statement?
4. Explain the "order of execution" of a program.
5. Which of the following are allowed as statement numbers in FORTRAN?
   (*a*) −2364
   (*b*) 998763
   (*c*) 2A3
   (*d*) 75.3
   (*e*) 0001
   (*f*) 0000
6. Write a program that computes 7^3.
7. Write a program that computes the cubes of the integers from 3 through 9.
8. Write a program that computes the cubes of the odd integers from 3 through 19.

3.2 INTEGER AND FLOATING-POINT CONSTANTS AND VARIABLES

One day, Howie went to visit an old friend from E. Z. High School. When he arrived at Benjamin's apartment, he was nowhere to be found. His roommate tried to explain to Howie.

"You're probably not going to believe this. Remember that Ben wasn't very popular socially. Ben pleaded each night that somehow, something would make him more popular. Well, one morning Ben told me that he had had a dream during the night, in which a voice told him that if he grew a beard he would be enormously popular. The voice also warned him that if he ever shaved off that beard, he would immediately be turned into a vase! Yes, I thought it was weird too. Anyway, Ben grew the beard and was enormously popular. So popular, in fact, that he couldn't stand it any longer. He longed for his once hated solitude. Finally, yesterday morning at breakfast he leaped up and stormed into the bathroom to shave away his claim to popularity. And that was the last I saw of him. Half an hour later when I went to look for him, all that was in the bathroom was his razor and a small white vase. And that was that!"

Howie didn't know what to say. "Well," he mumbled, "I guess, a Benny shaved is a Benny urned!"

"Yes, I guess so," said the roommate, looking at Howie rather strangely. "By the way, he said you might be able to help me with a problem. I'm doing some research on numbers and I want to derive the formula for the sum of the first N terms of $\frac{1}{2} + \frac{1}{3} + \frac{1}{4} + \frac{1}{5} + \frac{1}{6} + \ldots$. In other words, for $N = 3$, I want the value of $\frac{1}{2} + \frac{1}{3} + \frac{1}{4}$. For $N = 6$, I want the value of $\frac{1}{2} + \frac{1}{3} + \frac{1}{4} + \frac{1}{5} + \frac{1}{6} + \frac{1}{7}$. I think I have the formula worked out, Howie. I wonder if you could check out a few easy ones, like for N being 1, or 2, or 3."

"I'll do better than that," responded Howie boastfully. "I'll add the series for $N = 50$ and $N = 100$ and have the result tomorrow. It'll be a snap, because I learned all about fractions in my remedial math course."

"Well, give it a try, Howie," was the doubtful reply.

"See you tomorrow with the answer," Howie said as he departed.

Later, in his room, Howie decided that it would be easier for him to win a bicycle race on a bike that had the chain missing than it would be for him to add up these numbers without making a mistake. So he decided that he would write a computer program in FORTRAN and have the computer do the work. First, he drew the flowchart. He let N be the number of terms to add up. LUMP would be the amount he had added so far, and I would be the number of the term to be added next. Refer to the flowchart at the top of page 66.

"Let me check this out," Howie said to himself. "I can use $N = 50$ in the program, and when I want to run it for 100 terms, all I will have to do is change the first box to $N = 100$ and everything should still be the same. Let's see. Let me trace my logic here:

> N is 50
> LUMP is 0 (the amount I've added so far)
> I is 1 (this will be my counter)

Then, I let

$$\text{LUMP} = \text{LUMP} + 1/(I + 1)$$
$$\text{LUMP} = 0 + 1/(1 + 1)$$
$$\text{LUMP} = 1/2$$

Then, since I, which is 1, is less than 50, the counter I should be increased by 1. Now,

> I is 2

and

$$\text{LUMP} = \text{LUMP} + 1/(I + 1)$$
$$\text{LUMP} = 1/2 + 1/(2 + 1)$$
$$\text{LUMP} = 1/2 + 1/3$$

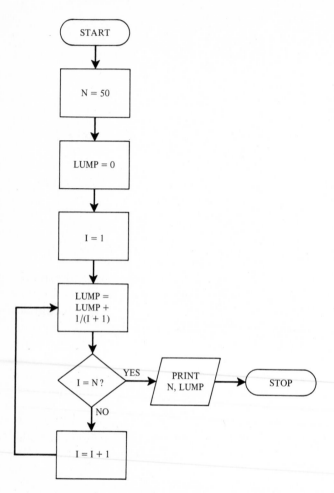

It looks like it is working. Now the program in FORTRAN." Howie wrote this program.

```
         N = 50
         LUMP = 0
         I = 1
   10    LUMP = LUMP + 1/(I + 1)
         IF (I .GE. N) GO TO 30
         I = I + 1
         GO TO 10
   30    PRINT, N, LUMP
         STOP
         END
```

Howie was excited with his project and ran to the computer center, where he correctly punched his card deck and submitted it. When the output came back, the output on the printout was:

```
        $JOB              'HOWIE',KP=29
  1            N=50
  2            LUMP=0
  3            I=1
  4     10     LUMP=LUMP+1/(I+1)
  5            IF (I.EQ.N) GO TO 30
  6            I=I+1
  7            GO TO 10
  8     30     PRINT,N,LUMP
  9            STOP
 10            END


        $ENTRY
         50                   0
```

Even Howie knew something was wrong. After looking at the program for a couple of billion nanoseconds, Howie knew he'd never be able to debug it so he went to see (you guessed it) his professor.

"At least you must be well rested," said Prof. Phil Ovitt to Howie after he looked at Howie's output.

"What do you mean?" asked Howie.

"Well, it's clear that you slept through my lecture yesterday on real variables and integer variables! Do you remember that real constants are numbers with decimals in them. Numbers like 46.0, +46.3, 10.7E3, $-5.1E+02$, and $+8.E-2$?"

Howie replied, "I'm not sure I know about the funny numbers with the E in them. Does E stand for extra hard?"

"No. The E stands for the exponent of the number. For example, the following are equivalent:

$$10.7E3 = 10.7 * 10^3 = 10700$$
$$-5.1E+02 = -5.1 * 10^2 = -510$$
$$+8.0E-02 = +8.0 * 10^{-2} = 0.08$$

Notice that, in each case, the number following the E was an integer (with no sign, a + sign, or a − sign). There can be no decimal in the exponent part of the real number. A real constant in the computer can have only seven digits in it but, of course, using the E notation you can write very big numbers. In fact most fourth-generation computers can handle numbers as big as about 10^{76} and as small as about 10^{-78}. Some examples of *errors* made while trying to write real constants are:

9.99999999	Too many digits. Remember, at most seven digits
9.99999900	Too many digits
100,000	No comma allowed
1.0E103	Number is too large
1.0E−103	Number is too small
18	No decimal point
18.E2.	Can't have decimal in exponent

Prof. Ovitt paused for a breath and Howie thought he'd make the most of the opportunity. "I think it must be time for me to go to the dorm for dinner," said Howie.

"But it's only 3 P.M.," replied the Prof.

"Then I'm real late for lunch," answered Howie.

"What about your program? Don't you want to debug it?"

"Oh yeah!"

"As I was saying," continued the venerable professor, "you know what real numbers are in FORTRAN. Integer numbers are numbers without a decimal point. The following are integer numbers:

50	+109
0	+123456789
−27	−89735

The largest integer number you can use with the newer computers is about 10^9 and the smallest is -10^9. Numbers that are not valid integer numbers are

1,000	Comma not allowed
10.	Period not allowed
988888888888	Too large
10E4	Exponents not allowed

"Yeah, I remember all that," interjected Howie. "But what about our broken down computer not running my program?"

"We're getting there, Howie Gettindere," responded the wise professor. "When we want to use variables in FORTRAN, we must give them a name. A valid FORTRAN variable name begins with a letter (any letter A through Z) and has from 0 to 5 additional letters or digits.[1] Examples of variable names are the following:

A
ABCDEF
$DOLR
X1A

[1] In the WATFIV version of FORTRAN, a $ may also be used as a letter.

Invalid names are

1A	Starts with a digit
DUMBELL	Too long
MONTH.	No special characters (like .) allowed

"Just as we have integer constants and real constants, we have integer variables and real variables. An *integer variable* is a variable that is going to have an integer value, and a *real variable* is a variable that is going to have a real value. In FORTRAN, integer variables have names that begin with I, J, K, L, M, or N; I, I2, JOHN, L2A are integer variable names. The other variable names are real variable names; A, $MONY, SUM are real variable names. Later we will talk about changing a program so that names beginning with I, J, K, L, M, or N can be real variable names, and names that don't begin with I, J, K, L, M, or N can be integer names."

"This is complicated," replied Howie.

"I have a 3 × 5 index card with some rules on it that I'll give you in a minute," the kind professor replied. "Now let's look at your program. The first time the computer executed the assignment statement

$$10 \quad \text{LUMP} = \text{LUMP} + 1/(I + 1)$$

the first thing it had to do is evaluate $1/(I + 1)$ when I was 1, an integer value. When the computer evaluates an integer expression it drops the decimal part off. So $1/(I + 1)$ became $1/(1 + 1)$ or $1/(2)$ which gets evaluated as 0 in integer arithmetic.

"The computer doesn't round off the answer in evaluating integer expressions; it just drops the decimal point. Thus, the first time your program executes statement $10 \text{ LUMP} = \text{LUMP} + 1/(I + 1)$, it results in $\text{LUMP} = 0$, not the 0.5 you desired."

"I guess I know why Al thought this was a hard problem," mumbled Howie. "It can't be done on a computer."

"Sure it can, Howie. You just need to know a little more about how the computer works when you program in FORTRAN. When a real expression like the one in your previous assignment (remember $A + B + C$) is evaluated, the results are a decimal number. You could change your program to use real variables and real expressions, and then you wouldn't lose all the decimal numbers you want.

"One quick way to fix the problem is to use a FORTRAN statement called the REAL statement. Any variable names you list after the word REAL will be treated as real variables even if they are given integer names. The REAL statement overrides the first letter convention. Thus your program could be written as follows." Prof. Ovitt inserted one statement in Howie's program and added some decimal points.

```
          REAL I, N, LUMP
          N = 50.0
          LUMP = 0.0
          I = 1.0
   10    LUMP = LUMP + 1.0/(I + 1.0)
          IF (I .EQ. N) GO TO 30
          I = I + 1.0
          GO TO 10
   30    PRINT, N, LUMP
          STOP
          END
```

"Howie . . . Howie . . . HOWIE!"

"Yes, Professor?" awoke Howie.

"Can you think of a FORTRAN statement that would convert real variables (i.e., they began with A to H or O to Z or $) to integer variables?"

"I suppose so," said Howie, "if given enough time."

Prof. Ovitt decided that he'd better leave while he was still calm. Phil left to join his close friend A. N. Chent, a history professor at UGH. They had decided to get together to talk over old times. As he left, he handed Howie an index card.

NAMING CONVENTIONS

Integer variables begin with I, J, K, L, M, or N.

Real variables begin with A to H, O to Z (or $).

Names must begin with a letter.

Names may contain only up to six characters.

Names may contain digits.

No special or odd characters may be used in names.

The INTEGER statement converts real names to integer names. The REAL statement converts integer names to real names. Integer and real statements are not considered executable statements.

For example, INTEGER Z, Z12, SALES will cause the variables Z, Z12, and SALES to be treated as integer variables (without decimals) rather than as real variables.

TOPIC SUMMARY FOR SECTION 3.2

FORTRAN real variables	FORTRAN naming conventions
FORTRAN integer variables	Length of FORTRAN names
E notation	Integer arithmetic
Size of real constants	INTEGER statement
Size of integer constants	REAL statement

Problems for Sec. 3.2

1. Answer the following questions by first straightening out the jumbled words making up the question.
   (*a*) THAW TCCHAARRSE RAE LWDOELA NI A TTTEEASNM MUBREN.
   (*b*) MEAS USENIQOT RFO AABEVRIL SMEAN.
   (*c*) WHO ANYM TTTEEASNMS RAE LWDOELA NO NOE DRAC?
   (*d*) HOW OD UYO UTNNOCIE A TTTEEASNM?
   (*e*) REEHT REA ON ROME USSENIQOT.
2. Howie had written a short composition for his English class that he was going to expand before handing it in. Take a look at his work and identify each "word" as
   (*a*) Valid FORTRAN variable name (integer or real)
   (*b*) Invalid FORTRAN name. Why?
   (*c*) Valid integer constant
   (*d*) Valid real constant

    I SPENT MY SUMMER VACATION RYDING WILD ELE-PHANTS IN BORNEO. WHILE I WAS ONLY THERE FOR 3 MOS. THAT WAS SUFFICIENT TO GET MORE THAN 35.631 SADDLE SORES.

    MY ADDRSS WAS 73.4E33 STREET WHICH MAY SOUND STRANGE SINCE E33 STREET IS IN N.Y. BUT THAT IS WHERE IT IS SINCE BORNEO IS EASILY FOUND IF YOU GO TO THE YEL-LOW PAGES. IT IS PART OF THE BRONX ZOO (SECTION-5). IF YOU CAN'T REMEMBER WHERE IT IS, TEAR OUT THE PAGE. AS THE KING COMMENTED TO HIS KNIGHT AS THE EVIL WHICH APPROACHED—PROMISE HER ANYTHING BUT GIVE HER OUR PAGE.

FORTRAN Integer Names	FORTRAN Real Names	Invalid FORTRAN Names	Valid Integer Constants	Valid Real Constants

3. Write a FORTRAN program that calculates $Y = X^3 + 4X^2 - (2/X)^2$ for $X = 1$.
4. Do Problem 2 for X equal to all the integers from 1 to 20.
5. Do Problem 2 for X equal to all the integers from -10 to $+10$ (be careful in this problem).
6. Punch up and run the FORTRAN program for the Wise Mathematician problem.
7. Write a FORTRAN program that computes the amount to charge in the car raffle in Section 2.1.
8. In order to raise money to support the student union, the student government has decided to have a lottery and has asked a member of the

student parliament, Voight Wareprohibited, to come up with rules to make the lottery interesting. Voight proposed that, to encourage people to buy a lot of tickets, each ticket be priced at $1, and that the person whose ticket gets drawn at lottery time be awarded an amount of money equal to 10 times the number of tickets he has bought. This rule was adopted and became known as the Voight Wareprohibited Bylaw. Write a FORTRAN program that calculates and prints the payoff to the winner, who bought 50 tickets. What do you think might happen in this lottery?

3.3 ASSIGNMENT STATEMENTS

Once upon a time there was a famous candy-maker named Pseudopoulos. His candy was so delicious and so artfully made that Pseudopoulos was asked to make candy for many large banquets in lands near and far. One day Pseudopoulos was asked to make candy for the royal wedding in the state of Athena. So pleased was the king of Athena with the candy that after the wedding he had Pseudopoulos make a large peppermint candy with the name Pseudopoulos on it. The king declared that candy to be the state candy. This is the first record that we have of a signed mint state mint.

The first record of ASSIGNMENT statements in this book is in Section 2.4, although ASSIGNMENT statements themselves were used as early as Section 1.3. Some of the ASSIGNMENT statements used already are the following:

$$A = 2.$$
$$X = A + B + C$$
$$DAY = DAY + 1.0$$

The general form of an ASSIGNMENT statement is "Variable = expression."

The variable on the left side of the [=] sign must be a single variable, such as A, X, or DAY in the preceding examples. The expression on the right side of the [=] sign can be a single number, like 2 or 5, or can be a more complicated expression, like A + B + C or DAY + 1.0. When the ASSIGNMENT statement is executed, the current values of the variables in the expression are used to evaluate the expression, and the resulting value is assigned to the variable on the left side. If the variables in the expression have not been previously assigned a value, when the computer tries to execute the assignment statement it will be unable to evaluate the expression and will print an error message.

The program that Howie wrote to print the first 15 powers of 2 in Section 3.1 has several assignment statements. The program was:

```
            I = 0
     6      I = I + 1
            J = 2 ** I
            PRINT, I, J
            IF (I .LT. 15) GO TO 6
            STOP
            END
```

In evaluating the expression in statement 6 the current value of I is added to 1, and this result is then assigned to I. The program executes as follows:

1. I is assigned the value 0.
2. In statement 6, the expression I + 1 is evaluated. The current value of I, which is 0, is added to 1 to get 1. This value is assigned to I (left side of [=] sign) so that I is now 1.
3. J = 2 ** 1 is calculated to be 2.
4. 1 and 2 are printed.
5. I is 1, which is less than 15, so GO TO 6 is executed; execution continues with statement 6.
6. In statement 6, the expression I + 1 is evaluated. The current value of I, which is 1, is added to 1 to get 2. This value is assigned to I, so that I is now 2.
7. J = 2 ** 2 is calculated to be 4.
   Etc.

Problems for Sec. 3.3

1. The following programs were submitted to the computer as complete programs. They did not run. Why didn't they? (The job control cards were all in order.)

```
(a)       C    AGE PROBLEM FROM ALGEBRA
               INTEGER TOM
               TOM = 1
               MARY = 2 * TOM
               MARY + 6 = TOM + 7
               PRINT, MARY, TOM
               STOP
               END
```

(b)
```
$5 = $3 + $2
PRINT, $5
STOP
END
```

(c)
```
INTEGER ONE, TWO, THREE, FOUR, FIVE
ONE = 1
TWO = 2
FOUR = 2 ** TWO
FIVE = TWO + THREE
PRINT, FOUR, FIVE
STOP
END
```

(d)
```
REAL NICKEL, NOT, MONEY
$5 = 5.
NICKEL = $5/100
NOT = -1.0
ALOT = 100.0
OF = 1.0
MONEY = 2NICKEL
$1 = NOT * ALOT * OF * MONEY
PRINT, $1
STOP
END
```

(e)
```
INTEGER ZERO, ONE, TWO, THREE
ZERO = 1
ONE = 0
TWO = ONE + ONE
THREE = 6/TWO
PRINT, THREE
STOP
END
```

(f)   INTEGER SUM, A
             SUM = 11
             SUM = SUM + SUM/3 + SUM/SUM
             A = SUM/(SUM − 15)
             PRINT, A
             STOP
             END

2. Check the appropriate column for the following FORTRAN ASSIGN-
MENT statements.

Statement	It's fine	Not Good	Don't Know
1. I = A			
2. 35 = SALES			
3. PAY = $150.92			
4. INTEREST = .05			
5. THREE = 2.0			
6. A ** 2 = B ** 2 + C ** 2			
7. SMALL = .12E+04/5.			
8. ANS = 3 * +5			
9. DUMB = HOWIE − BRAIN			
10. P387AB = X(3.5 − (B − 2.)			

3. Label each of the following FORTRAN names as integer variables, real
variables, or illegal variable names.

(a) 32   (g) NINE
(b) Z   (h) (XYZ)
(c) 5A   (i) J * 5
(d) N3602   (j) I
(e) NNNAAA5   (k) ABC
(f) B_25   (l) READ

4. How would the following expressions be written in FORTRAN?

(a) $M = \dfrac{3 + A}{Z + T}$

(b) $S = \dfrac{-b + (b^2 - 4AC)^{1/2}}{2a}$

(c) $K = \dfrac{3^A}{B} \dfrac{(X + 5)}{3} + \dfrac{1}{B}$

3.4 MIXED-MODE EXPRESSIONS AND MIXED-MODE ASSIGNMENT STATEMENTS

One day while Howie was gargling with mouthwash (he didn't have bad breath; he just wanted to see if his neck leaked), his friend Rudy Mentry walked up.

"Hi, How," said Rudy. "I just wrote a program to calculate the number of pets I have. I have three pet mice and two cats. Here's the program I wrote."

```
C   RUDY'S PET PROGRAM
    CATS = 2
    MICE = 3
    NUMBER = CATS + MICE
    PRINT, CATS, MICE, NUMBER
    STOP
    END
```

"Gee, Rudy, I used to think you were smart, but I don't know now. You should know that you can't put cats and mice together."

"No, Howie," replied Rudy. "I keep them separated. I'm just adding them in the program."

"Oh! Well, you can't even do that. CATS is a real variable name and MICE is an integer variable name. You should know that the values of these are stored differently in the computer and so you can't add them," said Howie haughtily.

"I know that they are stored differently, but remember what Prof. Ovitt said yesterday. An expression involving both integer values and real values is called a MIXED-MODE EXPRESSION. The computer can evaluate that expression. If a real valued number and an integer valued number are involved in a mathematical operation, the computer will convert the integer number to a real number and then perform the operation. In my program the integer value of MICE is converted to a real number, then added to CATS. For example in the expression

$$2.0 + 3$$

the 3 is converted to 3.0 and added to 2.0 to give 5.0. Here's an example that is trickier, though. If you had the expression

$$2/5 + 4.0$$

the 2/5 is evaluated first, and since both of those numbers are integers the result of 2/5 is 0; this 0 is to be added to 4.0, so the 0 is converted to 0.0 and added to 4.0 to give 4.0 as the result.

"If the expression had been written as

$$2.0/5 + 4.0$$

then the 2.0/5 would be evaluated by converting the 5 to 5.0 and 2.0/5.0 is 0.4. When this is added to 4.0, the result is 4.4. Similarly, (1/6) * 3.7 is evaluated as 0."

"I see," said Howie. "I'll bet (−2.0) ** 3 is converted to (−2.0) ** 3.0 and evaluated as −8.0."

"Well, Howie, the rules are a little different in evaluating exponents. If a real number is raised to an integer valued exponent, the exponent is not converted to a real value. Thus (−2.0) ** 3 is evaluated as −8.0 without converting the 3 to 3.0. When the computer raises a number other than zero, like 2.0, to an exponent that is real valued, it evaluates the expression using logarithms of the number (log 2.0 would be used). Since logarithms of negative numbers don't exist, the computer could not evaluate (−2.0) ** 3.0, and an error message would be printed. Thus when you use exponents, if the exponents are real numbers, be sure that the number to be raised to the exponent is not negative."

"In your pet program, what about your ASSIGNMENT statement CATS = 2? Did you mean to say CATS = 2.0?" Howie asked.

"No, Howie," Rudy responded. "That's an example of a MIXED-MODE ASSIGNMENT statement.[1] A mixed-mode assignment statement assigns to a variable on the left side of the [=] sign, a value from the right side that is a number of a different type or mode. In this case an integer expression on the right side of the [=] sign is to be assigned to a real variable. To execute that statement the computer converts the integer number to a decimal number, i.e., the 2 is converted to 2.0, and is assigned to CATS."

"How about 'NUMBER = CATS + MICE'?" asked Howie.

"NUMBER is an integer variable and CATS + MICE is evaluated as a real expression. When a real number is assigned to an integer variable, the computer just drops the decimal part of the number. In this case 2.0 + 3 is evaluated to be 5.0, and the value 5 is assigned to NUMBER.

"If the computer executes a statement I = 1.9, the value 1 would be assigned to I.

"Similarly, J = −7.0/4.0 would result in the expression −7.0/4.0 being −1.75 and J being assigned the value −1. Note that the decimal part of the number is dropped when a decimal number is assigned to an integer variable."

"This seems like a lot to remember," moaned Howie.

---

[1] The first record we have of this is the mention in Greek history of the day that Plato Mixed ran over the State Candy of Athena while cutting grass. The newspaper headlines the next day were "MIXED MOWED A SIGNED MINT STATE MINT," which Greek scholars have said could be translated into mixed-mode assignment statement.

"Yeah," said Rudy. "There was no reason to do so in this case, but I could have eliminated all mixed-mode work by writing the program as follows:

```
C   RUDY'S OTHER PET PROGRAM
    REAL MICE, NUMBER
    CATS = 2.0
    MICE = 3.0
    NUMBER = CATS + MICE
    PRINT, CATS, MICE, NUMBER
    STOP
    END
```

using the REAL DECLARATION statement.

"Or, I could have performed the entire program in integers as follows:

```
C   RUDY'S THIRD PET PROGRAM
    INTEGER CATS
    CATS = 2
    MICE = 3
    NUMBER = CATS + MICE
    PRINT, CATS, MICE, NUMBER
    STOP
    END
```

This program uses the INTEGER DECLARATION statement. But, like I said, the first program, using mixed-mode expressions and mixed-mode assignment statements, is perfectly good. One just has to know how the computer evaluates these things."

"Hey, Rudy," said Howie as he awakened, "want to go for a swim in the swimming hole?"

"The swimming hole is dry now, and it's too cold anyway," answered Rudy.

"That's great! I never could stand cold water, so it should be good. Let's give it a try," said Howie.

And off they went.

TOPIC SUMMARY FOR SECTION 3.4

MIXED-MODE expressions
MIXED-MODE ASSIGNMENT statement
REAL DECLARATION statement
INTEGER DECLARATION statement

Problems for Sec. 3.4

1. Explain the errors in the following assignment statements.
   (a) $3.6 = X$ (e) $I = A$
   (b) $X + Y = 9$ (f) $2 = 2$
   (c) $M8 = 8 + M8$ (g) $-A = 36.9$
   (d) $A = -B * + 6.$ (h) $I = I ** 3 ** 2$

2. Assume the following FORTRAN variables have been assigned values:
   $K = 72$
   $I = 19$
   $A = 7.$
   $B = 2.$
   Evaluate the following ASSIGNMENT statements:
   (a) $Y = K/I$ (d) $M = A/B * 2$
   (b) $Z = A/B$ (e) $K = K/A + K$
   (c) $L = A/B$

3. Write a program that determines if a number is even or odd. Print '1' if the number is odd and '2' if the number is even.

4. Read 20 data cards (with each one having one decimal number on it) and print the numbers with a 5 as the first digit to the right of the decimal point.

5. Let $A =$ any three digit number of your choice (under the condition that the first and third digits differ by more than 1). Call this number K and evaluate the following:
   (a) $L = K$ backwards
   (b)   IF (L .GT. K) GO TO 50
              $M = K - L$
              GO TO part (c)
        50    $M = L - K$
   (c) $N = M$ backwards
   (d) $J = ((N + M) * 10^9) - (2318 * 10^8 \ 36872552)$
   (e) Now, look at your answer and replace digits with letters according to the following scheme:

$0 = X$	$2 = D$	$4 = M$	$6 = R$	$8 = Y$
$1 = A$	$3 = E$	$5 = O$	$7 = U$	$9 = B$

3.5 UNFORMATTED INPUT AND OUTPUT

Prof. Phil Ovitt was having a quiet lunch in the school cafeteria when Prof. Whittier walked over.

"Hello, I. M.," said Phil with an expression indicating that he knew his serenity was over.

"Listen to what happened at my New Year's Eve party last week. Sorry, you couldn't make it, by the way. Well, I had everything prepared: the food was ready; my new octophonic stereo system was all set up; and the guests all started arriving when in walked my brother Mo with his dog. The dog walked over to the phonograph, put on a recording of popular nursery rhymes, and said in clear English, 'I want you all to hear my favorite record.'"

"That's incredible!" gasped the astonished Phil.

"I agree. Imagine, nursery rhymes on New Year's Eve."

Phil decided he'd had enough lunch and headed back to his office to prepare his lecture on the use of input statements in programming. While trying to forget Prof. Whittier's joke, he got an idea for his presentation on input statements. Phil jotted down these notes:

"When a person wants to listen to a record, he doesn't start designing and building the phonograph to play the record. Because this would take too long, the phonograph system is designed and built in advance. Furthermore, since people want to play different records at different times, the system is flexible enough to play any record that is *put in* the phonograph. Similarly, programmers may know that they are going to want to analyze some data as it becomes available and use that data for various purposes (like sales data for a store may be used to order new inventory). The programmers want to write programs in advance of their actual use of the program, and they want the program to have the flexibility of using any data that is put in the programming system. These goals can be accomplished with *input statements*. One form of a FORTRAN input statement is the *format-free* READ statement,[1] an example of which is the following:

$$READ, X, Y$$

This statement reads a data card and assigns the first value read to X and the second value read to Y. X and Y are variable names. The statement READ X, 2 would not be a valid statement since 2 is not a variable name."

The next day in class, Prof. Ovitt was explaining about the READ statements.

---

[1]The unformatted input and output statements introduced in this section are used with the WATFOR and WATFIV FORTRAN compilers. If you are not using one of these compilers, you will use the formatted input and output statements of Section 3.12. However, do not skip this section; the general ideas are still relevant.

"But where does the computer get the data cards it reads?" asked Howie, imagining the computer going to the source Howie usually goes to when he wants to see some computer cards.

"The programmer inserts the data at the end of his program deck, and after a $ENTRY card.[1] When the card reader begins reading the cards into the computer, the data will be read in also. The $ENTRY or similar card indicates where the instructions end and the data begin. For instance, a program to read three numbers and print their sum might look like this:

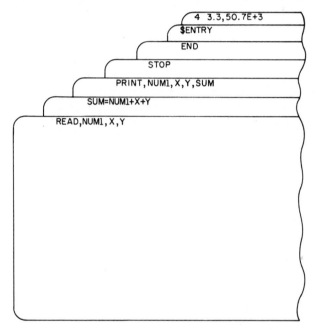

"When the READ statement in this program is executed, the computer will immediately read three items from a single data card (because there are three variable names in the list following the word READ). When it reads this data card it takes the first three numbers and stores them in the three listed locations. Thus, in this example

VARIABLE	VALUE READ
NUM1	4
X	3.3
Y	50.7E+3

"Notice that this program is somewhat general and was written to

[1]Your facility may use a slightly different card between the program and the data.

add any integer number and two decimal numbers, and could be used over and over for different numbers."

"How should the data card be prepared?" asked Clara.

"First let me say, if you want to read a number and assign it to an integer variable, like NUM1, the data should be typed with an integer number. If you want to read a number and assign it to a decimal variable, like X or Y, the data should be typed in as a decimal number; any acceptable decimal form will do, as in our example. The important thing to remember is to have integer names for integer numbers and real names for real numbers. The data type and the variable type must match. More than one piece of data can be typed on a data card, in any of the columns 1 through 80, with each piece of data separated by one or more blanks or by a comma.

"Everytime a read statement is executed a new data card is read. A data card will be read only once. If a READ statement is executed and there is no data card to be read, an error message will be printed and the program will stop executing. If a READ statement is to read, say, two values from a data card that has more than two numbers on it (say three numbers), then the extra numbers on the card will not be read. The next READ statement executed will start with a new data card.

"For example:

```
          READ, I
          READ, J
          K = I + J
          PRINT, K
          END
    $ENTRY
       2   3   4
       5   6
```

In execution the program will read into I the value 2, and into J the value 5. The numbers 3, 4, and 6 will not be read. They are not available for use in the program.

"If a READ statement is to read, say, four values and the data card has less than this number, a new data card will be read to complete the values necessary. Consider the following program:

```
          READ, I, J, K, L
          READ, M
          N = I + J + K + L + M
          PRINT, N
          END
    $ENTRY
       2   3   4
       5   6
       7   8
```

This program will read into I, J, K, L, and M the values 2, 3, 4, 5, and 7, respectively. The values 6 and 8 will be lost."

Prof. Ovitt summarized these rules on the blackboard:

FORMAT-FREE READ STATEMENTS

1. Every execution of a READ statement reads a new data card.
2. A data card is read only once.
3. If there are not enough data on a data card to satisfy the list of variables in the READ statement, a new data card will be read.
4. If there are more data on a data card than are necessary to fill the list of variables in a READ statement, the extra data are lost.
5. The data on a data card must correspond in type (integer or decimal) with the type of variable listed in the READ statement.
6. When using the format-free READ statement, data on data cards must be separated by one or more blanks or a comma.
7. Data may be typed anywhere in columns 1 to 80 on a card.
8. The word READ must always be followed by a comma.

"Whew! I am tired," exclaimed Phil. "Is there a volunteer in the class who would be willing to draw a parallel between the READ and PRINT statements?"

Now, volunteering was not the most popular sport in Prof. Ovitt's class. Last time somebody volunteered to "clean the boards" he spent the weekend at Prof. Ovitt's cottage washing the floors!

One of the students raised his hand. It was that transfer student Don Knowbetta. A chuckle rippled through the classroom. He spoke: "The format-free PRINT statement has already been used. It is commonly of the form

PRINT, Z

where Z is one of a possible list of variable names that are separated by commas and that have been assigned values before the PRINT statement is executed. For instance the previous program contains

PRINT, N

which will cause the value 21 to be printed as output. Print statements may print messages by using quotes. The previous program could have contained the statement

PRINT, 'THE ANSWER IS', N

and the output would have been

THE ANSWER IS 21

The first program you discussed in class today would give an output of

4   .3300000E01   .5070000E02   .5070730E05

Don went to the board and wrote:

FORMAT-FREE PRINT STATEMENTS

1. The word PRINT must always be followed by a comma.
2. Numbers may appear in PRINT statements; e.g., PRINT, 2, N, 4 is valid.
3. Expressions may be in PRINT statements if they do not begin with parentheses; e.g., PRINT, N + M is valid, but PRINT, (N + M) is not.[1]
4. A PRINT statement may print messages by having the message enclosed in quotes.

Who in heck was this guy? He sure knew his stuff.

TOPIC SUMMARY FOR SECTION 3.5

UNFORMATTED input
UNFORMATTED output
READ statements
PRINT statements

Problems for Sec. 3.5

1. Write a program that gives all of the divisors of a given integer number.
2. Write a program to print HOORAY IT WORKS 14 times.
3. (*a*) Write a program that will calculate the average of 10 numbers.
   (*b*) How many different ways may the data for the program at (a) have been prepared? Run the program using different data deck setups.
4. What, if anything, will the following program print if the numbers below are on one data card?

```
5   READ, A, I, J
    PRINT, 1, A, I, J, A * I + J
    GO TO 5
    STOP
    END

    3.0    5    6    8.2    9    2
```

---

[1]Some compilers may not allow expressions in PRINT statements.

5. A data deck contains an unknown number of cards. Write a program that reads the third number on each card (each card contains eight numbers) and calculates the average of those numbers.

3.6 IF STATEMENTS

Howie was walking with his friend Bill Watson when Rudy's sister Ella walked by and said hello to Howie. After Ella had passed, Bill asked, "Who is she, Howie?"

Howie responded, "Ella Mentry, my dear Watson."

Soon the two young men were joined by Rudy, and the three of them continued walking.

"If I pass this computer course, I'll send my grade into *Ripley's Believe It or Not*," said Howie, "otherwise I'll just calmly scream bloody murder at having to repeat the term!"

"Hey, Howie, that's a great example for our homework. Remember we were to find a real-life example of a conditional branch. Well, that's one. Look at this flowchart for what you just said." Rudy quickly sketched in the sand the following flowchart:

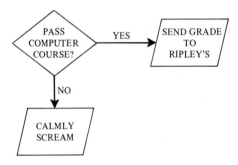

Bill interjected, "Yeah, Howie, you have made plans for your future, depending on the outcome of a condition (pass the computer course) that can't be evaluated yet. After the condition is evaluated, depending on the outcome, you can branch to one action 'send grade to Ripley's' or an alternative action, 'calmly scream.' This is just like a logical IF statement in FORTRAN. The logical IF statement is a conditional control statement, a statement which allows the programmer to control the order of the execution of the program based on decisions made during the execution."

The next day, in class, Prof. Ovitt was writing examples of logical IF statements on the chalkboard. He was saying, "A program to print all the odd integers less than 100 might be the following." He wrote on the board:

```
        X = 1
     5  PRINT, X
        X = X + 2
        IF (X .LT. 100) GO TO 5
    12  STOP
        END
```

Prof. Ovitt continued, "A slightly different version, but equal in content would be this program."

```
        X = 1
     5  PRINT, X
        X = X + 2
        IF (X .GE. 100) STOP
        GO TO 5
        END
```

The form of the logical IF statement was presented earlier and is repeated here for completeness. The general form is:

IF (LOGICAL TEST) Statement X
Statement Y

When a logical test is evaluated it will be either true or false. If it is true, statement X is executed; and if statement X does not transfer control elsewhere, then statement Y is executed. If the logical test is evaluated to be false, then statement X is not executed and control passes directly to statement Y. Statement X can be any executable FORTRAN statement except a DO statement or another logical IF statement. An example of a logical IF statement would be:

IF(X .GT. 5.2) SUM = SUM + X

The statement is read "If X is greater than 5.2, then SUM = SUM + X." The .GT. means "is greater than" and is called a relational operator. The relational operators in FORTRAN language used in logical IF statements are the following:

.EQ.	Equal to
.LT.	Less than
.LE.	Less than or equal to
.GT.	Greater than
.GE.	Greater than or equal to
.NE.	Not equal

Prof. Ovitt asked, "Does anyone know the form of another type of IF statement?"

"I do," said Howie. "The "no choice" IF statement, like IF your parachute doesn't open."

"NO!" replied Prof. Ovitt. "I really meant the arithmetic IF statement."

"Is that like 'One if by land, two if by sea'?" asked Warren Pease, the history major. That was the extent of Warren's arithmetic knowledge.

"NO!" replied Prof. Ovitt again, "an arithmetic IF statement is a *conditional branch statement* which can provide a *three-way branch*. Its form is:

$$IF\ (Z)\ I,\ J,\ K$$

Z is an arithmetic expression that can be evaluated at execution time, and I, J, and K are statement numbers for executable FORTRAN statements in the program. When the expression Z is evaluated, if Z is negative, control passes to statement number I; if Z is zero, control passes to statement J; and if Z is positive, control passes to statement K. In your FORTRAN program, you may only use actual statement numbers. Letters (such as I, J, K) may not be used. For example, if I had a program in which I wanted to perform different mathematical operations depending on whether a variable X had a negative value, a value of zero, or a positive value, I might use the FORTRAN statement

$$IF\ (X)\ 10,\ 20,\ 30$$

which would send control of the program to 10, 20, or 30, depending on whether the value of X was negative, zero, or positive, respectively. A flowchart for this would be"

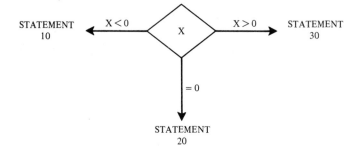

"That's cute, Prof. Ovitt," said Howard Hugh Applyit, "but how would you apply it?"

"Can anyone think of an application of a three-way branch?" asked Phil.

"How about this one. It's not a FORTRAN program," interjected Clara Fy. "A luxury automobile has an automatic temperature control system. The driver sets the device at the desired temperature, say 70°.

If the car gets too hot, the air conditioner goes on; if the car gets too cold, the heater goes on; if the car stays around 70°, the control system cuts off the air conditioner or the heater. (The system is continuously checking the temperature.)"

Clara went up to the chalkboard and began to draw.

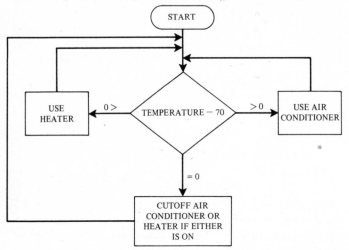

"Thank you, Clara, that's good," said the professor. "Any other examples, class?"

"I have another example," said Rudy. "The vending machines that sell soda for 15 cents a cup. If you put in too little money, the machine waits for more; if you put in the correct amount, you get a soda; if you put in too much money, you sometimes get change. The flowchart for that system is the following:"

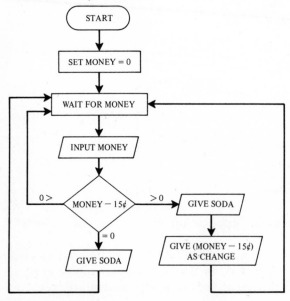

"That's also a good example, Rudy," replied Prof. Ovitt. "Too bad it doesn't work with the soda machine in Room 200. If you put more than 15 cents in that machine, you are out the balance. It's okay though, because you can keep the empty cup that comes down. These two fine examples demonstrate the logic of a three-way branch in common systems. Three-way branches are used in FORTRAN programs, usually in more advanced programs. The logical IF statement and the arithmetic IF statement are quite similar in applicability to a situation; there is rarely a case when you could not substitute one type for the other. Oh, I should mention that in an arithmetic IF statement the statements to which you may branch don't have to be all different. For example, if you wanted to evaluate an expression like $(4 + A)/(X - B)$ at the end of a long program, you would want to be sure you don't divide by zero, so you might use these statements as *part* of your program.

```
         IF (X − B) 10, 20, 10
   10    Y = (4 + A)/(X − B)
         PRINT, Y
   20    STOP
         END
```

TOPIC SUMMARY FOR SECTION 3.6

LOGICAL IF statement
Relational operators
ARITHMETIC IF statement

Problems for Sec. 3.6

1. Howie has set up a pricing policy at the hardware store where he has a part-time job. If a purchaser buys more than 100 nails he gets a 10 percent discount on the normal price of $.05 per unit for all those units over 100. If the number of units purchased exceeds 300, then the customer gets a 30 percent discount on all those units over 300.

    Write a program that reads two numbers from a data card. The first number is a customer identification number and the second is the number of units purchased. Have the program display the total cost for several customers.

2. The student senate at UGH has taken a poll to determine the opinion of the student body on 10 questions of interest to the university. The response to each question would be one of the following:

CODE	MEANING
1	In favor
2	Opposed
3	No opinion

For each student, a punched card is prepared containing the coded responses in the odd columns. The last card in the input deck has a 9 in each column as an *end-of-file indicator*.

Write a program that will tally, for each question, the percent in favor, opposed, and with no opinion.

3. Run a FORTRAN program that will tell you approximately the largest integer number your computer can handle.

4. Run a FORTRAN program that will tell you approximately the smallest decimal number your computer can handle.

3.7 GO TO STATEMENTS

"One control statement that has already been used extensively in class is the *unconditional* GO TO statement, an example of which is the following:

GO TO 11

Execution of this statement causes the computer to go to statement number 11 for the next statement to execute. Statement 11 must be an executable statement. The following program is not valid because statement 11 is not an executable statement.

```
11    REAL J
      READ, J
      PRINT, J
      IF (J .GT. 5.0) STOP
      GO TO 11
      STOP
      END
```

"Once again, the statement number must be an actual number, not . . ."

The bell signaling a 10-minute recess drowned out Prof. Ovitt's last few words.

As Howie got up from his seat to head for the soda machine, he felt a little dizzy and stumbled.

Rudy was concerned. "Do you have vertigo?" he asked.

"No," replied Howie, "not too far, just down to the soda machine."

When class resumed, Prof. Ovitt began lecturing. "As we have seen with IF statements, there are often occasions when it is desired to take different actions, depending on the results of previous work. The logical IF provides a FORTRAN statement that allows the programmer to put a two-way branch in the program. An arithmetic IF statement allows for up to a three-way branch. Can anyone think of a situation that might require more than a three-way branch?"

"Sure," cried Seymour, "exit 25 on Interstate 95 is a freeway branch!"

Clara Fy raised her hand. "I think I have a good example. The store I work at on Saturdays, 'Suit Yourself,' pays the sales people a commission on what they sell. The commission rate depends on the type of clothing sold, and the store has a program written to calculate a salesperson's commissions. Here's how it works. Attached to each piece of clothing is a computer card. Each card has on it the type of clothing, the price, the identification number, and the size of the piece of clothing. This data is used for inventory and reorder purposes, in addition to calculating commissions. For example a card may look like this

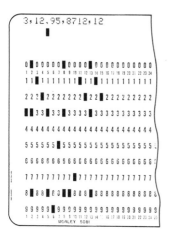

where

Type of clothing is	3
Price is	12.95
Identification number is	8712
Size is	12

"When a piece of clothing is sold, the salesperson puts the computer card in a drawer reserved for that person. At the end of the day, a person's cards are gathered together. A final card with all fives on it is placed at the bottom of the stack of cards. Since there is no clothing type '5' this can be used as a signal that there are no more sales transactions for this person. The set of cards are then run through the computer as data for a program.

"The computer reads the cards and calculates the commission by using the clothing type and the price. The commission structure is the following:

CLOTHING TYPE	COMMISSION RATE, %
1	12
2	9
3	8
4	9
5 code for no more data	

A program to calculate commissions for a salesperson would have to branch in one of four or five directions, depending on the clothing type."

"That's very good, Clara," responded Prof. Ovitt.

"Class, can we write a program to perform this task, namely, read the data cards and calculate the total commission?"

Rudy raised his hand. "Well, first read a card; and if the clothing type is 5, you are through reading cards."

"Correct, Rudy. Maybe we should draw a flowchart first," said Phil.

After considerable writing and erasing, the class came up with the following flowchart (letting COMM stand for commission). See page 93 for the flowchart.

"I'd like you to note a few interesting facets of this flowchart," said Prof. Ovitt. "First, note that we read four items at a time from a data card (TYPE, PRICE, ID, and SIZE). That was why we had *all fives* on that last data card. If we tell the computer to READ four items at a time, we must always give it four items. We only use the information TYPE = 5. However, the fact that PRICE = 5. and ID = 5 and SIZE = 5 does not bother us. At this point we wouldn't be using those variables.

"Also, we start out by testing to see if TYPE = 5; if it does, we are finished. It is certainly possible that a given salesperson has no sales at all and thus would have only one card in the drawer—the last one. Actually, the store probably doesn't bother putting such cases through the machine. However, we will see later that there are instances when it is more efficient to make such a test (an *end-of-file test*) early.

"Would you please also note that we test for TYPE 1, 2, 3, and 5 but not for TYPE 4. Don't be fooled. If the only possibilities are TYPES 1, 2, 3, 4, and 5, and the current TYPE is not 1, 2, 3, or 5, then it must be TYPE 4. Thus, we can save ourselves from making this test.

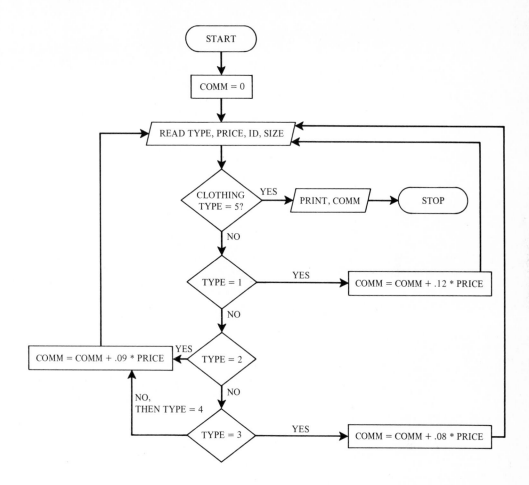

"Now, using this flowchart, I would like you all to take out a sheet of paper and write a FORTRAN program to solve this problem. This will be our first little quiz. You may use your books and notes if you wish."

Murmurs of discontent rumbled throughout the room. Iva Cribsheet was particularly dismayed at having spent all those hours stenciling notes on the back of his ruler, not to mention the time spent filling his hollow pencil with microdots. And now it's an open-book test. It just wasn't fair.

After 30 minutes had passed, Prof. Ovitt realized that no one had even raised his eyes from his paper. Three people were napping. Iva was assembling his miniature microdot reader, and even Clara was clearly having trouble with the exercise.

"Okay, time's up," called the professor. "Since many of you seem to be having a problem with this problem, we'll not count it as a quiz this time. I'll put a solution on the board and you can compare it with your own."

When Phil had finished, the following program was listed on the chalkboard:

```
        INTEGER TYPE, SIZE
        COMM = 0.0
10      READ, TYPE, PRICE, ID, SIZE
        IF (TYPE .EQ. 5) GO TO 3
        IF (TYPE .EQ. 1) GO TO 23
        IF (TYPE .EQ. 2) GO TO 28
        IF (TYPE .EQ. 3) GO TO 30
        GO TO 28
23      COMM = COMM + 0.12 * PRICE
        GO TO 10
28      COMM = COMM + 0.09 * PRICE
        GO TO 10
30      COMM = COMM + 0.08 * PRICE
        GO TO 10
3       PRINT, 'THE COMMISSION IS', COMM
        STOP
        END
```

"Now, are there any points worth noting in this program? Let's go around the room! Clara?"

"The variable names were carefully selected to correspond with the terms in the problem statement," she said.

"Seymour?"

"Well, you are not required to have statement numbers for every statement, and when you do, they do not have to be in increasing order. See that statement 3 at the end?"

"Very good, Seymour," said Prof. Ovitt. "Scott?"

"We gave COMM an initial value. In this case it was a zero."

"Howie?"

"The sum of the statement numbers equals my grade so far in the course," Howie commented.

Prof. Ovitt was quick. "Yes, Howie, except that you have the digits in the answer backwards!"

As the laughter subsided, Prof. Ovitt continued. "There is another FORTRAN statement that we could use in this situation. It is called the COMPUTED GO TO statement. Let me show you how this would change the program." He erased the first version and wrote:

```
        INTEGER TYPE, SIZE
        COMM = 0
10      READ, TYPE, PRICE, ID, SIZE
15      GO TO (23, 28, 30, 28, 3), TYPE
23      COMM = COMM + 0.12 * PRICE
        GO TO 10
28      COMM = COMM + 0.09 * PRICE
        GO TO 10
30      COMM = COMM + 0.08 * PRICE
        GO TO 10
3       PRINT, 'THE COMMISSION IS', COMM
        STOP
        END
```

"Now when statement 15 is executed, control transfers to one of the statement numbers listed in parentheses. *Which* one depends upon the variable TYPE found at the end of the statement. The value of TYPE will correspond to a place or position in the parenthesized list of statement numbers. If TYPE has the value 1, control transfers to the statement whose number is first in the list, namely 23; if TYPE is 3, 4, or 5, control passes to the statement numbered 30, 28, or 3, respectively. Notice that it is acceptable to have a statement number appear more than once in the list (28 appeared twice). If TYPE is any number other than 1, 2, 3, 4, or 5, then the very next statement would be executed. Copy down these rules."

COMPUTED GO TO STATEMENT

1. All statement numbers appearing in the parentheses must correspond to executable statements in the program.
2. The variable (like TYPE in this example) must be a simple integer variable, not a decimal variable, and not an arithmetic expression. If the variable has, at execution time, a value larger than the number of statement numbers in the GO TO statement, the GO TO statement is executed by ignoring the entire statement, control passing to the next statement in the program (statement 23 in this example, if TYPE were, say, 6 or more).

"While we are on GO TO statements, I'd like to cover one other form. This statement, similar to the COMPUTED GO TO statement, is the ASSIGNED GO TO statement, with its companion statement the ASSIGN statement. These statements are written as:

ASSIGN 30 TO NUM
GO TO NUM, (23, 28, 30, 28, 3)

Execution of these statements will cause NUM to be assigned the value 30; then the GO TO statement will cause control to transfer to statement 30, since that is the value of NUM. The rules for ASSIGNED GO TO statements are the following:"

ASSIGNED GO TO STATEMENT

1. The variable in the GO TO statement (NUM in this example) must be a simple integer variable which has been assigned a value by an ASSIGN statement prior to execution of the GO TO statement.
2. The variable in the ASSIGN statement should not be used elsewhere in the program (e.g., NUM = 4 should not also appear in a program with ASSIGN 3 TO NUM).
3. The value assigned to a variable in an ASSIGN statement must be the number of an executable FORTRAN statement in the program. When the ASSIGNED GO TO statement is executed, the variable must have been assigned a statement number in the list within the GO TO statement.

"Prof. Ovitt, can you tell us about the last program in which you used an ASSIGNED GO TO statement," asked Howie.

As he stood up, Prof. Ovitt hit the button in his desk that made the class bell ring. "Well," he paused as the bell rang, "I'd like to, but there goes the bell."

TOPIC SUMMARY FOR SECTION 3.7

GO TO statements
COMPUTED GO TO
ASSIGNED GO TO
ASSIGN statement

Problems for Sec. 3.7

1. The registrar's office at UGH needs a program that will compute the registration fees of students. If the student is from out of state, the registration fee is $15 plus $250 per course tuition. If he is a resident of the state, he pays $15 and $150 per course for tuition. Finally, a student on scholarship pays only the registration fee of $15.

   For each student, there is a data card containing

   (*a*) A student identification number
   (*b*) Number of courses being taken
   (*c*) A tuition code:

1 for out of state
2 for resident
3 for scholarship

Write a program for the registrar that inputs the cards and prints the tuition due for each student. Use a COMPUTED GO TO statement as part of your program.

2. Use an IF statement in Problem 1 above to list the identification numbers of all students signing up for more than five courses.
3. Write a program that will print out the largest of three numbers punched on the same data card.
4. Howie wants to invest $90 a year at 5 percent annual interest. How many years will it take for Howie to accumulate $20,000? Interest is compounded quarterly.
5. Write a FORTRAN program that identifies a number as odd or even.
6. Seymour often has to solve two simultaneous equations for his math homework. They are usually of the form

$$A * X + B * Y = C$$

$$D * X + E * Y = F$$

where A, B, C, D, E, F are known constants and X and Y are the quantities to be found. Write a program that will solve these for Seymour. Assume

$$A * E - B * D \neq 0$$

3.8 DO LOOPS

Howie had just gotten out of biology class and felt a bit bewildered.

"Mr. Gettindere," the teacher had said, "can you tell us which is the olfactory organ?"

"No, sir," Howie had replied.

"That is correct," said the teacher.

"Wonder what he meant?" thought Howie.

Howie decided that he would stop by Prof. Ovitt's office and see if he was there. There were a few questions Howie wanted cleared up concerning DO loops. When he arrived, the door to Prof. Ovitt's office was closed. Howie knocked.

"C'mon in," came the reply.

"Hi, Professor," Howie said. "Am I disturbing you?"

"No, Howard, not at all," replied Phil. "What can I do for you?"

"Well, to tell you the truth, Professor, I really don't understand DO loops very well. Would it be too much trouble for you to go over them with me?"

"DO loops? I'll be glad to," Ovitt responded. "No trouble at all. DO loops are simple but powerful statements for carrying out a set of instructions several times. There are many, many examples of instructions that must often be repeated; they are all around. Howie, do you know how to make a pizza?"

"Sure," he replied. "You take some dough, flatten it out, pour on some tomato sauce, top it off with some cheese, pop it into the oven, remove in 10 minutes, and, presto, you get Howie's delight."

"Well, you pasta that test," Prof. Ovitt reluctantly replied. "Now, suppose you were leaving instructions for a friend on how to prepare an order for 10 pizzas. You might leave a note like this:

Do all the instructions between here and the asterisks 10 times.

        Flatten the dough
        Pour on some tomato sauce
        Top it off with some cheese
        Pop it into the oven
        Remove it in 10 minutes
        * * * * * * * * * * * * * * * * * * *

"While our computer can't make a pizza, it handles loops in much the same way as this note on pizza-making. In fact, the computer version is even better because it has a built-in counter to keep track of how many times the steps have been done, whereas the little ol' pizza-maker had to use his fingers. If he had to make 12 pizzas, he would have had to take off his shoes, and if he had to make 25, he would need to hire part-time help.

"The DO statement in FORTRAN has the following form:

$$DO \ N_1 \quad Counter = N_2, N_3, N_4$$

For example, a FORTRAN statement might be

$$DO \ 4 \quad I = 1, 10, 1$$

"If we were to 'read' this statement aloud, we would say something like this: 'DO all the instructions from here to the statement numbered "4." Do these instructions until the counter reaches its maximum value. The counter is I and it starts at 1 and goes to 10 in increments of 1.

"Howie, you've had PRINT statements already; how would you get the computer to print your name 10 times?"

"That's easy," replied Howie. He began writing on the chalkboard in Ovitt's office.

$$PRINT, \ 'HOWIE'$$
$$PRINT, \ 'HOWIE'$$
$$PRINT, \ 'HOWIE'$$
$$PRINT, \ 'HOWIE'$$
$$PRINT, \ 'HOWIE'$$

```
PRINT, 'HOWIE'
PRINT, 'HOWIE'
PRINT, 'HOWIE'
PRINT, 'HOWIE'
PRINT, 'HOWIE'
```

"But, what if I asked you to have your name printed 1000 times, Howie?" asked Ovitt. "What then?"

"Well," Howie replied, "I would have 990 more to go, and you'd have to go get more chalk!"

"Stop for a minute and think, Howie," Phil pleaded. "Here we have a requirement to repeat something over and over again. A perfect job for the computer. A perfect application of DO loops."

"Oh, I get it now!" exclaimed Howie. "How about if I write something like this."

$$DO \ 6 \ I = 1, \ 1000, \ 1$$

```
6    PRINT, 'HOWIE'
```

"Very good, very good," sighed Phil. "These statements would result in your name being printed 1000 times. Since it is getting late, let's call it a day. I would like you to come prepared for class tomorrow with an example of the DO statement that you can share with your fellow students. Good night, Mr. Gettindere. I have every confidence that you will do a most outstanding job!"

Howie hurried home to prepare for the next day's class. Somehow he felt he had been had. Like his uncle the congressman, who went to deliver a speech at an Indian reservation.

"Our government will do its best to provide equal opportunity!" he started.

"Ook Goom Balla," the Indians cried.

"I shall propose legislation to improve your living conditions," he continued.

"Ook Goom Balla," shouted the Indians.

"I shall see to it that you get additional funding for your reservation," he went on.

"Ook Goom Balla," shouted the Indians.

"I shall work tirelessly in your behalf," he concluded.

"Ook Goom Balla," shouted the Indians.

Feeling quite pleased at having had such a successful speech, he remained for a while and spoke with several of the Indians. Suddenly, he noticed an area near the platform containing several very handsome prize bulls.

"What spectacular animals," he commented. "May I go over and have a closer look?"

"Sure," commented the chief, "but be careful not to step in any of the Ook Goom Balla!"

Howie remembered a problem he had worked on several weeks ago that he felt pretty comfortable with. It was the problem about adding up the following numbers:

$$\tfrac{1}{2} + \tfrac{1}{3} + \tfrac{1}{4} + \tfrac{1}{5} + \ldots + \tfrac{1}{50}$$

Howie spent the next several hours writing a FORTRAN program that used loops to solve this problem.

The next day in class, Howie was so nervous that he sat in his seat like the guy who swallowed his spoon. He couldn't stir.

Prof. Ovitt had not forgotten. "Mr. Gettindere, I believe you have an example of a FORTRAN program that uses DO loops. Would you put it on the board please," he asked.

As Howie walked to the front of the room, he explained to the class that the program he had chosen would add up the series $\tfrac{1}{2} + \tfrac{1}{3} + \tfrac{1}{4}$ and so on up to $\tfrac{1}{50}$. He wrote the following on the chalkboard:

```
        SUM = 0
        N = 50
        DO 15  B = +2,N
        B = B + 1
  15    IF (B − 50) 10,20,20
        PRINT, B, SUM
        STOP
        END
```

"Thank you, Howie," said Prof. Ovitt. "Your efforts have reminded me of several rules that I forgot to mention. Let's look at the general form of the DO statement.

DO LOOPS

DO N_1 Count = N_2, N_3, N_4

1. Count, which is the counter for the loop, must be an integer name.
2. N_2 is the starting value for the counter.
   N_3 is the value the counter should not exceed.
   N_4 is the amount that should be added to the counter each time through the loop. If the amount to be added is a one, this last number (N_4) may be omitted.
3. N_2, N_3, and N_4 must be unsigned, nonzero, integer numbers or variables.
4. The *counter* in the DO loop cannot be redefined anywhere in the body of the loop. That is, it may not appear on the left side of an equal sign.
5. The last statement in a DO loop (the one labeled as statement number N_1) must be an executable statement but may not be a STOP, DO, GO TO, arithmetic IF statement, or a logical IF containing any of the above statements.

"See if you can rewrite your program correcting these errors, Howie," Prof. Ovitt said.

"How about this one?" asked Howie as he rewrote the program.

```
         SUM = 0
         N = 50
         DO 15 I = 2, N
    15   SUM = SUM + 1.0/I
         PRINT, N, SUM
         STOP
         END
```

"That's good," said Phil. "Let me show you some other things you can do with DO loops. For example, I have 30 cards, one for each student, with a grade on each card. I want to find the highest grade and the first card on which this grade appears. Now, this certainly doesn't seem like a problem hard enough to warrant writing a program for, but remember it is just a simple illustration of the type of problem that might be part of a larger problem. Look at this program." Prof. Ovitt replaced Howie's program with the following.

```
         HIGH = -100.0
         DO 99  I = 1, 30
         READ, GRADE
         IF (GRADE .LE. HIGH) GO TO 99
         HIGH = GRADE
         NUM = I
    99   CONTINUE
         PRINT, NUM, HIGH
         STOP
         END
```

"Let's look closely at what this program does.

1. First, we store the number −100.0 into a memory location called HIGH.
2. Next, we start a loop that includes all the statements through statement 99. This loop is to be done 30 times (the counter I = 1, 30).
3. We then READ a grade from a data card (not shown).
4. IF the grade is less than or equal to the value in memory location HIGH, we know that location HIGH is the highest grade so far, so we GO TO 99, which continues the loop. Statement 99 is a CONTINUE statement. This is an executable statement which does nothing. It is useful in this

case because it provides an object for the DO loop and thus allows some statements to be skipped in the DO loop.

5. IF the current grade is not less than or equal to the contents of location HIGH, then it must be greater. It must be a new high. The program continues on and replaces the value in location HIGH with the current grade (HIGH = GRADE). We then store in memory location NUM the value of the counter. This will tell us which card first had this high value. We then get to the CONTINUE statement and continue with the loop. When the loop is finished (when it has been executed 30 times), the program continues to the PRINT statement and prints out the card number which first contained the highest grade (NUM) and then that highest grade itself (HIGH)."

Phyllis had a question. "Can you transfer control freely within a loop? Like that logical IF statement does."

"Yes, Phyllis," Prof. Ovitt replied. "You may even transfer control out of the loop. Take, for example, the following problem. Write a program that will READ up to 30 cards, and find the first card with a grade of 70 on it." Phil again went to the chalkboard.

```
        INTEGER GRADE
        DO 99  JCOUNT = 1, 30
        READ, GRADE
        IF (GRADE .EQ. 70) GO TO 100
   99   CONTINUE
        PRINT, 'NO GRADE OF 70 FOUND'
        STOP
  100   PRINT, 'A 70 WAS ON CARD', JCOUNT
        STOP
        END
```

"In this program, when a grade of 70 is found, control is transferred outside the loop (to statement 100). The loop need not be executed the full 30 times. Notice that in this case we then print out where the loop stopped (the contents of JCOUNT)."

When we transfer control out of a loop, the counter that we created is available for our use. When the loop has a normal termination, however, the counter created in the DO statement may not be considered well defined. Different compilers will give it different values, so it should not be used without considerable care.

"What happens in that program if it doesn't find anybody who got a 70?" asked Seymour.

"Well, look at the program," Prof. Ovitt replied. "If GRADE never equals 70, we will not have transferred control out of the loop and we will continue on with the program. The next statement to be executed after the loop prints NO GRADE OF 70 FOUND. The program then passes to the STOP statement.

"Before we take our break, I want you to know that you may not transfer control into the middle of a loop from elsewhere in the program. This would violate the rules for constructing DO statements."

During the break, Rudy remained at his desk and continued reading a paperback book with great interest.

"Whatcha reading?" Howie inquired.

"Oh, it's an adventure novel about a safari in Africa," Rudy replied. "It's really interesting right now; the leading character went out on a hunt several hours ago and hasn't returned yet."

"Maybe he disagreed with something that ate him!" Howie suggested. "Who's the author?"

Rudy looked at the binding. "Arthur Ballpoint," he replied.

"Is that his pen name?" asked Howie.

Rudy ignored him and continued reading. He was enjoying the book. After all, it came from the trite side of the racks.

Prof. Ovitt was calling the class to attention. "Shall we continue?" he asked.

TOPIC SUMMARY FOR SECTION 3.8

DO loops
Counters
DO parameters
Increment
Transfer control out of loop
Transfer control within loop

Problems for Sec. 3.8

1. Write a program that reads a data card with a number, N, on it and then a deck of N data cards containing one value on each card. Then print the numbers with their positions shifted up one place (the first number printed last). For example:

$$\text{INPUT} \quad 4$$
$$1$$
$$5$$

$$
\begin{array}{c}
3 \\
7 \\
\text{OUTPUT} \quad 5 \\
3 \\
7 \\
1
\end{array}
$$

(The 4 was N and does not get printed.)

Use DO loops.

2. Using DO loops, write a program that prints the first 100 integers and their square roots (the square root of a number is the number to the one-half power).

3. Write a program that prints the sum of the squares of the integers from 21 through 44 (inclusive).

4. Make a graph of the function $f(x) = (x^3 + 3x^2 + 2)/(x^2 + 1)^{1/2}$ for x between -10 and $+10$.

5. The Stella Kidd Elementary School is having a raffle to raise money for playground equipment. You have volunteered to print the raffle tickets. Each ticket should have the date of the raffle, the school name, the price of the ticket, and the ticket number on the ticket stub. A ticket should look like this:

```
********************************************************************
*   STELLA KIDD SCHOOL    *              TICKET NO. 5             *
*                         *                                       *
*   $1.00  TICKET         *   NAME:                               *
*                         *                                       *
*   TICKET NO. 5          *   ADDRESS:                            *
*                         *                                       *
*   NOV. 4, 1977          *   TELEPHONE:                          *
********************************************************************
```

    This piece is the stub.   This piece is for the raffle box.

Using DO loops, write a program to print tickets 1 through 20.

6. The Al Casseltza Pizza Company currently produces frozen pizzas for distribution in supermarkets. Business is mushrooming. Al is considering taking advantage of his good brand name by marketing frozen Chinese snack foods. Al has had some market analysts conduct some surveys. They have concluded that the total annual market for Chinese snack foods in this area is given by the following equation:

$$
M = 60{,}000 + 100{,}000(1 - 2^{-(A/10{,}000)})
$$

where M is the total sales and A is Al's advertising budget for the year. There is a 10 percent profit margin on sales of snack foods (before advertising expenses). Thus Al's annual profit is given by

$$
\text{Profit} = 0.1M - A
$$

Write a program that will find Al's optimal advertising budget.

3.9 NESTED LOOPS

Prof. Ovitt was talking.

"When I was preparing this lecture on nested loops, I was reminded of the time several bluebirds had built a nest in the mane of a champion race horse. The owner was a friend of mine and did everything he could to get rid of the birds. Nothing worked. He tried keeping the horse indoors, outdoors, several different places. He tried hosing the horse down, covering him with blankets. All to no avail. The birds remained. Finally, in desperation, he went to a hermit renowned for his ability to come up with solutions to just these kinds of problems. The hermit suggested that the owner put some yeast cakes in the mane next to the nest. The owner tried it and, lo and behold, it worked!"

"What's the point of that story?" asked Howie.

"It certainly goes to show that yeast is yeast and nest is nest and never the mane shall tweet."

It took Prof. Ovitt several minutes to restore order in the class. "Actually," Ovitt continued, "nested loops is a concept that refers to combining two or more DO loops. As an example, let us suppose that you want to write a program that will read the grades on the 10 quizzes that were given to our class and calculate each student's grade. For each student you will have a deck of 11 cards; the first will have the student's ID number, and the next 10 cards will have the student's 10 grades, one to a card.

"We have already seen programs that perform this type of process. Let's draw a very general flowchart of the logic we might want to use." Prof. Ovitt drew on the board:

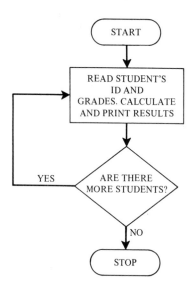

"What does that flowchart suggest?" Prof. Ovitt asked the class.

"It looks like a DO loop might be used in the program for the 30 students," volunteered Rudy.

"Right, Rudy," answered Prof. Ovitt. "To be specific, the program might look something like this:

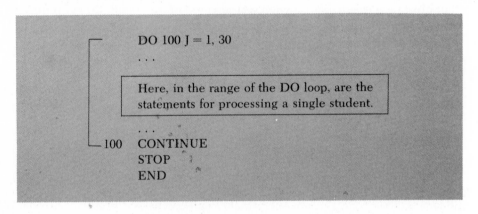

```
     ┌─   DO 100 J = 1, 30
     │
     │        . . .
     │
     │       ┌─────────────────────────────────────────────┐
     │       │ Here, in the range of the DO loop, are the  │
     │       │ statements for processing a single student.  │
     │       └─────────────────────────────────────────────┘
     │
     │        . . .
     └─ 100   CONTINUE
              STOP
              END
```

"Brandon, take a look inside the range of this loop. What is it that we want to process for each student?" Prof. Ovitt asked.

"I guess there are four major things to be done," replied Brandon. "As I see it, they are

1. Read the student's ID number.
2. Read his 10 grades.
3. Calculate his total and average.
4. Print out his ID and final grade.

"Good, Brandon. Clara, would you like to write the program for this middle section?"

Clara went to the chalkboard and wrote:

READ, ID

"Next I'd like to read the student's 10 grades; I'm going to use a DO loop to achieve this."

```
     READ, ID
     DO 90 I = 1, 10
          . . .
```

```
          ┌──────────────────────────────────┐
          │ In the range of this DO loop is the │
          │ required processing for each grade.  │
          └──────────────────────────────────┘
```

```
          . . .
  90   CONTINUE
```

"Shall I continue?" asked Clara.

"In a minute, Clara," Ovitt commented. "Phyllis would you like to draw the flowchart for the middle section of the program, being more specific than we were in our first flowchart? That is, please sketch in detail the flowchart for processing each student's grades, the portion in the rectangle in our previous flowchart."

Phyllis went to the chalkboard and sketched the following flowchart.

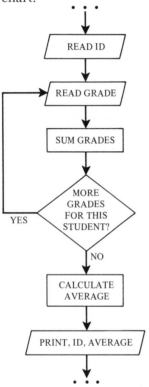

"Please continue, Clara," called Ovitt.

"Now then, in the range of the loop I shall put those statements that process each grade. That is, read the grade and add it to the running total.

```
            READ, ID
            DO 90 I = 1, 10
            READ, G
            TOTAL = TOTAL + G
    90      CONTINUE
```

"After I am finished with the 10 grades, I would get the average for this one student and print these results.

```
            READ, ID
            DO 90 I = 1, 10
```

```
        READ, G
        TOTAL = TOTAL + G
90      CONTINUE
        AVG = TOTAL/10
        PRINT, ID, AVG
```

"Also, before I process a student, I should make sure that location TOTAL has a zero in it so that each student's grade total begins at zero (otherwise I would be adding together all the students' grades)."

The entire program on the chalkboard now looked like this.

```
         DO 100 J = 1, 30
         READ, ID
         TOTAL = 0
         DO 90 I = 1, 10
         READ, G
         TOTAL = TOTAL + G
90       CONTINUE
         AVG = TOTAL/10
         PRINT, ID, AVG
100      CONTINUE
         STOP
         END
```

Prof. Ovitt began, "Here is an example of nested loops. One loop is nested within another."

```
┌        DO 100 J = 1, 30
│        . . .
│  ┌     DO 90 I = 1, 10
│  │     . . .
│  └ 90  CONTINUE
│        . . .
└ 100    CONTINUE
```

"In the execution of nested loops, the inner loop must always end before the outer loop ends. Thus our inner loop will be done 30 times (since it is inside the outer loop which goes from 1 to 30). If we set up a table representing memory locations, we can more easily see how this process works. Let us assume that the first student's grades are

        80   85   65   75   72   60   90   85   82   70

and his ID is 112 while the data for the second student is

        90   60   70   80   90   90   80   90   80   70

and her ID is 226. Here are the values the variables will assume during the execution of the program. See the table on page 110.

"I think you can begin to see how this table might look if we continued for 30 students. Now, class," Ovitt continued, "there are some specific rules that must be followed for nested loops, in addition to those you have been given for the DO statement. Please take out an index card and copy these down.

NESTED LOOPS

1. All statements that are in the range of the inner loop must also be in the range of the outer loop.
2. Nested DO loops may terminate on the same statement. The inner loop still must be satisfied before the outer loop continues.
3. If control is transferred during the execution of the outer loop, it must not be transferred into the range of the inner loop.

"Before the period ends I'd like to have a volunteer to give an example that clarifies these rules. Who will choose rule 1?" Prof. Ovitt asked.

Sid Down was up. "Rule 1 simply states that you can't end an inner loop after the outer loop has ended. Something like this is not allowed." Sid went to the board.

```
        DO 10 J = 1, 15
        . . .
   DO  5  I = 1, 3
   . . .
        10   CONTINUE
         5   CONTINUE
```

"That's correct," said Prof. Ovitt. "Mr. Gettindere, suppose you try the next one."

Howie explained how he couldn't write on the board because he had sprained his right wrist during a game of frisbee earlier that day when he accidentally stepped on his hand while reaching for the frisbee. Seymour volunteered to write for Howie.

"Well," Howie mumbled, "I guess it means nested DO loops may terminate on the same statement."

Seymour was writing on the board.

```
        DO 90 I = 1, 3
        DO 90 J = 1, 2
   90   PRINT, I, J
```

(VALUE OF J) TIME THROUGH OUTER LOOP	CONTENTS OF LOCATION ID	CONTENTS OF LOCATION TOTAL	(VALUE OF I) TIME THROUGH INNER LOOP	CONTENTS OF LOCATION G	CONTENTS OF LOCATION AVG
1	112	0 + 80 = 80	1	80	
		80 + 85 = 165	2	85	
		165 + 65 = 230	3	65	
		230 + 75 = 305	4	75	
		305 + 72 = 377	5	72	
		377 + 60 = 437	6	60	
		437 + 90 = 527	7	90	
		527 + 85 = 612	8	85	
		612 + 82 = 694	9	82	
		694 + 70 = 764	10	70	76.4
2	226	0 + 90 = 90	1	90	
		90 + 60 = 150	2	60	
		150 + 70 = 220	3	70	
		220 + 80 = 300	4	80	
		300 + 90 = 390	5	90	
		390 + 90 = 480	6	90	
		480 + 80 = 560	7	80	
		560 + 90 = 650	8	90	
		650 + 80 = 730	9	80	
		730 + 70 = 800	10	70	80.0

"Yes, that's it," guessed Howie.

"What would that program print out," asked Prof. Ovitt.

"It prints out I and J," replied Howie, as he sat down. Neil Down stood up and replied, "It prints." Neil wrote on the board:

1	1
1	2
2	1
2	2
3	1
3	2

"That's right, Neil," Prof. Ovitt responded. "And now how about the last one?" Neil Down sat down as Stan Dup arose. "I'll do the last one, Professor," he called. "If, for example, you have an IF or a GO TO to go to in your program, you can't GO TO or IF into the middle of a loop, you see."

Professor Ovitt was hoping the bell would ring. Eileen Dover leaned over and whispered into Stan's ear and Stan went to the board and wrote.

```
      ┌      DO 5 J = 1, 15
      │      . . .
      │      GO TO 10
      │      . . .
      │  ┌   DO 8 K = 1, 6
      │  │   . . .
      │  │ 10  READ, ID, GRADE, SUM
      │  │   . . .
      │  └  8  CONTINUE
      │      . . .
      └    5  CONTINUE
```

"This would not be allowed," Stan said to the class. "You have transferred control into the middle of a loop and thus have violated rule 3."

The bell rang and the class began to file out. As Prof. Ovitt was erasing the board, Seymour approached and asked a question, "Say, Prof. Ovitt, what about rule 4?"

"Rule 4? There was no rule 4," replied Ovitt. "What are you talking about?"

"You know, Professor," Seymour answered. "What you do if you're flying your plane and there is a hole in the bottom of your gas tank!"

"What's that?" asked Phil.

"Loop before you leak!" cracked Seymour, as he left, holding his side.

Problems for Sec. 3.9

1. Write a program that tabulates the function

$$\frac{3x^2 - 2xy + y^2}{x^3 + y^3}$$

for $x = 1, 2, 3, 4, 5, 6$ and $y = 8, 9, 10, 11, 12$.

2. (See Problem 6, Section 3.8.) Al's cross-town competitor, Ann Chovie is also planning to enter the Chinese snack market, with her own products under the Sue E. and Joe Main label. She also has studied the market potential and independently determined that the total market is given by the equation:

$$M = 60,000 + 100,000(1 - 2^{-(Z/10,000)})$$

where Z is the combined advertising budgets of Al and Ann and M is the total sales.

   If Ann's advertising budget is X and Al's is A then $Z = A + X$; Ann's share of the market is X/Z and Al's share is A/Z. Thus the profit Ann makes is $0.1(X/Z)M - X$ and the profit Al makes is $0.1(A/Z)M - A$. Assume that both Al and Ann know all of this. Write a program that will find an optimal advertising budget for Al; for Ann.

3. Each of the letters below represents a different digit. Write a program to perform the addition and determine the values associated with the letters.

$$
\begin{array}{r}
AB \\
CD \\
+\ EF \\
\underline{GH} \\
III
\end{array}
$$

3.10 SUBSCRIPTED VARIABLES

Prof. Ovitt was lunching with Prof. Whittier before his next class. Prof. Ovitt was having his favorite dish, oysters. Quite suddenly, in the middle of their conversation, Prof. Ovitt grasped his throat and began to jump wildly about. Whittier leaped up and began pounding Ovitt on the back in an attempt to dislodge what was apparently an obstruction in his throat.

   "Go ahead, cough it up!" Whittier pounded him again on the back, and behold, Ovitt coughed up the obstruction.

   "Will you look at that!" Whittier cried, "a pearl!"

   "Hope it's worth . . . something," gasped Ovitt.

   "Naw, this one is all pitted," came the reply.

   Prof. Ovitt regained his composure. "Boy, that sure made me feel sick."

   Whittier understood. "Well, you know, Phil, a gritty pearl is like a malady."

"Listen," pleaded Phil, "would you mind taking class for me today? My throat's a little sore."

"Sure thing, Phil," he replied.

Prof. Whittier substituted for Prof. Ovitt on several occasions. Each time, he liked to start his classes with a joke.

"Good afternoon, class. I'm taking over for Prof. Ovitt today. It is nice to have a captive audience such as this. It reminds me of the time I was doing some consulting at the state prison. There were these 10 prisoners in one of the cell blocks there. The prisoners wiled away the hours by telling their repertoire of 20 jokes they had exchanged over the years. While they had all heard the jokes before, they enjoyed their retelling during the week.

"After a while, the warden—who was a blood relative of Captain Bluebeard—decided that the inmates were enjoying themselves far too much, and he ordered that the joke-telling sessions cease.

"Well, as you might imagine, the inmates didn't take this too lightly. In their clever manner they devised a new system for telling the same old jokes. Instead of telling the jokes in the old narrative format, the teller would simply call out a number, say, 12, and the cell block would erupt in riotous laughter as the inmates recalled the contents of joke 12.

"One day, a new inmate was brought to the block. During his first evening, one of the other inmates quite suddenly yelled out '19!' at which time the walls reverberated with laughter. This went on for several days; then one day a prisoner yelled out '42.' The cellblock erupted in riotous laughter. Prisoners were rolling around on the floor of their cells. It took 20 minutes for the laughter to subside.

"What's the story?" the new inmate asked his neighbor. "Usually someone yells a number and everyone laughs a bit, but this time the laughter was much greater."

"Nobody heard that one before!" came the reply.

When the class settled down, Prof. Whittier began again. "I started today's class with that story because today we are to talk about subscripted variables in FORTRAN. Prof. Ovitt told me that he introduced the idea of subscripts in a previous class with a story similar to this one (Section 2.5). At that time he made a one-dimensional array, or list, with the jokes."

	JOKE LIST
Joke 1	Traveling salesman story
Joke 2	Farmer's son tale
Joke 3	Three little bears story
Joke 4	The knock, knock joke

"Note that if we have a list called JOKE, when we talk about Joke

3, we are talking about the third item on the joke list, namely the third joke.

In FORTRAN programming the use of subscripts is widespread, very useful, and not difficult. Recently, I asked our basketball coach, Jim Nasium, what the average weight of his team was. When he indicated that he had no idea, I devised a program to calculate the average. There are eight players on the basketball team. For each player there is a data card on which is typed the player's weight. One way to do this would be the following program." Prof. Whittier went to the board.

```
READ, A
READ, B
READ, C
READ, D
READ, E
READ, F
READ, G
READ, H
SUM = A + B + C + D + E + F + G + H
AVRGE = SUM/8
PRINT, AVRGE
STOP
END
```

"This is long, tedious, and impractical, especially if you were doing it for a football team of 30 players, or for the weights of a 200-person Philharmonic Orchestra. A better way to do this would be to use subscripts. Look at this program.

```
      DIMENSION WEIGHT(8)
      SUM = 0
      DO 20 I = 1, 8
      READ, WEIGHT(I)
  20  SUM = SUM + WEIGHT(I)
      AVRGE = SUM/8
      PRINT, AVRGE
      STOP
      END
```

"The first statement is a DIMENSION statement. It tells the computer that WEIGHT is a name for an array and that there will be up to eight items in that array. The computer needs to know this so that it can save enough memory locations for the data. The third statement is a DO statement, with which you are already familiar.

"Could one of you explain this section for our benefit? How about you, Tom Ree?" asked Whittier.

"It's a mystery to me," said Mr. Ree.

The class was a bit surprised when Lionel Trainz volunteered. It sure was a switch. He had to have a motive. On the other hand, maybe he was just plain crazy! It was probably a bit of each. He no doubt had a loco motive.

"The fourth statement, READ, WEIGHT(I), is in the middle of a loop. It will be executed eight times, since, in this case, the index of the loop indicates that the loop is to be done eight times. The index I keeps track of which iteration of the loop we are currently performing. This index I can, of course, be used in the body of the loop, as it is here. The first time this READ statement is executed, the value for I will be 1 so a data card will be read and the number on that card will be stored in the memory location with the address WEIGHT(1). Similarly, when I is a 7, the number on that data card will be stored in memory location WEIGHT(7), the seventh item in the WEIGHT array. When the loop is completed, eight cards will have been read and eight values will have been stored in locations WEIGHT(1) through WEIGHT(8). Now they are in memory and can be used when needed. For example, if you wanted to know the eighth player's weight, it would be sufficient to say

PRINT, WEIGHT(8)

Shall I continue?" asked Lionel.

"No, that's quite good," Whittier replied. "Please leave something for me."

"What about statement 20? What does that do?" asked Seymour.

"This statement calculates the sum of the weights. Notice that this statement is also in the range of the loop. Thus, it will also be executed eight times.

"Let's look at an instant replay of the computer's execution of the statement SUM = SUM + WEIGHT(I). The weights we will use as a sample are 100, 110, 100, 90, 115, 120, 70, 170.

"This example is worth reviewing since there are very many applications for the sum or total of a series of numbers. One trick to remember is that when you are getting a sum of this sort, the variable name being used to store the sum appears on both sides of the equal sign (e.g., SUM = SUM + WEIGHT(I)). This is read as follows: The updated value for SUM is set equal to the previous value of SUM plus whatever we are adding (in this case, weights).

TIME THROUGH LOOP	VALUE OF INDEX	OLD VALUE OF SUM	+	WEIGHT(I)	NEW VALUE OF SUM
First	1	0		100	100
Second	2	100		110	210
Third	3	210		100	310
Fourth	4	310		90	400
Fifth	5	400		115	515
Sixth	6	515		120	635
Seventh	7	635		70	705
Eighth	8	705		170	875

Whittier continued. "This program, after reading the eight cards, sums the weights and prints the average. Because of the simple nature of this particular problem, I am sure you see several ways to avoid using subscripted variables. However, this is not always the case. Consider the following minor change. There are 30 students on a football team, each with a card that has the student's weight on it. Write a program that reads the 30 cards and prints the number of people who are more than 10 pounds above the average weight.

"In this situation, the computer needs to go through all the data once to calculate the average, then go through the data again to see if each weight is more than 10 above the average. A program to perform this job would be this one. TOTAL counts up the number of people who weigh more than average + 10."

```
      DIMENSION WEIGHT (30)
      TOTAL = 0
      SUM = 0
      DO 20 I = 1, 30
      READ, WEIGHT(I)
 20   SUM = SUM + WEIGHT(I)
      AVRGE = SUM/30
      DO 40 I = 1, 30
      IF (WEIGHT(I) .GT. AVRGE + 10) TOTAL = TOTAL + 1
 40   CONTINUE
      PRINT, AVRGE, TOTAL
      STOP
      END
```

"Class, are there any special comments you'd like to make on this program?" asked Whittier.

Brandon observed, "Well, the DO loop is the same as in the first program and Lionel already explained it. The only difference is that it is now for 30 students rather than eight."

With a great deal of flourish, Sarah Mony arose and began to speak. "The only real difference is the second DO loop. In this loop, the IF statement is repeated 30 times. Each time it is comparing one of the weights in the WEIGHT array to the calculation average plus 10 pounds. If the particular weight during an iteration is greater than the average plus 10, then the statement TOTAL = TOTAL + 1 is executed. This is another 'sum' type statement and follows the hint you just gave, Professor. If the current weight is not greater than the average plus 10 then the next statement is executed and the loop would continue with the next weight. Of course, after you executed the TOTAL = TOTAL + 1 statement (if required), you would go to the next statement and, again, continue with the loop."

"Excellent explanation," Prof. Whittier commented. "There is only one thing I can add. Notice that there are two statements right up at the beginning, SUM = 0 and TOTAL = 0. Here, we are setting our two counters to zero. The reason is that the first time we use SUM or TOTAL, it must have a defined value. It is generally safe to say that if a variable name appears on the right side of a FORTRAN assignment statement or anywhere in an IF or PRINT statement, then prior to that statement that variable must have been given a value either

1. By being on the left side of an assignment statement
2. By being in a DATA statement
3. By being in a READ statement

We'll talk about DATA statements later."

"Are there any special rules for naming arrays?" asked Clara.

Before Prof. Whittier could respond, Howie blurted out, "I'll bet the array couldn't be called three."

"Why not, young man?" asked Prof. Whittier.

"How could you write a three DIMENSION statement?" responded Howie gleefully.

Prof. Whittier didn't smile. "Actually the rules for naming FORTRAN subscripted variables are the same as the rules for naming unsubscripted variables. Furthermore, arrays with names beginning with I, J, K, L, M, N are assumed to be integer arrays, although this rule can certainly be overridden by a DECLARATION statement as before. A little care should be taken to follow these simple rules, however. You may declare a variable to be integer, and DIMENSION it in one statement like

INTEGER WEIGHT(30)

This not only reserves 30 locations for the WEIGHT array but also treats all the values as integers. If you wanted to exercise your wrist by writing more you could use two statements."

DIMENSION WEIGHT(30)
INTEGER WEIGHT

You may not, however, DIMENSION the array twice by using the two statements together.

DIMENSION WEIGHT(3)
INTEGER WEIGHT(30)

Scott Free was curious. "Can you do the same with the REAL declaration statement?" he asked.

"Sure!" Whittier replied. "In that case you might have the following."

REAL NUMBER
DIMENSION NUMBER(10)

or

DIMENSION NUMBER(10)
REAL NUMBER

or

REAL NUMBER(10)

"But it is not correct to use these two statements:"

DIMENSION NUMBER(10)
REAL NUMBER(10)

By this time, Prof. Whittier began to sense some restlessness in the class. "There is just one final point I'd like to make. When I was a lad, an example of the values of a subscript occurred to me at a baseball game. We were up in the last of the ninth inning in the final game for the championship, facing the most feared of all the league's pitchers, Mel Famey. The bases were loaded. There were two out. And, yes, the ballgame was tied.

"The batter was tense as he stood at the plate awaiting the first dreaded pitch.

"'Strike one!' the umpire yelled. The fans began to grumble.

"'Ball one. Ball two!' the umpire called as the next two pitches were outside the mark.

"'Stee-rike two!'

"Mel wound up and threw the next pitch with all the force he could muster.

"'Ball tha-ree!' the umpire shouted.

"The stadium was quiet. The tenseness could be felt in the air. The catcher called time out and went out to the mound. The manager joined him and asked Mel how he felt.

"'Gee, I'm really nervous,' he said. 'Bases are loaded, two out, the count is three balls and two strikes, the whole season rides on this next pitch. Can I have a beer?'

"'Listen,' the manager said, 'you can have anything you want. Just relax now and take it easy.' He sent to the dugout for a beer.

"Well, Mel drank that beer right down and was ready to go. He completed his windup, threw the pitch . . .

"'Ball four!' shouted the umpire.

"Pandemonium erupted. We had won the ball game and the championship. And you know, to this day that drink he had is known as the 'beer that made Mel Famey walk us!'

"Now," Whittier tried to keep a straight face, "if we kept the score each inning for our team in an array called INNING, it could be dimensioned at INNING(9). The subscript may be any integer between 1 and the DIMENSION of the array (here the limit would be nine). We may not have a subscript of zero. While in this case, INNING(0) would not make sense, there are cases when you might like to use zero for a subscript. It is not allowed. Neither could we ever refer to INNING(10) in our program (even if the game went into extra innings), because the DIMENSION statement limits it to INNING(9). The DIMENSION statement clearly defines the range of subscripts that are permitted. The subscript always starts at 1 and ends at the number in parentheses for that variable in the DIMENSION statement.

"Some FORTRAN compilers allow subscripts to be real variables. If this is allowed, the computer will truncate the fractional portion of the number. Finally, it is often okay to use expressions as subscripts. The expression would be reduced to an integer number in order to identify a unique position in the array. Thus, if I = 2, JUGGLE = 1, and IT = 2, then the statement

PRINT, INNING(I + JUGGLE + IT)

would print out the contents of location 5 in the INNING array.

"Well, class, thank you for your attention today," Prof. Whittier concluded. "It was a pleasure teaching both of you!"

TOPIC SUMMARY FOR SECTION 3.10

Subscripted variables
DIMENSION statement
DECLARATION statement

Problems for Sec. 3.10

1. An integer array called DATA contains 100 numbers. Write a program that will do the following:

   (*a*) Print out the entire array in four columns.

(*b*) Print out the numbers in the even positions of the array.

(*c*) Print out the array with five numbers to each line.

(*d*) Print out the array in reverse order.

2. A set of data cards contains a series of integers that represent the age at last birthday of every resident in a small town. The age is punched in columns 1 to 3 on the data card.

Print out a list showing the number of people in each age group as follows:

Age Group	Number of Residents
0	
1	
2	
3	
4	
5-9	
10-14	
. . .	
95-99	
over 99	

This program can be written in less than 25 statements.

3. Identify the errors in the following sets of FORTRAN statements.

(*a*) INTEGER HOWIE
   REAL RUDY(5)
   HOWIE(1) = RUDY(4)

(*b*) INTEGER HOWIE(10)
   REAL RUDY
   DIMENSION RUDY(8), HOWIE(10)

(*c*) INTEGER HOWIE(15)
   Y = 10
   X = Y − HOWIE

(*d*) N = 4
   M = 3
   DIMENSION X(N,M)

4. Write a program that reads 20 data cards containing 40 single-digit numbers typed in columns 1, 3, 5, . . . , 77, 79. The program should print out the digits 0 through 9 and the frequency with which each digit appears in the data set.

5. Write a program that reads 40 data cards, each containing a single number. The program should compute the average and print the number of cards with a value higher than the average.

3.11 TWO-DIMENSIONAL ARRAYS

Phil returned for the next class and while he was standing in the corridor waiting for class to begin, one of the students approached.

"Hi, Prof. Ovitt," Hugh said. "What's the matter, you look kind of low."

"Well, Hugh," Ovitt replied, "last night four faculty members were trying to help out an old friend who was down on his luck. He was quite proud and certainly would not accept any money from us so we devised a scheme. We would all put up a 10 dollar ante and then put five slips of paper into a hat with the numbers 1 to 5 written on them. The five of us would draw and the person who drew the 5 from the hat would win the pot.

"Now, in order to ensure that our kindly unfortunate friend would win, we wrote the number five on all of the slips. We all drew our slips and quickly crumpled them up and discarded them. We anxiously awaited our compatriot's gleeful exclamation of success. There was only silence. After a few minutes, someone asked him what number he drew.

'I drew $7\frac{1}{8}$!' came the sad reply."

The bell rang signifying the start of class. Prof. Ovitt called the class to order. "I understand that Prof. Whittier did a fine job at the last class," he began.

"He couldn't have been wittier," someone murmured.

"Oh yes, it was, I assure you," Prof. Ovitt responded. "Well, anyway, there are a couple of points concerning arrays that I would like to make. As you may remember from a previous class (Section 2.5), we used two subscripts for the two-dimensional JOKE array.

"In FORTRAN we frequently use arrays with more than one subscript. For example, suppose each of you punched on a computer card the number of pets you have, by type. For example, the first number might be the number of dogs; the second number would be for cats; the third for fish; and the fourth for birds.

"I'll now put on the chalkboard a program that will read all the cards for the class and count the total number of cats. Our class size is 30 students.

```
      INTEGER PET, SUM
      DIMENSION PET(30,4)
      SUM = 0
      DO 20 I = 1, 30
      READ, PET(I,1), PET(I,2), PET(I,3), PET(I,4)
   20 SUM = SUM + PET(I,2)
      PRINT, SUM
      STOP
      END
```

Phil began his explanation. "Let's look at the DIMENSION statement. The first index for the PET array will refer to the person and, since there are 30 people, there is a '30' in the DIMENSION statement. The second index refers to the particular type of pet a person has. The '4' in the DIMENSION statement tells the computer that the second index will go up to four. In effect, this DIMENSION statement has reserved 120 locations (30 times 4). These locations have been given the addresses

PET (1,1)
PET (1,2)
PET (1,3)
PET (1,4)
PET (2,1)
PET (2,2)

. . .

PET (29,4)
PET (30,1)
PET (30,2)
PET (30,3)
PET (30,4)

"The READ statement is set up to read four values from a DATA card and place those values in the variables PET(I,1), PET(I,2), PET(I,3), PET(I,4). For example, if the first data card were punched with these values

2, 0, 4, 1

then the execution of the READ statement with I = 1 would result in the following assignments.

PET(1,1) = 2
PET(1,2) = 0
PET(1,3) = 4
PET(1,4) = 1

If the second data card had the values

0, 3, 1, 5

then, since I = 2 in the DO LOOP, the READ statement gets executed again, resulting in these values being assigned.

PET(2,1) = 0
PET(2,2) = 3
PET(2,3) = 1
PET(2,4) = 5

"You can visualize the computer reading a grid or matrix of values: Remember, PET(2,3) = 1 means that the number of pets owned by person 2 of pet type 3 is 1. The contents of memory location PET(2,3) is one.

"Notice that one of your classmates has 120 dogs and 1 cat!"

	PET TYPE			
PERSON	1	2	3	4
1	2	0	4	1
2	120	1	1	5
. . .	. . .	. . .	. . .	. . .
30	6	2	1	22

"One cat! He must be a lion!" someone shouted.

"No, he's a telling the truth," Phil replied. "Of course, with 120 dogs, who's going to argue with him. Let's look at the program I have put on the board. Statement 20 in the program should be familiar to you all by this time. It is a summation statement which, in this case, calculates the total number of cats the class has as pets. Note that the second subscript remains constant at 2 (denoting the second column of the array, i.e., pet type 2), and the first subscript changes because it is within the DO loop. Thus we will have:

TIME THROUGH LOOP	VALUE OF THE INDEX	OLD SUM	+	PET(I,2)	becomes	NEW SUM
First	1	0		0		0
Second	2	0		1		1
. . .	. . .	. . .		. . .		. . .
Thirtieth	30	26		2		28

"Let me show you a few more programs that demonstrate characteristics of loops. This first one will read the cards and calculate the total number of animals owned by person 15." Phil erased the board and began writing.

```
      INTEGER PET, SUM
      DIMENSION PET(30,4)
      SUM = 0
      DO 20 I = 1, 15
20    READ, PET(I,1),PET(I,2),PET(I,3),PET(I,4)
      DO 25 J = 1,4
25    SUM = SUM + PET(15,J)
      PRINT, SUM
      STOP
      END
```

"The first five statements are exactly the same as in the other program, right, class?" asked Ovitt.

Ben Dover stood up. "Yes, except that the loop is only done 15 times instead of 30. The index in the DO statement indicates that I will start at 1 and end at 15. That certainly is different from the last program!"

"Very good, Ben," Prof. Ovitt declared. "The program then reads only the first 15 of the 30 data cards into memory locations. It does not matter that we reserved room for 30 cards of data and only used 15; any memory locations that are unused merely remain unused. When we declare our array dimensions, we must be sure to have enough room for all our data. Declaring arrays too small will prevent execution (in this program we could not have READ 31 data cards if we saved only enough room for 30). Declaring them too large wastes memory locations but does not prevent execution of the program."

Another student stood up. "But, Prof. Ovitt, what about those other 15 cards. Since we only READ 15 cards won't they remain in the card reader and prevent the next program from being read in?"

"Good question, Sid Down," Phil replied.

Sid did.

"In practice, the card reader processes all the cards through the machine. However, the execution of the program does not use all of the data. It is also interesting to note that because the information desired is on card 15, the first 14 cards had to be read 'just to get them out of the way.' Once card 15 is read, the program continues on and enters the second DO loop. Will someone please explain what happens there?" asked Phil.

Marge Erine should have known butter, but she decided to give it a try. "I believe that this loop adds up the values in a row of the array. In this case, it is the fifteenth row." She went to the board. "Let us say that this particular person had 2 dogs, 1 cat, 4 fish, and 0 birds. Here is a table that shows how the values in the statement SUM = SUM + PET(15,J) change as the loop is executed."

TIME THROUGH THE LOOP	VALUE OF THE INDEX J	OLD SUM	+ PET(15,J)	becomes NEW SUM
First	1	0	2	2
Second	2	2	1	3
Third	3	3	4	7
Fourth	4	7	0	7

"Thank you, Marge," Phil replied. "In the previous program we selected a particular column and added up all the rows in that column. The procedure was to hold the column (the second subscript) constant at 2 and have a loop vary the row (the first subscript) from 1 to 30.

"In the program we have just completed, we selected a particular row and added across the columns in that row. The procedure was to hold the row (the first subscript) constant at 15 and have a loop vary the column (the second subscript) from 1 to 4.

"It is often helpful to think of subscripts in terms of rows and columns. If we wanted to get the total number of all types of pets owned by all students, we would want to add up all of the entries in the array. The procedure here would be to have a loop vary in both the row (the first subscript) and the column (the second subscript). Here is such a program."

```
      INTEGER PET, SUM
      DIMENSION PET(30,4)
      SUM = 0
      DO 20 I = 1, 30
      READ, PET(I,1),PET(I,2),PET(I,3),PET(I,4)
      DO 20 J = 1,4
   20 SUM = SUM + PET(I,J)
      PRINT, SUM
      STOP
      END
```

"The first thing to note about this program is that we have an example of nested loops. In this case, they both terminate at the same statement. Another way of writing this set of statements would be

```
      DO 20 I = 1,30
      READ, PET(I,1),PET(I,2),PET(I,3),PET(I,4)
      DO 19 J = 1,4
   19 SUM = SUM + PET(I,J)
   20 CONTINUE
```

"Both sets of statements do exactly the same thing. We shall refer to this last set, as it is a bit easier to follow the logic of the nested loop.

"First let me explain verbally what happens in this portion of the program, and then we shall look at a tabular display of the execution of these statements.

"In the first statement we initialize our index at 1 in preparation for reading our 30 cards. The second statement reads the data on a card into the proper memory locations. Now we come to another loop. This loop will add up all the columns for the present row of data. When this loop is finished, we proceed to the next statement, which continues on with the first loop. That is, we now get the second card, read in the data, add up the columns, and add this SUM to the previous SUM. This procedure continues for all 30 of the data cards. Here is how it might look:

OUTER LOOP	INNER LOOP						
Time through first loop	Time through second loop	Value of index I	Value of index J	Old SUM	+ PET(I,J)	becomes	New SUM
First	First	1	1	0	2		2
	Second	1	2	2	0		2
	Third	1	3	2	4		6
	Fourth	1	4	6	1		7
Second	First	2	1	7	120		127
	Second	2	2	127	1		128
	Third	2	3	128	1		129
	Fourth	2	4	129	5		134
. . .	. . .	. . .	. . .	. . .	. . .		. . .

"Continuing in this manner, we would eventually have the grand total in location SUM of all the pets owned by people in the class. Admittedly, this is a difficult concept, but it is a most important one. I suggest that you reread these notes and practice on some of these problems."

"Oh, before the break, there is one more thing that I wanted to mention," said Prof. Ovitt. "When you need to use loops in an input or an output statement, you can use a shortened version. This shortened version is called an IMPLIED LOOP and 'implies' that the word DO and a terminating statement number are present. The statement

PRINT, (A(J),J=1,5)

is an example of an implied loop. It will cause the values of A(1), A(2), A(3), A(4), and A(5) to be printed across the output page. The concept of the loop itself is somewhat similar to the normal DO LOOP, such as"

DO 10 J = 1,5
10   PRINT, A(J)

Rudy had his hand raised. "But, Prof. Ovitt," he started, "the DO LOOP you have written will print 5 separate lines of output. It's not exactly the same as the implied loop."

"That is of course correct, Rudy," Ovitt replied. "And that is a good point to remember about implied loops."

"Say, Prof. Ovitt," Howie asked, "can you use the concept of nested loops with the concept of implied loops?"

"Yes, you may," responded Ovitt. He went to the board and wrote the following statement.

PRINT, ((PET(I,J),J=1,4),I=1,5)

This will cause the following values to be printed across the page.

PET(1,1)
PET(1,2)
PET(1,3)
PET(1,4)
PET(2,1)

. . .

PET(5,1)
PET(5,2)
PET(5,3)
PET(5,4)

"As you can see, the J index of our implied loop was considered to be the inner loop, and the I index was associated with the outer loop.

"Of course, you may use implied loops with input also. As an example,

READ, ((PET(I,J),J=1,4),I=1,5)

will read 20 values into the PET array by rows. Well, I guess that's all for today."

Prof. Ovitt handed out a set of problems that he had prepared the previous day. Just as he finished, the bell rang, signaling the end of class.

As they were leaving, Phyllis was saying, "Boy, this sure looks like hard work! But, I guess hard work never killed anyone."

"Yeah," called Howie, "but who wants to take a chance on being its first victim!"

Problems for Sec. 3.11

1. Rudy has taken a part-time job as a dispatcher for a warehouse chain which delivers furniture to six different cities. Rudy obtained the distances between the cities from the following map (distances are in miles).

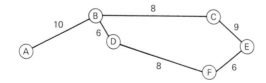

The warehouse is located in city A and each day Rudy has to prepare a route for the delivery truck that will cover the shortest distance. Write a program that will give the shortest route through the cities when the input is a list of those cities that must be visited. The truck must return to city A.

2. Howie, Seymour, and Hugh have taken a summer job at Bill Eumore's used car lot. At the end of each week, Bill gives the daily hours of each worker to Howie.

(a) Write a program that will read in the table of hours worked each day and calculate the following:

Worker	Straight time	Overtime
1		
2		
3		
Total		
Peak day is		

(b) Howie is paid $2.50 per hour, which is $.25 more than either of his two contemporaries. If a worker gets time and one-half for overtime hours, add a routine to your program above that will print out each worker's gross pay.

3. Assume that there are 30 students in Howie's class. Write a program that will read a student ID, and four exam grades from a punched card.

At the end of the data deck will be one more card containing a code that will specify a particular printing option. The codes and options are:

CODE	PRINTING OPTION
1	Print a class list with final grades
2	Print out the average grade for each of the four tests
3	Print out the mean grade for the class
4	All of the above

4. After the midterm exam, Seymour locked one of the UGH computer science faculty members in a building with only one exit. The floor plan of this one-story structure is depicted below.

The lights were turned out, and the victim was instructed to use only the light of a candle to find the way out. Immediately, the faculty member bumped into a computer system and decided to write a program to trace random paths through this maze. If he is equally likely to go in any direction allowable, how many decisions have to be made, on the average, before the exit is found?

3.12 FORMAT STATEMENTS

It was Friday evening, and Howie was eagerly anticipating the upcoming weekend. He had a few minutes before he had to be at the review session, so he thought he'd call home and let his folks know he was doing well in his computer course.

"Hello, operator?" Howie asked.

"Yes?" came the reply.

"I'd like to make a long-distance call, and I want to know how far I should stand from the phone." Howie chuckled.

"Do you wish to make a call, sir," the operator asked, "or are you just getting exercise by running at the mouth?"

"Yes, I would, operator," Howie replied, "I'd like to call home, Feeling, Ill."

"You sure you don't want to wait until ya' better?" asked the operator.

"I'm better now," Howie said, "I haven't called home in weeks!"

"What is the number, please?"

"Well, I don't know. It's a new number. Mr. Izzie Gettindere . . . on Queasy Street. Yes, operator, that's right, Q as in cucumber." Howie waited.

"Yes, I have that number," the operator replied. "Please dial CApitol 2-7635."

Howie was puzzled. "Say, operator, how do you dial a capital 2?" he asked.

Before the operator could respond, Howie had glanced at his watch and realized that he had to be at the review session in 5 minutes.

"Cancel that call, operator," he said. "I have to get going!" Howie quickly left for the session.

Farleigh Smart had volunteered the use of his home for the review session, and anyone who was in the computer class was welcome. Clara had agreed to come by and conduct the session on FORMAT statements. Most of the class was already there. Seymour was asking a question.

"Clara, I happened across my computer data card from one of those computer dating services. The numbers are typed on it without commas or spaces in between them. Look at it." He handed the card to Clara.

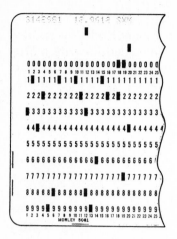

"How does the computer know where one number starts and another number ends? And there are letters on the card; how does the computer handle them?"

Before Clara could answer, Rudy was speaking. "I am working on a project that requires the use of a lot of data. The data is on a disk, and I have to read the disk. I'm not using the WATFOR or the WATFIV FORTRAN compiler; I'm using the standard FORTRAN compiler and need some help with the READ statements."

"Well . . . ," started Clara.

Before she could get started, she was interrupted by Howie's noisy entrance into the room. "Look at this!" He held up a sheet of computer paper.

```
3333333333333333333333
3333333333333333333332
3333333333333333333322
3333333333333333333222
33333333333333333332222                12
11111111111111111112222               11222
11111111111111111112222              11112222
11111111111111111112222             11111122222
11111111111111111112222            11111111222222
11111111111111111112222           11111111112222222
11111111111111111112222          1111111111111222222
1111111111111111111222          .111111111111111222
111111111111111111122          111111111111111111222
11111111111111111112          1111111111111111112
```

"It looks like it was printed by a computer. Could I learn to do some sophisticated stuff like this?"

Clara began to talk. "You have each asked me a question about input or output. Each of your questions has to do with FORMAT statements, the statements used in a computer program to tell the computer about the form of input data or the desired style for the output. We will be covering these statements later in class, but I think we can talk about your questions a bit now. Since Seymour was here first, let's deal with his question first. Look at this data card. Do you know what these numbers represent, Seymour?"

"Yes," responded Seymour. "The 3 is for the number of dates I have ever had; the 142981 is my file identification number; the 12.96 is my score on their IQ test; the 12 is my shoe size; and the SXM are my initials. They use this data to match me with a date."

Clara responded. "If we wanted to write a program to read this card and to properly select the numbers, we could have these statements." She wrote on a large pad mounted on an easel.

```
    INTEGER DATES, SIZE
10  FORMAT (I1, I6, 1X, F6.2, I2, A4)
    READ (5,10) DATES, ID, SCORE, SIZE, INITLS
```

Clara picked up the chalk and continued. "The READ statement has two numbers in parentheses. The first number stands for the input-output device being used; a '5' represents the card reader in most computer installations. The '10' is the number of the FORMAT statement to be used with this READ statement. This is a new form of the READ statement. Up to this point you have been used to seeing 'READ,' as the primary input command. As you will see, the new form is more flexible and quite a bit more useful. The variables to be given values by this READ statement are, of course, DATES, ID, SCORE, SIZE, and INITLS. When the READ statement is executed, the computer reads a card. Now, it reads this data quite differently from before. In all of the READ statements you have seen thus far, one number was distinguished from another by an intervening blank or comma. For example, take the following version of the READ statement with sample data.

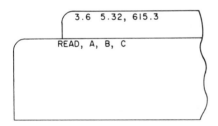

"When the above READ statement is executed, the computer begins reading the data card. It reads a 3.6, detects a blank, so it assigns this 3.6 to the first variable in the READ statement list. Since there are more variables in this list, the computer continues reading the data card. It now reads 5.32 and detects a comma. Since this is also a signal to stop, it assigns 5.32 to B. In a similar fashion, 615.3 is assigned to C thus exhausting the list of variables and terminating execution of the READ statement.

"We are now going to use FORMAT statements to describe what the data on the card look like. That is, the FORMAT statement will tell us whether each variable is an integer number, a real number, or alphabetic characters. It will also tell us how many columns on the data card are taken up by that number."

Lynn Olium was lying on the floor. "Is this going to be very complicated?" she asked.

"Not really, Lynn," Clara replied. "In fact, that is pretty much it. I'm sure you'll understand it much better after a few examples. For instance, let's take Seymour's data. Look at what I have written on the easel.

```
        INTEGER DATES, SIZE
  10    FORMAT (I1,I6,1X,F6.2,I2,A4)
        READ (5,10) DATES, ID, SCORE, SIZE, INITLS
```

"There is a one-to-one correspondence between items in the FORMAT list and variables in the READ list. An exception to this rule is a FORMAT character (an X) that specifies skipping a column on the data card. It has no corresponding variable in the READ list.

"In Seymour's example then, we have the following.

Variables in the READ list	DATES	ID		SCORE	SIZE	INITLS
FORMAT specifications	I1	I6	1X	F6.2	I2	A4

"Let's look closely at these FORMAT specifications. The letter that you see specifies the type of the variable.

I is used for integer variables and numbers.
F is used for floating-point (real) variables and numbers.
A is for alphanumeric variables and data.
X represents skipping a column on the data card.

"For integer (I) and alphanumeric (A) specifications, the use of a number immediately following the letter is easy to understand. This number represents how many columns on the data card have been used for that particular number of data item. Thus,

DATES is integer (I) and takes up one column.
ID is integer (I) and takes up six columns.
SIZE is integer (I) and takes up two columns.
INITLS is alphanumeric (A) and takes up four columns.

"The F format specification is slightly different. The first number after the letter F specifies how many columns this number uses on the data card. The second number indicates how many positions should be to the right of the decimal point. There is always a period between these two numbers. Thus,

SCORE is real (F) and takes up six columns.

The number should contain two decimal positions.

"The only other specification here is the X specification. As I said, this means to skip a column on the data card. The number in front of the X tells how many columns are to be skipped. Note that this number comes before the specification."

Seymour was eager to continue. "I think I understand this!" he exclaimed. He went up to the pad and began writing. "My computer match-up card would read like this."

Name ⟶	DATES	ID		SCORE	SIZE	INITLS
Format ⟶	I1	I6	1X	F6.2	I2	A4
Value ⟶	3	142981		12.96	12	SXM

"That is correct, Seymour," declared Clara. "You also recognized that the data card is read from left to right and every column must be accounted for except the extra columns on the right end of the card. A few more examples would be helpful, I am sure. Practice makes perfect!

"Suppose I wanted to write a READ statement that would read a three-digit integer number from columns 7, 8, and 9, and a four-digit integer number from columns 10, 11, 12, 13 from the same data card. How could I do it?"

"How about this?" asked Rudy.

21   FORMAT(6X,I3,I4)
READ(5,21) NUM1,NUM2

"Good," said Clara. "One thing I didn't mention. If you specify a number is to be three digits (this is called its field length) and it turns out to be only, say, one digit, the number should be typed in the rightmost positions of the data field. For example, if the numbers to be read in this example were 4 and 2, then the data card should be typed as

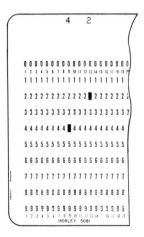

When the computer reads this card with the FORMAT specified in statement 21, NUM1 is assigned the value 4 and NUM2 is assigned the value 2. If the data card had been typed like this

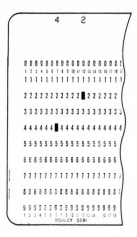

then the values assigned to NUM1 and NUM2 would have been 400 and 20, respectively. This is because the blanks are read as zeroes and the whole field is read. Any blanks to the right of the numbers, but still in the specified field to be read, are considered to be zeroes. The term for preparing data for this field is called *right-justified* or *right-adjusted*. In this example, the field for the first integer number is specified to be columns 7, 8, 9. Thus the number 4 should be typed in column 9. Just remember, the digits in a number should be punched on a data card in the rightmost columns of the field specified for the number."

"Suppose we wanted to write −411 as the first number and +25 as the second?" asked Rudy.

"We couldn't," responded Clara, "because −411 requires four columns to type. If you used our previous statement

21   FORMAT (6X,I3,I4)
       READ (5,21) NUM1,NUM2

and typed the data as

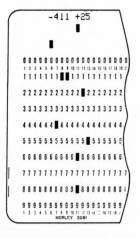

the values assigned to NUM1 and NUM2 would be 411 and +25, respectively. The FORMAT statement could be changed to FORMAT (5X,I4,I4) and no information would be lost."

"I see," said Howie. "Everything on the data card counts as taking up space, a number, a letter, a blank, a sign, a decimal point, or anything."

"Right you are," Clara replied. "Let's take a short break now.

"Oh, one more thing before we take a break. On our system, we could write a READ statement like this

READ (5, 21, END = 18, ERR = 27) NUM1, NUM2

The effect of adding these extra letters is as follows:

"If the READ statement is executed and there is no data card, control is transferred to statement number 18. If the READ statement is executed and there is some input error (like dust on a tape or something), control is transferred to statement 27. It should be noted that this particular program must contain executable statements numbered 18 and 27. (Any statement numbers may be used; 18 and 27 are just illustrative.) These extra features can prevent you from having the computer halt execution due to input error or lack of data. The END = N (where N is the statement number of an executable statement) feature in the READ statement allows a programmer to read a stack of data cards when the exact number of cards is unknown.

"The 'ERR =' clause can also be very useful, if there happens to be a mistake in the type of variable that is read and its FORMAT specification. That is, if the computer detected an error while trying to read an integer number with a floating-point specification, control could have been sent to another part of the program. Thus, rather than having the mistake kill the entire program execution, you could, perhaps, list where in the input file the error was detected.

"Okay," said Clara, "let's take a break now."

During the break, Howie went up to Clara to ask her a question. "Say, Clara," Howie began, "suppose I had a data card filled with 80 one-digit numbers, each corresponding to one of 80 variable names. When I prepared my FORMAT statement, would I have to repeat I1 80 times? That's a lot of writing. It would look like this."

20   FORMAT(I1,I1,I1,I1,I1, . . . ,I1)

"You could do it that way," Clara responded, "but there is an easier way. Anytime you have a repeating FORMAT specification, you may write it once, prefacing the specification with the number of times it is to be repeated. Thus, your example could appear as:

20   FORMAT (80I1)

Similarly, the FORMAT statement

35   FORMAT(2X,I3,I4,I4,A3,F6.2,F6.2,I3)

could be shortened to"

35   FORMAT(2X,I3,2I4,A3,2F6.2,I3)

Lynn was watching Howie trying to look good to Clara. She turned to Phyllis. "See Howie Gettindere over there?" she said. "Just trying to get Clara's attention. I went out with him last weekend and, let me tell you, he's no prize. I had to slap him six times!"

"Was he fresh?" asked Phyllis.

"No, I thought he was dead!" she replied.

Howie had started talking with Rudy. "Hey, see Phyllis over there next to that Lynn Olium? I met her at the end of the dance last weekend and asked to see her home. She said she'd send me a picture of it. I took Lynn home instead."

Clara was back and continued where she had left off. "We have been looking at integer formats and data. Let's spend some time on decimal numbers. If we use the F FORMAT specification, it is written as F5.2 of F8.3 or such. Look at this set of statements.

26   FORMAT (2X,F6.4,1X,F3.1)
READ (5,26) B,C

"Let's use these statements to read the following data card.

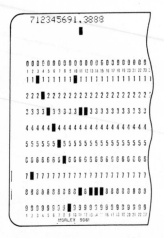

The 7 would be ignored because of the 2X specification in the FORMAT statement. The B would be assigned the value 123456, since the numbers 123456 occupy the six spaces specified by the F6.4 format and there are to be four decimal digits (that is, specified by the '.4' part of 'F6.4'). The 9 would be skipped because of the 1X in the FORMAT statement. The C would be assigned the value 1.3 since the field width for C is three columns. The 8 8 8 would be lost because it is not read into any variable name.

"When we looked at Seymour's example, the data for the SCORE field was 12.96. The decimal point was punched on the card. The format was F5.2, indicating five columns in the field with two decimal positions.

"Now we have an example of the data field being 123456. There is no decimal point punched on the card. The format is F6.4, indicating six columns in the field with four decimal positions. The number that is assigned is 12.3456. The decimal point may or may not be on the card. Usually you, the programmer, decide.

"If you are reading a decimal number and the decimal is on the data card but is not where the FORMAT statement indicated that it would be, the data card takes priority. For example, the statements

27   FORMAT (F10.4)
READ (5,27) D

would read this data card

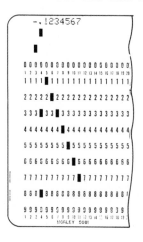

and assign the value −.123456 to D. The reason for this is that the field for D is columns 1 to 10. While the FORMAT statement says that there should be four digits after the decimal, the punched '.' in the data card overrides the FORMAT statement."

Clara was getting tired but she continued. "When I told you that the only FORMAT specifications were I, F, A, and X, I wasn't telling the whole story. A FORMAT form similar to the F FORMAT is the E FORMAT. An example of this format is

10   FORMAT (E10.5)
READ (5,10) B

This E10.5 specifies that the number to be read has a total field width of 10 columns (in this case columns 1 to 10), that B is to be a real number specified in exponential form, and that there are five digits to the right of the decimal. As with the F FORMAT, a decimal point punched on the data card being read will override the specification in the FORMAT statement as to the placement of the decimal point. Consider the following data cards read by FORMAT statement 10 above and the corresponding values that are assigned to B.

DATA CARD COLUMN	
1 2 3 4 5 6 7 8 9 10	B
1 2 3 4 5 6 7 8 E 2	1 2 3.4 5 6 7 8 $*$ 10^2
1 2 3 4 5 6 7 E + 2	1 2.3 4 5 6 7 $*$ 10^2
1 2 3 4 5 6 7 8 9 1	1 2 3 4 5.6 7 8 9 1
b b b b b 1 b b b b	.1
1 2 3 4 5 6 7 8 + 2	1 2 3.4 5 6 7 8 $*$ 10^2
1 2 3 4 5 6 E + 0 2	1.2 3 4 5 6 $*$ 10^2
1 2 3 4 5 6 E b b 2	1.2 3 4 5 6 $*$ 10^2
1 − b b b b b b b 3	.0 0 0 0 1 $*$ 10^{-3}
1 2 3 4 5 6 E b 3 b	1.2 3 4 5 6 $*$ 10^{+30}

"The final topic we will discuss tonight deals with output. The use of FORMAT statements to get neat, readable output is similar to the use of FORMAT statements for input of information. A program that calculates a value of sum to be 3.710 and then executes a statement

PRINT, SUM

will print an output that looks like this

.3710000E 01 .

A much neater and more readable output would be THE SUM IS 3.710. This can easily be achieved with FORMAT statements. In this case the statements that would work would be

9   FORMAT (' THE SUM IS', F5.3)
    WRITE (6,9) SUM

The WRITE statement is a more general form of the output statement than the 'PRINT,' statement. It can be used to obtain output on a tape, disk, card punch, or printer. The '6' in the WRITE statement indicates (in our system) that the results are to be obtained as printed output. (This is what we have been using when the PRINT statement was used.) If the output were desired on punched cards, a '7' could be used instead of the '6.' If tape output were desired, perhaps a '1' would be used, with some additional job control cards. Tape and disk output will probably be discussed in a later class. The '9' in the WRITE statement refers to the number of a FORMAT statement. When outputting data on the line printer, the character that is to be printed in column 1 of the page is not printed at all. Instead, this character, called the carriage control character, is used to instruct the line printer on how to print. The different carriage control characters and their uses are shown in the table at the top of page 139.

"Carriage control?" asked Howie. "Is that what drives the baby buggy?"

CHARACTER	PRINTER ACTION
	Start new line
0	Skip one line
—	Skip two lines
1	Go to new page
+	Stay on same line

"No, Howie, but try tickling its feet!" responded Clara. She continued. "The carriage control character should appear in quotes, as the first specification in the output FORMAT statement. For example,

10   FORMAT ('1' I4, F6.2)

would skip to the top of a new page before printing. The use in the FORMAT statements of the I, F, A, E, and X FORMAT specifications is the same as their use in FORMAT statements associated with READ statements. The only difference is that we are talking about an output line of 132 columns on a page of computer paper. (This is true of most line printers, although there may be differences at some installations that the programmer should be aware of.)

"A note of caution, if the number to be printed is larger than the space provided in the FORMAT statement, either an error message will result, the output field will look like ********, or some digits may be truncated without notification. In general, it is useful to let the output field specification be larger than you think you will need.

"Finally, we may print messages merely by including the message in quotes somewhere in the FORMAT statement. Thus, the following statements

WRITE (6,100)
100   FORMAT ('1' 'THIS IS THE TOP OF A NEW PAGE.')

would go to the top of a new page and print out the message

THIS IS THE TOP OF A NEW PAGE.

Note that we are permitted to have a WRITE statement without a list of variables.

"Another way to print messages is to use what is called the *Hollerith format*. This consists of the letter H (for Hollerith) followed by your message. Immediately before the H, you put the number of characters (including blanks) in your message. For example, the same message above could have been done as follows:

WRITE (6,100)
100   FORMAT ('1' 28HTHIS IS THE TOP OF THE PAGE.)

or you could have included the carriage control character in the Hollerith code.

WRITE (6,100)
100   FORMAT (29H1THIS IS THE TOP OF THE PAGE.)

"Well, it is 11 o'clock now, and I am beat," Clara sighed. "Let me suggest that the only way to get familiar with FORMAT statements is to work with several of them. I asked Prof. Ovitt for some practice problems and he gave me these. Why don't you take them with you and work on them when you get a chance."

"Thanks a lot for your help, Clara," called several voices, "we really appreciate it."

TOPIC SUMMARY FOR SECTION 3.12

FORMAT statements	X FORMAT
Formatted READ	E FORMAT
I FORMAT	Hollerith FORMAT
F FORMAT	Formatted WRITE
A FORMAT	Carriage control

Problems for Sec. 3.12

1. The Now York Times FORTRAN Format Crossword Puzzle

Solve the crossword puzzle by evaluating steps *i* through *ix* below.

(*i*)   'WHAT IS A CROWD?'ANDY ASKED

```
            READ 50, X, D, P, S, T, G
      50    FORMAT (1X, A4, 1X, A2, 3X, A4, 2(A1), 1X,A3)
```
(ii)
```
            PRINT 100, G
     100    FORMAT (' ' 6HPUT A, A1, 21HIN LOCATIONS E AND N.)
```

(iii)
```
            4TWO&3569ARE WHAT
            READ5, DATA1, NAME, DATA2, I4, Y, FFF
       5    FORMAT (F1.0, A3, A1, I4, A3, 1X, A4)
            K = DATA1
            C = NAME
            L = DATA2
            J = I4/1000
            I = ((J * 10) +5) − 30
            X = FFF
            STOP
            END
```

(iv) B = format specification symbol for real data.
(v)   A = format specification symbol for integer data.
(vi) Q = T and M = D
(vii) R is where the answer is.
(viii) In F, leave room for a lot.
(ix) K1 = ((I + K) / (K + I)) * 10 − 1

2. Write the correct values stored by the following (a 'b' represents a blank):

CARD FIELD (COLUMNS 1 TO 10)	READ BY FORMAT	RESULT STORED IN MEMORY
all blank	I3	
bb−3bbbbbb	I5	
b3b9b6bbb8	I6	
3962bbbbbb	F5.1	
3962bbbbbb	F9.2	
3962bbbbbb	F10.9	
bb3962bbbb	F4.8	
bb39.62bbb	F7.2	
bb39.62bbb	F7.3	
−b3b9b.6b2	F10.3	
3.96E+00bb	E10.0	
bbbb396Eb0	E12.3	
bbbb396E−4	E12.3	
HOWARDbbbb	A4	
HOWARDbbbb	A9	
HOWARDbbbb	A3	
bbbbbbbb25	A10	
25bbbbbbbb	A2	

3. Write the correct values printed by the following format specifications.

CONTENTS OF MEMORY	PRINTED BY FORMAT
15	I2
20	I3
−15	I2
20	I5
20695	I4
20695	I8
35.6	F8.2
−35.65	F3.2
−35.65	F6.3
−35.6	F6.3
−35.6	F9.1
365.2	E12.6
−365.248	E14.7
0.000365	E12.6
365.365	E15.15
HOWARD	A1
HOWARD	A3
HOWARD	A10

4. What would the following PRINT statements print? (A 'b' is a blank.)

  (a)   I1 = 10
            F1 = 10.0
            PRINT 100, I1, F1
      100   FORMAT (17H TEN INTEGER IS (, I2, 18H) AND TEN
            1REAL IS (, F4.1, ').')

  (b)   W ='UbAb'
            X ='R'
            Y = '1G'
            PRINT 50, W, X, X, Y
      50   FORMAT ('1',2HY0, A3, A1, 2HE, A1, A2, 3HHT.)

  (c)   PRINT 100
      100   FORMAT ( )

5. Write a program using FORMAT statements to print out a page-size version of your initials. The character used to print out a particular initial should be that initial.

3.13 SUBPROGRAMS

Howie and Rudy were leaving the FORTRAN review session at Clara's house together. Howie was talking, "Who was that other kid at the review session, Rudy? He looked familiar, but I can't place him."

"That's your roommate from last year, Izzie, don't you remember?" said an astonished Rudy.

"Oh, Izzie . . ."

"No, he was," responded Rudy.

"You know, there are three things I can't remember—names, faces, and I forget the third thing," mumbled Howie.

"I think Clara forgot a few things in the FORTRAN review session. Maybe we can talk about them now."

"Okay by me," said Howie. "You talk; I'll listen!"

"Well, we didn't talk about *subprograms* at all. You know, they're very useful for performing jobs that have to be done many times. Also, they enable one person to put into the computer a set of instructions that will be used as part of a program by many people."

"I wish someone would write a subprogram for our next assignment, so I could use it," said Howie.

"That is not exactly what I meant," continued Rudy. "As you know, in a lot of problems in statistics there are general procedures that have to be done by many people; for example, computing the average of a set of numbers, the largest number of a set, the variance of a set of numbers, a regression line, . . ."

"I think I'm regression I ever got into this discussion," Howie thought to himself.

"Well," continued Rudy, "instead of having every person who wants to use these programs write his own program, the programs can be stored in the computer for anyone to use. Let me give you an example, one that's too simple to be important, but it does illustrate the principle of subprograms. Suppose you wanted to compute the average weight for 30 people in class."

"Sounds heavy," thought Howie, again to himself.

"A program to do that might be the following." Rudy wrote on a scrap of paper:

```
      DIMENSION WEIGHT(30)
      SUM = 0
      DO 20 I = 1, 30
   20 READ, WEIGHT(I)
      DO 40 I = 1, 30
   40 SUM = SUM + WEIGHT(I)
      AVRG = SUM/30
      WRITE (6,10) AVRG
   10 FORMAT ('1 THE AVERAGE IS', F7.3)
      STOP
      END
```

"I understand that pretty well," said Howie. "First you read 30 weights, and then you use a DO loop to add them up. Dividing this SUM by 30 gives the average, which is then printed. That's a simple program."

"You could also write that program using a *subroutine*. It would look like this," continued Rudy.

```
        DIMENSION WEIGHT(30)
        DO 20 I = 1, 30
   20   READ, WEIGHT(I)
        CALL AV (30, WEIGHT, AVRGE)
        WRITE (6,10) AVRGE
   10   FORMAT ('1 THE AVERAGE IS', F7.3)
        STOP
        END
        SUBROUTINE AV(N, Y, Z)
        DIMENSION Y(N)
        TOTAL = 0.0
        DO 7 I = 1, N
    7   TOTAL = TOTAL + Y(I)
        Z = TOTAL/N
        RETURN
        END
```

"Wow, that sure made it much simpler," said Howie. "Like making a yo-yo out of a tractor tire!"

"It's not so bad, Howie," continued Rudy. "I'll show you what's going on. First, look at the subroutine itself.

```
        SUBROUTINE AV(N,Y,Z)
        DIMENSION Y(N)
        TOTAL = 0.0
        DO 7 I = 1, N
    7   TOTAL = TOTAL + Y(I)
        Z = TOTAL/N
        RETURN
        END
```

"The first statement identifies the program as a subroutine, gives it a name 'AV' (which I made up as representative of the word average) and states that the input-output variables of the subroutine are N, Y, and

Z. The input parameters are the values that are to be input to the subroutine, and the output parameters are the output of the subroutine, which will probably be used by the main program."

"If N, Y, and Z are input-output parameters, how can you tell which ones are input and which ones are output?" asked Howie.

"Good question. You look at the subroutine itself. If you view the subroutine as a program by itself, what values would be necessary for it to run?"

"Well," answered Howie, "I suppose the N in the DIMENSION statement, the DO statement, and the Y(I) in statement 7. That looks like all you'd need."

"Right. And the desired output is Z, the average," interjected Rudy. "So if N and the matrix Y are input into the subroutine, the SUBPROGRAM can calculate the average of the Y values."

"How does this subprogram relate to the main program, and what is a RETURN statement?" asked Howie.

"Look at the whole program," responded Rudy, wondering why he ever started with this. "Nothing through statement 20 is new; that part just reads in a list, WEIGHT, which has 30 items in it. The statement CALL AV(30, WEIGHT, AVRGE) tells the computer to get the subroutine named AV and have that subroutine operate on the parameters 30, WEIGHT, AVRGE. The computer sets up a one-to-one correspondence between the parameters in the CALL statement and the parameters in the SUBROUTINE identification statement. In this case, it goes like this.

$$\text{CALL AV(30, WEIGHT, AVRGE)}$$
$$\text{SUBROUTINE AV(N,} \quad \text{Y,} \quad \text{Z)}$$

When the CALL AV(30, WEIGHT, AVRGE) statement is executed, the computer goes to the subroutine and makes the association between the parameters in the CALL statement and the parameters in the SUBROUTINE statement. Notice that since WEIGHT in the main program is associated with Y in the subroutine, the dimensions of WEIGHT and Y must be the same. This is accomplished because N is 30 in the parameter list. The subroutine DIMENSION statement thus tells the computer that the dimension of Y is 30. Now, the computer starts execution of the subroutine. When the subroutine needs a value for an input parameter, say N, it uses the value of the associated parameter from the CALL statement (30 in this case). Similarly, when the Y list is needed, the associated variable in the CALL statement (the WEIGHT list) is used."

"Those are all the input parameters needed by the subroutine," said Howie, "but what about the use of the Z, and that RETURN statement?"

"The RETURN statement tells the computer to return to the statement in the main program immediately following the CALL statement. The Z in the SUBROUTINE statement is the output value. This is the actual calculation of the average weight. This variable is associated with AVRGE in the CALL statement, so that when the subroutine returns to the program, the variable AVRGE will have the value that was calculated for Z (the average weight). Now, the program proceeds to the WRITE statement with AVRGE having been calculated."

"I still don't see what's so great about that," said Howie, feeling that he could perceive the situation better than Rudy. "You changed a short, simple program into a long, hard one!"

"I said that this case wasn't a real application, Howie," retorted Rudy. "Besides, suppose you knew there was a subroutine called AV already in the computer that could calculate the average of a list of numbers; and suppose you had a sheet of paper describing what the input needed to be and how the output would appear; and suppose you happened to read that paper and the subroutine happened to be just like the one we have written here? Then your *whole* program might be written as follows."

```
          DIMENSION WEIGHT(30)
          DO 20 I = 1, 30
   20     READ, WEIGHT(I)
          CALL AV(30, WEIGHT, AVRGE)
          WRITE (6,10) AVRGE
   10     FORMAT ('1 THE AVERAGE IS', F7.3)
          STOP
          END
```

"OH!" Howie awakened to the possibilities. "This technique could be really useful for long programs that a lot of people need. Are there any other uses for subroutines?"

"Some people use them in their programs to simplify them, if they need to do the same calculations several times but in different places. Also, if a group of people are writing a program for a large problem that can be split into subproblems, they could each write their programs as subroutines and it would be easy for them to combine them."

"That could cause some problems, Rudy," Howie said. "What if different people used the same statement numbers that are used in another person's subroutine, or in the main program. Worse yet, what if the programmers used the same variable names in more than one subroutine?"

"No problem here, Howie, all variable names and statement numbers used in a subroutine are local to that subroutine. That means that the variable names and statement numbers used in a subroutine are not known or needed by any other subroutine or by the main program; in this respect, the subroutine is just like a totally different program!"

Just then Seymour came running up.

"Hi, Seymour!" greeted Howie, "I think I have a new name for Rudy; we should call him a 'Subroutine.'"

"Really?" said Seymour. "I haven't seen his act, but I'll take your word for it, Howie!"

"No, Seymour," interceded Howie, "I didn't mean that kind of routine, I meant we would call Rudy 'Mr. Subroutine' because he knows so much about FORTRAN subroutines."

"Oh! Well I wish he knew something about the statistics I have due tomorrow afternoon."

"What is it, Seymour?" asked Rudy.

"I have to calculate the variance of 50 numbers. Do you know about variance?"

"A little bit," responded Rudy. "I believe the *variance* of a set of numbers is related to the sum of the squares of their deviations from the average of the numbers. For example, if we consider the numbers to be $X_1, X_2, X_3, \ldots, X_{49}, X_{50}$, then we all know the average is $(X_1 + X_2 + X_3 + \ldots + X_{49} + X_{50})/50$. Call this number X_{AVG}. Then the variance of the set is $((X_1 - X_{AVG})^2 + (X_2 - X_{AVG})^2 + \ldots + (X_{50} - X_{AVG})^2)/49$."

"Yes, I guess you know 'a little bit' about the variance," said Howie.

"Howie, you know how to calculate the average of a set of numbers. Why don't we help Seymour write a program to find his answer? We can use subroutines for practice."

"Okay, Rudy, I'll take the first part," said Howie. "Look at this subroutine, Seymour, it calculates the average."

```
      SUBROUTINE AV(N,Y,Z)
      DIMENSION Y(N)
      TOTAL = 0.0
      DO 7 I = 1, N
    7 TOTAL = TOTAL + Y(I)
      Z = TOTAL/N
      RETURN
      END
```

"Now that I have calculated the average for you, you just have to program the remaining calculations. Are you following us, Seymour?" asked Howie.

"No, I always walk home this way," replied Seymour.

"Well, Howie, it'll be good practice for us, anyway," said Rudy. "Let me write a fancy program to calculate the variance. It will use your subroutine for the average."

The threesome stopped and Rudy began writing on the sidewalk with a piece of chalk.

```
                    DIMENSION X(50)
                    DO 10 I = 1, 50
            10      READ, X(I)
                    CALL VAR(50, X, VARINS)
                    PRINT, 'THE VARIANCE IS', VARINS
                    STOP
                    END
                    SUBROUTINE AV(N, Y, Z)
                    DIMENSION Y(N)
                    TOTAL = 0.0
                    DO 7 I = 1, N
             7      TOTAL = TOTAL + Y(I)
                    Z = TOTAL/N
                    RETURN
                    END
                    SUBROUTINE VAR(NUM, A, V)
                    DIMENSION A(NUM)
                    CALL AV(NUM, A, AVRGE)
                    V = 0.0
                    DO 10 I = 1, NUM
            10      V = V + (A(I) - AVRGE) ** 2
                    V = V/(NUM - 1)
                    RETURN
                    END
```

"What is that?" exclaimed Howie.

"It's not so bad, Howie," smiled Rudy. "Let's follow it through; it's an example of one subroutine calling another subroutine. First, the main program reads in the 50 values for the matrix X; then the subroutine VAR is called. The CALL statement for VAR and the naming statement of VAR cause the following association.

CALL VAR (50, X, VARINS)
SUBROUTINE VAR(NUM, A, V)

Thus, when VAR is called, NUM = 50 and the A matrix is the same as the matrix X. Also VARINS and V are associated. Now the subroutine VAR calls the subroutine AV. Look at the statements that call AV and name AV.

CALL AV(NUM, A, AVRGE)
SUBROUTINE AV(N, Y, Z)

So now when subroutine AV is executing, N has the value of NUM, which in turn has been assigned the value 50. Similarly Y is the same matrix as A which is the same as X, which has been input into the main program. Since the subroutine AV has been called, it is executed and calculates the average of the X values and assigns this value to Z. Now AV returns to the place from which it was called, in particular, to the subroutine VAR, with the value of Z being given to the variable in VAR named AVRGE. The subroutine VAR uses that value, the average of the X values, to calculate the variance, which it calls V. When subroutine VAR is finished, it returns to the place from which it was called, in particular, to the main program, with the variance V being assigned to VARINS in the main program. The answer is printed, and the program is finished."

"You've done it again, Rudy," sighed Howie.

"Well, Howie, actually, most computers have subroutines already in them that will do all this work. A complete program would really only have to look something like this.

```
          DIMENSION X(50)
          DO 10 I = 1, 50
    10    READ, X(I)
          CALL VAR(50, X, VARINS)
          PRINT, 'THE VARIANCE IS', VARINS
          STOP
          END
```

"By the way, Howie, did you pick up this list of rules for subroutines that Prof. Ovitt passed out?" asked Rudy. He showed them to Howie.

SUBROUTINE RULES

1. The name of a subroutine in a CALL statement must be the same as the name in a SUBROUTINE statement. Also, the list of input-output parameters in the CALL statement must match in number and type the list of parameters in the SUBROUTINE statement.
2. Expressions are not allowed in the SUBROUTINE statement list of input-output parameters, but expressions are allowed in the CALL statement input list.
3. When the RETURN statement is executed, control reverts to the next statement after the CALL statement that transferred control to the subroutine.
4. Variable names and statement numbers are local to a subroutine.
5. A subroutine may call a subroutine, but not itself and not a subroutine that in turn would call the original subroutine.
6. Subroutines may be placed in the computer by an individual or may be in the system already. This allows for repeated use of a program without the necessity of reading it in every time.
7. Only arrays that are in the parameter list of a SUBROUTINE can have a variable dimension, i.e., be dimensioned by a statement like DIMENSION X(N), where N is usually a parameter of the SUBROUTINE statement. This dimension (N) cannot be changed in the course of execution of the subroutine.

"By the way, Howie, there is one more thing I should mention while we are studying subroutines. Suppose in the SUBROUTINE MEAN we wanted to return to different places in the main program depending on the value of the mean. In WATFIV we could write the subroutine as follows.

```
      . . .
      CALL MEAN(K, WEIGHT, &6, &12, AVRGE)    } Main program
      . . .
      SUBROUTINE MEAN(N,Y,*,*,Z)
      DIMENSION Y(N)
      TOTAL = 0.0
      DO 7 I = 1, N
   7  TOTAL = TOTAL + Y(I)
      Z = TOTAL/N
      IF (Z .LE. 10) RETURN 1
      IF (Z .GE. 20) RETURN 2
      RETURN
      END
```

When the computer executes the subroutine, the place to which it returns in the main program depends on a value calculated in the subroutine. In this example, the possible places the subroutine can return to are statement number 6, statement number 12, and the place the subroutine was called from. Notice the statement numbers to which you might return are denoted by the &6 and &12 in the CALL statement and the corresponding parameter in the SUBROUTINE name statement is an '*'."

Rudy and Howie were approaching their rooms when Rudy first noticed that Seymour was no longer with them.

"I wonder what happened to Seymour?" Rudy asked.

"He did his magician's act," was Howie's curious reply.

"What do you mean, Howie?"

"Well," said Howie. "While we were walking along the sidewalk he turned into a movie theater."

Rudy gave a polite chuckle. "You know, Howie, that there are a couple more types of subprograms in FORTRAN."

Howie thought Rudy's dry humor was about to come in retaliation for his own joke, so Howie decided to play along. "Okay, Rudy, I'll bite. Please tell me about them."

Now, Rudy's humor was so dry some of his jokes were useful for stopping thunder showers. However, this time he wasn't kidding. "All right! People use built-in functions all the time. For example if you want the square root of a number in a program, you use the function SQRT. The following is a complete program.

```
        B = 7.0
        L = SQRT (B + 2.0)
        PRINT, L
        STOP
        END
```

"Someone else has written a program to solve square roots. They called it SQRT, and it is available for anyone to use merely by referring to the function name (i.e., SQRT). The program above would add B + 2.0 to get 9.0, take the square root which would be 3.0, store that in L as 3, then print that value."

"Are there many bulletin functions in FORTRAN?" asked Howie.

"You mean built-in functions. Yes. They can calculate the square root, trigonometric functions, logarithms, absolute values, largest value, smallest value, and others. Didn't you get the list Prof. Ovitt passed out?" (See Appendix B.)

"I thought that was just another homework assignment that I couldn't do."

"More importantly, perhaps," Rudy continued, "you, the programmer, can make up your own functions. In FORTRAN we have a subprogram known as the FUNCTION subprogram. It's a subprogram that calculates a value for a variable which is also the name of the FUNCTION."

Howie was being very attentive because he thought Rudy was about to spring the punch line. "I'm all ears, Rudy."

"I'll give you an example. We could rewrite the AVRGE program using a FUNCTION subprogram. Here we calculate AV which is the name of the FUNCTION subprogram."

```
        DIMENSION WEIGHT(30)
        DO 20 I = 1, 30
    20  READ, WEIGHT(I)
        AVERGE = AV(30, WEIGHT)
        PRINT, AVERGE
        STOP
        END
        FUNCTION AV(N,Y)
        DIMENSION Y(N)
        TOTAL = 0.0
        DO 7 I = 1, N
     7  TOTAL = TOTAL + Y(I)
        AV = TOTAL/N
        RETURN
        END
```

"That's not really very funny," said a surprised Howie.

"True, but it's very useful. While it looks very much like a sub-routine, it may be used in a program as if it were a function. This makes it a much more flexible feature. There is no CALL statement; the name itself does the calling. Thus, just as you could, in a program, say

$$X = SQRT(4) + SQRT(15) + 8 + B$$

we could get three times the average by replacing the statement

$$AVERGE = AV(30, WEIGHT)$$

with

$$AVERGE = AV(30, WEIGHT) + AV(30, WEIGHT) + AV(30, WEIGHT)$$

Notice that we don't have the repetitious call statements that would be characteristic of a SUBROUTINE. We have 'created our own function,' just as someone created the SQRT function.

"Here is a summary card with the rules for function subprograms."

FUNCTION SUBPROGRAMS

Function subprograms generally have the same rules as subroutine subprograms. Here are the few differences.

1. Since the function name (AV in the example) is a variable name, it has a type. (AV is a real variable since it begins with an A.) If the implicit declaration is not desired, the variable type may be changed by a declaration statement. In the above example the declaration statement to change AV to an integer variable would be

INTEGER FUNCTION AV(N,Y)

This statement would replace the statement FUNCTION AV(N,Y).

2. A function subprogram must have at least one parameter in its input list, while a subroutine subprogram need not have any input-output parameters.

3. The name of a function subprogram is assigned a value by the function subprogram. When the function subprogram is finished execution, control is returned to the place from which the function subprogram was called. The name of the function subprogram is not local to the subprogram.

"Does that stuff really function, Rudy?" asked Howie.

"It does; do you?" asked Rudy.

"Yeah, I guess so," Howie replied. "At least I've copied down all that you've said. Is that it?"

"One more thing," began Rudy, "just to make it complete. This is also available in FORTRAN as the FORTRAN STATEMENT FUNCTION, which permits a programmer to design a function with a single statement. For example, the amount of interest earned in a period is a function of the rate R times the principal amount P. The following program reads a data card containing the principal and computes the interest and new principal for a bank account.

```
EARN(P) = R * P
READ, A
R = 0.06
A = A + EARN(A)
PRINT, A
STOP
END
```

"Let me give this one a try," pleaded Howie. "I think I can tell you the function of this function. The first statement is the FORTRAN ARITHMETIC STATEMENT FUNCTION. It merely defines what the function is called (EARN) and what it does (R * P). I'll bet that the computer distinguishes between a statement function (such as EARN(P) . . .) and a subscripted variable (which could look like EARN (P) . . .) by the fact that EARN is not dimensioned!"

"Howie, you amaze me," Rudy cried. "Continue!"

"Well," Howie felt taller, "next you READ a value from a data card for principal and store it in A; the interest rate is set at 6 percent. The program then calculates the updated principal by adding to the old principal (A) the result of the function EARN after it has been executed. That is, the EARN says to look for a function defined as EARN. Then set P = A and use the function to calculate an answer (R * P). Return this answer to wherever the FUNCTION was used and continue with the program."

"Nice job, Howie," replied Rudy, "and of course you know that you can't use subscripted variables in an ARITHMETIC STATEMENT FUNCTION and that FUNCTION statements must appear before any executable statements in your program!"

"Of course," replied a confident Howie.

"Hey, you guys," called a refreshed Seymour as he returned to the group, "what did you talk about?"

"Well, we discussed SUBROUTINES, BUILT-IN FUNCTIONS, FUNCTION SUBPROGRAMS, and FUNCTION STATEMENTS. How about you? How was the movie?"

"It was great!" Seymour replied.

Rudy excused himself. "Hey guys, I've got to get going. I have a date with Edith tonight. See you around."

"Bye, Rudy, and thanks a lot," said Howie. "Say, Seymour, wasn't Rudy going steady with that girl Katie from West Street?"

"Yes, he is," replied Seymour. "But you know Rudy. He wants to have his Kate and Edith too!"

"Let's go home," said Howie.
"Okay," Seymour replied.

TOPIC SUMMARY FOR SECTION 3.13

Subprograms	RETURN statement
SUBROUTINE	Library subprograms
CALL statement	Multiple returns
Input-output parameters	FUNCTION subprograms
FORTRAN STATEMENT FUNCTION	

Problems for Sec. 3.13

1. Write a program using a statement function that will get the sum of any five numbers that are input.
2. Write a function subprogram that will find the sum of the first N integers.
3. Write a function subprogram that will find the range of a set of N numbers.
4. Write a function subprogram to calculate N factorial.
5. Write two separate subroutines that would calculate the mean and standard deviations, respectively, of an array of 100 items.
6. Write a program that will deal out two poker hands and select the winner. Assume that the ranking of hands is as follows:

> Four of a kind
> Full house (three of a kind and a pair)
> Three of a kind
> Two pair
> One pair
> None of the above

   Use the random number function or library routine to select cards for each hand.

7. Write a computer program that will play a simple version of computer basketball between two teams. The possession of the ball is determined by the following probabilities:

   (*a*) 10 percent chance of losing ball before shot
   (*b*) 35 percent chance of shooting and scoring
   (*c*) 45 percent chance of shooting and missing
   (*d*) 10 percent chance of being fouled while shooting

   If a player is fouled while shooting he takes two foul shots. There is a 75 percent probability of making any one foul shot.

   If a team shoots and fails to score, they have a 35 percent chance of getting the rebound.

Simulate the playing of the basketball game for a total of 150 shots (not counting foul shots).

How many "total shots taken" should be used to result in scores close to those obtained in professional basketball?

8. Rudy, Howie, and Clara were working on a project together. The purpose of the project was to write a program that would read data cards which contained dimensions of cylinders and cubes and calculate the volumes of the solids. The data cards were typed in the following manner.

If the number in column 1 were a 1, then that data card would represent the dimensions for a cylinder, the height being in column 10 and the radius of the base being in column 20.

If the number in column 1 were a 2, then that data card would present the dimensions for a cube, the length of each edge being in column 10.

If the number in column 1 were a 3, then that data card would indicate no more data.

To share the work, and work independently, Howie wrote a subroutine named CYLNDR, which received as input the height and radius of the cylinder and returned as output the volume $V = r^2h$. Clara wrote a subroutine named CUBE that received as input the length of an edge and returned the volume V.

Rudy wrote the main program that used the subroutines. Write the program and the subroutines the students might have used.

9. Have everyone in your class write his or her weight, height, and sex on a piece of paper. Collect these and use subroutines available on your computer to do the following.
   (a) Run a regression of weight as a function of height for everyone.
   (b) Run a regression of weight as a function of height for male students, then a separate regression for the female students.
   (c) Compare (a) with (b).
   (d) Since height is a linear dimension, and weight is a volume-related quantity, do you think some other regression would produce a better fit?

3.14 DATA STATEMENTS, DECLARATION STATEMENTS, MATRIX INPUT, MATRIX OUTPUT

Prof. Ovitt was lecturing: "Howie, besides using an ASSIGNMENT statement, how could you initialize a FORTRAN variable?"

"Well," sputtered Howie with a long pause, "I could put the letters H.G. next to it."

"Thanks, Howie, but what I was really referring to was the use of DATA statements. A DATA statement is a nonexecutable FORTRAN statement, appearing anywhere in the program (but usually at the beginning) that assigns, at compile time, a specified value to a variable or specified values to several variables. For example, if I wanted to have the variable N initialized at zero, I could use the statement

DATA N/0/

Any questions?"

"You said a DATA statement could assign values to several variables. How could you do that?" asked Phyllis.

"To assign the value 0 to N and the value 5.2 to X, I would use the statement

DATA N/0/,X/5.2/

or the statement

DATA N,X/0,5.2/

Both of these do the same thing. Notice that the variable type (real or integer) should agree with the data type. That is, N is integer and 0 is integer; X is real and 5.2 is real. Oh! Before I forget, let me mention that subprogram parameters and functions can not be initialized."

"Those DATA statements do offer an alternative way to initialize variables, but do they offer a really big saving in effort?" asked Seymour.

"They offer some saving of effort in initializing single variables, but their big advantage is in initializing matrices or arrays. Look at these statements." Prof. Ovitt wrote on the board.

INTEGER A(10), B(5,3), DIS(2,2)
DATA A/10 * 0/, B/6 * 0, 9 * 1/, DIS/1,2,3,4/, D/3.7/

"These statements would cause the matrix A to be a column of 10 zeros, since the 10 * 0 says that the value of 0 should be used 10 times. The '10' is called the replication factor. The matrix B is initialized to be

0	0	1
0	1	1
0	1	1
0	1	1
0	1	1

This is because the array is initialized by column so the six zeros are placed in the array first, going down column 1. Since that uses only five zeros (there are 5 rows in B) the sixth zero is placed in row 1, column 2.

Then the nine ones are placed in B going down column 2, then down column 3.

"Howie, would you initialize the DIS array?" asked Prof. Ovitt.

Howie started throwing books and papers around the room, and Prof. Ovitt quickly realized his mistake.

"Never mind. I declare," muttered the bewildered Professor.

"I think," started Ida Clair, thinking she had been called on, "that the array DIS would look like this." She went to the blackboard and wrote.

$$
\begin{array}{cc}
1 & 3 \\
2 & 4
\end{array}
$$

"Good," recovered Prof. Ovitt. "I should mention that initialization can also be done in DECLARATION statements. For example, the statements

INTEGER A(10), B(5,3), DIS(2,2)
DATA A/10 * 0/,B/6 * 0,9 * 1/DIS/1,2,3,4/,D/3.7/

are equivalent to the statements

INTEGER A(10)/10 * 0/,B(5,3)/6 * 0,9 * 1/,DIS(2,2)/1,2,3,4/
REAL D/3.7/

"When they are all the same like that, which one should you choose?" asked a curious Scott.

"That is usually up to the programmer and depends on what is available on the computer system he is using," replied Prof. Ovitt. "It would seem that combining the assignment of initial values with a DECLARATION statement is the simplest. However, it does depend upon the particular problem. Many times you have no need for a DECLARATION statement, so initializations are made with the DATA statement alone.

"While we are talking about getting values into arrays, I should mention some READ and WRITE statements that can be useful," continued Phil. "If you wanted to read the following card

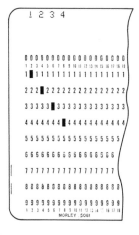

into the array DIS, you could use any of these READ statements."

Example 1:   INTEGER DIS(2,2)
             10   FORMAT (4I2)
                    READ (5,10) DIS

Example 2:   INTEGER DIS(2,2)
                    READ, DIS

Example 3:   INTEGER DIS(2,2)
             10   FORMAT (4I2)
                    READ (5,10)((DIS(I,J),I=1,2), J=1,2)

"The first example illustrates a new concept. We can READ in an array of values by referring to the array name only (in this example, the name DIS). This option is also available in a WRITE statement. At no other time can you use an array name without a subscript. There are two important points to remember. First, the array referenced in this fashion must have been declared as an array in a DIMENSION or DECLARATION statement. This is the only way that the machine can tell how much data to read. Second, any data that is READ using this option is stored in column order, that is, if we use the data card above, the DIS array will be

	Column 1	Column 2
Row 1	1	3
Row 2	2	4

This can be an important consideration in preparing the data."

"The second example is the same as the first," volunteered Phyllis, "except that the unformatted READ statement is used."

"That's right," Phil replied. "Now, what about the third example. Howie?"

"Gee, Prof, I didn't have a chance to do the assignment for today. You see, I had to go down to the delicatessen last night to pick up 200 pounds of limburger cheese for the wine and cheese party Friday night, and it took me quite a while."

"Two hundred pounds of limburger," Ovitt commented. "That's quite a phew!"

The class politely laughed and Prof. Ovitt forgot that he had asked the question and proceeded to explain Example 3.

"The third example uses IMPLIED DO LOOPS to read the numbers into the array. We have seen this form of a loop in a previous class, but it is worth reviewing at this time.

"This implied loop is really no more than a shorter way of writing the following nested loops.

```
                     DO 50 J=1,2
                     DO 60 I=1,2
              60     READ(5,10) DIS(I,J)
              50     CONTINUE
```

These statements do almost the same thing. They read the four numbers into locations DIS(1,1), DIS(1,2), DIS(2,1), and DIS(2,2), respectively. However, Example 3 reads from one data card and the above statements read four data cards.

"All of the above concepts also apply to output statements. Therefore we could write

$$\text{WRITE (6,2) DIS}$$

or using the unformatted output statement

$$\text{PRINT, DIS}$$

or using implied loops,

$$\text{WRITE(6,2), ((DIS(I,J),I=1,2),J=1,2)}$$

Again, remember that when the array name alone is used, the data is referenced in column order. The implied loop is a very useful shorthand for DO loops, but they may only be used in input or output statements."

The bell signaling the end of the period rang, and Prof. Ovitt hurried to pass out the assignment for the next class.

TOPIC SUMMARY FOR SECTION 3.14

DATA statements
Replication factor
Input and output of MATRICES
IMPLIED DO loops

Problems for Sec. 3.14

1. What do the following complete programs do in execution? Remember, initialization occurs only once and only at compile time.

(a)
```
    1    FORMAT (' K=' I2)
         WRITE(6,1)K
         STOP
         DATA K/7/
         END
```

(b)
```
    1    FORMAT (' X=' F5.2, ' Y=' F6.2)
         X = Y
         Y = Y ** 2
         DATA X, Y/6.0,7.0/
```

```
        WRITE (6,1) X,Y
        STOP
        END

(c)  1   FORMAT (' I=' I4, ' K='I4)
    10   DO 5 I = 1,2
         DATA K/9/
         WRITE (6,1) I,K
     5   K = K + 1
         STOP
         END
```

2. If A and B are matrices, then B is the transpose of A (written A^T) if element b_{ij} of B is the same as element a_{ji} of A.

   Write a program that inputs a 3×4 matrix and outputs its transpose.
3. (Continue with 2) Input a matrix A and see if $A = (A^T)^T$. How do you see if two matrices are equal?
4. Write a program that inputs a square matrix A and prints the inverse matrix of A (written A^{-1}). Use the computer library subroutines to calculate A^{-1}.
5. (Continue with 4) What is $A * A^{-1}$? Have the computer input a matrix A, calculate A^{-1}, then $A * A^{-1}$, and print the result.

3.15 ALPHANUMERIC CHARACTER MANIPULATION

Howie, Rudy, and Cole (Howie's roommate, Cole Shoulder) were having lunch in the cafeteria when Clara ran up to their table.

"Guess what!" gasped Clara excitedly.

"You found out what frogs get in their throats when they get hoarse!" said Howie before Clara could continue.

"Very funny, Howie," answered Clara. She continued, "the manager of the store where I work on Saturdays heard that I am studying computer science. He asked me to take some time off from selling and work on the information system the store uses for inventory control."

"Sounds great!" interjected Rudy. "Do you have a particular project to work on?"

"Yes," answered Clara. "The store currently uses punched cards to keep a record of everything that is sold. Remember in class I discussed that each punched card looked like this." Clara started writing on the paper napkin.

3   12.95   8712   12

Where

Type of clothing is	3
Price is	12.95

Identification No. is   8712
Size is   12

"Yes, I remember," said Rudy. "That was the class which Howie cut to go see a spiritualist."

"Was she any good?" asked Clara.

"Medium," Rudy replied.

"But what does your boss want you to do with the card system?"

"Well," answered Clara, "he thinks he can get a better idea of what to order for the store if he pays more attention to the colors of the clothes that are selling best. He wants me to plan the best way to add some characters to the punched cards in the future to indicate the color of the piece of clothing."

"What are you going to do?" asked Howie as he finished his pie and started to eat some cabbage salad.

Just then Cole bopped Howie on the ear and stomped out of the cafeteria. "What was that all about?" asked Clara.

"Apparently that was Cole's slaw," answered Rudy.

Howie was oblivious and continued his questioning of Clara. "What are you going to do about the information system for the store?"

"From now on each card is going to have punched on it the color of the garment. Then when a card is read, this information will be available to the person using the computer. We know that alphanumeric characters can be read using an A FORMAT. I brought along a sample card."

"Yellow and green clothes aren't selling too well this year anyway," said Howie, whose mind either worked in a strange way or not at all.

"Your mind either works in a strange way or not at all," said Clara perceptively. "What are you talking about?"

"Your store uses an IBM-360 or an IBM-370 computer, right?" asked Howie.

"Right!"

"Well, it probably stores one alphanumeric character per *byte* of memory and, since there are four bytes per word and each integer or real variable uses one word in memory, you can only store four characters in a variable name. Right?" asked Howie.

"Right again," replied Clara.

"Well, YELLOW has six characters in it and GREEN has five, so I guess you just won't be stocking yellow or green garments any more," finished Howie with a look of satisfaction.

"I think there may be other ways to handle that problem, Howie," began Rudy. "First of all, Clara could use abbreviations for the colors, like 'GRN' and 'YELO.' Or she could use other techniques. Let's first assume she uses abbreviations. Then her READ statement and her FORMAT statements could look like these." Rudy began writing on his paper placemat.

```
10   FORMAT(I2,3X,F6.2,3X,I4,3X,I2,3X,A4)
     READ(5,10) TYPE,PRICE,ID,SIZE,COLOR
```

"Say, that's good, Rudy," started Clara. "What would happen if the color on the card were RED? Since RED has only three characters, what would the variable COLOR contain for a value?"

"In that case, the variable COLOR would be padded on the right by a blank. I mean that if you read RED into COLOR, it would be the same as reading REDb (where b stands for blank) into COLOR," answered Rudy.

"What if I tried to read the five characters GREEN into COLOR, using statements like these?" asked Clara. She drew on a napkin

```
7    FORMAT(A5)
     READ(5,7)COLOR
```

"In that case the variable COLOR would contain the characters REEN (coded in numbers), leaving off the G because the memory location can only hold four characters," answered Rudy. "You know, I'll bet we could learn a lot about the way characters are stored in the computer by running a program or two instead of just talking about it. Let's go to the computer center and practice up a bit on character strings."

"Gee, I was going to go down to the alleys and bowl a few strings," said Clara.

"Do it later," replied Rudy, "you need this practice."

"That reminds me of my uncle, Willie B. Gettindere," said Howie. "He was a cotton farmer in the South, and one day while picking cotton, he came across two boll weevils. Now, cotton farmers and boll weevils are not exactly the best of friends, so Uncle Willie thoroughly sprayed his cotton field with insecticide. Since he had recently sprayed the field, he was curious as to how the boll weevils had gotten there in the first place.

"Later that afternoon, this character arrives at the farmhouse selling a special boll weevil spray. After much pressure Willie discovered that it was a con game and that this fellow had rented two boll weevils from a guy in town and had placed them in Willie's field.

"Willie was so enraged that he lost his temper and beat up the salesman; then he went into town and wrecked the offices of the guy who had rented the two insects.

"Of course, he was arrested. The judge was sympathetic, however, and said that Willie could at least choose whose charges he would face in court. He wisely chose the lessor of two weevils."

"Let's adjourn to the computer room and write some programs," pleaded Clara.

At the computer room the group—Howie, Rudy, and Clara—wrote this program to get a feel for how alphabetic data were printed when different format specifications were used.

```
      READ (5,12) ICOLOR, COLOR
12    FORMAT (A4,2X,A4)
      WRITE (6,15) ICOLOR,COLOR
15    FORMAT (' OUTPUT USING FORMAT 15 ' I20,10X,F24.4)
      WRITE (6,16) ICOLOR,COLOR
16    FORMAT (' OUTPUT USING FORMAT 16 ' 14X,A4,10X,A4)
      STOP
      END
$ENTRY
GRNbbbGRN
```

The output was the following:

```
OUTPUT FROM FORMAT 15    −942025408    −228414400.0000
OUTPUT FROM FORMAT 16    GRN    GRN
```

Rudy was explaining the output. "Notice that in this program we have read in GRNb into location ICOLOR and GRNb into location COLOR. Then, to illustrate that characters are stored internally as numbers, we use a FORMAT statement with an integer and a real specification for these two memory locations.

"Then, we use the normal A4 format to print out the data in character form. Howie, do you have your index card of character input and output?"

"Yes, right here," Howie handed it to Rudy.

CHARACTER INPUT/OUTPUT

1. If the number of characters to be input is greater than four, only the four rightmost characters are stored (unless other storage locations are provided by the programmer; this will be discussed later).[1]
2. If the number of characters to be input is less than four, the characters are put into memory with blanks added to the right.
3. If a print field width greater than four is provided for outputting four characters, the characters will be printed on the right side of the field, with the left side padded with blanks. If a print field width less than four is provided for outputting characters, the leftmost characters in the memory location will be printed in the field.

"Let's look at some examples," suggested Rudy.

RAW DATA	INPUT FORMAT	CONTENTS OF MEMORY LOCATION
HOWIE	A3	HOW
PHYLLIS	A4	PHYL
BRANDON	A9	ON
SEYMOUR	A5	EYMO

CONTENTS OF MEMORY LOCATION	OUTPUT FORMAT	PRINTED RESULTS
PHIL	A1	P
PHIL	A4	PHIL
PHIL	A6	PHIL
PHIL	A9	PHIL

"What do you think you will be doing with your punched cards at work, Clara? What type of programs will you be writing?" asked Rudy.

"First the manager wants a program to check the data cards and see if a particular color is becoming more popular. I wonder if we could write a little program that would do that?"

"Sure," said Rudy. "Suppose, for example, the manager wanted to look at the data cards for the clothes sold in the last 10 days and count the number of items of type 3 and color 'GRN.' A card with '5' in each data location could be used at the end of the data deck to signal that there are no more data cards. Let's see if we could write a flowchart for a program to do this."

[1] Some computer systems will store a different number (not four) of characters in a storage location.

After considerable scratching and erasing, the group came up with the following flowchart:

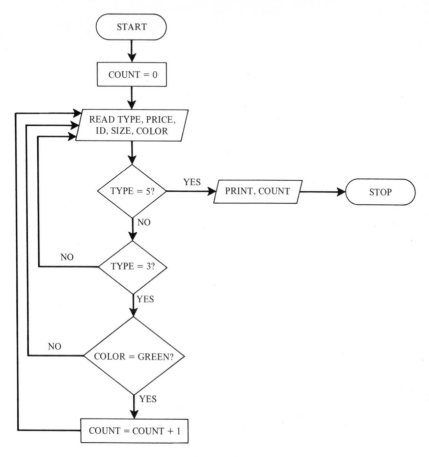

"Hey, that's good," said Howie. "Let's see if we can write a program to perform this task."

"I think we can, Howie," said Rudy. "It's not very different from what we've done in computer sciences already. How does this look?" Rudy wrote out the following program on the back of their old printout.

```
      INTEGER GREEN/'GRN'/,COUNT/0/,TYPE,SIZE,COLOR
10    FORMAT (I2,3X,F6.2,3X,I4,3X,I2.3X,A4)
15    READ (5,10) TYPE,PRICE,ID,SIZE,COLOR
      IF (TYPE .EQ. 5) GO TO 100
      IF (TYPE .NE. 3) GO TO 15
30    IF (COLOR .EQ. GREEN) COUNT = COUNT + 1
      GO TO 15
```

```
100    WRITE (6,20) COUNT
 20    FORMAT (' THE # ITEMS OF TYPE 3 THAT WERE GREEN = ' I4)
       STOP
       END
```

"First, we initialize location GREEN with the characters 'GRN' by using the INTEGER type statement. The data from the first data card is then read and stored in the appropriate location. Next, the program tests to see if the type is type 5. If it is type 5, then this must be the last card and we should stop processing and print the results. If it is not a 5, then the program tests to see if the type is type 3. If not, then the next card of data should be read. If the type was type 3, the program continues to the next statement and tests to see if the color is green (these were the two characteristics desired by the manager). If the COLOR is green, then increment a counter and get the next set of data."

"You were right, Rudy," remarked Howie. "That really isn't very different from the work we've already done. The difference is the initialization of GREEN in the INTEGER DECLARATION statement with the ' ' marks. I guess that's how the computer knows GRN is character data."

"Right, Howie," answered Rudy. "Note that it's important that the type of data be the same in the comparison in the logical IF statement."

"Rudy, suppose you really wanted to store more than four characters in a location. Is there anything you could do?" asked Clara.

"Yes, there are a couple of things. You could use *double-precision variables* or *complex variables*. I think Prof. Ovitt will probably cover these later. Or you could use two locations to hold one word. For example, if you had wanted to use eight characters for the color of a garment, and the whole word GREEN was on the DATA card, you could change your program to be this:

```
       INTEGER FIRST/' GREE'/,SECOND/' N'/,COUNT/0/,TYPE,SIZE,COLOR1,COLOR2
 10    FORMAT (I2,3X,F6.2,3X,I4,3X,I2,3X,A4,A4)
 15    READ (5,10) TYPE,PRICE,ID,SIZE,COLOR1,COLOR2
       IF(TYPE .EQ. 5) GO TO 100
       IF(TYPE .NE. 3) GO TO 15
 30    IF(COLOR1 .NE. FIRST) GO TO 15
       IF(COLOR2 .EQ. SECOND) COUNT = COUNT + 1
       GO TO 15
100    WRITE(6,20) COUNT
 20    FORMAT (' THE # ITEMS OF TYPE 3 THAT WERE GREEN = ' I4)
       STOP
       END
```

"Look closely at how this problem is handled in this program. In order to read in GREEN, which is longer than the allowable four characters, two storage locations are created. In the first (COLOR1) we put GREE and in the second (COLOR2) we have N. Since we now have two storage locations for a color, we must also have two comparisons to identify a color. Here you see the appropriate IF statements beginning at statement 30."

"Neat, Rudy," said Howie. "Any other tricks for dealing with these characters?"

"Just a few tips, Howie. If you had a problem and wanted to read the first four characters on a card and, if they were blank, transfer control to statement 80, do you know how to do it?"

"How's this?" asked Howie, showing Rudy this statement.

IF (WORD .EQ.   ) GO TO 80

"No, Howie. You'd have to give the computer something with which to compare WORD. You would use these statements.

INTEGER BLANK/' '/,WORD
IF (WORD .EQ. BLANK) GO TO 80

"Similarly, if you wanted to see if a character were a [.], you would use these statements.

INTEGER PERIOD/'.'/
IF (LETTER .EQ. PERIOD) GO TO 80

"Also, if you want to initialize a matrix of values, you could use a DECLARATION STATEMENT like this one

INTEGER A(5)/'A','B','C','D','E'/

"When you are programming in FORTRAN with the WATFIV compiler," continued Rudy, "there are some nice features for handling character strings. You can declare a FORTRAN variable to be a character variable and you can specify that the variable hold anywhere from 1 to 255 characters. If in Clara's problem the requirement was for an item description other than color, we would have a hard time fitting a long description in, even if we can make up several data names. For example, the CHARACTER DECLARATION statement

CHARACTER LINE * 80

would declare that the character variable LINE is to hold 80 characters. If we wanted to declare a test color to be GREEN, we could use the following statement.

CHARACTER TEST * 5/'GREEN'/

If there is no * and number after the character variable name in a CHARACTER statement, the character variable is assumed to be only one character long. A statement to initialize the first four characters of the alphabet might be the following:

CHARACTER ALPHA(4)/'A','B','C','D'/

This statement declares ALPHA to be a character array of dimension 4, each element to be of length one character (since no '∗ number' appeared after the name), and containing 'A', 'B', 'C', and 'D', respectively. If it were desired that ALPHA have two characters per element, the CHARACTER statement could be changed to

CHARACTER ALPHA ∗ 2(4)/'A1','B1','C1','D1'/

Character variables may be read and printed without FORMAT statements in WATFIV. If character variables are read without a FORMAT statement, the data for each variable should be in quotes. For example, to read a name and a course title from a data card would require the following statements:

CHARACTER NAME ∗ 18,COURSE ∗ 18
READ,NAME,COURSE

The data card would look like this:

The output statement could be merely

PRINT, NAME, COURSE

"Arithmetic operations cannot be performed with character variables. However, a character string can be assigned to a character variable in a character assignment statement. Also, character variables can be compared. If one character variable is longer than the other, the shorter variable is considered padded on the right with blanks."

"You know, Rudy," said Howie, "that wasn't at all funny."

TOPIC SUMMARY FOR SECTION 3.15

Alphanumeric characters	Input FORMAT
4 characters per variable name	Output FORMAT
Integer variables	Initialization
CHARACTER DECLARATION	

Problems for Sec. 3.15

1. The FBI has contacted Howie and asked him to help them evaluate coded strings of information.

   They would like a program that would:

   (a) Search a specified character string for the first appearance of a particular symbol or character

   (b) Replace a selected character or series of characters with another

   (c) Count the number of times a particular character (or characters) occurs

2. Write a program that will print a large 'banner' of a given input message. For example, if the input message was HAPPY NEW YEAR, then the program would produce an enlarged version of the message on computer output paper.

3. In FORTRAN, when characters are stored, the earlier a letter comes in the alphabet, the lower its number representation in memory will be. Use this information to write a program that will read a set of 10 data cards, each card having a four-letter name in columns 1 to 4, alphabetize the names, and print them in alphabetical order.

4. Do Problem 1 for an unknown number of data cards (less than 200 cards) but with the last card being blank to signal the end of the data.

5. Run this program and explain the results.

```
      DATA I/'WORD'/,X/'WORD'/
      IF (I .EQ. X) GO TO 10
      WRITE (6,4)
    4 FORMAT (' THEY ARE NOT EQUAL')
      STOP
   10 WRITE (6,5)
    5 FORMAT (' THEY ARE EQUAL')
      STOP
      END
```

6. In an English sentence two words are separated by a blank or a punctuation mark. Write a program that reads a data card containing an

English sentence and prints each word on a separate line. Assume only ',' and '.' punctuation marks are used. That means you can't use a sentence like the last one.

7. Write a program that decodes messages according to the following rules: Letters are to be replaced by their predecessors in the alphabet; A is replaced by Z (e.g., C is replaced by B). Other characters are to remain unchanged. (Hint: You might want to write a separate program to see how the letters A through Z are stored in the computer before you start this problem.) Have the computer decode this message:

ZPV BSF TVQQPTFE UP IBWF IUF DPNQVUFS EP UIFT.

3.16 ADDITIONAL FEATURES IN FORTRAN

Prof. Ovitt walked into the classroom carrying a bouquet of flowers.

"Hey, Professor," Howie called, "where did you get the flowers?"

"I bought them at a flower stand on the way in. They're for my wife. Oddly enough, I was the last customer."

"How come?" asked Clara.

"Well, this flower shop was operated by the Friars, you know, that religious group over at the monastery? Well, the attendant was telling me that the religious order had been in financial trouble and therefore had been looking for some ways to raise additional funds.

"The chancellor, after looking over several alternatives, approved the setting up of a flower shop outside of the monastery grounds. In fact, the flowers were growing right there already.

"Well, the flower shops in the town were outraged. They felt that they were at a serious disadvantage. People would probably prefer to buy from a religious group. Their purchases might be tax deductible, and the prices might even be lower.

"They tried everything to prevent the order from going into business. They took a list of 200 signatures to the mayor. That didn't work. They went to the monastery with their plea. It, too, was to no avail.

"In desperation, they contacted the florist's union, and they sent up their specialist, Attorney Hugh Marlowe.

"Hugh was a crackerjack lawyer. He worked all night preparing a legal brief and, in the morning, presented it to the judge and received an injunction preventing the group from starting their business.

"The injunction and court battle would have lasted several months so the Friars decided to go into another business."

"I think I understand," said Howie. "Only Hugh can prevent florist Friars."

"Today," recovered Prof. Ovitt, "the first topic we shall cover is conserving memory space. In an academic environment, we all too often are unconcerned with making our programs really efficient because there is usually an abundance of time and space available on the computer. In industry, however, where the memory size may be much smaller due to cost constraints, it may be necessary to be careful with the utilization of memory. There are two statements available to aid us in this regard. One of these statements is the EQUIVALENCE statement.

"In the parentheses that follow the word EQUIVALENCE we list all those variable names that we wish to share the same memory location. Thus, the statement

EQUIVALENCE (X, SALES, A1)

states that SALES and A1 are synonyms for X. Obviously, only one number can be stored in this memory location, so the value stored there should correspond to the variable name you are using at any particular time. It is most common to use the EQUIVALENCE statement to define the same storage area for large arrays. Thus, for example, if we had

DIMENSION SALES(100,50), PRICE(100,50)

we can save 5000 memory locations by saying

EQUIVALENCE (SALES, PRICE)

Of course, we should be through with one array before we use the other."

"Here are a couple of FORTRAN statements that will illustrate some additional features of EQUIVALENCE.

DIMENSION SALES(100,50), PRICE(100), DAY(30), PERSON(5000)
EQUIVALENCE (SALES, PRICE, PERSON), (SALES(1,3), DAY)

"Here is what these statements provide. The PRICE array occupies the same memory locations as the first column of the SALES matrix. Also, since there are 5000 SALES locations, the PERSON array overlays the entire SALES matrix. Note that we have a second set of equivalences in the EQUIVALENCE statement (the second set of parentheses). In this case, the DAY array occupies the first 30 locations of the third column of the SALES matrix, because the DAY array starts with location (1,3) in the SALES array where 1 means row 1 and 3 means column 3.

"As another example of the use of EQUIVALENCE, suppose you wanted to see if the third letter in the alphanumeric variable LOOK in a WATFIV program is a T. You could use these statements:

```
      CHARACTER * 1 LETTER (4), IS / 'T' /
      EQUIVALENCE (LOOK, LETTER)
      READ, LOOK
      IF (LETTER(3) .EQ. IS) GO TO 5
      PRINT,'NO'
      STOP
    5 PRINT,'YES'
      STOP
      END
```

The CHARACTER statement sets up the array LETTER with space for one character in each element of the array. The EQUIVALENCE statement makes the variable LOOK and the array LETTER occupy the same location. Thus, LETTER(3) can pick the third letter out of the contents of LOOK.

"The second statement available for conserving memory locations is the COMMON statement. A good example of its application can be found when using subroutines. Recall the subroutine on average weights we did in a previous class." Phil wrote the program on the board.

```
         DIMENSION WEIGHT(30)
         K = 30
         DO 20 I = 1, 30
   20    READ, WEIGHT(I)
         CALL AV(K, WEIGHT, AVRGE)
         WRITE (6,10) AVRGE
   10    FORMAT ( '1 THE AVERAGE IS', F7.3)
         STOP
         END
         SUBROUTINE AV(N,Y,Z)
         DIMENSION Y(N)
         TOTAL = 0
         DO 7 I = 1 , N
    7    TOTAL = TOTAL + Y(I)
         Z = TOTAL/N
         RETURN
         END
```

"The COMMON statement creates a common block in memory somewhat similar to the EQUIVALENCE statement. Let me rewrite this program using the COMMON statement."

```
         DIMENSION WEIGHT(30)
         COMMON K, WEIGHT, AVRGE
         K = 30
         DO 20 I = 1, 30
   20    READ, WEIGHT(I)
         CALL AV
         WRITE (6,10) AVRGE
   10    FORMAT ( '1 THE AVERAGE IS', F7.3)
         STOP
         END
```

```
      SUBROUTINE AV
      COMMON N, Y, Z
      DIMENSION Y(30)
      TOTAL = 0
      DO 7 I = 1, N
   7  TOTAL = TOTAL + Y(I)
      Z = TOTAL/N
      RETURN
      END
```

"Can anyone guess what has happened in this program?" asked Prof. Ovitt.

Rudy decided to give it a try. "I'd guess that the statement COMMON K, WEIGHT, AVRGE sets up a common block in memory that is 32 locations long (1 for K, 30 for WEIGHT, and 1 for AVRGE). The similar statement in the subroutine COMMON N, Y, Z says that N, Y, and Z are in the same common block. Thus, N actually is the same as K; the array Y is the same as the array WEIGHT; and AVRGE and Z are synonymous. What I like," Rudy continued, "is that you apparently can leave out the arguments in both the CALL statement and the SUBROUTINE statement; that's neat!"

"A very commendable job, Rudy," Prof. Ovitt commented.

"Prof. Ovitt," Hugh had his hand raised. "Are there any instances when you would want to use more memory locations rather than fewer?" he asked.

"Certainly," Phil Ovitt replied. "You recall that when we were covering character strings, we sometimes wanted a storage location to hold more than four characters. We had a statement to enlarge the storage capacity for letters. There are occasions where we would like to do arithmetic and retain more significant digits in our answer than usual."

"How many are retained now?" asked Ben.

"When using real constants, the computer retains seven significant digits," answered Ovitt. "*Double-precision constants* double the physical space used to store that information in memory, which actually allows 16 significant digits. The statement

DOUBLE PRECISION ORBIT, TRAJ, SPACE(40)

is a declaration statement that says the variables ORBIT and TRAJ are double-precision variables and the array SPACE is made up of 40 double-precision variables.

"In many scientific applications, the double-precision declaration is quite useful. Furthermore, you can do double-precision arithmetic and use double-precision functions and such by using variables that have been declared as such or by including the letter D as part of the statement. For example, the following are valid if ORBIT, TRAJ, and SPACE have all been declared as double precision.

$$ORBIT = TRAJ + SPACE(1,2)$$
$$TRAJ = (ORBIT ** 3) * 10$$
$$ORBIT = 3.7D9$$
$$TRAJ = DSQRT(ORBIT)$$

"Note that in ORBIT = 3.7D9 the D9 part is the same as the exponent E9 used with single-precision numbers.

"It is also legitimate to use the * convention that we used with the CHARACTER statement. Thus, the statement

$$REAL * 8 \ ORBIT, TRAJ, SPACE(40)$$

also declares the variables to be in double precision (eight bytes instead of the normal four).

"In printing the values of double-precision variables a format-free PRINT statement may be used. Alternatively an F format may be used or a D format, which is similar to an E format with the letter D instead of the letter E, may be used to print more significant digits."

"Say, Prof. Ovitt," asked Clara, "can we ask any questions we have on FORTRAN?"

"Sure, go right ahead," replied Ovitt.

"Well, don't you think that the selection of letters I through N as legitimate starting letters for integer variables is a bit arbitrary? I mean, suppose I prefer that everything in my program beginning with the letter A be an integer?"

"You would simply write IMPLICIT INTEGER A," replied Ovitt. "Then, any name in your program that began with the letter A would be considered an integer. Look at this statement."

$$IMPLICIT \ REAL(I - L, N), INTEGER \ (A - F, Z)$$

Here, any names beginning with the letters I through L or an N would be REAL variables, while names beginning with A through F or Z would be integer variables."

"That answers my question, all right," responded Clara.

"I wish that we could reread a card and get fancier output. It sure would be nice to have a backspace key and a tab key in the language," commented Howie.

"Essentially," replied Ovitt, "we have exactly that in WATFIV. If, in a FORMAT statement, we use the letter T it acts just like a TAB command. Take, for example, the following statements.

$$I = 50$$
$$J = 90$$
$$K = 10$$

PRINT 11, I, J, K
11   FORMAT (' 'T11, I2, T31, I2, T101, I2)

Remembering that the first column in the output record doesn't get printed, the line that would be printed would be

50   90   10
↑   ↑   ↑
column 10   column 30   column 100

Using this format, you can print a variety of fancy reports, lining up columns, headings, and such. In fact, you can use the T format to backspace. Thus, the statements here on the board actually result in the $ being inserted before the number 50.

I = 50
PRINT 19, I
19   FORMAT (' ' T50, I2, T49, '$')

The line printer doesn't actually backspace. What happens is, the output line is created in an area of memory called a *buffer area* by using the appropriate FORMAT statement. Then, the line created is sent to the printer.

"The T format can be used with READ statements also. Look at these statements." Prof. Ovitt wrote on the board.

READ 5, I, J, K
5   FORMAT (I2, T10, I2, T1, I2)

"And the data card."

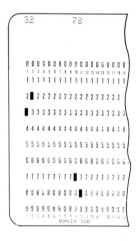

"The FORMAT statement results in the number 32 being assigned to I, the value 78 being assigned to J and then tab back to column 1 and assign 32 to the variable K. This is, in a sense, rereading the card. Again, the card reader doesn't read the card twice; it copies the card image into a buffer area and then 'looks' at it using the FORMAT statement."

"If there is a tab function in a format statement, shouldn't there also be something for skipping lines more easily?" asked Rudy.

"Yes, there should be, and there is," replied a pleased Phil. The class had obviously understood a lot of the previous lectures. "You may use a slash (/) anywhere in a FORMAT statement to indicate the end of one FORTRAN record and the beginning of another one. Thus, since a print line is considered to be a record, the statements

```
        I1 = 30
        K = 35
        L = 15
        PRINT 9, I1, K, L
    9   FORMAT (' ' I3/' ' I3///' ' I3)
```

would result in these lines being printed

> 30
> 35
>
>
> 15

Here is the use of multiple slashes. The rule is that if there are n consecutive slashes at the beginning or end of a FORMAT list, then n lines are skipped, but n slashes in the middle of a FORMAT line causes $n - 1$ lines to be skipped. Thus the three slashes actually skip 2 lines. These slashes may be used at the discretion of the programmer to space lines as desired.

"With input records, the slash format skips to new cards rather than lines. Thus, the following FORMAT statement will cause the first, second, fifth, and seventh cards to be READ.

```
        READ 5, I, J1, K, L
    5   FORMAT (I4/I3///I2//I4)
```

"That sure sounds logical," commented Seymour.

TOPIC SUMMARY FOR SECTION 3.16

EQUIVALENCE statements	IMPLICIT
COMMON	T FORMAT
Double precision	Slash FORMAT

Problems for Sec. 3.16

1. Write a program that uses an EQUIVALENCE statement to see how the computer stores the numbers 1374 and 1374. in different memory

locations. (Section 5.9 discusses different ways that decimal numbers may be stored.) Also investigate the way that letters are stored.

2. Write a program that reads a set of 100 data cards, each containing one number. Then in subroutine A, find the median of the numbers. In a different subroutine B find the squares of the numbers. Then use subroutine A to find the median of the squares. Use COMMON to save space.

3. Do Problem 2 with one subroutine and with EQUIVALENCE to save space. Use multiple returns from the subroutine.

4. Carefully prepare a problem that when solved on the computer with single-precision arithmetic will give inaccurate results, but when solved with double-precision will be much better. Program the problem each way.

3.17 LOGICAL AND COMPLEX OPERATIONS

"The last thing that I wanted to discuss today," said Prof. Ovitt, "is logical operations. In FORTRAN, we have two *logical constants*. They are .TRUE. and .FALSE.. If you want to assign the value true or false to a variable, that variable is called a *logical variable* and should be declared as such. Thus

LOGICAL S, Y, ANS

would declare S, Y, and ANS to be logical variables. If, in addition, it is desired to initialize the logical variables X and ANS to be .TRUE. and .FALSE., respectively, the declaration statement could be written as follows:

LOGICAL X/.TRUE./,Y,ANS/.FALSE./

Howie raised his hand. When he was called on he said, "If X is .TRUE. and ANS is .FALSE., then I'll bet Y = X + ANS is like the time I told my parents I spent $60 on books."

"What do you mean, Howie?" asked Phil.

"Well, I spent the $60," answered Howie, "but it wasn't on books; so my answer was true and false."

"No," chuckled Prof. Ovitt, "I'm afraid the statement Y = X + ANS isn't a valid one for logical variables. Since logical variables have values .TRUE. and .FALSE., expressions using these variables don't use arithmetic operators, but rather, they use the logical operators .AND., .OR., and .NOT.. For example, if the variables A and B are logical variables the expression A.AND.B is .TRUE. if and only if both A and B are .TRUE., otherwise A.AND.B is .FALSE.."

"What about A.OR.B?" asked Phyllis.

"A.OR.B is .FALSE. if and only if both A and B are .FALSE.; otherwise it is .TRUE.. Finally, .NOT.A is .FALSE. if A is .TRUE., and .NOT.A is .TRUE. if A is .FALSE.. We could make a table of all the possibilities for these expressions as follows." Prof. Ovitt wrote on the board.

A	B	A.AND.B	A.OR.B	.NOT.A
.TRUE.	.TRUE.	.TRUE.	.TRUE.	.FALSE.
.TRUE.	.FALSE.	.FALSE.	.TRUE.	.FALSE.
.FALSE.	.TRUE.	.FALSE.	.TRUE.	.TRUE.
.FALSE.	.FALSE.	.FALSE.	.FALSE.	.TRUE.

"The logical operators can be used with the relational operators that we have already used in FORTRAN. Remember the relational operators:

.EQ.   is equal to
.NE.   is not equal to
.LT.   is less than
.LE.   is less than or equal to
.GT.   is greater than
.GE.   is greater than or equal to

These relational operators compare two arithmetic expressions and produce a logical value. For example

S .LT. 2   produces a logical value of .FALSE. if S is 4.

L .GT. M   produces a logical value of .TRUE. if L is 5 and M is 2.

Now, we can construct logical expressions like the following

X .LT. Y .OR. M .GT. 6

where X, Y, and M are arithmetic variables. This would compare X with Y to produce a logical value, compare M with 6 to produce another logical value, then use the .OR. logical operator to produce one final logical value."[1]

"Can you give us an example of a logical operation?" asked Clara.

Howie couldn't resist, "How about last year when Seymour had a pain in his side so they took his appendix out. That was a logical operation."

"I'm not so sure, Howie," replied Seymour. "It had already been removed three years earlier."

"Can you give us an example of the use of logical values?" Clara asked Prof. Ovitt.

"Sure," replied Prof. Ovitt. "When I am preparing your final

[1]The order of clearing logical expressions from highest priority to lowest is: (1) functions are evaluated; (2) arithmetic operations are cleared; (3) relational operators; (4) .NOT.; (5) .AND.; (6) .OR.

grades for the course, I give out only the grades A, B, C, D, and F. There are no plusses and minuses. Well, with borderline cases like when a person's average is 70, I must decide whether to give the higher or the lower grade. In all fairness, I have decided that if a student has done the five computer programs given for homework, the student will get the higher grade. If the programs were not done, the lower grade will prevail. Let me show you the computer program I developed to do this grading for our class of 30 students." He began to write on the board.

```
      CHARACTER FNLGRD(30)
      LOGICAL PROGS
      DIMENSION AVG(30), NUMPRO(30), STUDID(30)
      DO 100 J=1, 30
100   READ, STUDID(J), AVG(J), NUMPRO(J)
      DO 600 I=1, 30
      PROGS=NUMPRO(I) .EQ. 5
      IF (AVG(I) .GE. 91 .OR. AVG(I) .EQ. 90 .AND. PROGS) GO TO 90
      IF (AVG(I) .GE. 81 .OR. AVG(I) .EQ. 80 .AND. PROGS) GO TO 80
      IF (AVG(I) .GE. 71 .OR. AVG(I) .EQ. 70 .AND. PROGS) GO TO 70
      IF (AVG(I) .GE. 61 .OR. AVG(I) .EQ. 60 .AND. PROGS) GO TO 60
      FNLGRD(I)='F'
      GO TO 500
60    FNLGRD(I)='D'
      GO TO 500
70    FNLGRD(I)='C'
      GO TO 500
80    FNLGRD(I)='B'
      GO TO 500
90    FNLGRD(I)='A'
500   PRINT, STUDID(I), FNLGRD(I)
600   CONTINUE
      STOP
      END
```

This program sets up a storage location called PROGS as a logical variable. That is, it may only contain the value .TRUE. or the value .FALSE.. After reading in the required data (a student's ID, current average, and number of programs written), the program begins to calculate the grade.

First, it will see if the number of programs written is equal to 5. If it is, then the value of PROGS will be set to .TRUE.. Note that we have used a logical comparison in an assignment statement. Of course, this allows us to assign only the values .TRUE. or .FALSE. to that variable.

"The next set of statements is a series of IF statements that determines what grade to assign. You can see that there are two ways to get an A. If the average is over 91 an A is given or, if the average is 90 *and* 5 programs were written. Thus, we have the .OR. relationship. Let's look at the possible ways to get an A.

PROGS	AVG.EQ.90	AVG.GE.91	AVG.EQ.90 .AND. PROGS	AVG.GE.91 .OR. AVG.EQ.90 .AND. PROGS	GET AN A?
TRUE	FALSE	TRUE	FALSE	TRUE	YES
TRUE	TRUE	FALSE	TRUE	TRUE	YES
TRUE	FALSE	FALSE	FALSE	FALSE	NO
FALSE	FALSE	TRUE	FALSE	TRUE	YES
FALSE	TRUE	FALSE	FALSE	FALSE	NO
FALSE	FALSE	FALSE	FALSE	FALSE	NO

"Here, you can see that three logical values are generated in this first IF statement. AVG(I) .GE. 91 can be true or false; and PROGS can be true or false. The .AND. and .OR. logical operators tell us what to do based on these comparisons. That is, what grade to assign."

"That's not as complex as I thought," commented Howie.

"No, Howie, its not really very complex, but *complex variables* are what I want to cover now. In mathematics we have numbers written in the form $a + bi$ where i is the square root of -1 and a and b are real numbers. We can represent complex numbers in FORTRAN by the two real numbers, a and b, separated by commas and in parentheses. For example

$$(6.5, 8.3) \text{ is the same as } 6.5 + 8.3i$$

$$(-3.0, 7.E-2) \text{ is the same as } -3.0 + 0.07i$$

A variable that has complex values is called a complex variable and is declared to be such by a type declaration statement. For example,

COMPLEX X, Y(50)

would declare X complex and Y a matrix for 50 complex numbers.

"The computer will evaluate complex arithmetic expressions with the usual rules of complex arithmetic. This is somewhat different from what you may be used to. For example,

$(a,b) + (c,d)$ equals $(a + c, b + d)$

$(a,b) - (c,d)$ equals $(a - c, b - d)$

$(a,b) \times (c,d)$ equals $(ac - bd, ad + bc)$

$(a,b) \mathbin{/} (c,d)$ equals $[(ac + bd) \mathbin{/} (c^2 + d^2), (-ad + bc) \mathbin{/} (c^2 + d^2)]$

"Now I know why they call it complex arithmetic," sighed Seymour.

"It's not that bad," Prof. Ovitt suggested. "Seymour, what if we wanted to multiply the complex number $5 + 3i$ by the complex number $6 + 2i$. What would be the answer?"

Seymour went up to the board and began to write.

1. $5 + 3i$ is the same as $(5,3)$
2. $6 + 2i$ is the same as $(6,2)$
3. $(5,3) \times (6,2)$ equals $[(5)(6) - (3)(2),(5)(2) + (3)(6)]$
4. My answer is $(24, 28)$ or $24 + 28i$

"Seymour, that is terrific," said Prof. Ovitt. "How did you manage to do it?"

"Nothing to it," replied Seymour. "I just copied down what was on the piece of paper Rudy gave me."

"I'd like to try one, Professor," volunteered Howie.

"Okay," came the reply. "What is the value for X in the following expression?

COMPLEX X
$X = (5,2) + (3,6) - 2$

"Well, I guess you'd convert the 2 to its complex form of $(2,0)$. Then, the answer would be $X = (6,8)$."

"Good, Howie," responded Prof. Ovitt.

"Can complex arithmetic be freely used in a program?" asked Rudy.

"Whenever you wish," Prof. Ovitt answered, "as long as the variables are declared as complex. The functions built into the computer can even be used with complex variables by putting a 'C' before the function name. For example,

CSQRT (X)

will calculate the square root of the complex variable X, the result being a complex number itself. However, if a complex function is used, even if it is a built-in FORTRAN function, it must be declared by a statement like the following:

COMPLEX X, CSQRT, Z, CMPLX

"How would this stuff be used?" asked Hugh. "Can you show us an example?"

Prof. Ovitt thought for a few minutes and then began to talk.

"Suppose a computer was being used to test the quality of a new golf club design. The club was set up on an automatic driving range and aimed to hit due east. Let (0,0) be the coordinates of the point on which the club was positioned on the ground and the target (the cup on the green) was at position (5,0), where the distances (in parentheses) are measured in units of 100 feet. Note that the coordinates of a point are two numbers: an east-west coordinate and a north-south coordinate. Twenty golf balls were hit and the coordinates of the points at which the balls came to rest were noted, then punched on data cards. You would like to know how many golf balls went a distance of not less than three units, not more than five units, and were no more than a distance of five units from the cup.

"Thus, you are reading the two coordinates of these sets of 20 data points as points in the x,y plane. You want to know if each data point is between the circle $x^2 + y^2 = 25$, the circle $x^2 + y^2 = 9$, and if the points are within five units of the point (5,0)."

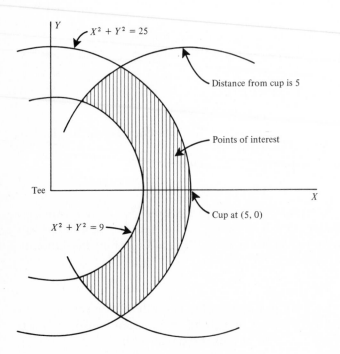

Then a program to do this would be the following:

```
      COMPLEX A, B
      B = (5., 0.)
      DO 12 I = 1, 20
      READ, A
      IF (CABS (A) .GT. 5.0 .OR. CABS(A) .LT. 3.) GO TO 12
      IF (CABS(A−B) .LT. 5.) PRINT, A
   12 CONTINUE
      STOP
      END
```

"The data cards for this program would be typed with the two decimal values for A enclosed in a set of parentheses and separated by a comma, like (3.2, 4.)," finished Prof. Ovitt.

"Wow, I'm glad I asked," mumbled Hugh.

Seymour was beginning to get a complex.

"Listen, Prof. Ovitt," Howie suggested, "I think that we should break early today so we can give our minds time to digest all this."

"Say, Seymour," Howie said as they were leaving, "it sure is nice to have an understanding of the FORTRAN language."

"Boy, it sure is," agreed Seymour. "I've already called to book reservations to Fortran. I figure I'll be able to talk like a native . . . and to think that I've also fulfilled my foreign language requirement . . ."

"Say, buddy," Howie interrupted. "sit down for a minute. There's something I want to explain to you!"

Problems for Sec. 3.17

1. Using the values $X = 3 + 5i$, $Y = -2 - 2i$, and $Z = 2 + i$ evaluate the following by hand and have the computer verify your answers.

    (a) X^2
    (b) $X + Y + Z$
    (c) $X + iX$
    (d) $X * Y * Z$
    (e) X/Y

2. A ball hit with force F by a bat starts its flight from a height of 4 feet, with an angle Z to the horizon. The initial velocity is $V = 200$. The ball's position at time t can be expressed as a complex number $P = X + iY$ in

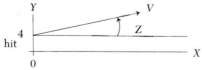

terms of its distance X and height Y. For this problem we then have

$$P = (200 \cos Z)t + [4 + (200 \sin Z - 16t)t]i$$

(*a*) Using complex numbers, have the computer help you find the angle
Z which produces the longest hig (assume the ball stops when it hits
the ground).

(*b*) Plot the trajectories of some of these hits.

3. If the clock strikes one, the mouse runs down.
   If the mouse runs down or it thunders, the lady will scream.
   If it is 1 o'clock and thundering, the 1 o'clock school bus will be late
   and will arrive at 1:30.
   If the lady screams or it thunders, the baby will wake up from its nap.
   If the girl gets home on the school bus, she will take care of the baby.
   It is 1:00 and clear outside. Have the computer tell you what will hap-
   pen now.

4. Phil, his sister, his son, and his daughter are tennis players. The best
   player's twin and the worst player are of opposite sex. The best player
   and the worst player are the same age. Who is the best player?

   Can the computer be used to solve this problem? Why or why
   not?

chapter
4

BASIC
programming

Before the concept of sharing time on computers became common, the process of submitting programs for solution was centered around a punched-card batch processing system. Now, it is quite common to communicate directly with the computer using a typewriterlike device. Not only does this provide for immediate entry of the program to be processed, but it also results in nearly instantaneous solutions being received by the user.

The language most often used in communicating with the computer in this manner is called BASIC (Beginner's All-purpose Symbolic Instruction Code). It is a relatively easy language to learn, and, although there are slight differences from computer system to computer system, the user will be able to adjust easily to slight variations by consulting the appropriate BASIC manuals at that installation.

4.1 INTRODUCTION TO TIME SHARING

Justin Time barely made it for his appointment with Howie. He was looking around the room, and Howie introduced himself.

"I'm Howie Gettindere, and I think you're looking for me," he said.

"Are you the one who called about getting familiar with our computer system?" Justin asked.

"Yes, it was I," Howie replied. "One of my roommates suggested that if I wanted to get a quick introduction to the computer system I should dial A-S-S-I-S-T on the university phone system and ask for an upperclassman to assist me. I called and explained my request to the guy who answered the phone. Who was he? His response was kind of cold."

"Luke Warm," Justin replied.

"That would have been better. Anyway, he told me to meet you over here, but he must have fouled up because there's nothing in this room but a bunch of typewriters," Howie exclaimed.

"No, this is the place," Justin said. "These are not ordinary typewriters. Yes, they do have keyboards that are quite similar to those of standard typewriters, but these are very special machines. They are used to communicate with the computer. They are called terminals."

"Are they sick?"

"No," answered an exasperated Justin, "you get inside them and wait for a bus! Listen, don't worry about why they call them terminals right now. They just do. Do you have to ask so many questions?"

"No, I don't," responded Howie. "How do you use these things?"

"Well, to make contact with the computer, a user picks up the telephone and calls a number that connects to the computer. The machine signals that it has answered the phone by generating a high-pitched tone over the receiver. The user then places the telephone receiver in a special cradle on the terminal, and he is then in contact with the computer. Anything he now types will be sent to the machine, and any messages from the machine will be automatically typed out at the terminal." Justin paused.

"Hey, no cards to punch, right?" asked Howie.

"That is correct," Justin answered. "But what I like is the fact that you get your results back right away. You don't have to come back later on."

"But what if I make some errors when I type in my instructions? You know, syntax errors?" Howie remembered what Bea had taught him.

Justin was waiting for the question. "If you make a syntax error while you're typing the instructions, the computer will tell you what the error is when you have completed typing the instructions. You could then retype it. The computer will ignore the previously typed instructions and use only the last version."

"Hey, I like this," smiled Howie. "But boy, I'll bet the line at the terminal is 10 blocks long. Everybody probably wants to use this terminal."

"The lines are not too long at all, Howie," Justin responded. "You see, there are 20 of these terminals located all over campus. Twenty people could be using them and each person would think that he was the sole user. They share the computer. That's why they refer to this type of computer processing as time sharing."

"How many people could share time?" Howie asked. "I mean how many terminals could you have?"

"On some of the larger computer systems, hundreds could be on line simultaneously," answered Justin.

"And all you need is a terminal and a telephone," mused Howie. "Say, does that mean that I could have one of these in my dorm room?"

"It sure does," replied Justin. "Or you could have one at home. In fact, several manufacturers now make models that are only slightly larger than an attache case . . . a really portable model that can be used wherever there is an electric outlet and a telephone."

"Do other computers have this setup?" asked Howie.

"Why sure," Justin continued, "they're all across the country and, if you have the right phone number, you can call any one of them up."

"But they can't let just anyone use the machine. There must be some restrictions?" questioned Howie.

"Yes, of course," Justin replied, "and you'll see ours in a minute. Essentially, after you make connection with the computer you must type in a number and a password. The number is used to bill the user for computer time used, and the password is used as a check against unauthorized people using the computer. Every system has these kinds of safeguards."

"Do you always have to use the phone to make contact or could a terminal be connected directly to the computer?" Howie asked.

Figure 4.1 The 2741 time sharing terminal.

"Yes, if the terminal is close enough, it is relatively simple to wire it directly to the computer, as with the IBM 2741 over against that wall."

"Can I ask one more question?" asked Howie.

"Yes. And that was it!" replied Justin. "I have to go to my 2 o'clock class."

"Gee," Howie mumbled aloud, "I wonder if you can still run programs with cards while other people are using the time sharing system?"

One of the students sitting at a terminal couldn't help but overhear Howie's comment. "Yes," a voice replied, "time sharing and batch processing can be going on at the same time. Different portions of the machine are devoted to each task."

"Thank you," Howie replied. "Say, would you mind showing me how to use this system?"

4.2 SIGNING ON

"I'll be glad to show you how to sign on as a user of our time sharing system," the student said. "By the way, my name is Bertha Vanation, what's yours?"

"Howie Gettindere."

"We don't have to go anywhere; the terminals are all here," Bertha replied.

"No, no, that's my name. It's Howie, Howie Gettindere."

"Nice to meet you, Howie." They shook hands. "Sit down. I'm about to sign on the system."

Bertha picked up the telephone. "The steps that I am going to go through vary from computer system to computer system, so be aware that commands, numbers, letters, or such may be slightly different."

She dialed the extension number for the computer and, when she heard the high-pitched tone, placed the telephone into the cradle on the terminal. She turned the terminal on and began to type:

LOGON-59320, BV

"This is the procedure for logging on (or signing on) the computer," she said. "I typed the word LOGON, followed by an account number that was assigned to me by the computer center, and finally added my own unique password which in this case is my initials, BV. When I hit the RETURN key, this message is sent to the machine for evaluation. If I use an illegal account number or password, the computer would not accept the connection." Bertha hit the RETURN key, and the terminal began to type on its own.

WELCOME TO THE BASIC SYSTEM.
NEW OR OLD?

"You see, my information was accepted and I have been connected with the system. Our system supports BASIC, a computer programming language that is used primarily in time sharing applications. The question 'NEW OR OLD?' refers to whether we wish to write a new program or retrieve an old one. I'll type OLD, and we will look at a program that I wrote yesterday and stored in the computer. I'll type my responses in lower case so you can distinguish them from what the computer types.

```
. . .
NEW OR OLD?          old
PROGRAM NAME?
. . .
```

"I called the program SIMPLE," Bertha said while typing the response.

```
. . .
PROGRAM NAME?     simple
READY
. . .
```

"The machine is now READY to respond to my commands," began Bertha. "I can LIST out a copy of the program, RUN it to get some results, or a variety of other things. Let's first get a copy of the program." She typed the word LIST and pressed the RETURN key.

```
. . .
list
SIMPLE
10    A = 2
20    B = 3
30    C = 4.5
40    X = A + B + C
50    Y = A − B − C
60    PRINT A,B,C,X,Y
70    END
```

"This, Howie," she continued, "is a copy of a program that I stored in memory.[1] There are many other programs stored there, some of which I wrote and many that were written by other people. We'll look at some of the general programs in the computer memory 'library' in just a minute.

"As you can probably tell, this program is quite simple and can practically be read like a sentence. We give three letters (A, B, C) values,

[1] Some BASIC systems may require the word LET in all ASSIGNMENT statements. For example, statement 10 would be 10 LET A = 2.

then add them up, subtract the last two from the first, and then print out the original numbers and the results of the two calculations. You'll get more complicated programs in class, I am sure. Here, why don't you keep this copy?" Bertha tore the page off and handed it to Howie.

"What else can you do?" asked Howie.

"Well, let's get a 'canned' program and run it," Bertha replied.

"Fine, where do they keep the cans?" Howie asked as he stood up and looked around.

"No, Howie, that's just a term used to describe programs that are 'canned' into the computer. They are put together in a nice neat package. These are the 'library' programs that I spoke of earlier that are stored inside the computer for anyone to use. First, let's get a listing of all the programs that are in the library. By typing the following, I can get a list of the names of the programs.

```
. . .
library
. . .
```

Bertha hit the RETURN key.

```
. . .
THE FOLLOWING PROGRAMS ARE IN THE USER LIBRARY.
ANGLES
BITEST
FILES
MATH01
MEAN
PLOT
SNOOPY
TICTAC
TTEST
XYGRAPH
PROGRAM NAME?
```

"Let's look at a MEAN program," suggested Bertha.

"Okay," said Howie, "which one do you think is the meanest?"

Bertha ignored him and typed one of the names from the list.

```
. . .
PROGRAM NAME?       mean
READY
. . .
```

"Now I'll type the word RUN, and the program, hopefully, will begin giving me instructions. I'll still type information in lower case so you can distinguish between what the computer has typed and what I have put in." She typed RUN and hit the RETURN key.

```
. . .
run
MEAN
DO YOU WANT INSTRUCTIONS?      "yes"¹
THE PROGRAM WILL CALCULATE THE AVERAGE OF UP TO
100 NUMBERS AND PRINT THIS RESULT.
HOW MANY NUMBERS DO YOU HAVE?      10
PLEASE TYPE THESE NUMBERS IN ONE AT A TIME
SEPARATED BY COMMAS.
? 5,32,15,15,30.5,10,15.3,5.10,6,9,9
YOU TYPED IN TOO MANY. EXTRA INPUT IGNORED.
THE MEAN IS EQUAL TO 14.290
DONE
```

"That's fantastic!" cried Howie. "But if there are programs already written and stored in the machine, why do I have to learn about programming?"

Bertha responded. "Well, first of all, it is the only real way to understand what a computer is all about. If you don't learn how to use it by writing programs, you will never really have a thorough understanding of how a computer works or of its capabilities and limitations. Besides, even though there are a lot of programs around, there may not be one written that will do what you want it to do. And also, often a 'canned' program must be changed a little bit to suit your particular needs. For example, if you wanted to get the average of 150 numbers, you would have to modify the MEAN program a little bit. To do that, you'd have to understand BASIC."

"Okay, you've convinced me," Howie said. "And gee, thanks a lot, you've really been a big help, Bertha."

"Before you go, Howie, let me show you how to sign off from the system," Bertha said. She then typed.

```
. . .
READY
logoff
YOU HAVE USED 15 MINUTES OF TERMINAL TIME. SIGNED
OFF at 2:15 PM.
. . .
```

She hung up the phone and turned off the terminal. "That's all there is to it," she said. "It was nice talking with you, Howie."

As they were walking out the door, Howie turned to Bertha and asked, "Is a time sharing system a very expensive setup?"

"Not as much as you would think, Howie," she replied. "Remember, if many different users can share the computer's time, they also can

¹Some BASIC systems may not require "   " marks around input that consists of letters. Some systems may use single quotes, like 'yes,' and others may allow either single or double quotes.

share its cost. The more people you have, the cheaper it will be for each user. It's quite popular in the academic and business world."

"I can see why," Howie mused. "Thanks again, Bertha."

"See you around," she answered.

TOPIC SUMMARY FOR SECTION 4.2

LOGON	PROGRAM NAME
RETURN key	NEW or OLD
LIST	Library programs
RUN	LOGOFF

Problems for Sec. 4.2

1. Have the computer terminal type a list of library programs on your system.
2. Access one of the library programs on your system and run it.
3. (*a*) Type and run Bertha's SIMPLE program.
   (*b*) After doing part (a), but before you have logged off the terminal, change line 30 of SIMPLE to 30 C = 7 by merely typing this line into the program. Now run SIMPLE with this change.
   (*c*) After doing parts (a) and (b), but before you have logged off the terminal, add this line to SIMPLE

$$55 \quad X = X/2$$

   Now run SIMPLE with this addition.
4. Explain the "order of execution" of a program.

4.3 AN OVERVIEW OF BASIC

Howie was sitting in his seat waiting for class to start when he noticed his friend Rudy Mentry was looking kind of glum.

"Hey, what's the matter, Rudy," he called.

"Aw, nothin' much," he replied. "I just got out of bed on the wrong side, and for me that's bad because it's against the wall. I'll be okay once class starts and I can get some sleep."

"Hey, you better not," commented Howie. "This stuff is really interesting. Bertha Vanation gave me a preview of it yesterday."

Prof. Phil Ovitt arrived, "Please come to order."

"I'll have two over light with toast and coffee!" ordered Hammond Deggs, one of the class clowns.

"Very funny, Mr. Deggs," replied Prof. Ovitt. "What's that yellow mess all over your shirt?" he asked.

"Well, I made a bet with my roommate that I could juggle four boiled eggs for 1 minute without dropping a one. When I wasn't looking, he substituted a raw egg for one of the others. When I was at the halfway point, I dropped one of the eggs and it hit me on the arm. Naturally, it was the raw egg. I guess the yolk's on me, eh, Professor!"

"Hey, listen," asked Phil, "if it's okay with everyone here . . . I mean, if you don't mind, maybe we could, well, start with class!

"Today we are going to familiarize ourselves with the procedure for writing a program in BASIC. You have all been exposed to the techniques of flowcharting. I would like a volunteer to go to the chalkboard and draw a flowchart describing the logic for getting the average of up to 100 numbers."

Clara Fy, always a volunteer, headed for the board. She drew the following flowchart.

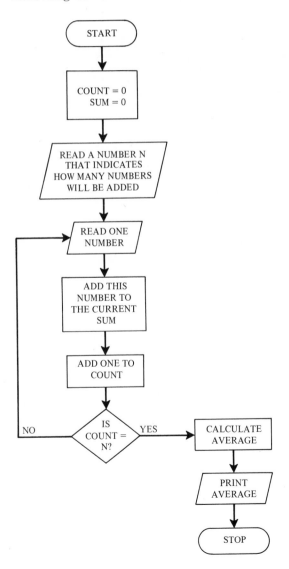

"That's a pretty fine job, Clara," Prof. Ovitt commented. "Now I will write a program in the BASIC language that will instruct the computer to solve the problem that has been described in Clara's flowchart. Please copy it down exactly as I write it on the board." Prof. Ovitt began to write.

```
10   REM THIS PROGRAM CALCULATES AN AVERAGE.
15   REM UP TO 100 NUMBERS MAY BE USED.
20   C = 0
25   S = 0
30   READ N1
40   R E A D  B
55   S = S + B
60   C = C + 1
70   IF C < N1 THEN 40
80   A = S/C
90   PRINT A
95   DATA 5
98   DATA 15,14,30.2,27E−1,−.53E2
100  END
```

"Now, normally," Phil continued, "you would type in this program, line by line, while sitting at a terminal. That way you would get line-by-line error messages, if appropriate, and also immediate results. However, just looking at this program can give us a pretty good overview of the BASIC language. I'd like you all to look at this program and note down your first impressions." Prof. Ovitt waited a few minutes and then called on Seymour Movies.

"What did you notice about this program?" he asked.

"There are two sentences at the beginning that tell what the program will do," answered Seymour. "But why do they start with the word 'REM'?"

"The REM stands for REMark," remarked Prof. Ovitt. "A RE-MARK statement is used by the programmer to give a message to a person who might read the program (including the programmer himself at some later time). REM statements do not cause the computer to perform any execution, so they may be placed anywhere in the program and are usually used to explain the program. What else do you notice about the program?"

Prof. Ovitt called on Clara.

"Well," Clara began, "for one thing, every line has a number. I assume that's required."

"Yes, it is," replied Prof. Ovitt. "Line numbers are required and can be any number between 1 and 99,999. Of course they must be integer numbers. It wouldn't do to number a line as 75.8."

"Are the numbers always used in ascending order as in this program?" asked Howie.

"Well, yes," Prof. Ovitt responded. "The line number has two important functions. First, they help specify the order in which the computer will execute the instructions. The computer executes them by referring to the line numbers in ascending order. Even if you typed in the program in reverse order, it would still execute properly since the machine would rearrange the instructions into ascending order by line number before executing the program."

"Why do you leave gaps between the statement numbers?" asked another student, Brandon Cattle, from Texas.

"Yes," Prof. Ovitt continued, "while it would seem simpler to number the statements consecutively (say from 1 to 16), it quite often happens that you want to add a statement to a program. If you have numbered the statements consecutively and you want to insert a statement after the first one, you would have to renumber (and retype) all of the higher numbered statements. If, on the other hand, you have left a gap (such as in our program), a statement can easily be inserted by merely giving it an unused line number between two of the statements used."

"You said that there were two important functions of line numbers, Professor, what's the other one?" asked Brandon.

"Well," Ovitt continued, "line numbers also serve as labels. Thus, if for some reason you wished to alter the order of execution of statements (line-by-line consecutive execution), you could refer to a specific line number to be executed next. In the program on the board, line 70 illustrates this usage. When this program is executed, the instructions are done line by line right up to the statement in line 70. Then, control is transferred to line 40 and execution again continues consecutively from that point."

Howie whispered to Scott Free, who was seated behind him, "Boy, Prof. Ovitt sure did a rush job writing those BASIC statements on the board. That last one was written almost on top of the one before it. I can't even see what that statement is!"

"That's an understatement," agreed Scott.

"Mr. Gettindere," Prof. Ovitt had seen Howie talking. "Suppose you tell us what you think is interesting about this program."

Howie hadn't written anything on his paper so he had to think fast. "Line 40 looks a little strange. There seem to be too many spaces inserted in the statement," he guessed.

"I wrote that statement with the extra spaces quite intentionally," Prof. Ovitt responded. "I wanted to illustrate the free-format feature of BASIC. We use spaces to indent and between words for our own convenience in reading. They have no meaning however, and may be inserted where desired in a statement."

"Can you explain the numbers in line 98?" asked Phyllis In.

Prof. Ovitt answered, "A DATA statement contains numbers to be READ during the execution of the program. We'll talk more about the use of READ and DATA statements soon. I will discuss the particular numbers in the DATA statement now. The 15 and 14 are integer numbers; the 30.2 is a decimal number. Numbers written with an 'E' in them are exponential numbers, written in a shorthand notation. The general form of an exponential number is aEb where 'a' is an integer number. Thus aEb is equivalent to $a * 10^b$. Thus

$$27E-1 \text{ is equal to } 27 * 10^{-1} = 2.7$$

and

$$-.53E2 \text{ is equal to } -0.53 * 10^2 = -53$$

"I know of a quick way to remember that," called Seymour. "I have my own little rule."

"How would you apply it?" asked Howard Hugh Applyit.

"Simple," Seymour responded. "Just look at the number after the E. This number tells you how many positions to move the decimal point. The sign of this number tells you which way. A minus sign means move the decimal point to the left; a plus sign means move the decimal point to the right. Thus 2.50+04 means move the decimal point four positions to the right, giving 25,000. And 2.5E−03 means move the decimal point three positions to the left, giving 0.0025 as the result."

"In a BASIC program you do not have to worry about which numbers in arithmetic expressions are integer numbers or decimal numbers or exponential numbers. The computer will handle all of the numbers, whatever they are—as long as they aren't too big or too little. In most systems numbers may not contain more than nine digits. Thus 0.0001234567 is too long (10 digits), although it could be used if written as 1.234567E−4. Numbers may not be written with commas; for example, one thousand should not be written as 1,000 but should be written 1000. The largest number in magnitude is about $\pm 10^{+38}$ and the smallest number in magnitude is about $\pm 10^{-39}$. Calculations are performed to about nine significant digits, so occasionally some round-off error might occur.

"I'm sure there are more questions about this program I have written," Phil continued, as he turned to erase the board. "But we will cover each of the statements in detail in subsequent classes and since it's getting close to the end of the hour, let's call it a day."

When Prof. Ovitt turned from the board the room was completely empty except for two pieces of notepaper that were fluttering toward the floor.

TOPIC SUMMARY FOR SECTION 4.3

REMARK statement	READ statements
Line numbers	DATA statements
Execution order	Size of numbers
Extra spaces in statements	Round off error

Problems for Sec. 4.3

1. Write a program that will READ three numbers from a DATA statement and PRINT their sum.
2. Write a program that will READ three numbers from a DATA statement and PRINT the largest number.
3. Write a program that will READ a number N from a DATA statement, then READ N observations of data from DATA statements and PRINT the largest number.
4. Run a program that is to read values into A, B, and C, although the DATA statement has only two numbers in it.
5. Run a program that READs values into A and B when the DATA statement has three numbers in it. Have A and B printed by the computer.

4.4 ASSIGNMENT STATEMENTS

Rudy, Seymour, and Howie were walking back to the dorm when Seymour stopped and pointed toward an elderly man with a walking stick who was slowly beginning to cross the street. "Hey, Howie," Seymour said, "look at that guy. Don't we know him from somewhere? Who is he?"

Howie thought for a minute and then replied, "I think you're right, Seymour. I can't remember his cane, but his pace is familiar."

"Say, what was our reading assignment?" Seymour interrupted.

"Assignment statements," replied Howie.

"I don't understand them," said Howie, who hadn't read about them yet, anyway.

"I've read the assignment," said Rudy. "Would you like a summary?"

"Will you be finished by the time we get to that theater?" asked Seymour, spotting a movie theater a block away.

"Sure," came the reply. "An ASSIGNMENT statement in BASIC assigns a value to a memory location in the computer. The person writing the program gives a name to a memory location by putting the name on the left side of an equal sign and then placing the value that is to be assigned to that memory location on the right side of the equal sign. In the program we had in class today there were several assignment statements." Rudy stopped and wrote on a fence post.

$$C = 0$$

$$S = 0$$

$$S = S + B$$

$$C = C + 1$$

$$A = S/C$$

"All of these were assignment statements. The first one assigns the value zero to the memory location named C. The next one assigns the value zero to the memory location called S. The statement $S = S + B$ assigns the result of the addition of the contents of location S and location B into location S."

Howie interjected. "And $C = C + 1$ means add 1 to C and place the result in location C. But what about that last one? Is that a division symbol?"

Rudy continued. "Well, in BASIC we have symbols for all operations in arithmetic. They are

$$+ \quad \text{for addition}$$
$$- \quad \text{for subtraction}$$
$$* \quad \text{for multiplication}$$
$$/ \quad \text{for division}$$
$$\uparrow \text{ (or } ** \text{)} \quad \text{for exponentiation}$$

Thus, in the last example, Howie, $A = S/C$ means divide S by C and place the results in memory location A."

"I get it," said Seymour. "And A was the average, right. But why didn't the programmer use the name 'AVERAGE' for the memory location instead of A?"

"In BASIC," Rudy replied, "there are strict rules on making up such names. First, there are two kinds of variables that are used in this language. The contents of a memory location may be numbers (numeric) or letters and numbers (alphanumeric). The names of the memory locations are designed to help us identify the kind of variable. All alphanumeric variable names are made up of two characters, a letter followed by a dollar sign. Thus, A\$, M\$, and X\$ are names of memory locations that would hold alphanumeric data.

"All other names in BASIC are either a single letter or a letter followed by a single digit. In this case, A, A1, X0, T, and L9 are all legitimate names."

Howie stopped and began to think up assignment statements. He took out a piece of chalk and began to write on the sidewalk. "These are all examples of assignment statements," he shouted.

$$A1 = 10$$
$$B\$ = \text{"YES"}$$
$$P = A1$$
$$E0 = M + 3 - G8$$
$$X = A/B + C$$

"That's right, Howie," Rudy agreed. "And you have brought up an interesting point. Let's look at your last assignment statement

$$X = A/B + C$$

Furthermore, let us assume that the contents of the named locations are as follows:

$$A = 15$$

$$B = 3$$

$$C = 2$$

"Then, as I see it, there are two possibilities for evaluating this statement.

First way	Second way
$X = \dfrac{A}{B} + C$	$X = \dfrac{A}{B + C}$
$X = \dfrac{15}{3} + 2$	$X = \dfrac{15}{3 + 2}$
$X = 7$	$X = 3$

"Thus, you see it can be confusing. Which did you mean, Howie?"

"I meant to do it the second way," Howie replied.

"Well, in that case, you should have written

$$X = A/(B + C)$$

Anytime there would be ambiguity just add parentheses. They can be quite freely used."

"What would the machine have done if I didn't have the parentheses there?" asked Howie.

"It would have solved the expression the first way," Rudy replied. "You see, the machine has a specified order in which it evaluates arithmetic expressions.

"First, the contents of parentheses are evaluated. Then, any exponentiation, followed by multiplication or division, and finally addition or subtraction. When there is a choice, the operations are performed left to right."

Seymour grabbed the chalk and drew an extended expression on the sidewalk.

$$X = (A + B/3) * (A/(3 + C)) + 3$$

"Assuming the same values for A, B, and C that you used, what would be assigned to X?" asked Seymour.

"Well," said Rudy, "remembering $A = 15$, $B = 3$, and $C = 2$, parentheses are done first and you also move left to right. So, the expression might be evaluated as follows:

Look at	$(A + B/3)$	
Division first	$B/3$	is 1

Addition next	$(A + 1)$	is 16
Look at	$(A/(3 + C))$	
Parentheses first	$(3 + C)$	is 5
Division next	$(A/5)$	is 3
Multiplication	$(16) * (3)$	is 48
Addition	$48 + 3$	is 51

"The number 51 would be placed in memory location X." When Rudy looked around nobody was there except a 6-foot 5-inch policeman who was looking somewhat chagrined at the mess on the sidewalk.

"Did you drop your chalk, sir?" quipped Rudy as he started to inch away. He thought to himself, "Nice guys, Howie and Seymour. They didn't even warn me he was watching. Guess I'll just chalk it up to experience."

TOPIC SUMMARY FOR SECTION 4.4

ASSIGNMENT statements
Naming variables
Alphanumeric variables
Order of operations
Use of parentheses

Problems for Sec. 4.4

1. Write a program that assigns the following values: $A = 2, B = 3, C = 7.1,$ $X = 5.E-1$ and calculate the value of $A^B + 2C - 5(X)$.
2. Which of the following are legal variable names?

   CAT   1C   Y27   Z1$ $A

   C1   E5   Z$ $3

   Use the computer to verify your conclusions.
3. Run this program:

$$\begin{array}{ll} 10 & L = M \\ 15 & PRINT\ L \\ 20 & END \end{array}$$

4. Write a program that will check to see if the contents of alphanumeric variables must be, may be, or must not be in single quotes (' '), or double quotes (" ") in assignment statements. Answer the following true-false questions.

   Use of quotes for alphanumeric variables

   (*a*) Single quotes may be used in assignment statements.
   (*b*) Double quotes may be used in assignment statements.
   (*c*) Quotes must be used in assignment statements.
   (*d*) Single quotes may be used in data statements.

(e) Double quotes may be used in data statements.

(f) Quotes must be used in data statements.

5. Evaluate the following expressions on the computer to confirm the hierarchy of operation:

(a) $1 / 2 / 2$ (c) $2 \uparrow 3 \uparrow 2$

(b) $3 - 2 / 4$ (d) $\dfrac{[14.6 - (9.4/18.1)]^2}{[3.4 - (2.2/14.6)]^2}$

4.5 INPUT AND OUTPUT

Prof. Ovitt called to his colleague Prof. O'Silver who had just arrived at the office.

"Hi, O'Silver," he called. "Do you have a minute?"

Prof. O'Silver took off his jacket and went into Prof. Ovitt's office. "Let me tell you, Phil," O'Silver began, "what took me so long getting in this morning. On my way in today some nut passed me on the expressway doing about 95 miles an hour. He was all over the road, swerving back and forth, like he had never driven before. Well, the cops finally caught up with him and pulled him over. I stopped also to give the guy a piece of my mind. And would you believe it—the guy had never been in a car before. He was about 85 years old and had lived like a hermit."

"What did the police do?" asked Ovitt.

"They charged him with recluse driving!"

O'Silver was holding onto his side and tears were in his eyes from laughing. "What did you want anyway, Phil?" he finally asked.

"I was wondering if you had any good examples of *input-output statements* in BASIC? I'm preparing my next lecture," he replied. But Prof. O'Silver had already left. Phil reviewed his lecture notes.

"Assignment statements can be used to put data (numeric or alphanumeric) into storage locations. Thus, A = 5 and B1 = 32.5 resulted in a 5 being placed in location A and 32.5 being placed in location B1. This could also have been done by using a READ statement and a DATA statement. For example the statement

10   READ A

is interpreted as 'READ a number from a DATA statement and place it into location A. Of course, there would have to be a DATA statement somewhere in the program. In this case, the statement

50   DATA 5

would result in the number 5 being placed into location A.

"The DATA statement (or statements) is used in place of the data cards you so often see associated with computer systems. In these statements, you make available the data that are going to be used in the program.

Each time a READ statement is executed a number is taken from the data list. If there are three names in the READ statement, then three numbers are taken from the list.

Continuing with our example, we could have written

> 10   READ A,B1
>
> . . .
>
> 50   DATA 5,32.5

The same assignments are achieved in each of the following methods:

10	READ A	10	READ A,B1
15	READ B1		. . .
	. . .	50	DATA 5
50	DATA 5,32.5	55	DATA 32.5

10	READ A	10	READ A,B1
15	READ B1		. . .
	. . .	50	DATA 5,32.5
50	DATA 5		
55	DATA 32.5		

If you wanted to place some alphanumeric information into a storage location, say A$, then the statements might look like these:

> 10   READ A$,B1
>
> . . .
>
> 50   DATA "YES", 32.5

Prof. Ovitt then looked over a copy of an index card he would pass out to the class.

DATA STATEMENTS

1. The word DATA is required.
2. May be placed anywhere in the program.
3. May contain one or several pieces of data.
4. Different data items in the statement must be separated by a blank or a comma.
5. The DATA statement with the lowest number is referenced first.
6. Alphanumeric information must be placed in quotes.

While waiting for class to start, the student behind Howie was relating a conversation he had overheard between a sergeant on the campus police force and a new patrolman.

"Say, Willie, you know that computer science professor, Phil Ovitt?" Sgt. Hans B. Hindubeck had asked.

"Prof. Ovitt? Yes, I think so," the recruit, Private Arrestum, replied.

"Funny thing happened today," the sergeant continued. "He called the station earlier and was quite upset. He said that when he got into his car this morning, the radio, steering wheel, and dashboard were all missing. He ran back into the house and immediately phoned us. Wow! Was he upset!"

"What happened?"

"Well, after he scolded us, I assured him that an all points bulletin would be put out for the thief. He hung up. A few minutes later, the phone rang again. It was Prof. Ovitt quietly requesting that we call off our search. It seems that when he got into his car this morning, he got into the back seat by mistake!"

At that point, Prof. Ovitt arrived and presented his lecture on READ and DATA statements.

When he was finished, Howie raised his hand. "It would be nice if we could reread the data that is in those DATA statements. For example, suppose I read in 1000 numbers somewhere. Normally that would not cause a problem, but suppose I was worried about using too much memory space? Are there any ways to read the data over again?"

"Yes, Howie," responded Prof. Ovitt. "You can use a RESTORE statement. In BASIC, when a RESTORE statement is encountered, the 'pointer' that is keeping track of which data items have been read is set back to the beginning. Thus, if you consider all of the data items in your DATA statements to be one big stack of numbers, the RESTORE statement goes back to the top of the stack. If another READ command is then executed, the first number in the stack will be read again. The example you mentioned could be programmed like this, Howie." Phil wrote down the following program.

```
10    REM MEAN AND STANDARD DEVIATION
20    S = 0
30    FOR I = 1 TO 1000
40    READ N
50    S = S + N
60    NEXT I
70    A = S/1000
80    RESTORE
90    T = 0
100   FOR I = 1 TO 1000
110   READ N
120   T = T + (N - A)↑2
130   NEXT I
```

```
140    D = SQR (T/999)
150    PRINT "AVERAGE = ", A, "STD. DEV. =", D
900    DATA . . .   (1000 numbers here)
999    END¹
```

"You see," Prof. Ovitt concluded, "the RESTORE statement in line 80 allows you to reread the data right from the first data item.

"Notice that the READ and DATA statements make data available in the program for use during execution of the program. The data is written into the program when the program itself is written. There is another type of input statement that allows the data to be placed in the computer during the execution of the program. This is the INPUT statement. For example, consider the following complete program:

```
10    INPUT A
12    B = A * 500
14    PRINT A,B
21    END
```

"When this program is run on the computer, the terminal will type a response like this:

?

"Yeah, I don't understand it either," interjected Howie.

"No, Howie," answered Prof. Ovitt, "it's not that the computer doesn't understand the program. The '?' is typed because the computer is waiting for the person at the terminal to give a value for A. For example, if the person at the terminal typed '11' after the computer's '?' and pressed the RETURN key, the computer would be able to calculate B and would print

11   5500

---

¹The standard deviation for a set of numbers $N(1), N(2), \ldots N(1000)$ is given by the formula

$$\left(\frac{1}{999} \sum_{i=1}^{1000} (N(i) - AV)^2\right)^{1/2}$$

where

$$AV = \frac{1}{1000} \sum_{i=1}^{1000} N(i)$$

"When would a person want to use a READ statement, and when would an INPUT statement be preferred?" Prof. Ovitt asked Seymour.

"I don't get it," responded Seymour.

"You don't get it?" replied Phil Ovitt.

"Let's see," started Hugh Dongettit, thinking he had been called. "If you know the data when you're writing the program initially, and the data aren't likely to change, then I suppose READ and DATA statements would be good. If you want to write a general program for repeated use with different data, it seems that an INPUT statement might be best."

"Very good, Hugh. One additional point, if you wanted to use a program many times with some of the data changing and some of the data remaining constant, you could put the data that remain constant in a DATA statement. The data that change each time you run the program could be input with an INPUT statement. However, there will be many instances when either type of input method will be acceptable."

"How do you know which number you're inputting when you type a number next to a question mark?" asked Phyllis.

"The program could be written to print instructions just before the question mark," said Phil. "Our previous program could have been written like this:

```
 5   PRINT 'PLEASE INPUT A'
10   INPUT A
12   B = A * 500
14   PRINT A,B
21   END
```

Then when the program is run the terminal will type this." Prof. Ovitt wrote on the board

PLEASE INPUT A

?

"What if you wanted to input, say, three values A, B, and C into a program? Would you use three input statements?" someone asked.

"You could," responded Phil, "or you could use the single INPUT statement INPUT A,B,C. When the computer typed '?' the person at the terminal would respond by typing three values, like this

? 50, 11, 23.7

"Any other questions?"

"The BASIC programs we've seen could be rewritten using IN-

PUT statements instead of the READ statements. Is that right?" asked Clara Fy.

"Yes," answered Phil.

"Could you tell us a little more about PRINT instructions?" questioned Scott.

"That is just the topic I wanted to cover next," began Phil. "When we want to print out any information, the command PRINT is used. Following the word PRINT, you would list the names of those memory locations whose contents you wished printed. Thus, if memory location A contained the number 60, location B$ the characters 'ANSWER,' and location C the number 3, then we might write

30   PRINT B$,A, C

This would result in the following output being typed at the terminal:

ANSWER   60   3

"What if you had written three PRINT statements?" asked Howie. "What would happen then?"

"Well," Prof. Ovitt replied, "if we had

10   PRINT B$
15   PRINT A
20   PRINT C

then the output would have been printed as follows:

ANSWER
60
3

"Each time a PRINT statement is encountered, a new line is printed, that is, unless a previous PRINT statement ended with a comma or a semicolon. I'll talk about those cases in a minute. Printing will continue on one line until the list of items in the PRINT statement is exhausted, or until there is no more room on the line (in which case printing will continue on the next line)."

"What if there is nothing listed in the PRINT statement?" asked Clara.

"Then nothing gets printed," Phil replied. "In effect, this results in skipping a line. For example, if we had the statements

40   PRINT
45   PRINT
50   PRINT A,B$,C
60   PRINT

two lines would be skipped, the contents of locations A, B, and C would be printed on one line, and then another line would be skipped."

Prof. Ovitt was getting warmed up. "There are a lot of very useful things that can be done with PRINT statements. If you write

10   PRINT 'THE ANSWER IS' A 'TO #1'

then the output at the terminal would be

THE ANSWER IS 60 TO #1

Anything that appears in quotes in a PRINT statement will be printed when the statement is executed. This can be a very useful method of printing labels or messages.

"PRINT statements are even more flexible. We are permitted to do arithmetic operations right in the statement. This can often save several statements in a program. Using the same data as before, the statement

50   PRINT 'THE AVERAGE IS', A/C

would display as output

THE AVERAGE IS 20

"Say, Professor," asked Seymour, "how do you know where on the page the answers will be printed?"

"There are five print zones," Prof. Ovitt responded. "Each zone is 15 columns wide.[1] The computer prints a line left to right, printing a single number in each print zone. If it runs out of print zones a new line is begun. The commas essentially indicate that it is time to go to a new print zone. If we replace the comma with a semicolon, each print zone is subdivided into five subzones of three columns each. In this way, we can print more information on one line than we can with the comma as punctuation."

"What about when a PRINT statement ends with a comma or semicolon? You were going to tell us about that," reminded Phyllis In.

"In that case, the execution of a PRINT statement won't start on a new line. The terminal will pick up as if it were still executing the last PRINT statement," answered Phil.

TOPIC SUMMARY FOR SECTION 4.5

READ statements	RESTORE statement
DATA statements	INPUT statement
Use of ' ' for alphanumeric data	PRINT zones, use of commas, semicolons

---

Problems for Sec. 4.5

1. What does the following program print?

---

[1]Some BASIC systems may divide the zones in slightly different ways.

```
10   READ A, B
20   PRINT "A" A, "B" B
30   A = 1
40   RESTORE
50   READ B, A
60   PRINT "NEXT TIME, A" A, "B" B
70   DATA 3, 4, 5, 6
80   END
```

2. What happens if you try to read "YES" into the variable A?
3. Write a program that INPUTs three numbers and prints the average.
4. Write a program that uses one INPUT statement to input numbers into A, B, and C and prints the numbers.
   (a) Try to input just two numbers and run the program.
   (b) Try to input four numbers and run the program.
5. Write a program that will compute the first four powers of 2 through 7 and print the following table (completed correctly). (Your computer may print the numbers in E notation or as decimal numbers.)

	POWER			
NUMBER	1	2	3	4
2	2	4	8	16
3	3	9	27	. . .
4	4	16	. . .	
. . .	. . .	. . .		
7				

6. Write a program to see if your computer allows single quotes or double quotes for the input of alphanumeric data.
7. Write a program that inputs alphanumeric data and then prints the data. What is the largest number of letters that can be input to one variable and then be printed out?
8. Write a program that inputs a length A yards, B feet, and C inches and converts this to millimeters. (See Problem 5, Section 2.2.)
9. Write a program that will convert a temperature in centigrade to the equivalent Fahrenheit degrees.

4.6 TRANSFER OF CONTROL STATEMENTS

When Howie arrived at Clara's house for the review session, the session was about half over.

"Sorry I'm late," Howie said as he entered the living room. One of the guys in the dorm needed help getting a part-time job so he could earn some spending money."

"Did you help him?" asked Rudy.

"Yeah. He had studied Flamenco dancing, so I got him a job as an exterminator."

Howie looked around the room and saw that most of the computer class was present. He noticed two guys over on the couch and walked up to introduce himself. "Hi, I'm Howie Gettindere," he said.

Both of them stood up to introduce themselves. "Ben Dover," "Neil Down," each said in turn.

"Well, make up your mind," cried Howie as he lost his balance and fell to the floor on top of another student.

Lynn Olium wasn't going to take that lying down. "Hey, watch it, will you, Howie," she pleaded. "Boy! I'll bet it was your baby picture that started planned parenthood."

"Go to the lake and jump in!" he replied.

"That is an *unconditional transfer statement*," called Seymour.

"What are you talking about?" asked Howie.

"Well," Seymour began, "you told Lynn to GO TO the lake. You didn't give her any choice, just go directly to the lake. In BASIC we have a similar statement."

"You mean there is a BASIC statement that says GO TO the lake?" asked a disbelieving Howie.

"No, in BASIC you would say GO TO 10, or GO TO 900, or some other line number," replied Seymour.

"That's right," Clara began, "let's summarize what we've covered, for Howie's benefit. As you know, the computer executes a program by arranging the statements in ascending order by line number and then executing one after the other in sequence. There are times, however, when we might want to alter this sequence. For example, suppose we have written a program to print the change a person gets when he buys something. We'll put the amount he gives the sales clerk and the cost of the item in a data statement. The program might look as follows:

```
10    REM CHANGE PROGRAM
15    REM P = PAYMENT AMOUNT, B = BILL, C = CHANGE
20    READ P,B
30    C = P - B
40    PRINT "BILL WAS $" B
45    PRINT "PAYMENT WAS $" P
50    PRINT "CHANGE IS $" C
60    DATA 5.00, 3.50
80    END
```

"This program would READ a 5.00 from the DATA statement into location P (the customer's payment) and READ the number 3.50 into location B (the customer's bill). The change due to the customer is calculated and stored in location C. Then, the following results are printed:

BILL WAS $3.50

PAYMENT WAS $5.00

CHANGE IS $1.50

"As you can see, this is only done for one customer. The unconditional transfer statement we have been discussing could be used to repeat this process over and over. This would change the program to the following.

```
10   REM CHANGE PROGRAM
15   REM P = PAYMENT AMOUNT, B = BILL, C = CHANGE
20   READ P, B
30   C = P - B
40   PRINT "BILL WAS $" B
45   PRINT "PAYMENT WAS $" P
50   PRINT "CHANGE WAS $" C
55   GO TO 20
60   DATA 5.00, 3.50, 1, .65
80   END
```

The GO TO statement in line 55 changes the sequential execution in the program. It indicates that the next instruction can be found at line 20. These GO TO statements can be placed anywhere in the program, at the discretion of the programmer. If, for example, we wanted to print only the change that resulted from the transaction, we could add the statement

35   GO TO 50

and thus skip the printing of the payment and price."

Howie understood the function of the GO TO statement, but was somewhat confused by another aspect of the program. "With that GO TO 20 statement in line 50," he said, "you never get to the end of the program. It'll run forever!"

"No, Howie," Rudy responded. "As soon as the READ statement is executed and there are no data available, execution will stop and an error message will be printed. With this program, we would get the following output:

BILL WAS $3.50

PAYMENT WAS $5.00

CHANGE IS $1.50

BILL WAS $.65

PAYMENT WAS $1.00

CHANGE IS $.35

OUT OF DATA IN LINE 20

"Of course, we can avoid this problem by building a counter into the program that will keep track of how many transactions there are."

Howie remembered about counters from his discussion of loops and counters while Prof. Ovitt was building chimneys. "Could the program be written with INPUT statements instead of READ statements?" asked Phyllis.

Clara stated: "Yes, here, I'll write it down." Clara wrote on a piece of poster paper:

```
10   REM CHANGE PROGRAM WITH INPUT STATEMENT
15   REM P = PAYMENT AMOUNT, B = BILL, C = CHANGE
20   INPUT P,B
30   C = P - B
40   PRINT "BILL WAS $" B
45   PRINT "PAYMENT WAS $" P
50   PRINT "CHANGE IS $" C
55   GO TO 20
80   END
```

"Now the terminal will wait for input each time line 20 is executed."

"How will this program ever stop?" asked Howie.

"One way," answered Rudy, "would be to press the ATTN[1] key on the terminal. That will cause the computer to stop executing a program and wait for further instructions. A better way might be to have certain numbers, when input, be a key to the computer that you want to stop. For example, you could have a statement, after the INPUT statement, that checks for the input of '−9,−9.' If that is the input, the computer should stop. The program would then look like this." Rudy added a statement to Clara's program.

[1]Different terminals may use a different key to perform this function.

```
10   REM CHANGE PROGRAM
15   REM P = PAYMENT AMOUNT, B = BILL, C = CHANGE
20   INPUT P,B
25   IF P = −9 THEN 80
30   C = P − B
40   PRINT "BILL WAS $" B
45   PRINT "PAYMENT WAS $" P
50   PRINT "CHANGE IS $" C
55   GO TO 20
80   END
```

"Statement 25 is called an IF statement and is used as a *conditional transfer* of control."

"What does line 25 do?" asked Howie.

Clara answered, "Each time line 25 is executed, the computer compares the current value of P with −9. If P is equal to −9, control is transferred to statement 80. If P is not equal to −9, control is transferred to the next executable statement after 25, statement 30 in this case. Notice that each time that the value input into P is not a −9, statement 25 will not cause control to transfer to statement 80.

"Hey, that's pretty neat," said Howie. "What kinds of comparisons

The general form of an IF-THEN statement in BASIC is:

L   IF (expression A) (relation) (expression B) THEN N

M   STATEMENT Y

where L, M, and N are actually statement numbers appearing in the program and statement Y is any BASIC statement. The execution of the IF-THEN statement is as follows:

Expression A and expression B are evaluated, then compared by the specified relation. If the comparison is TRUE, execution continues with the statement line N. If the comparison is FALSE, execution continues with statement #M. Some BASIC systems require that statement N be an executable statement (not a REM, DATA, DEF, or DIM statement). The relational operators in BASIC are these:

>	is greater than
<	is less than
>=	is greater than or equal to
<=	is less than or equal to
<>	is not equal to
=	is equal to

can I use in an IF statement? Could I say this to the computer?" Howie wrote down this line:

IF I MADE MISTAKES IN THIS PROGRAM THEN CORRECT THEM

"No, that would just be another mistake, Howie," replied Clara. "There are only particular relations that can be used in an IF statement. Here, I have a page I prepared on IF statements in BASIC."

"Can you have anything else after the word THEN, besides a line number?" asked Ophelia Pulse, the nursing student in the course.

"Some systems allow you to replace the word THEN with the words GO TO, but in both cases only line numbers may appear next," Clara replied.

Ophelia continued, "How about more elaborate tests? Suppose you wanted to test two things at once?"

"You cannot have more than one test in an IF statement," Clara answered. "But you can use several IF statements to achieve the desired results. For example, consider a program that reads a list of numbers and prints out the numbers that are between (and including) 10 and 20. If a 0 is read, the program stops."

Clara wrote out this program:

```
10    READ X
15    IF X = 0 THEN 70
20    IF X < 10 THEN 10
30    IF X > 20 THEN 10
40    PRINT X
50    GO TO 10
70    STOP
100   DATA 8,17,12,31,4,0
110   END
```

"Boy, look at all those IF statements," called Howie. "That computer sure can't make up its mind!"

"On the contrary," Clara commented, "it is very definitely 'making up its mind.' If X is equal to zero, then go to statement 70, which stops the program. If it is not equal to zero, keep on processing and check to see if X is less than 10. If it is less than 10, then go to statement 10 and READ a new value for X. If that first value for X was not less than 10, the program checks (in the next line) to see if X is greater than 20. If it is greater than 20, then go to statement 10 and READ a new X. Otherwise, this X must be within the desired range 10 to 20, so print out this value. After doing this, continue on with the program (get the next value for X). It has no trouble making up its mind at all," she concluded.

"Well, maybe you're right, and maybe you're not," said Howie, definitively.

"We've seen two ways of changing the sequence of execution: the GO TO statement and the IF statement," Ben commented. "Are there any others?" he asked.

"There is one more, Ben," Clara replied, "that is very much like the GO TO statement. It is called the ON GO TO statement (in some versions of BASIC it is referred to as the GO TO OF statement). This state-

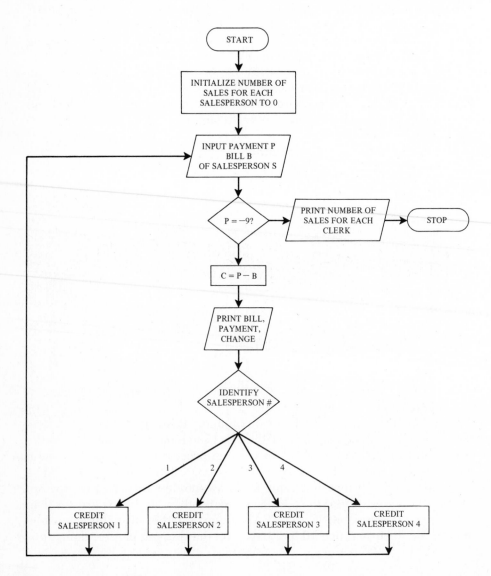

ment allows you to have a wider choice of places to transfer control to in your program.

"Let's modify one of our programs, the CHANGE PROGRAM with the INPUT statement, a little bit to illustrate how this new statement might be used. First, let us assume that there are four salespersons collecting these payments and that, at the end of the day, we would like to know which salesperson made the most sales. When we INPUT a payment and a bill, we will also INPUT the unique identification number of the salesperson (1, 2, 3, or 4) making the sales.

"In addition to calculating the change, then, we will need to keep four running totals of how many sales were made (one for each person). One way to approach this problem is to have four separate parts in our program. Each part will keep track of the number of sales made for a particular person. We will GO TO a particular one of these sections depending on the salesperson's number that was INPUT. Let's look at a flowchart for the program." (See page 214.)

"Now let's program the problem," said Rudy. Clara wrote down the following program.

```
10    REM FANCY CHANGE PROGRAM WITH INPUT STATEMENT
15    REM P = PAYMENT, B = CHARGE, C = CHANGE, S = SALESPERSON
16    S1 = 0
17    S2 = 0
18    S3 = 0
19    S4 = 0
20    INPUT P, B, S
25    IF P = -9 THEN 200
30    C = P - B
40    PRINT "BILL WAS $" B
45    PRINT "PAYMENT WAS $" P
46    PRINT "CHANGE IS $" C
50    REM NOW GIVE CREDIT TO SALESPERSON
60    ON S GO TO 90, 100, 110, 120
70    PRINT "NO SUCH SALESPERSON", S
80    GO TO 20
90    S1 = S1 + 1
95    GO TO 20
100   S2 = S2 + 1
105   GO TO 20
110   S3 = S3 + 1
115   GO TO 20
120   S4 = S4 + 1
125   GO TO 20
```

```
200   PRINT "THE NUMBER OF SALES FOR EACH PERSON"
210   PRINT 1, S1
220   PRINT 2, S2
230   PRINT 3, S3
240   PRINT 4, S4
250   END
```

"Wow, that's quite a program!" remarked Ben Dover. "I think line 60 warrants some explaining."

Neil's brother, Sid, stood up. "I agree," he said, "it looks awful complicated."

"I think I understand it," volunteered Seymour.

Complete and utter silence fell upon the room. The probability that Seymour could explain such a complicated program was about equal to the probability that a drowning banker would want to float alone.

Seymour began. "Statement 60[1] is the statement that transfers control to the proper section of the program for giving credit for the sale. Control will pass to line 90, 100, 110, or 120, depending on what is stored in S. This variable, S, you remember was INPUT from the terminal. Control is transferred using the following rule. If the variable (here it is the S) is a 1, GO TO the statement number that is first in the list. If the variable is a 2, GO TO the statement number that is second in the list. If the variable is a 3, GO TO the statement number that is third in the list, and so on for as many numbers in the list as you determine necessary.

"Thus, if the first value INPUT for S is a 1, control will transfer to statement number 90 which is a counter for salesperson 1's sales. After executing statement 90, the statement GO TO 20 returns to get another transaction. This second transaction may result in, say, a 3 (for salesperson 3) being INPUT into location S. At the ON _ GO TO statement, control is sent to statement 110, where sales clerk 3's number of sales is incremented by 1."

"What if someone put a phony ID number in with the data? Who would get credit for the sale?" Howie asked, trying to stump Seymour.

"Take a look again at the ON _ GO TO statement," Seymour replied. "In our example, the contents of location S are evaluated and control is transferred to statement 90, 100, 110, or 120, depending on whether the contents of S is 1, 2, 3, or 4. If the contents of S is anything else, control doesn't get transferred at all but proceeds to the next statement.

"Notice that Clara has taken this possibility into consideration in this program. If an ID is INPUT into location S that is a number other than

[1]On some systems that statement would be written 60 GO TO S OF 90, 100, 110, 120.

1, 2, 3, or 4, then the message 'NO SUCH SALESPERSON' will be printed out. After this, the next transaction will be evaluated."

"Say, Seymour, I think there is a mistake in the program. Look at line 210. It says there to PRINT 1, S1. Now I remember that S1 is the name of a memory location and saying PRINT S1 prints out the contents of that memory location. But what about the 1? You can't say PRINT 1 because 1 is not a legitimate name for a memory location."

Clara spoke up before Seymour had a chance. "Whenever a number appears in a PRINT statement that number is printed. It is used here to identify the sales clerk whose number of sales is printed. Our output from this portion of the program might be something like:

THE NUMBER OF SALES FOR EACH PERSON

1	2
2	2
3	2
4	0

"That's right," commented Seymour, confidently.

Needless to say, the room was abuzz with this historic event. Seymour had understood the program, as he claimed. As the students began to leave, many stopped to congratulate Seymour on his accomplishment.

When all of the other students had left, Seymour approached Clara. "It worked pretty well, eh Clara? No one ever saw the walkie talkie in my shirt, or the one you had in your pocketbook next to you."

"See you later, Seymour," she replied.

"Good night, Clara."

TOPIC SUMMARY FOR SECTION 4.6

Transfer of control
GO TO statement
IF-THEN statement
ON GO TO statement

Problems for Sec. 4.6

1. Write a program that will balance your checkbook. Each time the program is run, it should ask for your starting balance. Then it should repeatedly ask for your charges or deposits and print the balance after each charge or deposit. An input of 0 will tell the computer you are through.

2. Write a program that inputs a color into a variable C$. The program should print "YES" if the color input is "RED" and "NO" if the color input is not "RED."

3. Write a program for the Wise Mathematician problem of Section 2.2.

4. Write a program that calculates how much to pay the babysitter. The program inputs the starting time written as (A, B), where A is in hours and B is in minutes, and the finishing time (C, D), where C is hours and D is minutes. Assume the starting time will be between 6 o'clock and 10 o'clock and the ending time will be between 11 o'clock and 3 o'clock when you build your model. The pay rate is $1.00 per hour. The computer should print out the pay the babysitter deserves.

5. Assume the pay scale in Problem 4 is changed to $1.10 per hour from 6 P.M. to 8 P.M.; $.90 per hour from 8 P.M. to midnight and $1.25 per hour after midnight. Modify your program to incorporate these changes.

6. Write a program that will READ 20 numbers; find the largest number and where in the list of 20 numbers the largest value appears.

7. Write a program that will READ 20 numbers and list them in decreasing order with the position on the list printed beside the number. For example, the output might look like this:

Value	Where value appeared
112	17
103	1
92	6
81	12
Etc.	Etc.

8. (a) A department store has the following pricing policy on electric carving knives:

Number purchased	Price per knife
1	$11.95
2	10.25
3	9.75
4	9.50
5 or more	9.95

Write a program that will input the number of knives being purchased and output the amount of the bill. Use the form of the ON GO TO statement available at your facility.

(b) I have invited company for dinner and will need eight electric carving knives (one for each place setting). How should I make my purchase and what will it cost?

9. Run this program. What do the results mean? How can this be helpful?

```
10   A$ = "A"
12   B$ = "B"
14   IF A$ > B$ THEN 30
```

```
16   PRINT 'B > A'
20   STOP
30   PRINT 'A > B'
40   END
```

4.7 SUBSCRIPTED VARIABLES

Prof. O'Silver was calling the class to attention. "Prof. Ovitt cannot be here today. He asked me to present today's lesson. It seems that one of Prof. Ovitt's uncles died and left him 493 clocks. Phil is now busy winding up the estate.

"Today we are going to talk about *subscripts*. Does anyone know what a subscript is?"

"Yes," answered Brandon Cattle, "a subscript is what an understudy in a play is given to rehearse his lines."

Ed Jacation volunteered, "We used subscripts in freshman math. They were used to identify different values, for example, X_1, X_2, X_3, and X_4."

"That is much closer to the answer that I was looking for," commented O'Silver. "Let me explain subscripts by going through an example with you. Prof. Ovitt told me that you have solved the 'CHANGE' program so I will build upon it. Let us suppose that we want to determine which salesperson had the most sales. To make the problem more interesting, let us further assume that there are 100 clerks."

"Wow!" cried Seymour. "There won't be enough room on the chalkboard for a program that size. We'd have to have 100 names for the 100 storage locations that would be needed for the individual salesperson counts. Why, the ON _ GO TO statement itself would take the whole period to write. It would have to include 100 statement numbers. How about doing something like adding two numbers together?"

"No, Seymour, we'll stick to this problem," O'Silver replied, "and it will be much shorter than you think.

"Seymour's comment was a good one. It would appear at first glance that we need 100 names for our clerk totals. The people who designed BASIC anticipated such a problem and incorporated into the language a shorthand way to create many names.

"Here is how to proceed. Place a statement in the program to establish a large number of names and to reserve space in memory for them. This is done in a DIMENSION statement. For example, the statement

$$10 \quad \text{DIM Z}(100)$$

reserves 100 locations in memory and labels them Z(1), Z(2), Z(3), Z(4),

Z(5), . . . , Z(100). Thus, in one statement, we have made up 100 names and put aside the necessary memory locations to store data. If we want to refer to a particular location, we merely write that location name. For example, the statement

90   PRINT Z(40)

would print out the contents of location Z(40). Inside the parentheses is the subscript, which may be a number or a letter. If the subscript is a letter, it must have been given a value. Thus, the statements

50   A = 40

90   PRINT Z(A)

are equivalent to 90 PRINT Z(40). The subscript is merely a pointer that points to a particular position in a list (here, it is the Z list)."

"What are the rules for making up names for these subscripted variables?" asked Howie.

Prof. O'Silver answered, "The names for subscripted variables whose values will be numbers are a single letter of the alphabet. Thus, all of the following are legitimate names.

A(2)

Z(350)

K(1)

P(J)

"The only exception to this rule of having a single letter precede the parentheses is the use of subscripted variables to contain alphanumeric data (letters and numbers). Here, as in nonsubscripted variables, the $ is used as part of the name. Thus, for alphanumeric data the following are legitimate names."

A$(5)

Z$(530)

K$(3)

P$(L)

"How does this help us in our program?" asked Phyllis.

"When we input the salesperson number in our program, we can let that number be the subscript for one list of sales. I'll show you what I mean. Let Z be a subscripted variable that will contain a record of the number of sales made by each salesperson. Since there are 100 salespersons, we will dimension Z to be 100. Look at this flowchart for the problem of inputting the data and printing the number of sales for each salesperson, at the end of the day. Let $Z(I)$ be the number of sales of person I.

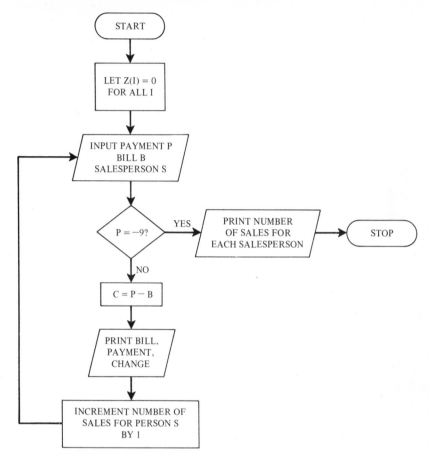

"I understand your flowchart," said Howie, "but it leaves a lot unsaid."

Prof. O'Silver continued, "That's true, the flowchart is not very detailed. I think you'll get a clear picture of the logic as I write the program. Remember that I want to let the subscripted variable Z contain the number of sales for the salespersons. Look at this program:

```
4   REM CHANGE PROBLEM, PLUS HOW MANY SALES FOR EACH SALESPERSON
5   DIM Z(100)
7   I = 1
```

```
10    Z(I) = 0
12    I = I + 1
15    IF I <= 100 THEN 10
20    INPUT P,B,S
25    IF P = −9 THEN 200
30    C = P − B
46    PRINT "CHANGE IS $" C
50    Z(S) = Z(S) + 1
60    GO TO 20
200   I = 1
210   PRINT I, Z(I)
215   I = I + 1
220   IF I <= 100 THEN 210
380   END
```

"Statement 5 tells the computer that the subscripted variable Z will have 100 elements. In other words, it's really like 100 different variables. What about statements 7 through 15, can anyone explain them?"

Rudy Mentry volunteered, "Those statements initialize the list Z to zero. In other words, when $I = 1$, $Z(1)$ is set equal to 0, then I is made equal to 2, and $Z(2)$ is set equal to 0. This is done until I is 100; then when I is 101, control passes to line 20. Since $Z(I)$ is the number of sales of person I, this sets the number of sales of all persons equal to 0 at the start of the program."

"Very good," commented O'Silver. "Statements 20 through 46 are very familiar now. What about statement 50?"

Rudy answered again, "Each time that statement is executed, it adds 1 to the current value for the number of sales for the person whose ID was just inputted, person S. This statement counts the sales, by person, by using the person's number S as the SUBSCRIPT of the list. Thus if person 12 made a sale, 12 would be input to S and $Z(12)$ would be incremented by 1."

Prof. O'Silver responded, "Right again. What's your name? You must not think this course is too hard."

"Rudy Mentry, Sir," responded Rudy.

"Well don't get too confident, young man. Anyway, the last statements, 200 through 220, are similar to the first statements in that they consider each element of the Z list, only this time the list is printed.

"Now that this is clear, how would you alter the program to find the salesperson with the maximum number of sales?"

Clara volunteered to go to the board and draw a flowchart of her approach. When she had finished, the following was on the board.

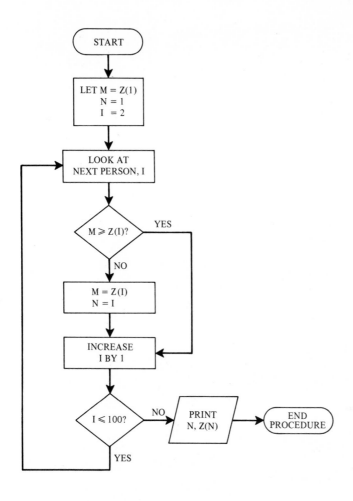

"Very good, Clara," O'Silver commented. "You have set the maximum arbitrarily at the first entry in the array. Then, you sequentially compare every other entry in the array with the maximum and its position in the list (identifying which person) is recorded. I'll write the statements that correspond to your flowchart."

	Statements	Comments
280	$M = Z(1)$	Set maximum equal to first value.
285	$N = 1$	Position in list is 1.
290	$I = 2$	Pointer starts with second location.
310	IF $M >= Z(I)$ THEN 330	Test for a new maximum.
320	$M = Z(I)$	Change maximum.
325	$N = I$	Identify position in list.
330	$I = I + 1$	Increment pointer.

	Statements	Comments
335	IF I <= 100 THEN 310	Finished yet?
350	PRINT 'PERSON',N	Print results.
355	PRINT 'HAD MAX SALES OF' M	

"Thus, if we put the whole program together it would look like this:

```
  3   REM CHANGE PROBLEM WHO HAD THE MOST SALES
  5   DIM Z(100)
  6   REM INITIALIZE SALES CLERK LIST AT ZERO
  7   I = 1
 10   Z(I) = 0
 12   I = I + 1
 15   IF I <= 100 THEN 10
 16   REM INPUT THE TRANSACTIONS
 17   REM CALCULATE AND PRINT THE CHANGE
 18   REM GIVE PROPER SALES CLERK CREDIT FOR SALE
 20   INPUT P, B, S
 25   IF P = -9 THEN 200
 30   C = P - B
 46   PRINT "CHANGE IS $" C
 50   Z(S) = Z(S) + 1
 60   GO TO 20
200   I = 1
205   REM PRINT OUT EACH SALES CLERK'S TOTAL NUMBER OF SALES
210   PRINT I, Z(I)
215   I = I + 1
220   IF I <= 100 THEN 210
250   REM FIND SALES CLERK WITH THE MOST SALES
280   M = Z(1)
285   N = 1
290   I = 2
310   IF M >= Z(I) THEN 330
320   M = Z(I)
325   N = I
330   I = I + 1
335   IF I <= 100 THEN 310
350   PRINT 'PERSON',N
355   PRINT 'HAD MAX SALES OF',M
380   END
```

Problems for Sec. 4.7

1. A store sells 10 items that have the following prices: 1.00, .72, 10000., 1.3.E+07, .06, 9.95, 83.125, 1007, 2.99, and .7. Write a program that READS these prices into a list P.
2. (See Problem 1.) Add statements to the program in Problem 1 that will input two numbers describing a customer's purchase. The first number will be the item number, the second number will be the quantity of that item being purchased. Using the price list of Problem 1, the program should calculate amount the customer shall pay.
3. (Add to Problem 2.) Assume a customer may purchase several types of goods. Your program should repeatedly INPUT pairs of numbers (item number, quantity) until (0,0) is INPUT, then the computer should total the bill and print the amount the customer should pay.
4. Write a program that INPUTS 20 numbers. Calculate the average of the numbers, then print the average and how many numbers are above the average.
5. If A is a row vector of N values (consider A the name of a list with N positions containing the numbers $a_1, a_2, \ldots, a_N$) and B is a column vector of N values (consider B the name of a list with N positions containing the values $b_1, b_2, \ldots, b_N$), then the multiplication A * B is performed by

$$a_1b_1 + a_2b_2 + \cdots + a_Nb_N$$

Write a program that inputs N, then inputs the vectors A and B and performs the multiplication A * B.

4.8 LOOPS IN BASIC

Prof. O'Silver stopped by Phil's house that evening to let him know what he had covered in class. Phil's wife answered the door.

"Hi, Sterling," she said. "Phil is in the study. Go right in."

O'Silver entered the study and found Phil talking with a young lady about graduate schools.

"Hi, O'Silver," Phil called, "do you know Theresa Crowd?" he asked.

"Sure, I can take a hint; I'll be back later." O'Silver turned to leave.

"No, no, this is Theresa Crowd," Phil explained. "That's her name, Theresa Crowd. She is a senior at UGH and is applying to graduate schools. I've been helping her with her application forms."

"Yes, and I'm really tired of filling out applications," she commented. "The same questions over and over again. The same essays, the same background data, the same answers, over and over."

"It's too bad you couldn't use a loop to do the repeating like you can in BASIC," commented Phil.

"You'll be able to cover loops in the next class," O'Silver commented. "I finished up subscripts today."

"Say, I was just working on that lecture," replied Prof. Ovitt. "How about lending me a hand?" he asked.

"Gee, I've got to go now, Professor," answered Theresa. "I have a sick roommate who needs to be cared for. See you later." O'Silver wasn't far behind. "Sorry, Phil," he called, "but I have to get home."

In class the next day, Prof. Ovitt was talking, "Now, let us all look at the problem PICKING THE MAXIMUM NUMBER OF SALES that Prof. O'Silver discussed in the last class.

"Were there any repetitive portions of the program? I mean procedures or statements that were done repeatedly?" he asked.

"Certainly," Rudy said definitively. "Look at the very beginning of the program. We had the statements:

```
6    REM FILL ARRAY WITH ZEROES
7    I = 1
10   Z(I) = 0
12   I = I + 1
15   IF I <= 100 THEN 10
```

Thus, we continually placed a zero into successive memory locations."

"Besides the actual assignment statement that places a zero into a specific memory location, what else was required in this program segment?" asked the professor.

Howie felt he'd better answer a question now rather than wait and be called on later.

"We had to have a pointer (statement 7) to indicate where in the array we wanted to put a zero," he said. "And we had to keep incrementing the pointer by 1 to get through the entire array (statement 12). Also, we needed a test statement to let us know when we had finished going through 100 memory locations (this was at statement 15)."

"Excellent, Howard," Ovitt called. "You have just described all of the characteristics of a loop in BASIC. Let me put on the board an example of how this very same segment of the program could be rewritten using loops.

```
6    REM FILL ARRAY WITH ZEROES
7    FOR I = 1 TO 100 STEP 1
10   Z(I) = 0
15   NEXT I
```

"This is called a FOR-NEXT loop in BASIC," Ovitt continued. "Let's look at a flowchart for it.

"The statements comprising a loop fall between the FOR statement and the NEXT statement. This is considered to be the range of the

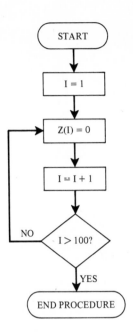

loop, and the statements within this range will be executed each time the computer executes the loop.

"The FOR statement has three parameters in it. It is of the general form

---

FOR variable name = starting value TO ending value STEP increment

The variable name (or index) that is used is like a counter or like the pointer in our program. The first time through the range of the loop the index, which in our example we called I, will have as its contents the 'starting value' (in this case, a 1). When the loop has completed the statements in the range and reaches the NEXT I statement, the 'increment' is added to the current value for I. A test is then made to see if the 'ending value' has been exceeded. If so, the range is not reentered and control passes to the statement following the NEXT statement of the loop. Otherwise, the loop is executed again.

"Let's look at some examples." He handed out some notes.

```
 5   REM EXAMPLE 1: PRINTS THE NUMBERS 1 TO 10
10   FOR I = 1 TO 10 STEP 1
20   PRINT I
30   NEXT I
40   END
```

```
 5   REM EXAMPLE 2: PRINTS THE ODD NUMBERS BETWEEN 1 AND 10
10   FOR B = 1 TO 10 STEP 2
20   PRINT B
30   NEXT B
40   END
```

```
 5   REM EXAMPLE 3: PRINTS THE NUMBERS FROM 20 TO 15
10   FOR X1 = 20 TO 15 STEP −1
20   PRINT X1
30   NEXT X1
40   END
```

```
 5   REM EXAMPLE 4: PRINTS A MESSAGE 6 TIMES
10   FOR Z = 5 TO 10
20   PRINT "DONT READ THIS MESSAGE."
30   NEXT Z
40   END
```

```
 5   REM EXAMPLE 5: PRINTING OUT DECIMAL VALUES
10   A = .5
15   B = 2.25
20   C = .25
25   FOR D = A TO B STEP C
30   PRINT D
35   NEXT D
40   END
```

```
 1   REM EXAMPLE 6: READ AN ARRAY AND PRINT IT BACKWARDS
 5   DIM X(10)
10   FOR J1 = 1 TO 10
20   READ X(J1)
30   NEXT J1
40   FOR K = 10 TO 1 STEP −1
50   PRINT X(K)
60   NEXT K
70   DATA 30, 5, 2, 3, 6, 1, 6, 8, 8, 5
80   END
```

"Let's look at these examples and see what each does. I think you'll find that each has a different point to illustrate. Let's go right up that first row of seats on my left. Each of you take an example and explain it."

Howie sighed a sigh of relief. He was in the seventh seat, and there were only six examples.

Seymour was in the first seat. "Example 1," he began, "illustrates that we can use the index in the FOR statement (in this case, the I) anywhere in the range of the loop. When it is encountered, its value is equal to whatever the index has been incremented to at that particular time. This segment of a program merely prints out the numbers 1 to 10 in a column."

Brandon was next. "Example 2 illustrates how we can have the index (in this case, B) take on different values by using the STEP clause in the FOR statement. In this case, the index B will take on the values 1, 3, 5, 7, and 9, thus going through the loop five times. The output would be these same numbers printed in a column."

"Example 3," Clara began, "shows that you can STEP backwards in a loop. That is, you can have negative values for a step. The range here is executed six times and the results are

```
20
19
18
17
16
15
```

"It is clear from example 4 that you don't have to use the index anywhere in the loop," called Cole Shoulder, the next in line. The index still acts as a counter keeping track of how many times the loop should be executed. This particular program segment prints the message 'DONT READ THIS MESSAGE' six times. Since the word STEP doesn't appear in the FOR statement, the increment is assumed to be 1 by the computer."

The fifth seat belonged to Phyllis. "There are two points to be made in the next example," she began. "First you may use letters (variable names) instead of numbers in a FOR statement as long as these names have been assigned a value before the FOR statement is executed. Second, decimal as well as integer numbers may be used as starting, ending, and incremental values. This segment would output:

```
.50
.75
1.00
1.25
1.50
1.75
2.00
2.25
```

When Howie looked up from the paper on which he was taking notes, he noticed that the chair in front of him was now empty! A voice came from behind him. It was Scott Free who, unnoticed to all, had sneaked behind Howie. "Looks like you're next, pal!" he said.

Before Howie could change seats Prof. Ovitt called, "Mr. Gettindere, would you please continue with example 6?"

"Ah, well (cough, cough), I just swallowed a Life Saver (cough) and I can't (cough) talk too well," Howie stuttered.

"Very well," said Prof. Ovitt. "You take it, Scott."

"Uh, Prof. Ovitt," replied Scott. "I really don't understand this stuff, I'll have to pass."

"Not at this rate!" Prof. Ovitt replied. "Can anyone help Scott out?"

"Sure," replied Seymour, "which way did he come in?"

Prof. Ovitt decided to explain the example himself. "Example 6," he began, "is given to illustrate the importance of loops when using subscripts. When we set up an array of numbers in memory, it is often necessary to search the array for a certain number or condition. We can use the FOR-NEXT loop to process the entire array.

"In this example, we first reserve space for 10 variable names in memory (the DIM statement). The variables will be called X(1) through X(10). The loop, starting in statement 10, will read 10 values from the DATA statement into the 10 array positions. The process goes something like this:

TIME THROUGH LOOP	VALUE OF INDEX J1	NUMBER READ FROM READ STATEMENT	NUMBER IS STORED IN LOCATION
1	1	30	X(1)
2	2	5	X(2)
3	3	2	X(3)
4	4	3	X(4)
5	5	6	X(5)
6	6	1	X(6)
7	7	6	X(7)
8	8	8	X(8)
9	9	8	X(9)
10	10	5	X(10)

"Note that the READ statement was in the range of the loop and thus was actually executed 10 times. After this, another loop is started that prints out the values just read in, but in reverse order. Note that we can use a different variable name for the subscript (like K instead of J1), since the subscript is only a pointer rather than a part of the name itself. Whatever is found in parentheses must be evaluated as a number that can point to a specific location in memory. This particular portion of the program performs something like this:

TIME THROUGH LOOP	VALUE OF INDEX K	LOCATION REFERENCED	NUMBER PRINTED
1	10	X(10)	5
2	9	X(9)	8
3	8	X(8)	8
4	7	X(7)	6
5	6	X(6)	1
6	5	X(5)	6
7	4	X(4)	3
8	3	X(3)	2
9	2	X(2)	5
10	1	X(1)	30

"Okay, class," Ovitt continued, "as a group I'd like you to review the CHANGE PROBLEM WHO HAD THE MOST SALES using loops wherever helpful. That's all for today class; you may leave early." The bell rang signaling the end of the class period.

"Nothing like these short classes, eh, Howie?" Rudy joked. "Want to stop by the student lounge and look over the program Prof. Ovitt suggested?"

Now Howie wasn't about to refuse additional help. "Sure, I'll probably get to see more if we study together."

"Yes, Seymour is coming too," Rudy replied.

When they arrived at the student lounge, they found Clara, Seymour, and Brandon waiting to begin work on the problem.

"Hi, Rudy, Howie," called Clara. "We were just deciding how we would approach the study suggestion. Got any ideas?"

"Well," Rudy replied, "the first part of the program was solved in class." He began to write on a large pad of flip charts precariously attached to an easel.

```
3    REM CHANGE PROBLEM WHO HAD THE MOST SALES
4    REM USE LOOPS
5    DIM Z (100)
6    REM INITIALIZE SALESPERSON LIST AT ZERO
7    FOR I = 1 TO 100 STEP 1
10   Z(I) = 0
15   NEXT I
```

"Now we have to determine what else in the program is repetitive and might be appropriate for loops. Anybody got any ideas?" he asked.

Brandon spoke up. "Well, you have to INPUT the payment, the bill, and the salesperson number for many transactions. That sounds repetitive."

"Sure," Clara said, "but we don't know how many transactions there will be, so how can we indicate how many times the loop should be done?"

"We could just make an assumption," Seymour assumed, "and say that there would be no more than 500 transactions or something!"

"All right, what would the loop be?" asked Rudy, trying to get Seymour to answer the question.

Seymour walked up to the easel and added some more statements.

```
16   REM INPUT UP TO 500 TRANSACTIONS
17   REM CALCULATE & PRINT THE CHANGE
18   REM GIVE PROPER SALESPERSON CREDIT FOR SALE
20   FOR J = 1 TO 500
22   INPUT P, B, S
25   IF P = -9 THEN 200
30   C = P - B
46   PRINT "CHANGE IS $" C
50   Z(S) = Z(S) + 1
60   NEXT J
```

"Hey, this isn't very hard at all," cried Seymour. "Howie, why don't you try it?"

"Sure," replied Howie, "the next section just prints out the total number of sales for each salesperson.

```
200   REM PRINT OUT EACH SALES CLERK'S TOTAL NUMBER OF SALES
210   FOR J = 1 TO 100
215   PRINT Z(J)
220   NEXT J
```

"I've already worked out the last loop," called Clara. "That's the one that finds the salesperson with the maximum number of sales. Here, let me add it to Howie's statements. After arbitrarily picking the first person as having the maximum sales,

```
280   M = Z(1)
285   N = 1
```

we must look at persons 2 through 100 to see if this maximum should be replaced.

```
290   FOR K = 2 TO 100
300   IF M = Z(K) THEN 330
310   M >= Z(K)
320   N = K
330   NEXT K
```

and finish up with,

```
350   PRINT 'PERSON' N, 'HAD THE MAXIMUM SALES = ' M
380   END
```

"Thus the whole program can be written as follows:

```
3    REM CHANGE PROBLEM WHO HAD THE MOST SALES
4    REM USE LOOP
5    DIM Z(100)
6    REM INITIALIZE SALESPERSON LIST AT ZERO
7    FOR I = 1 TO 100
10   Z(I) = 0
15   NEXT I
16   REM INPUT UP TO 500 TRANSACTIONS
17   REM CALCULATE & PRINT THE CHANGE
18   REM GIVE PROPER SALESPERSON CREDIT FOR SALE
20   FOR J = 1 TO 500
22   INPUT P, B, S
25   IF P = -9 THEN 200
30   C = P - B
46   PRINT "CHANGE IS $" C
50   Z(S) = Z(S) + 1
60   NEXT J
200  REM PRINT OUT EACH SALES CLERK'S TOTAL NUMBER OF SALES
210  FOR J = 1 TO 100
215  PRINT Z(J)
220  NEXT J
280  M = Z(1)
285  N = 1
290  FOR K = 2 TO 100
300  IF M >= Z(K) THEN 330
310  M = Z(K)
320  N = K
330  NEXT K
350  PRINT 'PERSON' N, HAD THE MAX NUMBER SALES =', M
380  END
```

TOPIC SUMMARY FOR SECTION 4.8

LOOPS	Increment
FOR NEXT LOOPS	Step backwards
Parameters	Step by decimal amounts
Counter	

Problems for Sec. 4.8

1. Write a program that uses loops to print the square of each odd integer from 11 through 37.

2. How can you write a program that uses FOR-NEXT loops to read N pieces of data when you don't know N until program execution time; you only know in advance N is less than 100.

3. If A is a row vector of N values (consider A the name of a list with N positions containing the numbers a_1, a_2, ..., a_N), and B is a column vector of N values (consider B the name of a list with N positions containing the values b_1, b_2, ..., b_N) then the multiplication A * B is evaluated as

$$a_1 b_1 + a_2 b_2 + \cdots + a_N b_N$$

Using FOR-NEXT loops, write a program that inputs N, then inputs the vectors A and B and performs the multiplication A * B.

4. Write a program that inputs N and a list A(1), A(2), ... A(N), then shifts each value in the list forward one space, and makes A(N) become A(1). For example, if before the shift

$$A = (1, 5, 7, 3, 2)$$

then after the shift

$$A = (2, 1, 5, 7, 3)$$

5. Write a program that inputs N and two lists A and B, each of length N, and outputs a list C. The list C shall be determined as follows: Element i in list C will be the number of the elements in the B list that have the same value as the ith element of the A list.

C is called the element number equivalent of B to A. For example, if $N = 5$ and

$$A = \begin{bmatrix} 1 \\ 9 \\ 5 \\ -1 \\ 4 \end{bmatrix} \qquad B = \begin{bmatrix} 5 \\ 7 \\ -1 \\ 5 \\ 4 \end{bmatrix}$$

then

$$C = \begin{bmatrix} 0 \\ 0 \\ 2 \\ 1 \\ 1 \end{bmatrix}$$

4.9 TABLES AND CHAIRS IN BASIC

At the start of the next class, Howie began speaking. "Say, Professor, I was reading the assignment last night on two-dimensional arrays, and I'm not sure I understand them."

"Okay, Howard," Prof. Ovitt replied. "We covered singly subscripted arrays in the last class. In some instances, however, these simple lists are not enough. In those cases, we might use double subscripts."

"Yes, I understand that," Howie began, "and the fact that double subscripts usually refer to a table with rows and columns."

"That's right, Howard," Prof. Ovitt interjected, "it's common to let the first subscript represent a row pointer and the second subscript represent a column pointer. I'll bet it will help you if we consider an application of the concept. Let's suppose we gather data from the people in our computer class on the number of pets they have. We'll consider four types of pets: dogs, cats, mosquitos, and camels."

"What about parrots?" asked Howie.

"Does anyone have a parrot?" Prof. Ovitt asked the class.

"I do," said Howie. "He's a rather strange bird."

"What do you mean?" asked Scott.

"Well, one day I noticed the parrot was praying," continued Howie. "So I said to the bird, 'Are you religious?'

"'Yes, I am,' answered the parrot. 'And, on Christmas Day I would like to go to church to pray.'

"Naturally, I was a little surprised, but I agreed to take the parrot to church that Christmas Day. The other people in the church were quite curious about the parrot being there, and when I explained that he wanted to pray they were really skeptical. Well, to make a long story short, everyone wanted to bet me that the parrot would not actually pray. One thing led to another, and I had $60 bet with various people that the parrot would, in fact, recite some prayers.

"I sat with the parrot through the entire service and he did NOTHING! I had to pay off $60. I was furious.

"When I got the parrot home, I was quite upset.

"'I thought you were going to pray. You dumb parrot, you cost me $60! What do you have to say for yourself?'

"'Think of the odds you're going to get on Easter!' answered the parrot, confidently."

"Thank you, Howard, but we'll stick with dogs, cats, mosquitos, and camels for now," said Prof. Ovitt. "Each DATA statement contains this information for one of the 30 students. For example, the statements

902   DATA 2, 1, 0, 1
903   DATA 0, 0, 0, 0

indicate that the student whose DATA is in line 902 has 2 dogs, 1 cat, no mosquitos, and 1 camel, while the next student has no pets at all. Let me write up a program that will READ the data for the whole class and print out the total number of camels.

```
100    DIM P(30,4)
200    S = 0
250    FOR I = 1 TO 30
260    READ P(I,1),P(I,2),P(I,3),P(I,4)
270    S = S + P(I,4)
275    NEXT I
280    PRINT S
900    DATA . . .
999    END
```

"Let's look at the DIM statement. The first index for the P array . . ."

"Why didn't you call it 'PET' or something like that?" interrupted Howie.

"You may use only a single letter to name an array, Howard," replied Phil Ovitt.

"But I don't want to name it Howard. I'd like to call it PET," Howie said.

"May I continue?" asked Ovitt. Without waiting for an answer, he continued. "Let's look at the DIM statement. The first index of the P array will refer to the person and, since there are 30 people, there is a '30' in the DIM statement. The second index refers to the particular types of pets that a person has. The '4' in the DIM statement tells the computer that for each value of the first index, the second index can have four values. In effect, this DIM statement has reserved 120 locations (30 times 4). These locations have been given the addresses

P(1,1)
P(1,2)
P(1,3)
P(1,4)
P(2,1)
P(2,2)
. . .
P(29,4)
P(30,1)
P(30,2)
P(30,3)
P(30,4)

"The READ statement is set up to read four values from a DATA statement and place those values in the variables P(I,1), P(I,2), P(I,3), and P(I,4). For example, if the first DATA statement were

$$900 \quad \text{DATA } 2, 0, 4, 1$$

then the execution of the READ statement with $I = 1$ would result in the following assignments:

$$P(1,1) = 2$$
$$P(1,2) = 0$$
$$P(1,3) = 4$$
$$P(1,4) = 1$$

If the next DATA statement was

$$901 \quad \text{DATA } 120, 1, 1, 5$$

then, since $I = 2$ in the FOR statement, the READ gets executed again and the result is

$$P(2,1) = 120$$
$$P(2,2) = 1$$
$$P(2,3) = 1$$
$$P(2,4) = 5$$

"If all 30 data statements were used, the following table would be created in memory.

	PET TYPE			
PERSON	1	2	3	4
1	2	0	4	1
2	120	1	1	5
3	2	1	0	1
4	0	0	0	0
. . .				
30	3	1	1	10

"Remember, $P(2,3)$ means that the number of pets owned by person 2 of pet type 3 is 1. The contents of memory location $P(2,3)$ is 1. Person 2 has 1 mosquito.

"Notice that one of your classmates has 120 dogs and 1 cat!"

"One cat! He must be a lion!" someone shouted.

"No, he's a telling the truth," Phil replied. "Anyway, with 120 dogs, who is going to argue with him? Let's look at the program that I have put on the board. Statement 270 should be familiar to you all by this time. It is a summation statement which, in this case, calculates the total number of camels the class has as pets. Note that the second subscript remains constant at 4 (representing column 4 of the table), and the first subscript changes because it is within the FOR-NEXT loop. Thus, we will have

TIME THROUGH LOOP	VALUE OF INDEX	OLD S	+	P(I,4)	becomes	NEW S
1	1	0		1		1
2	2	1		5		6
. . .	. . .	. . .		. . .		. . .
30	30	53		10		63

"Let me show you a few more programs that demonstrate characteristics of loops. The first one will read the data and calculate the number of animals owned by person 12."

Phil began to write on the board.

```
10   DIM P(30,4)
20   S = 0
30   FOR I = 1 TO 12
40   READ P(I,1),P(I,2),P(I,3),P(I,4)
50   NEXT I
60   FOR J = 1 TO 4
70   S = S + P(12,J)
80   NEXT J
90   PRINT S
900   DATA 2, 0, 4, 1
901   DATA 120, 1, 1, 5
902   DATA 2, 1, 0, 1
. . .   . . .
929   DATA 3, 1, 1, 10
999   END
```

"The first four statements are exactly the same as in the other program, right, class?" asked Ovitt.

Ben Dover stood up. "Yes, except that the loop is only done 12 times instead of 30. The index in the FOR statement indicates that I will start at 1 and end at 12. That certainly is different from the last program!"

"Very good, Ben," Prof. Ovitt declared. "The program then reads only the first 12 of the 30 DATA statements into memory locations. It does not matter that we reserved room for 30 lines of data and only used 12; any memory locations that are unused merely remain unused. When we declare our array dimensions, we must be sure to have enough room for all our data. Declaring arrays too small will prevent execution (in this program we could not have READ 31 DATA statements if we saved only enough room for 30). Declaring them too large wastes memory locations but does not prevent execution of the program."

Another student stood up. "But Prof. Ovitt, what about those other 18 DATA statements?"

"Good question, Sid Down," Phil replied.

Sid did.

"The execution of the program simply does not need all of the data. It is also interesting to note that because the information desired is in DATA statement 12, the first 11 DATA statements had to be read 'just to get them out of the way.' Once DATA statement 12 is read, the program continues on and enters the second FOR-NEXT loop. Will someone please explain what happens there?" asked Phil.

Marge Erine should have known better, but she decided to give it a try. "I believe that this loop adds up the values in a row of the array. In this case, it is the twelfth row." She went to the board. "Let us say that this particular person had 2 dogs, 1 cat, 4 mosquitos, and 0 camels. Here is a table that shows how the values in the statement $S = S + P(12,J)$ change as the loop is executed."

TIME THROUGH LOOP	VALUE OF THE INDEX J	OLD S	+	P(12,J)	becomes	NEW S
1	1	0		2		2
2	2	2		1		3
3	3	3		4		7
4	4	7		0		7

"Thank you, Marge," Phil replied. "In the previous program we selected a particular column and added up all the rows in that column. The procedure was to hold the column (the second subscript) constant at 2 and have a loop vary the row (the first subscript) from 1 to 30.

"In the program we have just completed, we selected a particular row and added up all of the columns in that row. The procedure was to hold the row (the first subscript) constant at 12 and have a loop vary the column (the second subscript) from 1 to 4.

"It is often helpful to think of subscripts in terms of rows and columns. If we wanted to get the total number of all types of pets owned by all students, we would want to add up all of the entries in the array. The procedure here would be to have a loop vary both the row (the first subscript) and the column (the second subscript). Here is such a program."

```
10    DIM P(30,4)
20    S = 0
30    FOR I = 1 TO 30
40    FOR J = 1 TO 4
50    READ P(I,J)
60    S = S + P(I,J)
70    NEXT J
80    NEXT I
90    PRINT S
900   DATA . . .
999   END
```

"In BASIC, when we have two or more loops combined in this manner, they are referred to as *nested loops*. Before I explain what this program does, I'd like you to copy down the following rules for nested loops."

NESTED LOOPS

Rule 1. The inner loop must end or be terminated before the outer loop ends.

Rule 2. Control can never be transferred into the middle of a loop.

"Now, let me explain verbally what happens in this portion of the program, and then we shall look at a tabular display of the execution of these statements.

"In the second statement we initialize our sum at 0 in preparation for adding our data. Line 30 sets up a loop for reading and adding the pets for the 30 people. Statement 40 defines a loop which will be used to read the numbers of the four types of pets a particular person might have. This is a nested loop configuration. The way that execution proceeds is as follows.

Line	Execution
20	S is set to 0
30	I is set to 1
40	J is set to 1
50	READ a number into P(1,1)
60	S = S + P(1,1)
70	NEXT J, J becomes 2
50	READ a number into P(1,2)
60	S = S + P(1,2)

70   NEXT J, J becomes 3
50   READ a number into P(1,3)
60   S = S + P(1,3)
70   NEXT J, J becomes 4
50   READ a number into P(1,4)
60   S = S + P(1,4)
70   NEXT J,This loop is finished.
80   NEXT I, I becomes 2
40   J is set to 1
50   READ a number into P(2,1)
      Etc.

This procedure continues for all 30 of the data sets. Here is how it might look.

OUTER LOOP	INNER LOOP						
Time through first loop	Time through second loop	Value of index I	Value of index J	old S	+ P(I,J)	becomes	new S
First	First	1	1	0	2		2
	Second	1	2	2	0		2
	Third	1	3	2	4		6
	Fourth	1	4	6	1		7
Second	First	2	1	7	120		127
	Second	2	2	127	1		128
	Third	2	3	128	1		129
	Fourth	2	4	129	5		134
. . .	. . .	. . .	. . .	. . .	. . .		. . .

"Continuing in this manner, we would eventually have the grand total of all the pets owned by people in the class. Admittedly, these are difficult concepts that we have covered today. But they are important, so I suggest that you reread these notes and practice on some of these problems."

Prof. Ovitt handed out a set of problems that he had prepared the previous day. Just as he finished, the bell rang, signaling the end of class.

Problems for Sec. 4.9

1. Write a program that inputs a matrix A and prints the elements of the diagonal (the elements of the diagonal are the elements whose row number equals the column number).
2. The matrix A is a table with N rows and M columns. For example

$$A = \begin{bmatrix} 3 & 1 \\ 2 & 4 \\ 9 & 5 \end{bmatrix}$$

has three rows and two columns. The transpose of a matrix is defined as follows: If B is the transpose matrix of A (written A^T) then $b_{ij} = a_{ji}$. That is, the element in ith row and jth column of B is the same as the element in the jth row and ith column of A. Thus for the matrix above,

$$A^T = \begin{bmatrix} 3 & 2 & 9 \\ 1 & 4 & 5 \end{bmatrix}$$

Write a program that inputs a 4×5 matrix (4 rows and 5 columns) and prints its transpose.

3. Write a program that inputs two numbers N and M, then inputs an N by M matrix A. The program should print the transpose of A.
4. In matrix multiplication, if C, A, and B are matrices and $C = A * B$ then:
   (a) The column dimension of A must equal the row dimension of B. Call that dimension N.
   (b) The row dimension of C is equal to the row dimension of A.
   (c) The column dimension of C is equal to the column dimension of B.
   (d) Element C_{ij} of C is calculated by the following formula:

$$C_{ij} = a_{i1}b_{1j} + a_{i2}b_{2j} + \cdots + a_{in}b_{nj}$$

Write a program that inputs any 3×5 matrix and multiplies it by any 5×2 matrix and prints the results.
5. Continuing with Problem 4. Write a program that inputs three numbers N, M, P, then inputs an $N \times M$ matrix A, and an $M \times P$ matrix B. The program should print $C = A * B$.
6. Continuing with Problem 4. If $N = M = P$, does $A * B = B * A$ in general? Show why, using your program for Problem 4.

4.10 FUNCTIONS AND SUBROUTINES

The computer exam was only two days away, and Howie was beginning to panic. He called Rudy and Clara and invited them over for a party. When they arrived, Howie had a list of questions that covered several pages.

"I had a hunch you were looking for a review session," laughed Rudy.

"Well, I'm beginning to panic," shook Howie. "I was trying to write some programs to practice for the exam, and I really got hung up on one to calculate the square root of a number."

"You don't have to write a program to calculate a square root," Clara said.

"What? Have you seen the exam?" Howie questioned.

"No, what I mean," Clara continued, "is that there is a program already in the computer that calculates square roots."

"So, what good does that do me?" asked Howie.

"All you have to do to use that program is to reference the three letters SQR (for square root)." Clara replied. "Here, let me show you." She begin writing on Howie's mirror with a bar of soap.

```
10   FOR I = 1 TO 16
20   A = SQR(I)
30   PRINT A
40   NEXT I
50   END
```

"This short program," Clara continued, "will calculate and print the square root of every number from 1 to 16. You see, whenever you use the name SQR you get the square root of whatever is in the parentheses. This is called a function (the square root function) and is built into the BASIC language."

"Are there any other built-in functions?" asked Howie.

"Yes, there are quite a few," volunteered Rudy. "Some of the more common are these." Rudy handed Howie a list that he had prepared on an index card.

SOME BUILT-IN FUNCTIONS IN BASIC

Function	Result
SQR(Y)	The square root of Y
LOG(Y)	The natural logarithm of Y
ABS(Y)	The absolute value of Y
INT(Y)	The integer part of Y
EXP(Y)	The value of e^Y
RND	Returns a random number from the uniform distribution (between 0 and 1)
SGN(Y)	If Y > 0 then SGN(Y) = 1
	If Y = 0 then SGN(Y) = 0
	If Y < 0 then SGN(Y) = −1

"Thanks, Rudy," Howie commented, as he looked over the list. "They look important. Say, what does that RND function do?"

"Well," Clara said, "the random number function is a very useful one. You see, a computer may be used to simulate events whose outcomes are not known in advance; that is, there is some randomness involved. As a quick example, suppose you wanted the computer to roll two dice for a game you are playing. Assuming the game is to be fair, you could use the RND function to select the outcome of the dice roll. Before I show you how this works, let's look at how RND works.[1] I'll write a short program that just prints out five random numbers." Clara picked up a tube of cake frosting and wrote on the top of Howie's party cake:

```
10    FOR K = 1 TO 5
20    N = RND
30    PRINT N
40    NEXT K
50    END
```

"The output from this short program might be:

.034275
.961302
.541581
.230477
.423349

Thus, we have five random numbers. When we look at the dice problem, we discover that we need random integers between (and including) 1 and 6 (to represent all the possible faces of one die). A nine would make no sense. Since the RND function only returns numbers between 0 and 1, it will have to be modified. Any ideas how that might be done?" she asked.

"Sure," said Howie. "We could modify the RND function by writing it as DNR."

Clara continued as if she hadn't asked the question. "Look what happens if we multiply our random number by some other number—let's say a 6.

Number generated	Multiplied by 6
.034275	0.205650
.961302	5.767812
.541581	3.249486
.230477	1.382862
.423349	2.540094

If we use the integer function INT to truncate the decimal portion, we get an integer random number.

[1]Some systems will require the RND function to be written with an argument.

NUMBER GENERATED	RND * 6	INT(RND * 6)
.034275	0.205650	0
.961302	5.767812	5
.541581	3.249486	3
.230477	1.382862	1
.423349	2.540094	2

"I'm sure you see that this results in random integers uniformly distributed between 0 and 5. That means any integer, 0, 1, . . . , 5, occurs with probability 1/6. For the dice problem, we need random numbers between 1 and 6. Let's try the following.

$$A = 1 + INT(RND * 6)$$

SAMPLE RND	RND * 6	INT(RND * 6)	1 + INT(RND * 6)
.034275	0.205650	0	1
.961302	5.767812	5	6
.541581	3.249486	3	4
.230477	1.382862	1	2
.423349	2.540094	2	3

"Hey, I get it!" cried a confident Howie. "Let me try to write the program for the dice problem." He began to write in the dust on his desk top.

```
500   REM THROW THE DICE
510   D1 = 1 + INT(RND * 6)
520   D2 = 1 + INT(RND * 6)
525   PRINT "THE RESULT OF THE THROW IS", D1 "AND", D2
530   END
```

"Boy, these sure are useful hints you're giving me," declared a grateful Howie.

"Say, Rudy," Clara called, "why don't you do a subroutine for Howie!"

Howie was miffed. "Well, if you're not going to do your best routine, don't do anything at all."

Rudy was shaking his head. "No, Howie, subroutines are used in programming. Let us suppose that the procedure Clara just discussed had to appear in several places of your program. It would be tedious to have to rewrite the statements over and over again and too complicated to keep transferring control around. The concept of subroutines allows you to write the procedure once and refer to it whenever you wish.

"To write Clara's program as a subroutine we would write the following." Rudy began to write in the dust on Howie's end tables.

```
500   REM THROW THE DICE
510   D1 = 1 + INT(RND * 6)
520   D2 = 1 + INT(RND * 6)
525   PRINT "THE RESULT OF THE THROW IS", D1, "AND" D2
530   RETURN
```

Howie was a little surprised. "The only thing you did was to add the word RETURN," he commented.

"Let me continue," pleaded Rudy. "Now, anytime you wanted to print out a throw of the dice you could say (in the main program)

10   GOSUB 500

This is very much like a GO TO statement except that when control is transferred to the subroutine, the computer remembers the point at which it left the main program. When the RETURN statement is executed, it returns to that point in the program. Look at the following program.

```
10    REM PRINT THE SUM OF THE DICE
20    GOSUB 500
30    S = D1 + D2
35    PRINT "THE SUM OF THIS ROLL IS", S
40    PRINT "NEXT PLAYERS TURN"
45    GOSUB 500
50    S = D1 + D2
60    PRINT "SECOND PLAYERS SCORE IS", S
70    STOP
500   REM THROW THE DICE
510   D1 = 1 + INT(RND * 6)
520   D2 = 1 + INT(RND * 6)
525   PRINT "THE RESULTS OF THE THROWS ARE," D1, "AND," D2
530   RETURN
550   END
```

This program would print out the following.

```
THE RESULTS OF THE THROWS ARE 5 AND 3
THE SUM OF THIS ROLL IS 8
NEXT PLAYERS TURN
THE RESULTS OF THE THROWS ARE 1 AND 4
SECOND PLAYERS SCORE IS 5
```

"These are great little tricks," commented Howie. "I wonder how come Prof. Ovitt didn't cover them in class?"

"But he did, Howie," Clara replied. "That was the day you cut class to bring your suit to the Greek tailor for repair. Remember?"

"Oh yeah, I recall," recalled Howie. "While I was there a tall man came in with a torn pair of pants and said, 'Eumenides?' and the tailor replied, 'Euripides?' I guess they knew each other from the old country.

"I can see how built-in functions and subroutines can be quite helpful in my programming," Howie commented. "It would be nice if I could make up my own functions. For example, I have a problem that requires using a formula over and over. I get tired of writing it."

"What is the formula?" asked Clara.

"Well, several times in one of my programs, I have to calculate the sum of the N numbers from 1 to N. The formula I use is

$$S = \frac{N(N + 1)}{2}$$

Rudy used his felt tip pen to write some statements on the back of Howie's hand.

```
10    DEF FNS(N) = (N * (N + 1))/2
```

"This statement," he explained, "is called a DEFine FunctioN (DEF FN) statement. Once you define your own function using this statement, you can reference just the function name. It works just like the SQR function does. Thus if you wanted to get the sum of the numbers from 1 to 15, from 1 to 186, and from 1 to 8, the following statements would suffice.

```
10    DEF FNS(N) = (N * (N + 1))/2
20    A = FNS(15)
30    X = 186
40    B = FNS(X)
50    C = FNS(8)
60    PRINT A,B,C
70    END
```

"You just put the appropriate formula in a DEF FN statement. You add your own function name after the letters FN. Then, if there are variables in the formula, the variables appear in parentheses."

"Hey, I bet that I could define a function to calculate the roots of a quadratic equation!" cried Howie. "That was a problem I wrote a whole program for earlier. The statements[1]

```
10   DEF FNA(A,B,C) = (−B + SQR(B ** 2 − 4 * A * C))/(2 * A)
20   DEF FNB(A,B,C) = (−B − SQR(B ** 2 − 4 * A * C))/(2 * A)
```

will do it, or even these,

```
10   DEF FNX(A,B,C) = SQR(B ** 2 − 4 * A * C)
15   DEF FNA(A,B,C) = (−B + FNX(A,B,C))/(2 * A)
20   DEF FNB(A,B,C) = (−B − FNX(A,B,C))/(2 * A)
```

"Boy, Howie, you really catch on fast," said Rudy. "You won't have any trouble at all with the test. Well, we've got to be going now. See you in class next week."

"Yeah, and thanks a lot, Clara, Rudy; it was great having you over. It really helped," responded Howie. "Now I think I'll turn on the TV and watch the solar landing tonight."

"It's a moon landing, Howie. How could a spacecraft land on the sun? It's too bright and hot."

"Oh," responded Howie, "I thought it would be okay since it's nighttime."

TOPIC SUMMARY FOR SECTION 4.10

FUNCTION	RETURN
Built-In FUNCTION	GO SUB
Random numbers	DEFINE FUNCTION
SUBROUTINE	

Problems for Sec. 4.10

1. Write a program that inputs a number and prints the absolute value of the number, using the BASIC built-in function.
2. Write a subroutine (not using any built-in functions) that calculates the absolute value of a number.
3. You have found that it is necessary to calculate $N * (N − 1) * (N − 2) * \ldots * 1$ in many places in solving a problem. Write a program with a subroutine that will calculate that product for any $N > 2$. That product is called N factorial and is usually written as $N!$.

---

[1]Some BASIC systems allow only one variable as the argument for a function.

4. The trigonometric functions sine, cosine, and tangent are built-in functions named SIN, COS, TAN, respectively. Write a program that tabulates sin (X) for X equal to 0, 1, 2, 3, 4 . . . . What does this tell you about the units of X when you use the SIN function?

5. Cotangent = cosine/sine. Write a user-defined function for cotangent in a program that inputs numbers and prints their sine, cosine, and cotangent. A good program will work for the input of 3.14159.

6. Write a program that simulates the game of "craps," the popular Las Vegas dice game. Run the program a sufficient number of times to determine if the game "seems" to be fair or not.

7. Write a program that will allow a person to play blackjack against the computer. Assume that the deck is not shuffled after each hand. Is there a strategy that can "beat the dealer?"

8. There's a new game in town called Twenty. Here's how it is played. There are 20 cards numbered 1 to 10 (two cards of each number) in a deck. You get two cards and your opponent gets two cards, one of which you can see and the other you cannot see. If you do not like your cards you may ask for additional cards one at a time, but you may not dispose of any cards. The object of the game is to have the value of the cards you hold be closer to 20 than your opponent's value. If a person's score exceeds 20, the game immediately ends and the other person wins. Your opponent has the inflexible rule that he must wait until you have received all the cards you desire, then he must draw more cards as long as his total is less than 15. Write a program using the random number function that allows you to play against the computer. Try to develop a winning strategy.

9. Each of the letters below represents a different digit. Write a program to perform the addition and determine the values associated with the letters.

$$
\begin{array}{r}
AB \\
CD \\
+ \ EF \\
\underline{GH} \\
III
\end{array}
$$

4.11 CHARACTER STRING FUNCTIONS

Seymour and Clara were at the movies watching one of the nominees for picture of the year, "The Buccaneer," a story about skyrocketing prices of corn. It was intermission and Seymour was talking to Clara about one of the actors. "What do you think of the Colonel in the story?" he asked.

"He's quite a character," she replied. "He doesn't pay much attention to what his friends are trying to tell him; in one ear and out the other!"

"Maybe the other characters are stringing him along," Seymour suggested.

"Say, that reminds me, Seymour," Clara started, "did you do the assignment on *character strings* for Prof. Ovitt's class?"

"No, not yet," Seymour replied. "I just got used to the fact that you have to use quotes around your data when you use character strings in a program."

Clara took an index card out of her pocketbook. "Yes, I remember now; anything enclosed in quotes in BASIC was considered to be a character string. Here, look at this example." She showed a piece of notepaper to Seymour.

Example	Comment
'CLARA FY'	The name Clara Fy is a character string.
B$ = "ANSWER"	The character string 'answer' is stored in location B$.

"Say, Clara," suggested Seymour, "we've got a few minutes before the picture starts again, so how about reviewing the reading and printing of character strings for me?"

"Sure," she replied. She began to write on the inside of an empty popcorn box.

"Remember that when we make up a name for a storage location that is to contain a character string, it must have a $ as the second character. We can READ character strings from DATA statements if we put the string in quotes like this."

```
10   READ A$, J, D$
90   DATA 'JANUARY', 30, 'TUESDAY'
```

"The string JANUARY is stored in location A$, and the string TUESDAY is stored in location D$. Another way to input is, of course, the INPUT statement. In this case, we type in a response when a question mark appears at the terminal. If the INPUT statement is looking for character data, the character data should be enclosed in quotes. Thus, we might see

```
10   PRINT "PLEASE TYPE YOUR FIRST NAME"
20   INPUT A$
```

and our response would be

```
?'CLARA'
```

"Say, Clara, I noticed that you use both single and double quotes in your examples," commented Seymour. "Don't you have to be consistent?"

"You really should be," she replied, "but most systems treat the two symbols as synonymous. By the way, I was reading a book on BASIC that I got from the library last night, and there are two functions that deal with character strings."

"Oh really," yawned Seymour, "what are they?" He was hoping that the movie would start soon.

"One of them is the LENGTH function. It can be used to find out how many characters are in a character string. For example, the statement

40   N$ = 'CLARA FY'
50   A1 = LENGTH (N$)

would result in an 8 being stored in location A1. That's because there are 8 characters in the string N$."

"There are 15 characters in this movie," commented Seymour, vainly attempting to change the subject.

"Also," Clara continued, "there is an INDEX function.[1] This function finds the position of a character (or set of characters) in a selected string. Look at these statements.

10   A$ = 'SEYMOUR'
20   N = INDEX (A$,'OUR')

"The value of N will be 5. See the two values in parentheses? The function is asking where in the first string (A$) you find the first occurrence of the second string ('OUR'). That position is returned from the function. Hence, a 5 is assigned to N."

"Would you like a candy bar or something?" asked Seymour.

Clara was now oblivious to Seymour. She was standing and addressing all the theater patrons.

"There is one other function that I read about, the *substring* function. It allows you to extract a portion of a string and assign it to another storage location. There are three parameters needed by this function.

1. The name of the string to be looked at
2. The character on which the extraction is to begin
3. The number of characters to be extracted.

"As an example, look at these statements.

10   N$ = 'SEYMOUR MOVIES'
20   B$ = SUBSTR(N$, 9, 6)

"This would result in the substring MOVIES[2] being stored in location B$."

Clara was suddenly aware that the audience was applauding her performance. Embarrassed, she quickly sat down.

The person seated directly behind her tapped her on the shoulder.

---

[1]This function will not be available on all systems.
[2]The SUBSTR function will not be available on all systems.

"Say, Clara," he said, "while those functions are part of many BASIC systems, we don't have all of them on our system. You knew that, didn't you?"

"Yes, I did," she replied. "I always use our reference manual if I have any question as to what's available."

The curtain opened and "The Buccaneer" began again.

TOPIC SUMMARY FOR SECTION 4.11

| Character strings | LENGTH function |
| Use of " " and ' ' | INDEX function |

Problems for Sec. 4.11

1. Write a program that will allow you to discover how many characters your system will allow as input into a character variable.
2. See how much flexibility your BASIC system will allow with the subscripting of character strings. Are lists allowed? Are tables of character variables allowed?
3. Run this program:

```
10   A$ = "A"
20   B$ = "B"
30   IF A$<B$ GO TO 70
40   PRINT "A$>B$"
50   STOP
70   PRINT "A$<B$"
80   END
```

What might be the implications of the program? What if statement 10 were changed to A$ = "AT"? Would that change anything?

4. Write a program that inputs five names and prints them in alphabetic order.
5. Write a program that inputs a name and finds the first occurrence of the letter T. Try your program on 'H. Gettindere.'
6. Write a program that will read the names:

> H. Gettindere
> T. Shoelaces
> Clara Fy
> Bill Eumore
> Bea Keeper

and extract letters from these names to print the following sentence:

THIS BOOK IS _____.

(Have the computer fill in the blank as you like.)

7. Write a program that decodes messages according to the following rules: Letters are replaced by their predecessors in the alphabet (e.g., C is replaced by B); A is replaced by Z. Other characters are to remain unchanged. Have the computer decode this message:

ZPV BSF TVQQPTFE UP IBWF IVF DPNQVUFS EP VIFT

4.12 MATRIX COMMANDS

Prof. Ovitt had arrived and was spreading his notes across the desk. "I'm sorry I'm late, class," he began, "but on the way over here from the parking lot I stopped to watch two silkworms having a race. They ended up in a tie!"

The class groaned in unison.

Prof. Ovitt began, "Today's lecture will deal with matrices. You are all familiar with matrices. We covered them in the class on subscripts and again during our discussion of FOR-NEXT loops. The reason we are going to cover them again today is to show you a shorthand way of dealing with such tables. To give you an idea of what I mean, look at the following statements." Prof. Ovitt began writing on the board.

```
10   DIM B(2,3)
20   MAT READ B
```

"This new statement," Phil explained, "has the word MAT in it. This is short for matrix and will be used in several other statements. In this case it reads in the entire matrix B. It knows how large the matrix is because the matrix has been dimensioned."

"How does it read the data," asked Clara, "by row or by column?"

"Always by row," replied Ovitt. "Thus, if our table is supposed to be

2	19.6	8
19	25	3

then the DATA statements should be

```
900   DATA 2, 19.6, 8
901   DATA 19. 25, 3
```

Can someone tell the class what the equivalent would be if FOR-NEXT statements were used instead of the MAT READ statement?" he asked.

Xavier Greenstamps answered his first question of the semester. "I believe that they would be

```
10    FOR I = 1 TO 2
20    FOR J = 1 TO 3
30    READ B(I,J)
40    NEXT J
50    NEXT I
```

"That is correct," said Prof. Ovitt. "Your loops also read the data in by row. Of course, you could read more than one matrix in the same MAT READ statement if you wished. Thus,

```
10    DIM B(10,10), X(15), N(3,5)
15    MAT READ B, X, N
```

would read 100 items into B (by row), then 15 items into X and finally, 15 items (by row) into matrix N.

"Can anyone think of another input statement that might be similar to a MAT READ statement?" he asked.

"I'm only guessing," volunteered Seymour, "but could you use

```
20    MAT INPUT B
```

in place of the MAT READ statement?"

"Absolutely," answered Ovitt. "The only difference is that now the data is entered during execution of the program. That is, when the MAT INPUT statement is reached, a '?' is printed at the terminal and you must type in the matrix data (by row) at that time. Now let me show you some shortcuts with matrices." Phil erased the board and began to write.

STATEMENT	RESULT
15 MAT B = ZER	Fills matrix B with zeros.
15 MAT B = CON	Fills matrix B with ones.
15 MAT B = IDN	Fills diagonal of matrix with ones, all other cells with zeros. Only works for a square matrix.

"In addition to the above statements, programs can be considerably shortened by using matrix arithmetic where possible. If two or more matrices have the same dimensions, they may be added or subtracted. Thus, the following statements may appear in a program."

```
10    DIM A(2,3), B(2,3), C(2,3), D(2,3)
20    MAT READ A,B
30    MAT C = A + B
40    MAT D = A − B
         . . .
```

"If matrix A and B were read in as follows:

MATRIX A		
1	3	9
15	2	6

MATRIX B		
3	36.5	8
9	20	7

Then, after the execution of the above statements, we would have

MATRIX C		
4	39.5	17
24	22	13

MATRIX D		
−2	−33.5	1
6	−18	−1

"Matrix multiplication is also permitted," continued Ovitt. "The rule is, as always, that the number of columns in the first matrix must equal the number of rows in the second matrix. Thus, if we had the following statements

```
10   DIM X(2,3), Y(3,1), A(2,1)
20   MAT A = X * Y
```

with the data

MATRIX X		
3	8	5
2	4	1

MATRIX Y
2
3
2

the result of the multiplication would be

MATRIX A
40
18

"Say, Prof. Ovitt," interrupted Howie, "where did you get those numbers for matrix A?"

"There are a few things you must know in order to multiply matrices, Howard," replied Prof. Ovitt. "Remembering that the number of columns of the first matrix must equal the number of rows of the second matrix, you can determine the dimensions of the final matrix by using the other two dimensions of the original matrices. The row dimension of the product matrix is the row dimension of the first multiplying matrix, and the column dimension of the product matrix is the column dimension of the second multiplying matrix. If X is 3×4 and Y is 4×7 then X * Y will be 3×7. If X is 4×2 and Y is 2×4 then X * Y will be 4×4.

"The entries in the product matrix are determined by applying the following formula:

$$A(I,J) = \sum_{K=1}^{N} X(I,K) * Y(K,J)$$

where N is the number of columns in X and the number of rows in Y. In our previous example, entry 2,1 (row 2, column 1) of matrix A would have been obtained as follows." Prof. Ovitt sketched the following on the board.

I	J	K	X(I,K)	Y(K,J)	PRODUCT
2	1	1	2	2	4
		2	4	3	12
		3	1	2	2

"Thus, A(2,1) was calculated to be

$$X(2,1) * Y(1,1) + X(2,2) * Y(2,1) + X(2,3) * Y(3,1)$$

$$(2) \quad * \quad (2) \quad + \quad (4) \quad * \quad (3) \quad + \quad (1) \quad * \quad (2)$$

which is 18.

"Matrix multiplication can be extremely useful in many problems. For example, let us write a program that reads in the sales of three salespersons for four different products and then, using a price schedule for each product, calculates each person's total sales."

Brandon volunteered to put the program on the board and wrote the following.

```
10   DIM S(3,4), P(4,1), A(3,1)
20   MAT READ S, P
30   MAT A = S * P
40   PRINT, "SALESMAN 1 HAS SALES OF", A(1,1)
50   PRINT "SALESMAN 2 HAS SALES OF", A(2,1)
60   PRINT "SALESMAN 3 HAS SALES OF", A(3,1)
70   DATA 5, 20, 3, 3
80   DATA 4, 0, 2, 1
```

```
 90    DATA 2, 2, 5, 8
 95    REM PRICES FOR EACH ITEM
100    DATA 2.50, 1.25, .95, 3.25
110    END
```

"I suggest that you work through this program to be sure you understand how matrices are used in BASIC. You may also multiply an entire matrix by a constant. Each of the following statements is allowed in BASIC."

STATEMENT	RESULT
10 MAT F = (2) * A	Multiplies each element in matrix A by 2
10 MAT F = (1/2) * A	Divides each element in matrix A by 2
10 N = 5 15 M = 7 17 MAT F = ((N + M)/6) * A	Multiplies each element in matrix A by 2

"Now, class," continued Ovitt. "the bell is about to ring, but I'd like you all to stay until I've finished with today's topic.

"The only matrix operation we haven't covered is printing." Ovitt turned to write on the board.

The bell rang.

"The statements I am now writing on the board will print out the contents of a matrix. Of course, the matrix must have been dimensioned.

20   MAT PRINT A

If A was a matrix with the values

$$\begin{bmatrix} 10 & 20 \\ 5 & 36 \end{bmatrix}$$

then the output would be

$$\begin{matrix} 10 & 20 \\ 5 & 36 \end{matrix}$$

Note that the output is printed by row."

Prof. Ovitt turned from the board and saw a student with her hand raised.

"Althea Tamaro," he called.

The classroom emptied out faster than a bag of peanuts at an elephant convention.

TOPIC SUMMARY FOR SECTION 4.12

Matrix commands	MAT INPUT
MAT READ	MAT ASSIGNMENT statements
	MAT PRINT

Problems for Sec. 4.12

1. There are functions built into BASIC to perform important operations on matrices. If A is a matrix

$$\text{MAT C} = \text{TRN(A)}$$

will cause matrix C to be the transpose of matrix A (see Problem 2, Section 4.9), and

$$\text{MAT D} = \text{INV(A)}$$

will cause matrix D to be the inverse of matrix A (written A^{-1}); A must be a square matrix and D has the same dimension as A.

Write a program that inputs the matrix

$$A = \begin{bmatrix} 5 & 3 & 1 \\ 2 & 7 & 9 \\ 6 & 8 & 2 \end{bmatrix}$$

and prints its transpose and its inverse.

2. See Problem 1. What is AA^{-1}? Remember, A^{-1} is the inverse matrix of A. Calculate AA^{-1} by using the statements

$$\begin{aligned} 20 \quad & \text{MAT C} = \text{INV(A)} \\ 25 \quad & \text{MAT D} = A * C \end{aligned}$$

3. Many systems do not allow statements like this

$$10 \quad \text{MAT A} = A * B$$

even though A and B are well-defined matrices of the appropriate dimensions. What reason can you give for this?

4. Simultaneous linear equations are of the form $AX = B$, where A is an $M \times N$ matrix of known constants, X is an $N \times 1$ array of unknown (but to be solved for) values, and B is an $M \times 1$ array of known constants. The solution of that set of simultaneous equations is $X = A^{-1}B$.

Write a program that inputs numbers N and M, then the arrays A and B and prints X.

Solve this set of equations

$$5X_1 + 3X_2 + X_3 = 7$$

$$2X_1 + 7X_2 + 9X_3 = 8$$

$$6X_1 + 8X_2 + 2X_3 = -6$$

4.13 ADDITIONAL PRINTING OPTIONS IN BASIC

Howie was practicing his programming in the room where several of the computer terminals were located. He noticed several students creating something of a commotion around one of the terminals. When he wandered over to investigate he saw the following printed on the output page.

THE NUMBER HIDDEN IS BETWEEN 1 AND 1000.
NEXT PERSONS TRY
?456
THE NUMBER HIDDEN IS BETWEEN 456 AND 1000.
NEXT PERSONS TRY
?502
THE NUMBER HIDDEN IS BETWEEN 456 AND 502.
NEXT PERSONS TRY

"What's going on?" asked Howie.

"We're playing COFFEE!" Rudy replied.

"What's that?" asked Howie.

"Well," Rudy began to explain. "The program COFFEE is a canned program stored in the computer, and we're playing it. Here's how it goes. The computer selects a random number between 1 and 1000. Then, each person who is playing steps up to the machine and types a number. The object is NOT to guess the number that the computer has selected. If you are unfortunate enough to guess it, you buy coffee for all the players in the game. If you fail to guess it, the computer shortens the interval of available numbers and the next person guesses."

"Hey, can I play?" asked an enthusiastic Howie.

"Sure," Rudy answered. "You can go after Seymour!" They watched as Seymour typed.

?500
THE NUMBER HIDDEN IS BETWEEN 500 AND 502
NEXT PERSONS TRY

Howie found himself in front of the terminal.

"Your turn, Howie," chuckled Rudy.

Howie realized immediately that he didn't have much to choose from and decided he'd type in any old number.

    ?236
    THAT IS OUTSIDE THE RANGE, PLEASE TRY AGAIN
    ?

Reluctantly, Howie typed.

    ?501
    P.T. BARNUM SAYS THERE IS ONE BORN EVERY MINUTE. TODAY, YOU ARE IT.
    YOU WON IT. PAY UP!

When Howie turned around, there were 14 students crowded around the terminal waiting for coffee.

Half an hour later, after everyone had finished their coffee, the room was practically empty. Howie went over to the terminal. He was quite curious to see how the COFFEE program worked.

After logging on to the system, he typed the system command for using a canned program.

    PROGRAM NAME?   coffee
    READY

He then typed in the system command for getting a copy of the program.

    list

The following program was listed at the terminal.

```
100    REM THE COFFEE GAME
110    PRINT "DO YOU WANT INSTRUCTIONS?"
120    INPUT A$
130    IF A$ = 'YES' THEN 800
140    N1 = INT(RND * 1000) + 1
150    L = 1
160    U = 1000
170    PRINT USING 190, L, U
190    : THE NUMBER HIDDEN IS BETWEEN ### AND ####
200    PRINT "NEXT PERSONS TRY"
210    INPUT N
```

```
220    IF N < L THEN 300
230    IF N > U THEN 300
240    IF N = N1 THEN 400
250    IF N < N1 THEN 280
260    U = N
270    GO TO 170
280    L = N
290    GO TO 170
300    PRINT "THAT IS OUTSIDE THE RANGE, PLEASE TRY AGAIN."
310    GO TO 210
400    PRINT "P.T. BARNUM SAYS THERE IS ONE BORN EVERY"
410    PRINT "MINUTE. TODAY, YOU ARE IT. YOU WON IT."
420    PRINT "PAY UP!"
430    GO TO 900
800    PRINT "THE WINNER OF THIS GAME IS REALLY"
810    PRINT "THE LOSER. HE BUYS COFFEE FOR"
820    PRINT "ALL PLAYERS. THE GAME STARTS"
830    PRINT "WITH THE COMPUTER RANDOMLY SELECTING"
840    PRINT "A NUMBER BETWEEN 1 AND 1000."
850    PRINT "PLAYERS THEN TRY NOT TO GUESS"
860    PRINT "THAT NUMBER. THE COMPUTER"
870    PRINT "SHORTENS THE INTERVAL AS GUESSES"
880    PRINT "ARE MADE."
890    GO TO 140
900    END
```

Howie understood most of the program but was a bit surprised to see a new statement. He tore off the output page and headed for Prof. Ovitt's office.

"Prof. Ovitt," he asked, "could you spend a few minutes explaining something to me?"

"Sure, Howard. What is the problem?" he asked.

"Well, take a look at this output. Here is a statement that I have never seen before." Howie pointed to the following statements.

```
170    PRINT USING 190, L, U
190    : THE NUMBER HIDDEN IS BETWEEN ### AND ####
```

"Oh, yes," Prof. Ovitt responded. "That is a PRINT USING statement. It is an alternate form of the PRINT statement that is available on some BASIC systems."

"How does it work?" asked Howie.

"Well," Prof. Ovitt began, "the USING portion of the statement refers us to another statement that will indicate how the output line should look. This statement, called an image statement, is written with a colon followed by whatever characters you might want to be printed with your output.

"Furthermore, there is a special symbol, the pound sign (#), that is used to indicate where data should be printed. That is, in the example you've shown me, whatever is stored in memory location L is printed where those first three pound signs are. Then, the contents of location U are printed where those next four pound signs are. This type of statement allows for a very precise description of an output line."

"Yes," recalled Howie, "I remember when we talked about *print zones* on the page. This new statement actually allows us to print something in every single column on the page, right?"

"That's right, Howie," Ovitt answered. "Here, let me give you another example of its use. You can explain to me what the output would be." Phil began to write on the chalkboard in his office.

```
10   N$ = 'HOWIE'
20   B$ = 'IL'
30   J = 80
40   K1 = 1
50   PRINT USING 60, N$, B$, J, K1
60   : ##### W##L PASS THIS COURSE, ODDS ARE ##.# TO #.
70   END
```

"That's easy," Howie started, "this program will print this message."

HOWIE WILL PASS THIS COURSE, ODDS ARE 80.0 TO 1

"Let me ask you something, Professor," Howie ventured. "Suppose that I changed the IMAGE statement in your program to this one.

60   : ### W###L PASS THIS COURSE, ODDS ARE # TO ##

"What would be printed?"
Prof. Ovitt wrote again on the chalkboard.

HOW WIL L PASS THIS COURSE, ODDS ARE * TO   1.

"Well," Howie commented, "you really can create your own output line!"

"I hope you noticed, Howie," said Prof. Ovitt, "that when the number of pound signs you leave are too few to accommodate the data to be printed an * will appear. Alphabetic data are left justified and numeric data are right justified."

"Oh, of course," Howie weakly responded. "Say, are there other printing options that are available?"

"There is also a MAT PRINT USING statement in BASIC for formatted output of matrices. The image statement will have the format for each row of the matrix output.

"For example, suppose the matrix

$$A = \begin{bmatrix} 1 & 2 & 3 \\ 4 & 5 & 6 \end{bmatrix}$$

were printed by the following statements:

```
10   : ## #.# #
50   MAT PRINT USING 10, A
```

The output would be

```
1  2.0  3
4  5.0  6
```

This instruction can be useful for printing matrices in an orderly way."

"I guess that's it," said a bewildered Howie.

"There's one other printing option, Howie," replied Prof. Ovitt. "Many systems permit you to use a TAB command right in the PRINT statement. It works just like a tab on a typewriter. That is, it allows you to skip across the page to specific columns. For example, the statement

```
10   PRINT TAB (10), X, TAB (35), Y
```

will print the value of X beginning in column 10 and the value of Y beginning in column 35."

"Thanks, Prof. Ovitt, I really appreciate your help," said Howie.

As he was leaving, Howie felt quite pleased at having learned some new material. If only he hadn't lost that COFFEE game . . . He walked by the terminal room and saw Seymour working at one of the machines. Howie had an idea. He quietly edged over to one of the terminals and called up the COFFEE program. He then added the statement 215 GO TO 400 to the program and called to Seymour.

"Hey, Seymour, how about a quick game of COFFEE. The loser buys lunch. I'll even let you go first!" he called.

"You're on!" replied a confident Seymour.

TOPIC SUMMARY FOR SECTION 4.13

PRINT USING statement	MAT PRINT USING
IMAGE statement	TAB

Problems for Sec. 4.13

1. Write a program in BASIC that plays the following version of HANG-
   MAN. The first player walks up to the terminal and types in a 5-letter
   word and then tears off the output page. The second player then tries
   to guess the word by typing in one letter at a time. If a guess is correct,
   the computer prints the letter in its position in the word. The other positions are dashes. Use appropriate messages for the winner and loser,
   etc. A game is considered complete when *both* players have competed.
   The winner is the player with the fewest guesses.
2. Consider amending the program in Problem 1 to allow guessing the
   word at any time. Bonus points or penalty points may be assessed as
   warranted.
3. Try printing the following matrix with and without a PRINT USING
   statement.

$$\begin{bmatrix} 3. & 2.7 & 4. & .08 & .7 & 6.7 & 5.1 \\ .9 & 25.3 & .6 & .5 & .9 & 12.1 & 4.1 \\ 1.2 & 3. & .7 & .2 & 1.7 & .5 & .2 \end{bmatrix}$$

4.14 FILE PROCESSING IN BASIC

Prof. Ovitt had sent one of his graduate students, Mark Papers, to give a
review session on file processing in BASIC. When Mark arrived, there
wasn't a seat left in the room. The students had gotten about as much out
of Prof. Ovitt's lecture on files as the hippopotamus got out of its correspondence course on waltzing. Even Clara and Rudy were there.

"My name is Mark Papers," he began. "I just came from the area
that they have selected for the new optometry building and I tell you, it's
a site for sore eyes."

The room was silent.

Mark continued, "Today we are going to review *files* in BASIC.
Up to now when you have written computer programs, you have used
either an INPUT statement to obtain your data or a READ statement with
DATA statements to obtain it.

"There are a great many programs, however, that use a data file
already stored inside the computer. The file medium itself may be tape or
disk. Prof. Ovitt is planning to spend a good deal of time on file structures
later on in the course.

"Today we will discuss the commands that can be used in a BASIC
program to interact with data files.

"I'd like to emphasize one point before I begin. I have used several different BASIC computer systems and have found the language to be
relatively consistent from system to system. However, there are occasional
changes that have to be made in using data files. I'm sure that you will have
no trouble adapting to these changes, particularly now that you know that
they may exist.

"First, I'd like to write on the board an example of how we might get some data into a file that is to be stored in the computer for future reference." Mark spoke as he wrote. "This program will place data on five students into a file. For each student, there is a student code number (C), age (A), height in inches (H), weight (W), and sex (S), where a '1' represents a male and a '2' represents a female.

```
        OPEN-CLASS
10      FILES CLASS
20      FOR I = 1 TO 5
30      READ C,A,H,W,S
40      PRINT #1; C,A,H,W,S
50      NEXT I
90      DATA 113, 18, 67, 150, 2
91      DATA 182, 19, 73, 202, 1
92      DATA 365, 18, 70, 175, 1
93      DATA 987, 17, 71, 122, 2
94      DATA 011, 21, 58, 200, 1
95      END
```

"Hey, Mark," someone called, "you forgot to put a statement number on the first statement."

"I'd appreciate it if each of you would give your name when you ask a question. I'm afraid I don't know any of you," said Mark.

"Seymour Movies," the same voice responded.

"I don't see how that will help," replied a bewildered Mark. "Anyway, that first statement is not really part of the BASIC program. It is what we call a system command. You used some of these already when you signed on at the terminal. Remember LOGON?

"The OPEN command creates an empty file by reserving a predetermined number of locations in memory and naming this file CLASS (or whatever you place after the word OPEN).[1]

"Then, in the BASIC program itself, I have a FILES statement that lists all of the previously set up files that will be used by this program. Here, we will only be using one, so only one name (CLASS) appears in this statement. Each name in this list also has a number assigned to it. This number is its position in the list. Thus, CLASS is file #1, since I listed it first.

"To READ or PRINT on a file, we merely refer to the file number

[1]Some BASIC systems have an OPEN command as a statement of the language, e.g., 10 OPEN-CLASS. In these, and some other versions, a CLOSE statement should be used at the end of a program to properly close the files used.

in the appropriate input-output statement. Look at the program I have just put on the board. The FOR-NEXT loop reads the original data from DATA statements and then places them on the file. Note that no output gets printed at the terminal, the PRINT #1 statement records the data on the file. Once again, remember that other systems may use PUT #1 or even PUT to place data into a file.

"If we ran this program, when we were through the data would be stored in the computer. We could come back the next day or a week later and use this data in another program. Are there any questions thus far?

"Howard Hugh Applyit," began a student.

Before Howard could ask his question, Mark interrupted, "I'll show you. Let me erase this program and write another one on the board. This one will print a list of all students who weigh more than 150 pounds. To read a previously established file, I use a form of the READ statement; some other computer facilities may use the word GET instead."

```
10   FILES CLASS
20   FOR I = 1 TO 5
30   READ #1; C,A,H,W,S
40   IF W <= 150 THEN 60
50   PRINT C
60   NEXT I
70   END
```

"Does everyone understand the procedure now?" Mark asked.

"Hugh Dongettit," Hugh started, "and I . . ."

"I most certainly do!" Mark indignantly replied.

"No, that's my name," Hugh assured him. "And my question may be silly, but can you read one file, write on another, and print out data also?

"Sure you can," Mark responded. "Let's write a program that reads the CLASS file, separates all males, puts their information on a file named MALE, and puts all the data on female students on a file named FEMALE. Also, let's print out the student codes of the male students." Mark erased the board and began to write again.

"First you will have to 'open' the two new files that are needed."

OPEN-MALE
OPEN-FEMALE

"The program will be the following:"

```
10   FILES CLASS, MALE, FEMALE
20   FOR I = 1 TO 5
30   READ #1; A,B,C,D,E
40   IF E = 1 THEN 70
50   PRINT #3; A,B,C,D,E
60   GO TO 90
70   PRINT #2; A,B,C,D,E
80   PRINT A
90   NEXT I
95   END
```

"I see how that works," cried Howie. "You read the data file and, if it's a male, you put the data on the MALE file, print out the student ID, and continue. But I thought that the variable names were C, A, H, W, and S not A, B, C, D, and E!"

"The variable names are not stored on the file, just the numbers," replied Mark, "so you may use whatever names you wish."

"Ida Clair. Why are these file things so useful?" she asked.

"What is your name, please?" Mark queried.

"Ida Clair!" she said again. "That's my name!"

"Oh, sorry!" said an embarrassed Mark.

"Don't be sorry—I like it fine!" she said. "I'm glad it's my name because that's what everybody calls me."

"To answer your question," Mark began, "files of data can be used by a great variety of programs. They can be used as a data base to store a great deal of information for a decision maker. A program and a file constitute a kind of information system. Some of the questions that we could ask of our file are

1. How many male students are there?
2. Select all those students over 6 feet tall.
3. Print the students in ascending numerical order.
4. Find the student with code 112.
5. How many students are over 21?
6. Delete student 213 from the file.
7. Add student 118 to the list.

"You may begin to see that if this file were an employee payroll file, a warehouse inventory file, or a patient's medical history file, there are numerous questions that can be asked. Yet, since the file is stored in memory, we don't have to keep typing the data in DATA statements."

"Does a file stay in the computer forever?" asked Tyrone.

Mark decided not to ask his name. "There are two ways that the file may be deleted. The first way is under programmer control. You may use another SYSTEM command to delete an entire file. The command

PURGE-CLASS

would erase the file CLASS from the computer's memory.

"The second way is usually a computer center procedure. On a periodic basis, it is normal to purge data files. That is, erase them. Thus, a particular computer facility may, unless otherwise instructed, purge all files from memory on a monthly basis."

"Thank you," Tyrone replied.

"Let me finish up for today by asking if there are any other questions," Mark said.

"Are there any other statements used for processing files," asked Clara.

"Yes, but that point needs to be clarified," Mark answered. "Each system has its own set of commands, but generally you can do the following with special statements in BASIC:

1. READ directly a specific record from a specific file.
2. PRINT directly a specific record from a specific file.
3. Reset the file pointer to a particular record in a file.
4. Place an end-of-file mark at the end of the data.
5. INPUT the name of the file to be accessed while the program is executing.

"Say listen," Mark hastily began, "I'd like to continue but I have to get going or I'll be late for my work-study job."

As they were filing out of the classroom, Howie approached Mark and walked along with him.

"Where do you work?" Howie asked.

"In the behavioral sciences lab," Mark replied, "over in the biology building."

"Sounds interesting; what do you do?" Howie queried.

"We're doing work on the behavior of animals," Mark replied. "I guess you might say that I pull habits out of rats."

Mark hurried away.

"Boy," Seymour said, as they were leaving the room. "I'm sure glad I've fulfilled this course requirement."

"What do you mean, Seymour?" asked Howie. "This is an elective, not a required course!"

"But my advisor in the history department told me that to be a history major I was required to take the basic course!" explained Seymour.

"Say, buddy," Howie began, "I've got some good news and some bad news . . ."

TOPIC SUMMARY FOR SECTION 4.14

FILE PROCESSING	PRINT #
OPEN FILE	Adding to files
PUT #	Deleting from files
READ #	KILL

Problems for Sec. 4.14

1. A professional football team is preparing data on college players with professional potential. Prepare an alphanumeric data file to store the height, weight, speed, position, and name of each player.
   Input the following data to the file:

HEIGHT	WEIGHT	SPEED	POSITION	NAME
77	220	4.6	LB	Crunch
72	240	4.9	C	Strong
79	260	4.9	DE	Lookout
71	250	4.6	C	Starr
60	290	4.9	LB	Goode
80	210	5.1	DE	Beane
71	250	5.2	LB	Slow
75	260	4.9	LB	Masher

   plus your own data.

2. Write a program that will read the file created in Problem 1 and find all players at position LB that have speed less than 5.0 and weigh more than 237.

3. Write a program that creates a file with the following inventory data:

PART NUMBER	CURRENT INVENTORY	REORDER POINT
5	1000	900
12	3	2
1	47	40
17	18	15
2	126	300
19	1942	1000

   Each day the day's sales are input and subtracted from current inventory. Then the production of the day is added to current inventory.
      Write a program that updates the inventory with the following data:

PART	SALES	PART	PRODUCTION
12	1	5	100
1	30	1	10
17	10	17	3
19	200	2	19

4. Continue with Problem 3. The program should print out the part numbers of all parts whose current inventory is below the reorder point after the day's sales and production have been incorporated in the current inventory.
5. Continue with Problem 3. The new inventory manager would like to change the inventory numbers as follows:

OLD NUMBER	NEW NUMBER
1	1
2	2
5	3
12	4
17	5
19	6

Create a new file utilizing these new numbers and kill the old file.

chapter 5

How computers store and process information

While the knowledge of a high-level language such as FORTRAN or BASIC is sufficient to utilize a computer, this knowledge does not give detailed information about the method of computer operation. The purpose of this chapter is to explore the operations performed in the computer. This presentation is accomplished by examining the machine language used by a computer 'invented' by one of Howie's classmates, Tyrone. At the end of the chapter Tyrone relates his machine to commercially produced computers.

5.1 TYRONE'S COMPUTER

Tyrone Shoelaces was considered to be one of the university's brightest students. Not only did he maintain a straight A academic average, but he was an outstanding amateur inventor in his spare time. It was Tyrone who held the patents on that new dogfood that tasted like a mailman's leg. Very successful. His greatest accomplishment, however, and the one most often sought after, was his Homemade Instructional Computer Coordinating Users Programming Systems (HICCUPS). Of course, HICCUPS wasn't for sale commercially. It was an experiment that Tyrone kept in his barn.

Howie saw this as a golden opportunity. If he could understand how HICCUPS worked, it should be quite helpful in his computer course. After all, while you could give instructions to the machine in an "English-like" language, the machine certainly didn't understand English. Now, Tyrone's HICCUPS wasn't exactly like the university computer, yet there would certainly be many similarities. If he could work with HICCUPS, he would no doubt fly through the course. Howie left for 2 Binary Place, Tyrone's off-campus address.

When nobody answered the door, Howie wandered around back and saw some lights on in the barn. He looked closer and saw that the door was not a door; it was ajar. He let himself in.

"Hi there, Howie," Tyrone called. "Welcome to HICCUPS Haven."

"Wow, this is a swell place you have here . . . a huge barn and lots of land . . ."

"Yes, it's very nice, Howie. It's an old farm with all the trimmings," said Tyrone. "It used to belong to Farmer Inadel."

"Sorry to barge in on you like this," excused Howie. "But I had heard about your computer and thought I could really learn something by becoming familiar with it. Hope you don't mind?"

"Not at all, not at all! In fact, you're just in time for the tour and demonstration. The others are over here. C'mon and join us."

As they were walking down to the back of the barn, they passed a girl who was obviously leaving.

"I'll see ya tomorrow," he called.

"Okay," she answered.

"Who was that?" Howie asked.

"Althea Tamaro," said Tyrone.

"Okay, I'll be back then." Howie turned to leave.

"Where are you going?" asked Tyrone.

"But . . ."

"C'mon, let's go. It's getting late." Tyrone turned and headed down back.

Howie couldn't help but notice the entire wall was covered with wires and lights and switches extending far up into the hayloft.

Howie recognized two of the people waiting down back. There was Hugh Dongettit, who wasn't going to pass the computer course until next semester, and his gossipy classmate, Phyllis In.

It seemed that Tyrone had regularly scheduled classes and tours here. He apparently was extremely punctual for he had an assistant, Hugo Fligh, who kept a close watch on his watch. The next class was due to start at exactly 10:05 A.M.

"The time now is exactly 10 hours, 3 minutes, and 45 seconds," Fligh chanted.

"My, how Fligh times," thought Howie out loud.

5.2 COMPUTER MEMORY

Tyrone started explaining about his computer, "All computers have some fixed number of memory locations. These are places where numbers or data can be stored. We'll go upstairs in a minute and look at what HIC-CUPS uses, but let me just explain the concept of memory a bit further. Each memory location contains a fixed number of digit positions. In my computer, each memory location can hold five digits (0 through 9) and a sign, and I have 500 memory locations in my machine. Let's go up in the hayloft and take a look."

Memory location 001	Memory location 011
Memory location 002	Memory location 012
Memory location 003	Memory location 013
Memory location 004	Memory location 014
Memory location 005	Memory location 015
Memory location 006	Memory location 016
Memory location 007	Memory location 017
Memory location 008	Memory location 018
Memory location 009	Memory location 019
Memory location 010	Memory location 020

The group ascended the ladder that led to the hayloft. The memory section of the computer took up most of the attic. There were 500 rectangular boxes, each with six small windows. The boxes were numbered consecutively from 1 to 500.

"Each of these boxes is a memory location. The numbers that uniquely identify each memory location are called addresses. Here, we have addresses from 001 to 500. The sign (+ or −) and numbers showing in the six windows of a memory location or address are called the contents of that location or address. Often, the contents of a memory location are called a word. Does anyone have any questions?"

"Yes," Hugh responded. "Is there much of a difference between your machine and a real computer memory? You know, I mean a larger, commercial machine."

"In size, certainly," Tyrone answered. "And I don't mean physical size, since microminiature circuits have made modern computers relatively small. Rather, there are many more memory locations in a commercial machine, and they have a greater capacity. Here is a comparison." Tyrone pointed to a poster hanging on the far wall.

	COMPUTER MEMORY	
	HICCUPS	Typical commercial machines
Number of memory locations	500	4000 up to 1 million or more
Capacity of a memory location	5 decimal digits plus a sign	32 binary digits (a binary digit is a zero or a one)
Range of integer numbers that can be stored	−99999 to +99999	−2,147,483,648 to +2,147,483,648 (31 binary digits for a number and 1 binary digit for a sign)

TOPIC SUMMARY FOR SECTION 5.2

Memory locations
Addresses
Contents of memory location

5.3 THE ARITHMETIC UNIT

Tyrone continued with his explanation about his computer. "As you know, the purpose of the computer is to perform a task. Performing that task will involve two things: (1) the instructions that the computer should follow, and (2) the numbers or data that the instructions should operate on. For example, if you wanted to add the number 5 to the number 3, the instructions you would have to give the computer would be these:

1. Input the first number into a memory location.
2. Input the second number into a different memory location.
3. Add the numbers together.
4. Print the result.

The numbers or data you would have to give the computer would be 3 and 5."

"Can the numbers you input into your machine be put into any memory location?" asked Phyllis.

"Yes, all the memory locations are just the same," replied Tyrone.

"Wow!" said Phyllis. "You must have used an enormous amount of wire."

"Why?" asked Tyrone.

"You use electric current to add the numbers together, right?" asked Phyllis.

"Yes," replied Tyrone.

"Well, then to add two numbers, the memory locations that those numbers are in would have to be connected, and since there are 500 memory locations, for all of them to be connected to each other would require $500 \times 499/2$ or 124,750 connections," said Phyllis.

"That's good thinking, Phyllis," said the astonished Tyrone. "I started to do it that way but realized I'd never finish, so I made an extra memory location, called the *arithmetic unit*. This memory looks just like the other memory locations, but it's wired to do all the arithmetic operations: the addition, subtraction, multiplication, and division."

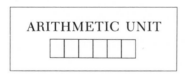

"I see," interjected, Phyllis. "The arithmetic unit is wired to all the other memory locations, only 500 wirings. Then when two numbers are to be added, one could be put into the arithmetic unit, and the other could be added to it in the arithmetic unit."

"Right," replied Tyrone, feeling that his day might not be as bad as he had feared.

5.4 INSTRUCTIONS FOR HICCUPS

While the group was walking back downstairs, Howie wandered over to the water cooler for a drink. The bottle on top of the cooler had a 500-gallon capacity.

"Wow, that's a healthy water supply," he commented.

"Yes, it's well water," Tyrone replied.

"How does HICCUPS know what to do, though?" asked Hugh.

"The computer is fed instructions that have been punched on cards, one instruction per card. The cards are read by this machine (the machine looked like a regular card reader) and loaded into consecutive memory locations. The instructions are written in a numerical code. For example, let's write a set of instructions to perform the work we have already talked about: input two numbers, add them together, and print the result. To input or read a number, I use instruction code 10, followed by three numbers which specify where the number should be input. The instruction +10123 would read a data card (that's the +10 part) into location 123 (that's the 123 part of the instruction)."

"Are there many instructions?" asked Howie.

"Here, I have a set of the machine language instructions you can look at. We'll talk about them shortly." (See page 277.)

"Take a few minutes to look these over, and then I'll answer any questions you might have," Tyrone concluded.

"How do you remember all these instructions?" asked Hugh.

"Well, there are only 13, so it isn't too hard. Even so, I tried to make it easier by putting the 'operation to be done' column in alphabetical order and using an ascending numerical order for the related operation codes."

"Getting back to our problem of adding two numbers," Tyrone continued, "first we have to read the first number into a memory location. We know the instruction could be +10123. We punch that on a card starting in column 12. Now we need to read another data card into a second location; let's use this: +10124. Execution of these two instructions will cause the computer to read a data card into location 123 and a data card into location 124. We know that to add two numbers together we must load one of the numbers into the arithmetic unit. How can we do that?"

"How about +07123?" asked Phyllis.

"Right. The +07 part tells the computer to load the arithmetic unit with the contents of location 123, which contains the value of the first card read. This instruction erases what used to be in the arithmetic unit before it loads the number from location 123 into the arithmetic unit. After the execution of this instruction the arithmetic unit and location 123 will have the same value in them, since this instruction does not erase the contents of location 123. Now we have to add to the arithmetic unit the contents of location 124. That can be accomplished by instruction +01124, which does not alter the contents of location 124; it just adds a copy of the contents to the arithmetic unit. Are you still with us, Hugh?"

"Yeah, of course I am, the water isn't sick," replied Hugh.

MACHINE LANGUAGE INSTRUCTIONS FOR HICCUPS

Operation to be done	Numerical operation code	How operation is performed
ADDITION	+01xyz	ADD WHAT IS IN LOCATION xyz TO THE ARITHMETIC UNIT.
BRANCH	+02xyz	GO TO LOCATION xyz FOR YOUR NEXT INSTRUCTION.
BRANCH ON NEGATIVE	+03xyz	GO TO LOCATION xyz FOR YOUR NEXT INSTRUCTION IF THE ARITHMETIC UNIT CONTAINS A NEGATIVE NUMBER.
BRANCH ON POSITIVE	+04xyz	GO TO LOCATION xyz FOR YOUR NEXT INSTRUCTION IF THE ARITHMETIC UNIT CONTAINS A POSITIVE NUMBER.
BRANCH ON ZERO	+05xyz	GO TO LOCATION xyz FOR YOUR NEXT INSTRUCTION IF THE ARITHMETIC UNIT CONTAINS A ZERO.
DIVISION	+06xyz	DIVIDE THE CONTENTS OF THE ARITH-METIC UNIT BY THE CONTENTS OF LOCATION xyz. DROP DECIMAL PART OF QUOTIENT.
LOADING	+07xyz	MOVE A NUMBER FROM LOCATION xyz INTO THE ARITHMETIC UNIT. LOCATION xyz REMAINS UNCHANGED.
MULTIPLICATION	+08xyz	MULTIPLY THE CONTENTS OF THE ARITHMETIC UNIT BY THE CONTENTS OF LOCATION xyz. RETAIN 5 MOST SIG-NIFICANT DIGITS.
PRINTING	+09xyz	PRINT OUT WHAT YOU FIND IN LOCATION xyz.
READING	+10xyz	READ A CARD FROM THE CARD READER AND STORE THE NUMBER ON IT IN LOCATION xyz.
STOP	+11000	STOP EXECUTING INSTRUCTIONS.
STORING	+12xyz	STORE WHAT IS IN THE ARITHMETIC UNIT INTO LOCATION xyz (PREVIOUS CONTENTS ARE ERASED).
SUBTRACTION	+13xyz	SUBTRACT THE CONTENTS OF LOCA-TION xyz FROM THE ARITHMETIC UNIT.

Tyrone decided that Howie and Phyllis were the only ones following him. "Let's forge ahead," said Tyrone.

"Oh, you do sculpturing here also?" asked Howie.

Tyrone decided that Phyllis was his best audience and turned to her to continue, "When we want to print the results, if they are in the arithmetic unit, they must be transferred to a regular memory location, then printed. The instructions to do this would be

$$+12125$$
$$+09125$$

Now we want the machine to stop, so we use the instruction $+11000$. Let's write all of our instructions on this chalkboard." (Tyrone wrote on the board.)

$$+10123$$
$$+10124$$
$$+07123$$
$$+01124$$
$$+12125$$
$$+09125$$
$$+11000$$

"How do those instructions get into the computer?" asked Howie.

"We put a card that says LOAD on it in front of our instruction deck, and we put location numbers on the cards in columns 1 to 3. After the card reader reads the cards, it loads the instructions into the memory locations written in columns 1 to 3. The cards for our instructions might look like this:

```
LOAD
200   +10123
201   +10124
202   +07123
203   +01124
204   +12125
205   +09125
206   +11000
```

Now the computer will load the instructions into locations 200 to 206."

"What about actually getting the numbers we want to add and the answer?" asked Hugh, trying to get involved.

"We need just a couple more cards," said Tyrone, "an *execute card* to tell the computer which memory location to start execution at, some data cards, and a card to tell the computer that it has reached the end of the cards for this job. The program, completed, looks like this."

```
LOAD
200   +10123
201   +10124
202   +07123
203   +01124
204   +12125
205   +09125
206   +11000
EXECUTE 200
+00005
+00003
ENDJOB
```

"I think I understand," said Howie. "But could you go through the program one more time?"

"Okay, Howie," said Tyrone. "We'll take it card by card. The LOAD card tells HICCUPS that a program is to be loaded into memory locations. The instructions are therefore loaded into memory locations 200 through 206. The EXECUTE 200 card tells the computer that execution of the instructions should start at location 200."

"What about the next two cards?" asked Howie.

"Those are data cards. They are read while the program is being loaded; the values on those cards are saved in the computer (or in larger computers in an *input buffer*) until the computer executes a READ statement (like the +10123 instruction). Then the values on those cards are called up sequentially, a new value being called up every time a READ statement is executed. The ENDJOB card tells HICCUPS to stop the card reader, that all the cards for this job have been read."

"I understand that at this point all the cards have been read by the card reader and are loaded into memory locations. Is that correct?" asked Phyllis.

"Yes," responded Tyrone. "Now HICCUPS is ready to execute the program, so it goes to memory location 200 for an instruction. The instruction is +10123 which, as you know, reads the first piece of data into location 123. Thus memory location 123 looks like this after that instruction.

```
MEMORY LOCATION 123
+ 0 0 0 0 5
```

"The next instruction to be executed is the instruction at location

201. The computer keeps executing instructions sequentially, one memory location after another, until it executes a +11000 instruction, when it stops."

"What if we had forgotten to put an instruction in location 201?" asked Howie.

"Then the computer would have gone to 201 anyway and used whatever was left there from the last program it ran. Since this probably would not be very relevant to our program, we would probably start getting out garbage, or errors, or something."

"Oh," replied Howie.

"Let's continue; we're almost finished," said Tyrone. "In executing instruction +10124 from location 201, the computer puts the next piece of data, +00003, in location 124. The instruction at 202 causes the value from location 123, that value being +00005, to be put in the arithmetic unit. Then the instruction at 203 adds the value at 124 to the value in the arithmetic unit. Before the instruction at 203 (+01124) is executed, we have these memory locations looking like this:

MEMORY LOCATION 124	ARITHMETIC UNIT
+ 0 0 0 0 3	+ 0 0 0 0 5

After +01124 is executed, the memory locations look like this:

MEMORY LOCATION 124	ARITHMETIC UNIT
+ 0 0 0 0 3	+ 0 0 0 0 8

The execution of instruction +12125 copies the contents of the arithmetic unit, +00008, into location 125 (leaving the arithmetic unit at +00008 also). The +09125 tells the line printer, over here (Tyrone pointed to line printer), to print the contents of memory location 125. This is done because the computer can't print directly from the arithmetic unit. Finally the instruction in location 206 is executed. Since it is +11000, HICCUPS stops and rests. Any questions?" asked Tyrone.

"Nope, Tyrone, that was clear as the sun during a solar eclipse!" joked Howie.

"How about if you write a program to add your last three test grades, Howie?" suggested Tyrone.

"UH . . . , well . . . , I could add them on my fingers . . . ," stammered Howie.

"Give it a try," prodded Hugh.

"Okay, where do I want the first instruction to be located?" asked Howie.

"Anywhere you like," answered Tyrone. "You just load the instructions where you like; the execute card will tell HICCUPS where they are."

"How's this?" ventured Howie, as he wrote on the board.

LOAD
100   +10300
101   +10301
102   +10302
103   +07300
104   +01301
105   +01302
106   +12400
107   +09400
108   +11000
EXECUTE 100
+00002
−00064
+00037
ENDJOB

"That's great, Howie," responded Tyrone. "Notice that the same program could be used, with different data cards, to add Phyllis' grades." At this point Tyrone noticed his audience getting a little restless, so he said, "Maybe we should take a short break."

TOPIC SUMMARY FOR SECTION 5.4

Instructions	ENDJOB
Loading into memory	READ instruction
Machine language	ADDITION instruction
Operation code OPCODE	STORING instruction
Operand	STOP instruction
Execute card	PRINTING instruction

CROSSWORD PUZZLE

Across

1. Ophelia Pulse is studying to be an _____ .
2. Are you incompetent?
4. Opcode 00.
6. To start the HICCUPS machine you must turn it _____ .
7. Either (a) the meaning of operation code 12 or (b) where you buy stuff.
10. An article.
11. If you can't get this one, just use 3 Down.
15. How you put sand in a dumptruck or instructions into HICCUPS.
16. The grade you expect to get in your computer course.
17. The grade you will get in your computer course.

Down

1. The operation code 10 is for _____ .
2. Do you want to bet on 2 Across?
3. The last part of a machine language instruction in HICCUPS.
4. When you get behind in your programs, send an _____ .
5. A holiday gift for your computer instructor.
8. Where the ENDJOB card goes.
9. A HICCUPS command is an _____ code.
12. An elevated train.
13. Ro frontwards or backwards.
14. The organization that N. E. Briates should join.

Problems for Sec. 5.4

1. What is the difference between the address of a memory location and the contents of the location?
2. What is the purpose of the arithmetic unit?

3. Which of the following numbers can be stored as integers in a memory location in HICCUPS?
   (a) .05
   (b) 8721
   (c) −8721
   (d) 111,291
   (e) 1/2
   (f) $3 * 10^7$
4. If memory location 219 contained +10379, would that be an instruction or data?
5. Write a program for HICCUPS that will read in four values from four data cards, add them, add 100 to the total, and print the results.
6. Write a program for HICCUPS that prints the values of the first six powers of 2.
7. When is it better to read the data into memory locations rather than to load it?
8. Draw a flowchart for calculating the median of a set of 15 numbers.
9. What do you think would happen if you added two numbers together (in HICCUPS) and got a 6-digit number?

5.5 BRANCH INSTRUCTIONS

During the break, Howie was talking to Hugh about the farm and barn. Howie turned to Tyrone, "I wonder why a farmer would want to sell this place. What's the farmer doing now?"

"He went into business making synthetic hay. In fact, that's what I have scattered around here for atmosphere. He's not doing so well, though, and his oldest boy is trying to help out by shining shoes at the cobbler shop."

"That farmer's got a good philosophy," Howie said, "make hay while the son shines."

Tyrone ignored that last remark and started again, "Let's talk about making decisions in the computer. The capability of making decisions is a very desirable characteristic to have in a program. I have a set of BRANCH instructions available for the HICCUPS computer that gives it this capability. As you may recall, program instructions are executed by the computer consecutively, one after the other, in order. The only way to change this sequence is by using a BRANCH instruction. Now, every instruction has its own memory location, its own address. We simply use the BRANCH instruction to inform the computer that it should not continue with the very next instruction but go to another address for a command and then continue consecutively from the new address. Look at the following as an example. Assume that this program was loaded into memory beginning at location 100.

ADDRESS	INSTRUCTION
100	+10300
101	+10301
102	+10302
103	+07300
104	+01301
105	+01302
106	+12400
107	+09400
108	+02100
109	+11000

"I have added a statement. It is the second one from the end in memory location 108. The instruction is +02100 or BRANCH directly to location 100 for your next instruction. What does this addition do for us?" Tyrone asked.

Hugh was first to respond. "Well, after you calculate and print the sum of somebody's three exams, you go back to the beginning of the program and do it all over again. It looks like you could get the sum of my grades, Howie's, and Phyllis', and I guess everybody's because you never ever get to that STOP instruction in location 109."

"That's right," said Tyrone. "And because of that problem, this is only an illustration, not a whole program anymore. You should also note that every time the program starts over again, there must be three more data cards. If not, the program could not continue and an error message would be printed."

"Let's make the program complete. Suppose that we only want to do this for the three of you. It is here that we can find the other BRANCH statements on that page I gave you quite useful. There are a couple of ways we can detect when we are through and have the program transfer control to that STOP statement. Let's look at the first way. We could add a data card with a negative grade on it as the last data card. Then we could put an instruction into the program that would detect any negative grades. If a negative grade is detected, the program would BRANCH to a memory location with +11000 and stop. The program would look like this:

LOAD	
100	+10300
101	+07300
102	+03110
103	+10301
104	+10302
105	+01301
106	+01302

```
107   +12400
108   +09400
109   +02100
110   +11000
EXECUTE 100
+00004  ⎫
+00002  ⎬  Hugh's grades
+00001  ⎭
+00002  ⎫
+00064  ⎬  Howie's grades
+00037  ⎭
+00072  ⎫
+00084  ⎬  Phyllis' grades
+00091  ⎭
−00001      The last card indicator
ENDJOB
```

"The program reads one card, loads it into the arithmetic unit, then branches to a STOP instruction if that card is negative. If the card isn't negative, the computer reads two more cards and adds them to the first value, which is already in the arithmetic unit. It proceeds in memory location order until it executes the instruction at location 109, at which time it branches back to 100 and proceeds again from there."

"Say, that's pretty neat," responded Howie. "You said there were more ways to do this?"

"Yes," replied Tyrone. "Another way would be to build a *counter* into the computer program."

"Sounds good to me," said Hugh. "Let's do that. Then we will sit down at it and have some lunch. I'm starved."

"Not that kind of counter, Hugh," stated Tyrone. "We'll reserve a memory location, say location 200, in the computer to keep a count of the number of times we have read three grades; that will be the counter. Each time we read three grades, we will add one to the counter. When the counter has the value 3, we will BRANCH to the STOP instruction."

"But we don't have a BRANCH statement that says BRANCH on a 3!" exclaimed Howie.

"You are correct, Howie," replied Tyrone, "but you'll see that we can make the test with the BRANCH statements we have. Look at the following set of instructions. Remember that location 200 has our counter and suppose HICCUPS has a +00003 in location 090 and +11000 in location 114.

+07200   Load the current value of the counter into the arithmetic unit.

+13090   Subtract +00003 from the value in the arithmetic unit.

+05114   If the result in the arithmetic unit contains +00000, jump to location 114, which will end the execution.

"I see," said Phyllis. "If the answer in the arithmetic unit is zero after +13090 is executed, we must have read the grades for three people."

"Wait a minute, how did you get that 3 into location 090? You didn't READ it in," asked Hugh.

Tyrone was anticipating the question. "Of course, we could have READ +00003 into location 090. However, there is another way to enter data into memory—during the LOAD phase. If one of the cards we have in our deck is 090 +00003, it would be loaded into memory just as the instructions were. We must take care not to have this card in the execution sequence, since +00003 is not a legitimate instruction. We also need a number +00001 somewhere to add to our counter (let's use location 097), and we should start our counter at zero (no people yet processed). Our program would look like the following:

Program	Comments
LOAD	
090 +00003	Our test value, 3
097 00001	The increment of 1
100 10300	
101 10301	
102 10302	
103 07300	The main program
104 01301	(adding up a person's grades and printing the result)
105 01302	
106 12400	
107 09400	
108 07200	LOAD the counter
109 01097	ADD 1 to it
110 12200	STORE it
111 13090	SUBTRACT 3 to see if three people have been processed.
112 05114	If the answer is zero, three people have been processed so BRANCH to the STOP instruction, *otherwise continue on.*
113 02100	BRANCH to get next person's grades.
114 11000	STOP processing
200 00000	The counter with a starting value of zero
EXECUTE 100	The first instruction is in location 100.
	Data cards
ENDJOB	

"You all see that the instructions of the program are all together in consecutive locations, but the constants (e.g., the number 3, the number 1) can be anywhere in memory. We, the programmers, control where."

"Perhaps the best way to become familiar with these concepts is by taking a look at some examples I have mimeographed."

"Since it is so close to lunchtime, why don't you all take those sheets with you and come on back at 1:30 or so. I'll see you then."

The group of three decided to look over Tyrone's handouts first, and then have lunch. They left for Hugh's apartment.

Problems for Sec. 5.5

1. Write a program, using the BRANCH instruction, that prints the first six powers of 2. Compare this program to the program for Problem 6, Section 5.4.
2. Write a program that interchanges the values in memory locations 300 and 275.
3. Write a program that reads five numbers and prints the largest number.
4. Write a program that reads 2000 cards, each containing an integer between 1 and 5, and prints the number of cards with each number.

5.6 WORKING OUT SOME EXAMPLES

Fortunately, Hugh's apartment was directly over a butcher shop so that after they had a chance to look over Tyrone's mimeographed sheets, they could go down for a quick bite to eat before returning for the continuation of the tour. When they arrived at the door, there was a package for Hugh sitting on the doorstep.

"It's from my Mom," Hugh said as he picked up the package. They all went inside, and Phyllis and Howie sat down while Hugh opened his piece of mail. After unwrapping the package, he reached in and withdrew three light blue, handmade socks. He opened a note attached to them and read aloud.

"Dear son. I hope you enjoy the socks I knitted for you. I thought that you would need them, especially after you mentioned in your last letter that since you've been away you've grown another foot. Take care of yourself. Love, Mom."

"Say, can we get to work?" asked Howie. "We've only got an hour for lunch."

"Sure," replied Hugh. "And why don't you go through the first example, Howie." Phyllis agreed. Howie looked at the first page. There was nothing but a program on it and the question "what is the main learning point of this program?" Howie spent a few minutes working it out. The program was pictured as follows:

```
                    LOAD
                    003   +00009
                    004   +00004
                    005   +04000
                    006   +07003
                    007   +01004
                    008   +01005
                    009   +12005
                    010   +12011
                    011   +09005
                    012   +09004
                    013   +09003
                    014   +11000
                    EXECUTE 006
                    ENDJOB
```

"Okay," started Howie, "I'll go through this program one line at a time and explain what is happening. After the loading is completed, we have put the following numbers into memory.

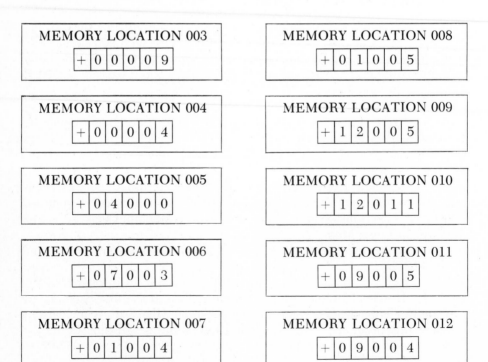

MEMORY LOCATION 003	MEMORY LOCATION 008
+ 0 0 0 0 9	+ 0 1 0 0 5

MEMORY LOCATION 004	MEMORY LOCATION 009
+ 0 0 0 0 4	+ 1 2 0 0 5

MEMORY LOCATION 005	MEMORY LOCATION 010
+ 0 4 0 0 0	+ 1 2 0 1 1

MEMORY LOCATION 006	MEMORY LOCATION 011
+ 0 7 0 0 3	+ 0 9 0 0 5

MEMORY LOCATION 007	MEMORY LOCATION 012
+ 0 1 0 0 4	+ 0 9 0 0 4

MEMORY LOCATION 013	MEMORY LOCATION 014
+ 0 9 0 0 3	+ 1 1 0 0 0

"Next, the EXECUTE card indicates that the first instruction will be found in location 006. Thus, we begin with

INSTRUCTION LOCATION	INSTRUCTION	WHAT HAPPENS	RESULT
006	+07003	Load the arithmetic unit with the contents of location 003	ARITHMETIC UNIT + 0 0 0 0 9
007	+01004	Add to the arithmetic unit the contents of location 004	ARITHMETIC UNIT + 0 0 0 1 3
008	+01005	Add to the arithmetic unit the contents of location 005	ARITHMETIC UNIT + 0 4 0 1 3
009	+12005	Store a copy of the contents of the arithmetic unit in location 005	MEMORY LOCATION 005 + 0 4 0 1 3
010	+12011	Store a copy of the contents of the arithmetic unit in location 011	MEMORY LOCATION 011 + 0 4 0 1 3

"Oops! I think we may have a problem," Howie exclaimed. "I can see from looking at the program that we are supposed to execute all the instructions between 006 (where we started) and 014 (where I see the STOP command). Location 011 is within this range. I haven't executed the instruction at 011 yet, and this last command (+12011) tells me to store something new there. Should I do it?"

Phyllis felt confident. "Sure, why not. It is only a machine. It does what it is told. If you follow your last instruction, you will store a +04013 into location 011. Whatever was there before (in this case, a PRINT instruction) is erased. Go ahead, continue, Howie! What instruction gets executed next?"

"Well," Howie said, "oddly enough, the next instruction to be performed is the one just changed, the one at location 011.

011	+04013	Branch to location 013 for your next instruction if the contents of the arithmetic unit are positive	It is positive, so the next instruction is the one at 013
013	+09003	Print out the contents of location 003	A +00009 is printed
014	+11000	Stop executing instructions	That's all, folks!

"Well, it's my guess that this example was given to show that in execution the program could modify its own instructions," commented Howie.

"Yes, I agree," Hugh chimed in. "It was also a pretty good illustration of performing instructions in sequence unless otherwise directed. Hey, can I do this next one?"

"Sure, go right ahead," Howie replied.

"It's okay with me," Phyllis agreed.

"Does everyone have a copy?" asked Hugh.

"The question is, which of these programs will execute properly?

(1)	(2)
LOAD	LOAD
100 +10400	106 +00002
101 +07400	105 +11000
102 +06106	104 +09400
103 +12400	103 +12400
104 +09400	102 +06106
105 +11000	101 +07400
106 +00002	100 +10400
EXECUTE 100	EXECUTE 100
+50000	+50000
ENDJOB	ENDJOB

(3)	(4)
LOAD	LOAD
100 +10400	100 +10400
101 +07400	105 +11000
102 +06106	103 +12400
103 +12400	101 +07400
104 +09400	104 +09400
105 +11000	102 +06106
106 +00002	106 +00002
EXECUTE 105	EXECUTE 100
+50000	+50000
ENDJOB	ENDJOB

They all have the same instructions so if they worked, they would all perform the same task. Any ideas?"

"Well, number 2 will never work," cried Howie, "the dumb cards are backwards . . . and look at number 4. Someone must have dropped that set. Yea, number 2 and number 4 won't . . ."

"Wait, Howie," Phyllis interrupted. "You forgot that before the instructions are executed in order, they are loaded into memory. Once loaded into memory, the EXECUTE card signifies the starting point and then they are done in order. Therefore, what difference does it make what order the cards are in as long as the instructions are in the proper sequence in memory when the program is to be executed? I think they all work."

"Well, I agree; they all work," Hugh commented. "I mean they all would be executed without any errors. However, I don't think they all will do the same task. Phyllis, look carefully at number 3. Note that the execute card says to begin execution at location 105. When the computer begins there, it executes the instruction +11000 and stops executing. The program works, but it does nothing. There's only one more; why don't you try it, Phyllis?"

"Okay," she began, "but I hope this isn't the hardest one. Let's see, it says to write a HICCUPS machine language program to print out the first 10 powers of the number 2. Excuse me for a few seconds, guys, while I work on this problem. First I will write out what needs to be done and then draw a flowchart.

1. Put the number 2 into some memory location, say, location 300.
2. Set up a counter in some memory location (say, 305) to keep track of how many powers of 2 we have printed. Set this counter equal to zero to begin with.
3. Put a constant, number 1, into a memory location (try 400) to be used to increment your counter each time you print a power of 2.
4. Reserve a space for my answer (let's use location 500). Start it out with a one (my first answer is 2 times 1).
5. Put a 15 into a memory location (location 200) as a reminder of how many powers of 2 we want to print.
6. Now write the commands for performing the mathematics requested.
   (a) Do the arithmetic.
      • Load my last answer into the arithmetic unit.
      • Multiply the contents of the arithmetic unit by 2.
      • Store this result in the answer location.
      • Print out the contents of the answer location.
   (b) Test to see if 15 powers have been printed.
      • Load the arithmetic unit with the contents of the counter.
      • Add 1 to the contents of the arithmetic unit.
      • Store the updated contents of the arithmetic unit in the counter location.
      • Subtract 15 from the contents of the arithmetic unit.
      • If the arithmetic unit contains a zero, branch to a stop command, otherwise continue.
      • Repeat the process again, beginning with the arithmetic step above.

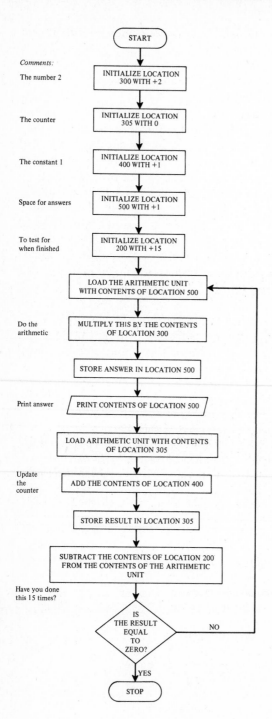

Comments:

The number 2 — INITIALIZE LOCATION 300 WITH +2

The counter — INITIALIZE LOCATION 305 WITH 0

The constant 1 — INITIALIZE LOCATION 400 WITH +1

Space for answers — INITIALIZE LOCATION 500 WITH +1

To test for when finished — INITIALIZE LOCATION 200 WITH +15

LOAD THE ARITHMETIC UNIT WITH CONTENTS OF LOCATION 500

Do the arithmetic — MULTIPLY THIS BY THE CONTENTS OF LOCATION 300

STORE ANSWER IN LOCATION 500

Print answer — PRINT CONTENTS OF LOCATION 500

LOAD ARITHMETIC UNIT WITH CONTENTS OF LOCATION 305

Update the counter — ADD THE CONTENTS OF LOCATION 400

STORE RESULT IN LOCATION 305

SUBTRACT THE CONTENTS OF LOCATION 200 FROM THE CONTENTS OF THE ARITHMETIC UNIT

Have you done this 15 times? — IS THE RESULT EQUAL TO ZERO? — NO / YES

START / STOP

"Phew," she sighed, "now I'm ready to write the flowchart." She took a large piece of paper and began to draw a flowchart by constantly referring to her handwritten notes above.

She held up her copy of the flowchart and began to write the program on another sheet of paper.

"C'mon over here," she directed, "and watch how I can code the program directly from the flowchart." As Howie and Hugh watched over her shoulder, Phyllis wrote.

```
        LOAD
        300   +00002
        305   +00000
        400   +00001
        500   +00001
        200   +00015
        100   +07500
        101   +08300
        102   +12500
        103   +09500
        104   +07305
        105   +01400
        106   +12305
        107   +13200
        108   +05110
        109   +02100
        110   +11000
        EXECUTE 100
        ENDJOB
```

"Hey," exclaimed Howie, "that was real neat. If you write each box on the flowchart carefully, then coding it into the HICCUPS machine language isn't all that bad. I'll have to remember that."

Hugh began to put his coat on. "We'd better hurry if we want to get lunch before getting back to Tyrone's. Let's go on downstairs," he said.

Problems for Sec. 5.6

1. Write a HICCUPS program that prints the odd integers between 1 and 20.

2. What does the following HICCUPS machine language program print?

```
200   +07210
201   +04205
202   +02206
203   +12210
204   +02214
205   +11000
206   +01211
207   +05205
208   +03206
209   +02203
210   −00007
211   +00002
212   +35000
213   +02000
214   +09211
215   +11000
EXECUTE 200
```

3. Draw a flowchart for calculating the median of 15 numbers.
4. Write a program in HICCUPS that will READ 10 data cards and print out how many negative numbers were found and also the sum of the positive numbers.

5.7 ASSEMBLY LANGUAGE

When Howie, Hugh, and Phyllis returned to Tyrone's barn, Tyrone responded, "You're a little late, what happened?"

"Well," said Howie, "there was a lot of excitement in the deli while we had lunch. The owner was reaching into the freezer for some sandwich meat and a large piece of ice sliced a deep cut into his arm. They called a doctor, but the poor guy died before the doctor arrived."

"What did the doctor say when he did arrive?" asked Tyrone.

"The doctor said the deli owner died from cold cuts," answered Howie.

"Such baloney," muttered Tyrone, eager to get started with the computer tour again. "This morning, we spoke primarily about the machine language for HICCUPS. You recall the set of numerical commands that were instructions for the machine. After I had worked with those numerical commands for a few months, I saw some ways I might change the commands. I decided that it would be easier to remember commands and easier for my assistants if commands were written with letters instead of numbers. Also, I found that if I wrote a long program and later wanted to add even one statement in the middle, I would have to change many statements because the locations that the later statements of the program were loaded into were all shifted one memory location. Thus, many statements like +08300 might have to be changed to something like +08301, because of the extra statement added somewhere, say in location 286. Clearly, this was a very tedious task. I decided that I could resolve both of these difficulties by using alphabetic instruction codes and by not requiring that instructions be loaded into specific memory locations. Let me explain in more detail what I mean. Take a look at this chart, which compares the old numeric instruction codes with the new alphabetic equivalents.

MACHINE LANGUAGE AND ASSEMBLY LANGUAGE OPERATION CODES

OPERATION TO BE DONE	NUMERICAL OPERATION CODE	ALPHABETIC OPERATION CODE
ADDITION	+01	A
BRANCH	+02	B
BRANCH ON NEGATIVE	+03	BN
BRANCH ON POSITIVE	+04	BP
BRANCH ON ZERO	+05	BZ
DIVISION	+06	D
LOADING	+07	L
MULTIPLICATION	+08	M
PRINTING	+09	P
READING	+10	R
STOP	+11	STP
STORING	+12	ST
SUBTRACTION	+13	S

"I am sure you see that it will be a little easier to use these new codes in place of the numbers."

"Those numbers didn't give me as much trouble as keeping track of the various memory locations," commented Howie.

"Yes, that's the other problem I was referring to," Tyrone replied. "From now on, instead of using the actual address numbers (like location 301 for example) you may use names that you make up. We'll let the computer assign these names as addresses in memory."

"I am afraid I don't quite follow you," said Phyllis. "Could you show us a sample program?"

"Sure," responded Tyrone. "I have here a program written in machine language and also using the alphabetic codes. You've seen it before; it is the problem we discussed this morning—the one that added up three exam grades. Here are the programs."

Machine language program		Assembly language program		
LOAD		ASSEMBLE		
100	+10300	BEGIN	R	GRADE1
101	+10301		R	GRADE2
102	+10302		R	GRADE3
103	+07300		L	GRADE1
104	+01301		A	GRADE2
105	+01302		A	GRADE3
106	+12400		ST	ANSWER
107	+09400		P	ANSWER
108	+11000		STP	
EXECUTE 100		GRADE1		
+00002		GRADE2		
+00064		GRADE3		
+00037		ANSWER		
ENDJOB		EXECUTE BEGIN		
		+00002		
		+00064		
		+00037		
		ENDJOB		

"It does look easier to understand," Hugh commented, "but there are some new words we haven't seen before. Will you explain them later?"

"Yes, of course," Tyrone replied, "but first, can you tell me what you notice about this new program?"

Phyllis started first. "Well, for one thing, there are no memory location numbers (addresses) specified for each instruction."

"That is correct, Phyllis," Tyrone continued, "since now the machine will be placing the program into memory rather than you, the programmer. Anything else?"

"Instead of having numbers immediately following the operation code, we have words. The words seem to be chosen carefully as representative of what the problem was trying to do," mentioned Howie.

"Very good observation, Howie," Tyrone said. "One can choose any names he wants for address labels, but it is clearly helpful to use names that relate to the problem being solved. Let me now explain a few concepts. We call this new language ASSEMBLY language. This is because the program of alphabetic codes has to be *assembled* into machine language (that is, the computer must translate the alphabetic codes into numeric ones). The computer does this in a rather interesting way. There is a program stored inside the machine that does the translating—that is, it changes an A (for addition) to an 01 (its numeric code). The procedure adopted by the machine is to put the contents of the first card of your program into location 000 and simply enter all succeeding instructions into successive memory locations.

"Now, let us look at our two sample programs as containing three 'columns' of information. In the machine language version, the first 'column' contains the memory location for the instruction; the second 'column' contains the operation code; and the third 'column' contains an address in memory. For example, the first column has the address 100 in it; the second column has the operation code +10; and the third column has a memory location to be used, location 300.

"The assembly language program has three similar columns. The first column is again used for the memory location of the instruction. However, we only use this column if we are going to refer to a specific location in the logic of our program. Thus, you see the BEGIN is used as a label (or address) in the program. We do refer to this, as you see, on the EXECUTE card in the program. This is essentially saying go to the memory location with the address BEGIN to find your first instruction. The second column contains the alphabetic equivalent of the two-digit operation code; the third column contains an address in memory but by name rather than by number."

"How does the program get translated?" asked Hugh.

"Well," Tyrone continued, "it is done by a process known as two-pass assembly. The first time the machine starts assembling, it assembles the left-hand column into successive memory locations beginning at location 000. In this case, we would have

```
        ASSEMBLE
        001   R     GRADE1
        002   R     GRADE2
        003   R     GRADE3
        004   L     GRADE1
        005   A     GRADE2
        006   A     GRADE3
        007   ST    ANSWER
        008   P     ANSWER
        009   STP
        010
```

```
011
012
013
EXECUTE 001
+00002
+00064
+00037
ENDJOB
```

"After this first pass is completed, note that any 'words' that appeared in the first column now have a number as well as a name. For example, the label 'BEGIN' is now associated with the location 001, the label 'GRADE1' is associated with the location 010, etc.

"The second pass during the assembly process translates the operation codes of the second column and the memory locations referred to in the third column. Note that all of the names (addresses) referred to in this third column can be easily given a number since they all were given numbers during the first pass. Remember, 'BEGIN' was given the number 001, and 'GRADE1' was given the number 010. The program would now look like this.

```
        ASSEMBLE
001    +10010
002    +10011
003    +10012
004    +07010
005    +01011
006    +01012
007    +12013
008    +09013
009    +11000
010
011
012
013
EXECUTE 001
+00002
+00064
+00037
ENDJOB
```

"I have three questions," cried Howie. "First, am I correct in assuming that in an assembly language program, every name that is referenced (in that third column) must appear in the first column?"

"Yes, Howie, that is correct," Tyrone replied. "It is the only way that actual numbers can be assigned to these labels, thus tying the labels to a unique memory location."

"Second," Howie continued, "if I didn't want the program to be loaded into the machine starting at memory location 001, could I have said something like ASSEMBLE 200 and have the program loaded into the computer beginning at memory location 200?"

"Right again, Howie, you are two for two," said Tyrone.

"Third," said Howie, "how do you get a constant, say 3, in a location?"

"Good question, Howie," answered Tyrone. "You could read the number into the location. Or, you could use the operation code called SET to LOAD a number in a location. For example, the card

THRE SET +00003

when loaded would put the number +00003 in the location named THRE. There is no need for an equivalent operation code in machine language because the numbers are always loaded into specific locations anyway."

"Okay, Tyrone," Howie continued, "I understand that your machine, HICCUPS, can be given instructions in either machine language (numerical codes) or assembly language. But now I'm a little curious about larger machines. You know, like the one at school. How does HICCUPS compare with it?"

"That's a good question, Howie," replied Tyrone. "Of course there are differences. For one thing, the set of commands in the instruction set is much greater in the university's computer. There are instructions for doing arithmetic with numbers having decimals as well as special commands for performing loops. All in all there are many times as many instruction codes."

"That goes for assembly language too, right?" asked Hugh.

"That's right," continued Tyrone. "But if we are going to talk about the larger machines, we should talk about the languages most people use when they program these machines. These languages have been set up so that people can write instructions with words (like READ) and symbols (like +) similar to the words and symbols with which they are already familiar. Also, more than one computer operation can be written in each statement (like A = B + C + D). These advanced programming languages are called *higher-level languages*."

Howie interrupted. "I remember from the tour I took of the computer center at the beginning of the term that there were many of these

higher-level languages. I think I have a few of them written down somewhere here." Howie pulled out one of his notebook pages. It read:

LANGUAGE		PRIMARY USE
COBOL	COmmon Business Oriented Language	Business data processing
FORTRAN	FORmula TRANslation	Scientific applications and business applications
BASIC	Beginner's All-purpose Symbolic Instruction Code	Communicating with the machine via teletype rather than cards
PL/1	Programming Language 1	Combining many good features of FORTRAN and COBOL
APL	A Programming Language	A new problem-oriented language

"Can the larger machines use all of these languages?" asked
Howie.

"Most of them can, Howie," replied Tyrone. "You see, just as my
machine has a translator to convert HICCUPS assembly language into
machine language, every one of those languages has associated with it a
translator to convert it into machine language. It is essentially a computer
program stored within the computer. They call it a *compiler*. Therefore,
there is a COBOL compiler, a FORTRAN compiler, and so forth. A particular computer installation may have one or several of these compilers,
depending upon the type of machine it has, its size, and the like."

"What about machine language in the computer at school? Is it
just like the machine language for HICCUPS?" asked Phyllis.

"No, Phyllis. It is similar but with some important differences. I
don't want to go into all that, though, unless you're really interested."

"I'd sure like to hear about it," exclaimed Howie, "I'm kind of
curious about how our university computer really works."

"Well, I'll be happy to discuss some of the concepts," said Tyrone.
"We really ought to start with how our numbers and letters are actually
represented inside the machine."

TOPIC SUMMARY FOR SECTION 5.7

Assembly language	COBOL
Translation	FORTRAN
Two-pass assembly	BASIC
High-level languages	PL/1
	APL

Problems for Sec. 5.7

1. Write a program in assembly language that reads 2000 cards and prints the average.
2. Write a program in assembly language that reads 10 numbers and prints the largest number.
3. Use assembly language to do Problem 4 of Section 5.6.
4. Using only SET instructions, calculate the sum of the numbers 7, 21, and 432.
5. Write an assembly language program that will read data cards and print the numbers that have been read and are evenly divisible by 5.
6. Write an assembly language program in HICCUPS that will print out the sum of the numbers from 1 to N. N will be read from a data card.
7. Translate any three HICCUPS machine language programs that you have written into HICCUPS assembly language programs.
8. If you have already studied BASIC or FORTRAN, write a program in that language that will READ, as data, a HICCUPS assembly language program and print out the machine language translation.
9. Continuing with Problem 8. Have your program execute the machine language program.

5.8 NUMBER SYSTEMS

"If we are going to talk about the method of operation of commercially produced computers, let me talk about the number systems first. Do you all understand binary and hexadecimal notation?" asked Tyrone.

"Of course," commented Howie, "but I'm sure a little review would be helpful." Howie understood about as much about binary and hexadecimal notation as Hugh Dongettit, and Hugh was 15 before he found out that a zebra was not a horse that had escaped from prison.

"Okay, we'll have a short review," said Tyrone. "Now we are all used to the decimal system which has a base of 10 and uses 10 symbols, 0, 1, 2, . . . , 9. When a number like one thousand three hundred sixty-five is written 1365, this is a short version of

$$1 * 10^3 + 3 * 10^2 + 6 * 10^1 + 5 * 10^0$$

(Remember $10^0 = 1$.)

"In fact any number written in the decimal system can be expanded in that way. Look at 76,291.73. It is

$$\begin{array}{r} 7 * 10^4 \\ +6 * 10^3 \\ +2 * 10^2 \\ +9 * 10 \\ +1 * 10^0 \\ +7 * 10^{-1} \\ +3 * 10^{-2} \\ \hline 76,291.73 \end{array}$$

"Consider the number written as 76,291.73. Each digit is in a column that has associated with it a power of 10. The digit in the first column to the left of the decimal is multiplied by 10 to the power of 0, the digit in the second column to the left of the decimal is multiplied by 10 to the power of 1, etc. Here, look at the number with the powers of 10 written above the digits." Tyrone wrote

10^4	10^3	10^2	10^1	10^0	10^{-1}	10^{-2}
7	6	2	9	1.	7	3

"I thought you were going to discuss binary and hexadecimal numbers," interrupted Howie.

"I was just getting to that," answered Tyrone. "In the binary system the base is 2, so we have two symbols, 0 and 1."

"Does that mean I don't have 5 fingers on my right hand if I count in binary?" asked Hugh.

Tyrone continued, "Certainly the number of fingers on your hand doesn't change, regardless of the number system you use, but the way you represent that number would change. Just as in a number written in the decimal system each digit is in a column that has associated with it a power of 10, in a number written in binary form each digit is in a column that has associated with it a power of 2. For example, if we had the binary number 101 and we wanted to see what it represents, we can write the powers of 2 above each column as follows

2^2	2^1	2^0
1	0	1.

So that 101 in binary is really

$$1 * 2^2 + 0 * 2^1 + 1 * 2^0$$

If we wanted to know what that means in the decimal system, we could carry out the multiplication and addition to get

$$1 * 2^2 + 0 * 2^1 + 1 * 2^0 =$$

$$1 * 4 + 0 * 2 + 1 * 1 =$$

$$4 + 0 + 1 = 5$$

Thus if we wanted to talk in binary about the number of fingers on Hugh's right hand, we would say it is 101."

"Let's try a harder number," encouraged Phyllis, "What does the number 10111001.1 in binary represent? I mean what is its decimal number equivalent?"

"Well, we just write the number out with the powers of 2 over each column, then add up the values. Here, I'll show you.

2^7	2^6	2^5	2^4	2^3	2^2	2^1	2^0	2^{-1}
1	0	1	1	1	0	0	1.	1

So the number is

$$1 * 2^7 + 0 * 2^6 + 1 * 2^5 + 1 * 2^4 + 1 * 2^3 + 0 * 2^2 + 0 * 2^1 + 1 * 2^0 + 1 * 2^{-1}$$

or in decimal notation it is

$$1 * 128 + 0 * 64 + 1 * 32 + 1 * 16 + 1 * 8 + 0 * 4 + 0 * 2 + 1 * 1 + 1 * \tfrac{1}{2} =$$
$$128 + 32 + 16 + 8 + 1 + 0.5 = 185.5$$

"That's pretty straightforward. How would you take a number in decimal, say 75, and write it in binary?" asked Phyllis.

Tyrone answered, "You could make a table of the powers of 2 like this:

POWERS OF 2	DECIMAL VALUE
2^0	1
2^1	2
2^2	4
2^3	8
2^4	16
2^5	32
2^6	64
2^7	128

"We need to find which powers of 2 will be used to make up 75. Now we know that 75 is less than 2^7 but greater than 2^6. So take 2^6 away from 75 (i.e., take $64 = 2^6$ away from the 75) and that leaves 11. Since 2^5 is 32, there is no 2^5 in 11. Similarly, for 2^4. But 2^3 is 8, which is less than 11, so there is a 2^3 in the composition of 11. Take 2^3 away from 11 and it leaves 3, which is $2^0 + 2^1$. Thus we see that $75 = 1 * 2^6 + 0 * 2^5 + 0 * 2^4 + 1 * 2^3 + 0 * 2^2 + 1 * 2^1 + 1 * 2^0$. Thus 75 written in binary would be

2^6	2^5	2^4	2^3	2^2	2^1	2^0
1	0	0	1	0	1	1

Without writing the powers of 2 above the number, we would simply write the binary number as 1001011. There is an easier way to figure out how a decimal number is written in binary. Just divide the decimal number repeatedly by 2 and remember the remainder each time. Those remainders will be the digits of the binary number (if written down from right to left). For example

$75/2 = 37$ with remainder $= 1$ that will be multiplied by 2^0
$37/2 = 18$ with remainder $= 1$ that will be multiplied by 2^1
$18/2 = 9$ with remainder $= 0$ that will be multiplied by 2^2
$9/2 = 4$ with remainder $= 1$ that will be multiplied by 2^3
$4/2 = 2$ with remainder $= 0$ that will be multiplied by 2^4
$2/2 = 1$ with remainder $= 0$ that will be multiplied by 2^5
$1/2 = 0$ with remainder $= 1$ that will be multiplied by 2^6
$0/2 = 0$ with remainder $= 0$ Finished.

Thus the number 75 in binary is 1001011, as before."

"This is all very interesting, Tyrone, but how does it relate to computers?" asked Howie.

"The computer has two states for each memory location. This is done because electronic circuitry is most efficient and accurate if each element has only two possible states. Thus, in a core memory each core is magnetized or not; in other memories a circuit may be open or closed. Since the computer memory units have two states, it is appropriate to use mathematics which have only two symbols. Thus we use the binary number system to represent numbers in a computer. You may recall that one number in the computer is called a bit. That's short for BInary digiT."

"You mean," stated Howie, "that the computer at school uses binary arithmetic for all its numbers."

"Yes, Howie," answered Tyrone. "In fact the instructions are coded in binary also. For example, the instructions to load the accumulator (that's a location like Tyrone's arithmetic unit) may have the operation code of 0101 1000 0010 0000 0000, and an address of the number to be coded into the accumulator would be 0111 1100 1001. Now, if a memory location is 32 bits, this instruction and operand in memory would look like this:

0101 1000 0010 0000 0000   0111 1100 1001

instruction code   operand address

"Wow, that's hard to read," said Hugh.

"That's right, Hugh," said Tyrone, "so we might want to represent that number in another number system. Since a computer frequently groups bits in units of four, it would be convenient to use a number system that could represent any four-bit binary number by a single symbol. Since a four-bit binary number can be anything from

0000

which is 0 to

1111

which is 15 in decimal, we need 16 symbols to represent any four-bit binary number by a single symbol. Thus the base 16 number system, the hexadecimal system, is used. The 16 symbols used for numbers, and their decimal and binary equivalents are these:

Hexadecimal symbol	Decimal	Binary
0	0	0
1	1	1
2	2	10
3	3	11
4	4	100
5	5	101
6	6	110
7	7	111
8	8	1000
9	9	1001
A	10	1010
B	11	1011
C	12	1100
D	13	1101
E	14	1110
F	15	1111

"To convert a binary number to a hexadecimal number, you look at the binary number four bits at a time, starting with the first four bits to the left of the decimal. Thus the binary number

0111 1100 1001

would be converted to hexadecimal

7   C   9

and the number

0101 1000 0010 0000 0000

would be

5   8   2   0   0

in hexadecimal.

"Thus our operation code and address, which was so hard to read in binary, would become, in hexadecimal

582007C9

which is much easier to read."

"Let me get this straight," said Phyllis, "An instruction on the school computer is really in memory in binary form, but for convenience, if we are using machine language, we may want to think of it in hexadecimal form."

"That's pretty much right, Phyllis." answered Tyrone. "In fact, if you get a *dump* of the contents of memory, the computer may print it in hexadecimal form for you so that you can read it more easily. However, there are actually several ways in which data are represented in the computer. I have a sheet of practice problems. Why don't you take a look at them, then we'll continue with data representation in the computer."

Problems for Sec. 5.8

1. Write the following decimal numbers in binary notation.
   (*a*) 33
   (*b*) 160
   (*c*) 75
   (*d*) 63.152
2. Convert the numbers in Problem 1 to their hexadecimal equivalent.
3. How does the octal number system (base is 8) represent the numbers 1 to 10? Can you write the decimal numbers of Problem 1 in octal?
4. Write a program in any language of your choice that will convert from decimal to binary to hexadecimal and the reverse. Try it with the data from Problem 1.
5. What decimal numbers are represented below in binary notation?
   (*a*) 110111011.11101111
   (*b*) 100001.0000
   (*c*) 111110111110

5.9 DATA REPRESENTATION

After the break, Tyrone started the discussion again. "When the input data enters the machine from a card, it comes in Hollerith code.

"Here's a picture of a card punched in Hollerith code. (See page 307.)

As you know from one of your first visits to the computer center, the data are then converted to one of a variety of other codes and stored in the computer. I'll briefly mention three of these codes—Binary-Coded Decimal (BCD), Extended Binary-Coded Decimal Interchange Code

(EBCDIC), and the U.S.A. Standard Code for Information Interchange (USASCII).

"In BCD all characters (numbers and letters) are represented by using six bits for the data. As you know any decimal digit can be represented by four bits, as shown here."

NUMBER	BITS
0	0000
1	0001
2	0010
3	0011
4	0100
5	0101
6	0110
7	0111
8	1000
9	1001

"By adding two extra bit portions at the front, we can expand our character set from just numbers, to include letters and special characters. These two bits can be 00 or 10 or 01 or 11. When combined with the other four bits, a character can be represented. Thus we have six bits, each of which can take on two states (a 0 or a 1). This gives us 2^6 (= 64) possible codes. Ten of them are for numbers, 26 for the alphabetic characters, and the remaining 28 are for special characters such as a $, #, (, and so forth.

"What do the actual codes look like?" asked Phyllis.

Tyrone handed each of them a laminated card with the codes on it.

"Here you go," he said. "You can use this for a bookmark. It is just the codes for some of the more familiar characters as represented in our machine."

CHARACTER	BCD CODE
blank	00 0000
;	11 1011
(	01 1100
)	11 1100
<	11 1110
+	11 0000
$	10 1011
*	10 1100
A	11 0001
B	11 0010
C	11 0011
D	11 0100
E	11 0101
F	11 0110
G	11 0111
H	11 1000
I	11 1001
J	10 0001
K	10 0010
L	10 0011
M	10 0100
N	10 0101
O	10 0110
P	10 0111
Q	10 1000
R	10 1001
S	01 0010
T	01 0011
U	01 0100
V	01 0101
W	01 0110
X	01 0111
Y	01 1000
Z	01 1001
0	00 1010
1	00 0001
2	00 0010
3	00 0011
4	00 0100
5	00 0101
6	00 0110
7	00 0111
8	00 1000
9	00 1001

"Hey, that's pretty neat," commented Howie. "Now I'm beginning to understand what happens inside the computer. What about EBCDIC? That must be similar."

"Yes, EBCDIC is very similar to BCD; the main difference is that with the EBCDIC code, eight bit portions are used. The concept is the same. Using eight bits expands the number of possible characters to 2^8 (= 256). In addition to alphabetic characters, numbers, and the special characters cited earlier, we now can have lower case letters, some special device control characters, and even a lot of unused codes reserved for some future use. In EBCDIC a decimal digit will have 1111 as its first four bits, and the next four bits will be the decimal digit in binary form."

"What about USASCII?" asked Phyllis. "That really sounds different."

"Not really," replied Tyrone. "The USASCII code is a seven-bit code (an eight-bit code has also been developed) that was designed to simplify machine-to-machine communications. The USASCII code is commonly associated with teleprocessing or time sharing systems."

"How about taking a number that is on a punched card and going through what happens to the data from the card to the internal storage?" asked Hugh.

"Sure," replied Tyrone. "Let's use the number 4096. It gets processed through the card reader and during the READ cycle is converted to binary. As each 'hole' in the card passes by the reading element, a current is sent to an appropriate location to indicate an 'on' condition.

"Suppose that 4096 had been read as alphanumeric data. Let's look at this value using EBCDIC code. We will represent each decimal digit with eight binary digits, with the first four binary digits being 1111 in the EBCDIC representation of numbers. Thus, 4 is 1111 0100. In EBCDIC code,

a decimal digit 0 is 1111 0000
a decimal digit 9 is 1111 1001
a decimal digit 6 is 1111 0110

Therefore, using the EBCDIC code, we could represent 4096 in memory as

1111 0100 1111 0000 1111 1001 1111 0110

Note that this could be written as the hexadecimal number F4F0F9F6 by making the four for one substitution mentioned earlier.

"This, you should understand is a brief look at how data is represented internally. There are instructions available for conserving storage space by storing the data in fewer locations. Data stored in this way is called *packed*."

"I'm a little confused," said Howie. "First you talked about representing a number in binary, then you talked about binary-coded decimals. Now you are talking about packed data."

"Let me summarize," began Tyrone. "Integer numbers are usually in memory in binary form; remember, the number 75 in the decimal system is 1001011 in binary. Alphanumeric data may be represented in a binary-coded decimal form. For example, 75 written in EBCDIC would be

$$1111 \qquad 0111 \qquad 1111 \qquad 0101$$

a	7	a	5
number		number	

This is inefficient in terms of storage locations used since the computer is storing 1111 before every digit, so there are ways of packing the binary-coded decimal numbers to eliminate this duplication."

"How many bits are there at each memory location?" asked Phyllis.

"Actually," answered Tyrone, "Some computers operate with a fixed number of bits per location, say 32, and are called *fixed-word-length machines*. Other computers can address each character in memory, and are therefore *character-addressable machines*. These computers are usually called *variable-word-length* machines. The newer machines (from third generation) can process both fixed-word-length and variable-word-length data."

"Thanks, I'm glad I asked," responded Phyllis.

"Now I know why a fixed-word-length, 32-bit-per-location machine only stores four letters per memory location," said Howie.

"Right, Howie," interrupted Tyrone, pleased that his day had been productive. "It's because the computer uses eight bits per letter, and so four letters require 32 bits."

"Oh," said Howie. "I thought it was because there are 26 letters in the alphabet and each hexadecimal digit represents four binary digits so 26 plus 4 is 30 bits."

"First of all, Howie, that doesn't make sense," responded Tyrone. "Furthermore you said 30 bits and each location has 32 bits. What are you going to do with the extra two bits?"

"I thought I'd go for an ice cream cone," answered Howie.

Tyrone ran screaming from the room.

TOPIC SUMMARY FOR SECTION 5.9

Data representation	Packing
Binary-coded decimal (BCD)	Fixed word length
Extended binary-coded decimal interchange code (EBCDIC)	Character addressable
U.S.A. standard code for information interchange (USASCII)	Variable word length

---

Problems for Sec. 5.9

1. Determine how your system is affected by the BCD, EBCDIC, and USASCII codes.

2. Identify what a 'dump' is and prepare a paper discussing its use in programming.
3. Is your machine a fixed-word-length machine or a variable-word-length machine? What are its characteristics?
4. Find out how a number on a data card is stored when read in by one of your programs.

chapter
6

This chapter deals primarily with file structures, particularly as they relate to tape and disk processing.

The first section introduces some of the fundamental concepts involved in designing files and is followed by an explanation of, first, magnetic tapes and then magnetic disks. These are the two auxiliary storage media most often used in computer applications.

A few comments are then presented on selecting between these two media. Following this, the differences between the sequential, indexed sequential, and direct-access file organization techniques are discussed.

Finally, the statements that are used in programming a particular computer system to interact with these types of files are given, along with some of the required computer center job control statements.

6.1 FILE STRUCTURE

Howie was hoping that the lecture would be over soon so that he could get on down to the rehearsals at the drama club. He began to copy down what Prof. Ovitt was saying.

"A file," Phil was saying, "can be considered to be any collection of data. If I wrote 100 numbers on the board, I could refer to them as a file of numbers."

"Can anyone suggest examples of files?" he asked.

Hugh began to talk. "The telephone book is a file of names, addresses, and phone numbers," he said.

"And the inventory at the store where I work is a file," Clara volunteered. "It is a file of sizes, colors, and such."

"You're both right," Prof. Ovitt agreed. "Any other ideas?"

"The information on personnel that is used to prepare a payroll is a file," commented Rudy.

"I have a nail file," volunteered Seymour.

"That wasn't exactly what I meant by a file, Seymour," Phil replied.

"Why? I have 32 different kinds of nails, and I keep a record of them on a list," Seymour answered.

"Oh, okay, Seymour," Prof. Ovitt continued. "Files usually contain some kind of information. Furthermore, one can usually identify *records* and *fields* in the file.

"A record is a block of information. For example a 'record' from the telephone book file would be a single person's name, address, and telephone number. The record thus describes all there is to know about one of the set of common items in the file.

"The field concept is an even finer designation. Records are usually composed of one or more fields. Again, using our telephone directory example, the phone number would be considered to be a field."

"I once made a record in left field," interjected Seymour, "when I dropped three consecutive fly balls."

Prof. Ovitt continued as if uninterrupted. "Look at this example on the board," he directed.

DELIA CARDS   10   40   A   2.75

"Here is a record from a firm's payroll file. There is a similar record for each employee. Each record has five fields.

Typed field	Contents in example
Name field	DELIA CARDS
Overtime hours field	10
Hours worked field	40
Department code field	A
Pay rate field	2.75

"What kinds of files are used in programming?" asked Howie.

"We must be careful to define precisely what we mean by files, Mr. Gettindere," Prof. Ovitt replied. "Any collection of data can be called a file, irrespective of whether or not computers are involved. On the other hand, there are physical computer files. A deck of cards containing data is a card file. A magnetic tape full of information is a file also. A disk pack of data can be considered to be a file.

"When we put our data files on these physical devices, we will need to keep track of things like fields and records. We'll see more on this later. If there are no more questions, I'll see you all next class."

6.2 A THEATER PRODUCTION ABOUT MAGNETIC TAPES

Howie enjoyed his extracurricular activities, especially his job as stagehand for the drama club. He had always wanted to be in show business, and this was probably as close as he would ever get. He spent as much time as possible at the club's theater. He even decided to leave his job at the candle factory so that he would not have to work on wick ends.

On this particular night, the actors in the club were rehearsing a musical production that had been, essentially, Howie's idea. Howie had felt that, with the popularity of computers everywhere, and also with 350 students taking the core computer course each semester, a musical production might be well received. The officers had agreed to give the idea tentative approval and assigned their composer and lyricist to the project. Howie was to act as the technical consultant.

Howie felt somewhat strange sitting alone out in front of the stage rather than in his usual position out back. His discomfort subsided as the director spoke to the crew.

"Okay, everybody, we're set to go," said Stan Still, the director. "This is the Tape scene from the second act. Let's get it right."

As he walked off stage, the curtain rose, and the leading man began to sing (sung to the tune of "I'd Like to Get the World to Sing").

> I'd like to get magnetic tape,
> To store my data on.
> I'd like to know how much to store,
> Before the room's all gone.
>
> I know that tapes have density,
> To measure bits per inch.
> And forty million characters,
> Can be stored in a pinch.
>
> But what else do I need to know,
> About this half-inch tape?
> Like speeds and length and codes and such,
> And how much is the freight?
>
> That's the way it is—
> I just need to know more,
> So just tell me the score,
> That's the way it is.

Howie was dutifully reflecting on the technical details of the song when Stan called from the stage, "Hey, Howie, what do you think?"

Howie quickly withdrew one of his index cards from class to review. After all, he had a responsibility now and might as well be sure he was right.

MAGNETIC TAPE

Plastic, with a metallic coating on one side

One-half inch wide

2400 feet per reel

Density: the number of characters that can be stored per inch of tape (BPI: bits per inch)

Common densities: 200 BPI   556 BPI   6400 BPI
                     800 BPI   1600 BPI

Recording tracks: Most common tapes have either seven tracks (or channels) or nine tracks.

Storage capacity: 1 million to 180 million characters

Speeds: records from 36 to 200 inches per second

Cost: approximately $15 to $30 per reel

File type: sequential

"Yes," Howie called. "It's all right so far. Go on with it."

The play continued, and another actor arrived on stage apparently playing a salesman and responding to the leading man's question as only a salesman could. He began to sing (to the tune of the "Notre Dame Fight Song").

> *Cheer cheer for mag tapes today!*
> *They are the best in the whole U.S.A.*
> *Easy handling, low cost too,*
> *Can be reused, yes, through and through.*
> *If you make errors, you can correct 'em,*
> *Not even Sherlock Holmes could detect them*
> > *With them little space is lost,*
> > *So buy them and you will see!*

Howie's mind was working overtime. "Yes," he thought, "tapes can be reused and cards cannot; if you make errors on tape they can simply be rewritten, while with cards you need a new card . . ."

"Hey, Howie," Stan called, "is that space line correct? Do you save space?"

"Very definitely," Howie responded. "Why, one 2400-foot reel of tape full of data is equivalent to 500,000 punched cards! That certainly saves space! It isn't as bulky either, wouldn't you agree? It's also a bit more flexible. With cards, you are limited to 80 columns of data storage. With tape, each record can be as long or as short as you need. That wasn't in the song."

"Well, we can't fit everything in," came the reply. "We haven't covered the disadvantages yet. Let's continue!"

The leading man had turned to his assistant for advice. "What do you think?" he asked.

The response came (sung to the tune of "I'm Looking Over a Four Leaf Clover").

It is essential,
To process sequential,
When you use magnetic tapes.

Cause it is certain,
The order is firm,
One follows another.
Sequential's the term.

There are some drawbacks,
Like when some dust attacks.
Heat and humidity hurt too.

Sometimes the tape breaks,
Or numbers press through.
And just remember,
They're invisible to you.

No need explaining,
The ones remaining,
Without tapes there's cards galore . . .

Howie was beginning to wonder whether this was such a good idea after all, when Lena Times, the composer, and Otto Biographee, the writer, approached.

"Say, Howie," Otto began, "if we are to continue with our writing, we're going to have to get more familiar with tapes. I think you'd better explain them to us. Can you tell us what one looks like?"

"Better than that," Howie replied, "I can show you a picture of a tape and the unit that processes them." He reached into his back pocket and withdrew his wallet. There, in the little plastic holders, were the pictures Howie had referred to. (See page 318.)

"Well, that helps," Lena admitted. "But we have to know more about it than that."

Howie began to fidget. He had already exhausted his knowledge about tapes and certainly couldn't fake it now.

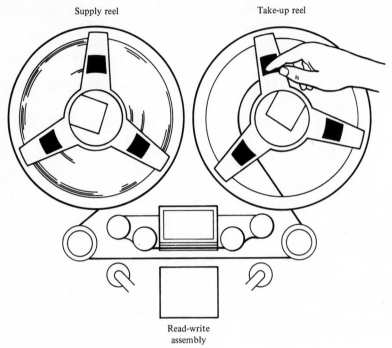

Figure 6.1 Schematic of a mounted tape reel.

"Say, why don't you both come over to my room tonight and I'll prepare a little presentation for you?" Howie suggested.

"Fine, we'll be there about 8 o'clock," responded Otto, speaking for both of them.

Later that day, Howie called several of his classmates over for supper in his room. They all eagerly accepted.

"Say, that was a great meal," Rudy complimented Howie. "Thanks for inviting us."

"Yes, thank you," came the chorus.

"Hey, ready for a little game before dessert?" asked Howie. "I've written several topics on separate pieces of paper and have placed them under each dinner plate. Let's see if you can talk on your topic extemporaneously for 3 minutes."

"Sounds like fun, who goes first?" asked Brandon.

"You start, if you like!" Howie responded.

"Wow, this is a strange topic!" commented Brandon. "I'm supposed to talk on the representation of data on magnetic tape!" Brandon stood up and cleared his throat.

"Well, my friends," he began, "a magnetic tape usually has seven or nine tracks (or parallel channels) where the data are recorded. Here, let

Figure 6.2 The tape drive.

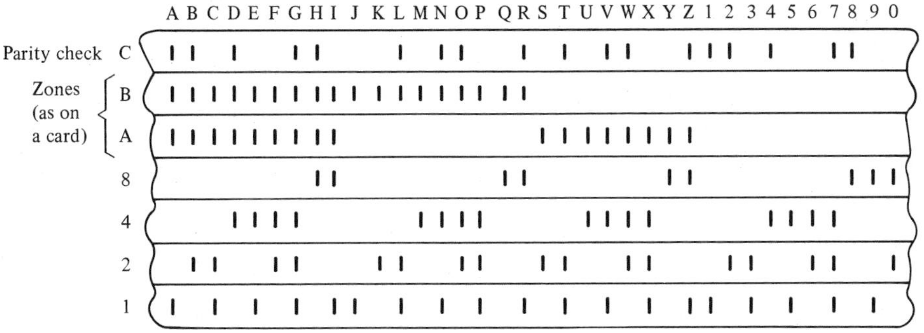

A B C D E F G H I J K L M N O P Q R S T U V W X Y Z 1 2 3 4 5 6 7 8 9 0

| | Parity check C | Zones (as on a card) B A | 8 | 4 | 2 | 1 |

Figure 6.3 Schematic of a strip of 7-track magnetic tape. The letter J would be represented by a magnetic spot on Track 'B' and Track 1. The number 6 would be represented by a magnetic spot on Track '4' and Track '2'.

me draw a sketch of a strip of magnetic tape with some coded characters on it." Brandon began to write on the tablecloth.

"As you see, an individual track can have a spot on it that is either magnetized or unmagnetized. By combining these 'spots' a variety of characters can be represented."

"What's that *parity check track* that you labeled?" asked Howie.

"That's just a check on the accuracy of the data," replied Brandon. "If the total of the magnetic spots in any column is odd, a magnetic spot is put in the parity check track."

"Why is that?" asked Howie.

"The objective is to have every character on a tape represented by an even number of bits, then the computer will not process them if they are odd as a check on data accuracy.[1] Let me continue before my time is up.

"Recorded data on a tape also has a density."

"I know what that is," called Howie, remembering one of the songs. He began to sing.

I know that tapes have density,
To measure bits per inch.

Brandon looked at Howie a bit strangely.

"Anyway," he continued, "there are different density factors, the most common being 556 or 800 characters per inch. That's a lot of characters on a 2400-foot reel of tape."

"Times up!" called Howie.

Rudy picked up his plate and began his turn.

"Hey, mine says IRG! What does that stand for?" he kidded.

"Interrecord gap," suggested Howie.

"Oh, that's right," Rudy admitted, "that is the space on the tape that separates one record from another."

"Is this a record or a tape?" asked Seymour, who was invited so there would be someone to do the dishes.

"No, Seymour," Rudy continued, "an IRG is a space on the tape about three-fourths of an inch wide that separates one logical tape record from another. It's needed for two reasons. First, it separates records (so you know when one stops and the next begins). Second, it allows for that bit of tape that is wasted when the tape reader starts and stops as it processes the records on the tape."

"What do you really mean by a record?" asked Seymour.

"Well," Rudy replied. "A record is a collection of information

---

[1]This is for a computer system utilizing even parity. Some systems may utilize an odd parity check. The principle is still the same.

about something. The university has a record on you, Seymour. It contains several fields of information. It has your name, address, social security number, and so on. This record is often referred to as a 'logical' record."

"Is a logical record distinguished from an illogical record like Seymour's?" asked Brandon.

"No," Rudy continued, "a logical record is distinguished from a physical record. The machine can usually work on chunks of data at a time. Thus, it could read a string of five logical records. In this example, this string of five logical records would be one physical record."

Tyrone had been doing some quick calculations on his paper cup. "Say," he called for the attention of the group. "If you have 200 records (even very short ones), you'll have 200 IRGs. If each IRG is three-fourths of an inch wide, then this small application wastes over 12 feet of tape. Sounds inefficient to me."

"You're right, it is," confirmed Rudy. "Usually, records are grouped together to form a block. This technique is called *blocking*. Thus, if you take your 200 records and put 10 in a block, you would only need 20 gaps in between (one for each block) and waste far less tape. By the way, these 20 blocks are the 'physical records.'

"You will often find a 'blocking factor' associated with a tape. If the blocking factor is 35, there are 35 logical records in a block. As long as the records are of fixed length, there is little difficulty in accessing a record. Blocking records also saves time since the tape unit will not stop and start as many times."

Howie was taking notes as fast as he possibly could.

Tyrone looked under his plate. "I've got 'labels' as my topic. Let's see, there are gummed labels attached to the outside of the tape reel that describe what is on the tape and other information for identifying the file. It is common practice to put additional information on the tape itself (at the beginning) such as tape name, file size, number of records, and so forth. This is then referred to as a header label. It's just a precaution in case the outside label comes off. That's all I can think of. It's your turn, Seymour."

Seymour anxiously turned his plate over. He read aloud. "Dishes, I'm supposed to do dishes!"

"Hey, that's great of you!" the group chimed as they left for the other room.

Problems for Sec. 6.2

1. Determine whether your computer system has even or odd parity.
2. Review this chapter by solving the following crossword.

Across

1. A track on a magnetic tape is often referred to as a _____.
5. It can be odd (answer is *not:* this book).
6. Number of feet on a 2400-foot reel of tape.
8. They are bringing the _____ for the authors.
11. The sun god of Greece.
12. If we transfer 10 records at a time, we are moving _____ records.
16. The space between records.
17. Grouping records together forms a _____.
19. Type of file a magnetic tape contains.

Down

2. A _____ label is a label at the beginning of a magnetic tape.
3. 2000 pounds backwards.
4. Largest BPI.
7. Number of characters that 'can be stored in a pinch' (in millions).
9. What are we talking about?
10. What Farmer Inadel makes while his son shines.
13. One record in any physical record is usually a _____ record.
14. Where data is put on a tape, or where trains put their wheels.
15. The star of this book.
18. Density.

3. List the advantages and disadvantages of magnetic tape.
4. What environmental conditions need there be in a tape processing system?

5. Find out from your computer center why a plastic ring is sometimes used with a magnetic tape.

6.3 MAGNETIC DISKS

It was 8 o'clock, and Lena and Otto had just arrived at Howie's. Howie had memorized all the notes on tapes that he had copied from his previous guests during supper.

"Well, I'm all set. Go ahead and ask me anything you wish about tapes," Howie beamed.

"Thanks, Howie," Lena replied, "but we're really interested in disks. We already have written the tape production."

Howie was beginning to fidget. "What is it that you wanted to know?" he weakly asked.

"I guess just some corroboration for some facts we have here," Otto answered. "Before we came here we stopped by the computer center to get a look at what a disk is. The operator, Preston Buttons, was really very nice. Not only did he give us some pictures, but he also described the characteristics of a disk."

"Did you find out how much data can be stored on a disk pack?" Howie asked.

"Yes," Lena replied, "up to 7 million characters. And he told us

Figure 6.4 A disk pack with read/write access arms.

Figure 6.5 A disk pack.

that one of the major manufacturers has recently released a disk storage unit that can store up to 800 million characters of information."

"Let me tell you how the disk works," volunteered Howie, hoping he would be interrupted.

"No need to!" Otto obliged. "Look at the pictures he gave us." Lena handed two photographs to Howie.

"He told us that a magnetic disk was a thin circular metal plate which is coated on both sides with a recording material," Otto said. "It looks a lot like a phonograph record. On the surface are a series of concentric circles, called tracks, where the actual data are written. "When you stack six of these together, you have what is called a *disk pack*. If you look closely at that picture, Howie, you can see the read-write heads that process the data."

It was clear that Otto was excited about what he had learned, so Howie let him continue.

"The disks are constantly spinning past those read-write heads. Even I can see that it would be quicker to find a piece of information on a disk than it would be on a tape. With a tape, you have to read sequentially. This seems to give you much more flexibility. You could access any random piece of information."

"Prof. Ovitt told us that tapes are sequential-access files and disks can be sequential-access files or random-access files," interjected Howie. "Another term for random-access file would be direct-access files."

"He was right!" confirmed Lena.

"Well, what facts do you have on disks?" asked Howie. The session was going rather well.

"Funny thing," observed Otto, "but Preston gave us an index card and told us we could reference it if we had any questions like that. Here it is." He handed the card to Howie.

Howie had to restrain himself from leaping for it. He studied it carefully.

DISK DATA FOR A TYPICAL DISK PACK

Capacity:

- 10 recording surfaces
- 200 tracks per surface
- 13,000 characters per track
- Total capacity of 26 million characters

Disk packs are removable, thus providing unlimited off line memory.
Data transfer time (from disk to computer) averages 156,000 characters per second.

"Hey, that should be a real help to you," commented Howie. "But it doesn't tell you how to choose between disk or tape for a particular application."

Lena looked at Otto. As if on signal, they both stood up, locked arms, and burst into song (to the tune of "Tea for Two").

See how we
Will choose the two—
It's tape for me
And disk for you,
Yes, tape for me
And disk for you
Today.

Separate uses
With different speeds,
And separate files,
With different needs—
Yours is sequential,
While mine is for random, access.

Tapes this year
Are slow I fear,
But data is near
With disks in gear
Disks that here
Will process spee-di-ly.

Otto and Lena were dancing the 'ole soft shoe' now, with imaginary top hat and cane. Howie opened the front door. They were still singing.

They can live in harmony
If their limits you can clearly see.
So bye Howie
We're happy as can be.

They side-shuffled out the door and, as they continued down the hall, went into a new number.

"They must have flipped," Howie thought, as he closed the door. Howie shut off the light and headed for bed.

"Hey, who shut out the lights?" Seymour called from the kitchen, where he was finishing up the dishes.

"Are you still there, Seymour?" Howie asked aloud.

"No, Howie, your dog is a ventriloquist," came the reply.

TOPIC SUMMARY FOR SECTION 6.3

Tracks	Direct access
Disk pack	10 recording surfaces
Random access	200 tracks per surface

Problems for Sec. 6.3

1. What are the major differences between a sequential- and a random-access file?
2. What are the advantages of a disk processing system over a tape processing system? Tape over disk?
3. Identify the disk unit used at your computer center and note down its characteristics (storage capacity, speed, name, etc.).

6.4 SELECTING THE FILE MEDIUM

Before he was due to rehease again, Howie thought that it would be a good idea to enroll in a one-day seminar, sponsored by the computer center, that dealt with files and file processing.

It was 8 o'clock in the morning, and Howie reluctantly began to hear the first speaker.

"Good morning, everyone," boomed a voice. "My name is U. Shelley Boring, and I'd like to welcome you all here today. A funny thing happened to me on the way in today. As I was passing by an open field, I saw a bull over near a construction trailer eating some TNT. I rushed right down to the local constable and informed him of this serious matter.

"'That's abominable,'" he told me!

"I agreed.

"Now, please control yourselves. After all, we have some serious work to do today.

"You all signed up for this seminar in anticipation of learning more about file processing. Once you can identify certain characteristics of your file, you will be better able to choose the proper hardware to use. The first question to ask yourselves is whether random or sequential processing is necessary. There are many data processing jobs that are best done by processing the records in the file in a given order. Can someone suggest such an application?" Shelley asked.

"Yes," replied Adam Up, a math major. "A payroll job is a sequential file and best done so. You go through an employee list and extract any necessary data for preparing a check. There is no need to directly locate employees in the file."

"Very good, Ad," commented Shelley, "but then, this is the third time you've taken this seminar. Now, if a payroll problem is a good example of a sequential file, what jobs would be better done using a random- or direct-access approach?"

One of the students from the School of Communicable Diseases, Betty Ketchsit, volunteered. "I'd guess that any time you needed information from the file right away, it would be unwise to use sequential processing techniques or hardware. For example, when I go to the savings bank to make a deposit, I don't want to wait while the computer goes through 10,000 customer accounts until it finds mine. I want to be finished quickly."

"An airlines reservation system is a good example," suggested Howie. "When a customer wants information on a specific flight, he wants that information immediately. The reservation file should be a direct-access file."

Shelley continued. "Those are excellent examples. Thank you. Another factor that must be considered is the size of the file. How many tapes would be required to hold the file? Would additional disk packs be needed? One thing to remember here is to determine how much of the file must be 'on line' (that is, immediately available).

"Somewhat related to the file size idea is record and field sizes. Most importantly, are all the records of fixed length (that is, do they have the same number of fields) or are they variable length records? Magnetic tape can easily accommodate variable length records whereas some random-access files cannot."

"Shouldn't you consider how often records in the file are used when deciding which type of file to have?" asked Ad.

"Thanks, Ad, the timing was perfect," Shelley whispered. "We get that information from a FAR."

"How far?" wondered Howie, out loud.

"No, a FAR is a File Activity Ratio," replied Shelley. "It is a simple arithmetic formula that gives you a feel for what proportion of the file is being used. Here, let me put the formula on the board." He began to write.

$$\text{File Activity Ratio} = \frac{\text{Total number of records used}}{\text{Total number of records scanned}}$$

"If this ratio is very high, there really isn't much difference between using a tape or a disk. That is, if you're using most of the records in each run, the FAR is not a consideration in the file-type decision. If it's low, however, there are a few records that are getting all the attention. Thus, in this case, it would be more efficient to use a direct-access device."

"How low is low?" asked Betty.

"There is no fixed percent," Shelley responded. "I'd say under 10 or 12 percent is low enough."

"What if you didn't have a disk drive to use but did have a tape. What could you do?" asked Ed.

"At the very least," suggested Shelley, "you could put all the active records at the beginning of the file. That would certainly save processing time. This applies to all files. It's good practice to store frequently accessed items where the access time will be shortest. Just a minute of saved time can be important."

"Are you saying that access speed is also one of the criteria?" asked Chester Minute.

"Sure," replied Shelley. "It makes sense that if an item is referenced frequently, the speed with which it is obtained should be as high as possible. This might dictate several small files rather than one large one. Perhaps several tape drives are necessary and desirable."

Shelley went on. "Let's continue with the factors that should influence the type of file selected for an application. Many times, records in a file have to be frequently updated. For example, the airline reservations application mentioned earlier illustrates a file with a large number of additions and deletions. On the other hand, the savings bank example is one where there are less frequent changes.

"If there are frequent changes, you will have to consider some means for reorganizing the file to consolidate the empty spaces. Can anybody suggest other criteria that we haven't covered?"

"Shouldn't you consider the possible growth of the file?" asked Howie. "Its future size may affect the decision as to which type of file to use."

Betty also had a suggestion. "I think that one should consider file protection. Hardware failures are infrequent, but programming errors may erase portions of a file. Duplicate tapes would seem feasible and perhaps, though more expensive, duplicate disk packs might be used."

"Very good," commented Shelley. "Those were very good suggestions. Shall we summarize the factors that impinge on the choice of file medium?" He wrote again on the board.

1. Random or sequential processing
2. File size
3. Record sizes (fixed or variable length)
4. File activity ratio
5. Frequency with which records are referenced
6. Speed with which records are accessed
7. Number of deletions and additions
8. Growth potential of the file
9. File protection considerations
10. Cost of hardware

"Well, that's all for this morning," summarized Shelley. "Let's get together again after lunch."

TOPIC SUMMARY FOR SECTION 6.4

Sequential and random processing	Access speed
Optimal file size	File protection
File activity ratio (FAR)	Duplicate tapes

Problems for Sec. 6.4

1. Inquire at your computer center about some of the administrative jobs that are processed for the university. Determine which are tape files and which are disk files. Why was a particular file medium selected?
2. Draw up a list of those applications that you feel would be best accomplished using magnetic tape, or disks, or cards.

6.5 FILE ORGANIZATION

On his way back to the afternoon seminar Howie noticed an inebriated man walk up to a parking meter and deposit a dime. The indicator went up to 60, and the drunk screamed.

"What's the matter?" asked Howie as he rushed over.

"I've lost a hundred pounds!" he exclaimed.

Howie thought he'd be a good samaritan and invited the gentleman to come to the seminar with him and get some rest (and some free coffee).

"This afternoon, let's discuss techniques of file organization," encouraged Betty. "We know tape files are always sequential. One record is processed after another in order. Disk files, on the other hand, are much more flexible. They can be organized in one of three different ways, as

1. Sequential files
2. Indexed sequential files
3. Direct-access files

Let's look more closely at the disk file. How would a sequential file be organized on disk equipment?" she asked.

Adam responded. "By storing the records in adjacent locations on the disk. This file is just like a tape file. When you add or delete records, you must rewrite the entire master file on an interim location while the corrections are made."

"But you would sometimes get a much faster processing time with the disk, wouldn't you?" asked someone else.

"That's right," Adam agreed, "but the cost of storing the data on disk would be much greater and probably outweigh any advantage gained from faster processing!"

Shelley was wondering why he had bothered attending this seminar when someone knocked on the door.

"Door is open!" he called.

"How did you know it was me?" asked Doris Opin as she entered the room. "You must be clairvoyant!"

"No, but a lot of people think I look like her," Shelley responded.

"What were you discussing?" she asked.

"We were about to begin talking about indexed sequential files," Shelley said. "Would you care to contribute something?"

"Not really," she replied. "I barely have enough to get home."

"Okay, I'll continue," Shelley began. "To understand the concept of indexed sequential file organization, we must consider a disk to have two separate areas of space. One is called the prime area and the other, an overflow area. In the prime area we store the main records in a file. Look at this slide I have of the surface of a disk pack." He shut off the lights and turned on the projector.

"On this chart, let's assume that the data for a personnel file is stored in the prime area. When data are stored on the disk using, say, the first track, approximately 13,000 bytes or characters would be stored on surface zero. Now, remembering that there are 10 recordable surfaces on a disk pack (you can't record on the top of the first disk or the bottom of the last disk in a 6-disk pack), we could place our file on the first track of each surface. In this way, a large amount of data can be accessed with one positioning of the access arms (the ones with the read-write heads). When we record data in this manner it is often referred to as the cylinder concept."

"Can you reference a particular cylinder?" asked Howie.

"Sure, each cylinder has a number," Shelley replied. "Cylinder 1 contains the first track from every surface. Cylinder 55 contains track 55 from every surface."

"Why is it called 'indexed sequential'?" asked Betty.

"When you add a record to any sequential file," began Shelley, "you normally insert it in some specific position. This position is determined by a key associated with your file.

"For example, in an inventory file application, you might have ar-

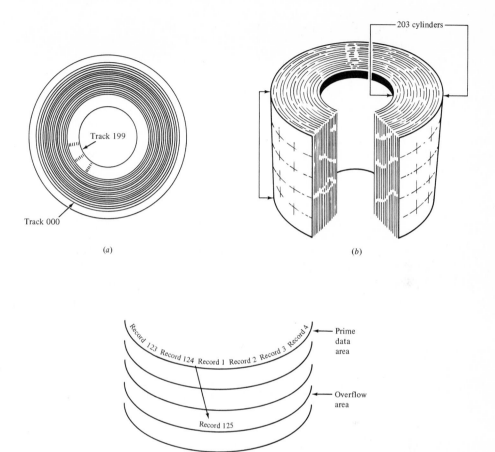

Figure 6.6 Track, cylinder, and overflow areas. (a) One surface of the disk showing the 200 tracks. (b) One cylinder is made up of the same track from all surfaces. Here we have the 200 "cylinders" of a disk pack depicted. (c) If you add a record to a full track (say record 2 is added), then the record that was last before the addition is bumped into the overflow area.

ranged the inventory in ascending order by item number. To add a new item number into its proper sequential position in the file is quite easy. However, this causes the positions of the records that follow this insertion to shift their position on the track, perhaps bumping the last record off the track entirely.

"The shifted record (or records) is put in that other area that I mentioned earlier, the *overflow area*. This would be an empty area somewhere else on the disk."

"But how do you know which records are in the overflow area?" asked Adam.

"On each track on a cylinder," replied Shelley, "is a field called the track index, and it contains the highest key associated with that track. Thus, if the track index was 125, it would indicate that items 0 to 125 were associated with this track (although it might be in the overflow area).

"To locate a record, the read-write heads, on programmer command, move to a cylinder and examine the track index. For example, if we were looking for item 36, the track index of 125 would indicate that item 36 was, in fact, located on surface 1 in that cylinder. If item 126 was being searched for, then the next track index of, say, 500 would indicate that item 126 was associated with surface 2 of that cylinder."

"But how do you know what records might be on an overflow area," queried Howie.

"Well, actually, the track index also will have information about this. It will tell you what record (item) is the highest one physically present on the track and then indicate on what cylinder and track the records continue (that is, where the overflow area begins)," replied Shelley.

"That means that my records in the file could be retrieved either sequentially or randomly," cried Howie.

"That's precisely correct!" applauded Shelley. "You've got the idea. Could you list all the advantages of index sequential files?"

Howie took his notes and went to the board.

ADVANTAGES OF INDEXED SEQUENTIAL FILE ORGANIZATION

1. You may process files randomly or sequentially.
2. Unlike tape sequential processing, you don't have to examine each previous record.
3. Additions do not require the whole file to be recreated.
4. Inquiries to the file need not be sorted to increase efficiency (as is often needed with tape files).

"They're not without disadvantages," suggested Adam. "If there are deletions, you never fill up the deleted space. This must cause some inefficiency. Furthermore, I can see that if there are a large number of additions and deletions to a file, this type of processing may become complex and inefficient with cumbersome overflow areas and cross references."

"Of course, you're right, Adam," replied Shelley. "And now let's look at the last type of file organization, direct organization. With this type of organization a record is placed at a location on the disk that is related to its key. Thus, if we had an item number 603, we could store it on cylinder 60, track 3. Item 362 would go on cylinder 36, track 2. If we can make such a relationship between the key and the disk indexes, it can greatly enhance the efficiency with which the file is used. Simple relations such as the previous example do not often exist, yet some such relationship can usually be developed."

Adam began talking. "It would seem to be a particularly efficient file organization for files with large amounts of unsorted transactions or even for files with a lot of additions and deletions."

"Right, Adam," said Shelley, "but you can end up wasting a lot of disk space because of the gaps between records. The killer is when you don't have enough."

Howie's friend sat up. "No tequila for me, thank you, I've had enough." He fell to the floor.

Adam rushed to help. "It's okay, Adam," Howie assured him. "He's just had a little too much to drink."

"Better get some water," suggested Shelley. "Here, fill up the glass." He handed an empty glass to Betty.

"Did someone call my name?" asked Philip DeGlass from his position on the floor.

"No, Philip," Howie assured him. "We're going to take you home now. You've been away too long."

"Yes," Philip replied, "but I've found that absinthe makes the heart grow fonder."

TOPIC SUMMARY FOR SECTION 6.5

Sequential file   Cylinder
Indexed sequential file   Tracks
Direct-access file   File key
Disk overflow area   Direct organization

Problems for Sec. 6.5

1. Draw a schematic of a cylinder from a disk pack. What is its capacity? How many tracks in each cylinder?
2. If, when a track is full, items get 'bumped' into the cylinder overflow area, what happens when the overflow area is full?
3. Name three applications for each type of file (using disks), i.e., sequential file, indexed sequential file, and direct-access file.
4. Visit your computer center and determine the file organization techniques most often used for administrative jobs.

6.6 STORAGE AND RETRIEVAL USING TAPES AND DISKS

Howie and Rudy were waiting for class to begin, when they noticed Seymour looking rather glum.

"Wow, look at that!" exclaimed Howie. "Seymour's got a black eye. What happened Seymour? Did you run into a door at the party at Catherine's mansion last night?"

"No!" replied Seymour, "I was struck by the beauty of the place!"

Prof. Ovitt arrived before either Howie or Rudy could respond. He began his lecture.

"We have all seen how enormously fast the computer operates. Its internal processing speeds are really quite impressive. Unfortunately, modern input and output devices cannot operate nearly as fast. In addition, most real world applications using computers utilize large amounts of data. Because of this, storage and retrieval media that are faster than punched cards are needed."

"That's why they have tapes and disks as part of a computer system, right?" asked Howie.

"That is correct," replied Ovitt. "As you know, tapes are a sequential-access medium. That means that the access time for retrieving a record from a tape file is dependent upon its position in that file. All prior records must be passed before access can be made.

"Disks, on the other hand, are direct-access devices, and access time is independent of the position of the record on the disk.

"As a programmer, you can read information from tapes and disks, as well as write information on them. Normally, you would be programming in a batch processing environment when you use these media, since time sharing or real time processing is less conducive to handling large volumes of data."

"Are there special commands for dealing with tapes and disks?" asked Clara.

"Yes, there are," Phil replied. "Each batch processing language (such as FORTRAN) has its own set of commands for dealing with these storage media. In addition, you are normally required to include some descriptive information about the tape or disk file on the job control cards at your facility. We'll see some examples of this later. Right now, I'd like to discuss some of the commands that are available when one is processing a tape.

"If you wanted to write information on a tape, you would use the PRINT command of the particular language being utilized. Normally, a number will follow the PRINT command; this identifies a particular tape drive at the computer center. For example, if the computer center had a tape drive which they assigned the number 7, then the following statement would write four pieces of data onto the tape.

WRITE (7) A, B1, J, L

"Now, visualize, if you will, this WRITE statement as it might appear in a loop. In this loop, we will read four items from each of 30 data cards and write them onto a tape.

```
        . . .
        DO 5 I = 1, 30
        READ, A, B1, J, L
   5    WRITE (7) A, B1, J, L
        . . .
```

"The information would be read one card at a time and stored sequentially on the tape as one long string of data. Once it is on the tape, it remains there until something is written on top of it or the data are erased."

"Is it like a home tape unit?" asked Seymour. "I mean, can you backspace and rewind and such?"

"Wow!" responded Prof. Ovitt. "That's quite a shiner you have there, Seymour. What happened?"

"Well, you see, Professor," replied Seymour, "it's like this! While I was over at the computer center last night working late on my programs, a big guy came in and began wrecking the machines. Enraged, I grabbed him by the . . ."

"Seymour," Prof. Ovitt interrupted. "The computer center was closed last night."

"I walked into a door," mumbled Seymour.

"To answer your question," Phil continued, "you can do what you suggest. The statement

REWIND 7

would rewind the tape mounted on tape drive 7 back to the beginning."

"What if I don't want to go all the way back to the start of the tape?" wondered Seymour.

"In that case," Phil replied, "you could use the backspace statement. For example,

BACKSPACE 7

would backspace the tape mounted on tape unit 7 by one record. The statements,

```
        DO 10 J = 1, 20
   10   BACKSPACE 7
```

would backspace 20 records."

Rudy raised his hand. "Prof. Ovitt, I know from the last class that a record is a series of fields that the programmer defines as a logical piece of information. In the example you've used today, we could consider A, B1, J, and L as a single record. The loop then put 20 records on the tape. I understand that, but how does the computer know how long my records are?"

"A good question," praised Ovitt. "After a WRITE statement has been executed, a space is left on the tape. This is the IRG or InterRecord

Gap that we spoke of in an earlier class. The computer can detect these gaps and thus can 'count them,' if you will. In addition, you can put information on record length into the job control statements. As I said, we'll see some examples of this later. Let me show you a brief program that performs a very simple operation using the commands I have mentioned. While this particular program is written in FORTRAN, I think you'll see that the concepts are easily adaptable to another language." Prof. Ovitt began to write on the board.

```
C    DEMONSTRATION PROGRAM
     DIMENSION N(50)
     DO 5 K = 1, 50
     N(K) = K
5    WRITE (7) N(K)
     REWIND 7
     READ (7) N
     PRINT, N
     DO 10 L = 1,5
10   BACKSPACE 7
     DO 15 M = 1, 5
     READ (7) N(M)
15   PRINT, N(M)
     REWIND 7
     STOP
     END
```

"This program," Ovitt continued, "writes the numbers 1 to 50 onto a tape mounted on tape unit 7. It then rewinds the tape and reads all 50 numbers. The entire set of 50 numbers is then printed. Next, the tape is backspaced five records, and these five records are printed out.

"Now, this program is only a contrived example, but I think it illustrates the kinds of things that you can do with tapes."

"Prof. Ovitt, why do you have to specify the number of the drive you're using?" asked Brandon.

"For two reasons," replied Prof. Ovitt. "First, you may, in your program, wish to use several tapes. The number that appears with these tape commands is the only uniquely identifying characteristic. Second, a computer center may have several tape drives, and your tape can only be mounted on one of them. That one must be identified so the computer system can find your tape."

"Thank you," replied Brandon.

"Let's take a 5-minute break before we begin to discuss disk processing," suggested Phil.

"Say, Howie," called Seymour, "I heard you recently got a pet parrot. Is that right?"

"Yes," Howie responded. "I picked him up from a local taxidermist. He said his pet was very nervous. Just a case of mounting apprehension, I guess!"

Fortunately, Prof. Ovitt began to lecture again. "As I'm sure you've seen, processing with tapes often requires rewinding and backspacing across a tape and can use a large amount of computer time. It would be nice if you could access a desired record directly from memory, but the cost of such a memory for very large data files is still prohibitive. Disk units, however, are less expensive and can accommodate large files.

"We've already discussed how a disk is made up of tracks and cylinders. We'll look now at statements that might be used for accessing the data. Before you can read or write on a disk file, you must *define* the characteristics of the file in a statement of your program. In one language, FORTRAN, the define file statement is as follows." Prof. Ovitt began to write on the board.

DEFINE FILE 9 (1500,100,U)

"The number 9 is the number assigned to the disk unit by the computer center. This is the same concept that we had with tape files. Inside the parentheses are three parameters. The first is the maximum number of records to be stored (in this case 1500). The second parameter indicates how many characters are in each record. The third parameter is a letter, in this case the letter U, which indicates that reading and writing operations may or may not reference a format statement; that is, the file will be unformatted. (A format statement describes the data in detail.)

"How would we write information onto a disk?" asked Clara.

Prof. Ovitt began to explain the write commands. "In the statement

WRITE (9'NREC)

the 9 is once again the unit identification. The variable NREC contains a number which indicates where the record is to be written. Notice that these two parameters are separated by a '. This, in a way, distinguishes this statement as a disk input-output statement."

"Is the READ statement pretty much the same?" asked Howie.

"Yes," Phil replied, "it is of the form

READ (9'I)

and this time I is the place on the disk where this record is written. Perhaps an example will illustrate the use of these three statements.

"Let's read an inventory item number and the amount of that item in inventory from a data card. We will then write this information on a disk file. Let us assume that the items are identified by a number between 1 and 2500."

Phil began to write a program on the board.

```
C   WRITING INVENTORY ON A DISK
    DEFINE FILE 18 (2500,20,U)
    DO 5 I = 1, 2500
    READ, ITEMNO, INV
5   WRITE (18'ITEMNO) INV
    STOP
    END
```

"Can anyone explain this program?" Phil asked.

"I'll give it a try," volunteered Tyrone Shoelaces. "The file is defined as having 2500 records with each record being 20 characters long. The amount of inventory for each item might use up, say, 5 characters, thus leaving 15 characters for information to be added later. Perhaps a re-order point could be identified in this extra space. Anyway, it is reserved and filled with blanks.

"The loop reads in the 2500 inventory item cards and writes each one in a particular location on the disk. That location is the item number. It is interesting to note that the cards could be in any order. They still would be stored in the proper place. The define file statement had created room for 2500 records."

"Mr. Shoelaces," called Prof. Ovitt, "what if the loop were structured to read in only 1500 cards. What would happen then?"

"Well," began Tyrone, "the items that were read in would be placed in their unique location in the file (somewhere between 1 and 2500). Any space that was not used would be empty. It would still be part of the file but would currently not contain any information. Some files are deliberately designed this way to provide for future expansion."

"Very good," commented Prof. Ovitt. "Let me just cover one more statement that is useful for processing data on a disk. This statement is called the FIND statement.

"If you wish to locate a particular record, the following statement could be used.

FIND (15'250)

"This will find record 250 on disk file 15. This moves the access arm to the proper location. If this statement appears several statements before a READ command, it can increase the speed at which records are accessed.

"Now, I know that this may be confusing to those of you who are unfamiliar with FORTRAN, but I feel that the examples used are easy enough to follow. The concepts are the important part. Since most data processing applications utilize both tapes and disks, it is important to understand how to use these media. While we have not exhausted all of the possible commands available for such interaction, the ones we have covered today are the most frequently used."

"Say, Prof. Ovitt," said Howie, "you mentioned earlier that you would comment on the tape and disk information that is required in job control statements. Will you be covering that today?"

"Yes, Howie," he replied, "it's rather brief, but after all we've been discussing in the last few classes I think you'll understand the concepts rather quickly.

"There is one statement in particular that warrants our attention. This job control statement is the *data definition statement,* often referred to as the DD statement. Let me show you an example of one of these statements as it relates to processing files." Prof. Ovitt erased the board and began to write.

//MYFILE DD UNIT=3330,VOL=SER=USER02,DSN=PHILNO,
  DCB=(RECFM=FB,LRECL=80,BLKSIZE=5600,SPACE=(TRK,(5,1))

"Let me explain each of these parameters," Phil continued.

"The // characters identify this statement as a job control (JCL) statement. Immediately after these characters I put a name that identifies this particular statement to me. The letters DD define this particular JCL statement as a data definition statement.

"Now we define the characteristics of our file. The UNIT is the device we are using. A 3330 is a disk unit at our facility. The tape drive is designated as 2400, so we would say UNIT = 2400 if this was a tape processing job. These numbers are essentially manufacturer's model numbers.

"VOL stands for volume and SER stands for series; these are merely identifiers that specify which particular tape or disk to use. In this example, the disk pack we are using has been given the name USER02 by the computer center.

"Since there can be several data sets on a tape or a disk, we must specify which data set we are using. The data set name parameter (DSN) accomplished this. I've named my data set PHILNO.

"The *data control block* (DCB) specifies in more detail what my file will look like. Let's use the following example to illustrate this portion of the JCL statement."

"Say, Prof. Ovitt," asked Brandon, "could you go a bit slower. I'm behind in my notes."

"Okay, Mr. Cattle," replied Prof. Ovitt. "Let's say that we have a record described by an 80-column punched card and we decide to block in 70 record units. Remember, blocking allows us to combine records so that we can transfer large chunks of data, rather than individual records, back and forth. It usually saves both time and space.

"Now we can look at the data control block in the JCL statement. RECFM=FB indicates that the record format is Fixed Blocked records. The Logical RECord Length (LRECL) is 80 bytes, as we specified, and the BLocK SIZE (BLKSIZE) for seventy 80-byte records is 5600 bytes."

"What is that final parameter concerning SPACE?" asked Howie.

"That refers to our disk file, Howard," responded Prof. Ovitt. "You remember that a disk surface was made up of tracks on which the data was stored. Well, this parameter reserves space for your file.

"There are two numbers in parentheses after the letters TRK for track. The first number (in this case a 5) indicates how many tracks you expect to use. The second parameter allows you to add additional tracks if needed. This parameter says 'add 1 track at a time as required up to a maximum of 15 additional times.' If the parameter had been TRK(5,2) then we would have allocated 5 tracks and added 2 tracks at a time as needed, again doing this up to 15 times (perhaps adding up to 30 tracks to the file). This second parameter is very useful for ensuring that valuable disk space is not wasted.

"As you can see, this statement rather completely describes your file to the computer system."

"Prof. Ovitt," called Rudy, "the bell rang 20 minutes ago. We're late for our next class."

"Yes, of course," replied Phil. "What is your next class?"

"It's a course titled The Sequential Random Access of Virtual Memory Using Hash Coding Techniques on Buffered Input from Systems within a Radius Greater Than 400 Miles."

"Sounds technical," said Phil.

"No, it is an introductory survey course," answered Howie.

TOPIC SUMMARY FOR SECTION 6.6

Writing onto tape	DCB
Reading from tape	LRECL
REWIND	BLKSIZE
BACKSPACE	TRK
DEFINE FILE	UNIT
Writing onto disk	VOL
Reading from a disk	SER
FIND statement	Blocking records
DD statement	Contingency tracks
DSN	

Problems for Sec. 6.6

1. Find out from your computer center what numbers are assigned to the tape units. Do the same for disk units.

2. What are the model numbers of the tape drives and disk drives used at your facility?
3. Obtain from your computer facility the procedure that you must follow to borrow and utilize a tape.
4. If you have had FORTRAN, see if you can write a program similar to the DEMONSTRATION PROGRAM in Section 6.6 that will run at your facility.
5. Obtain the necessary job control cards for creating and accessing a disk file. If you are familiar with FORTRAN, write a short program that will READ and WRITE an inventory file similar to that described in the last section.
6. If you are familiar with BASIC, find out how both your programs and any 'canned' programs are stored in your system.

chapter
7

Computer applications

On almost any Sunday, the big city newspapers will contain many articles concerning the growing use of computers in numerous fields, including medicine, education, sports, industry, and law enforcement. It would take many volumes to list the ways in which computers have been applied. Rather than attempt to start such a list, this chapter will present some of the ideas underlying a few of these applications. From this the reader should have a better understanding of the conceptual foundation of such applications and be better able to develop his own systems; a person with the knowledge of a programming language, flowcharting techniques, and an understanding of simple systems is able to comprehend and develop more sophisticated systems.

This chapter will include sections on computer simulation, computer-assisted instruction, and optical character recognition, as well as applications in mathematics and in management.

7.1 SIMULATION

Howie came back to his room after his first Saturday at his new part-time job at the campus bakery.

"Hey, Howie. Wow! Those sure are pretty birthday cakes. How come you have four of them?" asked Cole, Howie's roommate.

"They're my first day's pay. The baker made a bunch of cakes and told me to put frosting on them. I made one chocolate cake and eight birthday cakes. I guess I made a mistake because we sold the chocolate cake but only four birthday cakes. The baker seemed kind of mad and told me that the leftover birthday cakes were my first day's pay. How was I to know how many birthday cakes people would want?"

"Why don't you use the computer and make a model to tell you how many cakes to decorate as birthday cakes?" asked Cole, somewhat facetiously.

"Hey, that's a good idea. The bakery keeps a record of the number of birthday cakes it sells. If I study those records I can see how many cakes are sold each day."

Monday, Howie went to the bakery and studied the records of last year. He found that on the past 50 Saturdays the bakery had sold the following numbers of birthday cakes:

3 cakes on 5 Saturdays
4 cakes on 10 Saturdays
5 cakes on 10 Saturdays
6 cakes on 25 Saturdays

The baker said that while there were different students on campus this year, the overall number of students was about unchanged and so these figures would probably be representative of the demand for birthday cakes on future Saturdays. He then told Howie that from now on just make three birthday cakes each Saturday, because then they would all be sold.

"Yes, they would all be sold," responded Howie, "but then there would be customers who would come in to buy a birthday cake and would have to go off campus because we would be sold out. In fact your figures probably don't represent true demand for last year, since some days you could probably have sold more than you baked."

"That's true, Howie. What do you suggest we do?"

"Let's estimate the number of Saturdays in the next 50 Saturdays that the bakery could sell 3, 4, 5, 6, 7, etc., cakes, if we had enough to fill any demand "

"Okay," began baker Rollin Dough. "Out of the next 50 Saturdays I think I could sell these numbers of cakes." The baker wrote on a cake box.

DEMAND (Number of birthday cakes)	NUMBER OF SATURDAYS ON WHICH THAT DEMAND OCCURRED (out of 50 Saturdays)	PROPORTION OF SATURDAYS ON WHICH THAT DEMAND OCCURRED
3	5	0.1
4	10	0.2
5	10	0.2
6	10	0.2
7	10	0.2
8	5	0.1

"Now what?" asked the baker.

"How much does it cost to bake a cake?" asked Howie.

"About $1.10. I know this because I was just trying to figure out where my money is going," responded Rollin.

"And the cake sells for $3.50," Howie interjected. "I think I can write a program that will help us decide how many birthday cakes to bake so that we maximize our average profit."

Howie left the bakery and realized he didn't have any idea how to solve this problem. He went to see Prof. Ovitt.

After he had listened to Howie's explanation of the problem, Prof. Ovitt began to speak. "I see. The problem is that you would like to bake just the number of birthday cakes that you are going to be able to sell that day, but since you don't know what demand will be, and since you prepare the birthday cakes in advance, you have to guess."

"That's right," said Howie.

"If you bake three each Saturday, you'll almost never have left-overs, but you'll be short about 90 percent of the time. If you bake eight each Saturday, you'll never be short, but you'll have leftovers about 90 percent of the time, based on the baker's estimates."

"I guess maybe we should average it out and bake $5\frac{1}{2}$ each day," interjected Howie.

"Why don't you run a simulation program?"

"What's that," Howie asked.

"A *simulation program* is a program that constructs in the computer a set of conditions analogous to a situation in the real world. By studying the behavior of the computer system, some insight may be gained about the possible outcomes for the real world system. In your problem, the bakery is the real world situation. The model we make to simulate the bakery should have some critical similarities with the real system.

"That sounds like it has possibilities," Howie paused, "but I still don't know how to solve the problem."

"Do you remember the random-number generators that we said are built into most programming languages?" asked Prof. Ovitt.

"Probably. Could you refresh my memory?"

"A perfect random-number generator is able to produce numbers from 0.000000 to 0.999999 so that every number in that range has an equal chance of being produced. The FORTRAN and BASIC languages have random-number generators built into them that are, for most practical purposes, perfect random number generators.[1] Consider a number N that has been generated at random (i.e., by our random number generator). What is the probability that N is less than 0.1?"

"Let's see," said Howie. "If you look at the interval from 0 to 0.9999 . . . like this

```
L_____J
0                                              0.9999 . . .
```

then I guess the interval 0 to 0.1 is this segment of it.

```
L___._____J
0   0.1                                        0.9999 . . .
```

This segment has one-tenth of the numbers from 0 to 0.9999 . . . , so I guess the probability that N is less than 0.1 is one-tenth or 0.1."

"Good, Howie. Try this one. What is the probability that N is between 0.1 and 0.3?"

"The segment from 0.1 to 0.3 is two-tenths of the line from 0 to 0.9999 . . . . That means the segment from 0.1 to 0.3 has two-tenths of the numbers from 0 to 0.9999 . . . . I guess the probability that N is between 0.1 and 0.3 is two-tenths or 0.2."

"Right again, Howie. I think you understand that pretty well. Now let's construct a computer model of the bakery situation. We have assumed from the baker's figures that the probability of demand for birthday cakes on a particular day is the following:

Number of birthday cakes	Probability of demand
3	0.1
4	0.2
5	0.2
6	0.2
7	0.2
8	0.1

What we will do in the computer is generate a random number and let

[1]Actually, in running simulation programs of importance, some care must be taken to check the "randomness" of the output from a random-number generator. This topic is treated more thoroughly in books which treat simulation in greater detail.

the value of that random number tell us what the demand for cakes might be. For example, we might let any random number generated that is between 0.0 and 0.1 correspond to a demand of three birthday cakes. The probability that the random number will be in that range is 0.1, and the probability that the demand is 3 is also 0.1. Thus we have defined a situation in the computer (namely the random number is between 0.0 and 0.1) that has a correspondence in the real world (the demand is three), and both events have the same probability."

"Let me get this straight," interrupted Howie. "For each possible outcome in the real world (like the demand for birthday cakes being three), we are going to define a possible outcome for the random number (like the random number is less than 0.1) such that the real world event has the same probability of occurring as the computer-generated event."

"I couldn't have said it better, Howie."

"What computer event could correspond to the real event of the demand for birthday cakes being four?" asked Howie.

"The probability of the demand for the cakes being four is 0.2. Thus we need a computer event that has a probability of 0.2 of occurring. Look at the event—the random number is between 0.1 and 0.3. That has a probability of 0.2 of occurring and is a different event from the event we have set up to correspond to the demand being 3. Thus we might use the event—the random number is between 0.1 and 0.3—to correspond to the demand for birthday cakes being four."

"How about the other demands?" asked Howie.

"We can make these correlations (Prof. Ovitt wrote on the board):

REAL WORLD DEMAND	VALUE OF RANDOM NUMBER	PROBABILITY OF EACH
3	0.0–0.0999 . . .	0.1
4	0.1–0.2999 . . .	0.2
5	0.3–0.4999 . . .	0.2
6	0.5–0.6999 . . .	0.2
7	0.7–0.8999 . . .	0.2
8	0.9–0.9999 . . .	0.1

"I'm a little uneasy," said Howie.

"Let me go on, and maybe it will clear up," responded Prof. Ovitt. "The simulation procedure then consists of generating a random number, finding which range that random number falls into, and using that knowledge to assume a demand for cakes. For example, if the random number is 0.83172, and since that number is in the 0.7–0.899999 range, it would correspond to a demand of seven cakes. If you had baked seven or more cakes, then the bakery would sell seven cakes. Of course, if the bakery had baked only five cakes and the demand were seven, you could sell only five cakes."

"A little clearer," said Howie. "When do we do this simulation, though?"

"We could do it now. Remember, we want to simulate the bakery in advance so that we can use the output for planning."

"How do we know how many cakes we bake?" asked Howie.

"We could assume a number of birthday cakes were prepared, say five. Then we simulate a day at the bakery, using the random-number generator to determine the demand for cakes. Say the simulated demand is four. Then we have baked five cakes and sold four in the model."

"I don't see how those results will help much," commented Howie. "Suppose the simulation came up with a demand of eight when we run it. Then the best answer would be to have prepared eight birthday cakes. But, I know what can happen when you do that because I did it once."

"After you assume a number of cakes, say five, you run the simulation and record your results. Then you run the simulation again and again, maybe 1000 times, each time assuming that five cakes were prepared. You tabulate all the results and then, because you have run it a lot of times, you can see what happened on the average. Also you can see what the best days might produce, the worst days, the variance, etc."

"You'll really get a feeling for what might happen if you bake five birthday cakes," Howie was warming up. "Then I bet you do the whole thing over assuming that you bake four cakes."

"Right, Howie, you could simulate the situation for each of the possible baking decisions and tabulate the results in each case. After we have considered all the reasonable decisions, we can look over the results and see which strategy we like best. Let's see if we can be specific about this. How much does a cake sell for?"

"$3.50," responded Howie.

"And how much do you think it costs to bake a cake?"

"The baker said it costs $1.10," continued Howie.

"Let's see if you can draw a flowchart for the entire simulation," encouraged Prof. Ovitt.

Howie drew on some paper. (See page 349.)

"That's good," said Prof. Ovitt. "You could now write a program and run it."

Howie went to the computer room and returned to Prof. Ovitt's office in a couple of hours.

"Look at these results," he announced.

The printout looked like this:

NUMBER BIRTHDAY CAKES BAKED = 3
MAX PROFIT = 7.20   AVERAGE PROFIT = 7.20
MIN PROFIT = 7.20   VARIANCE = 0

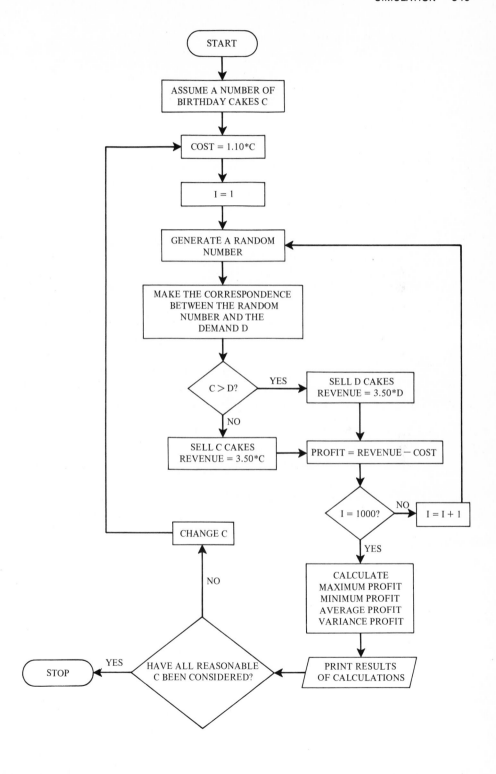

NUMBER BIRTHDAY CAKES BAKED = 4
MAX PROFIT = 9.60   AVERAGE PROFIT = 9.23
MIN PROFIT = 6.10   VARIANCE = 1.14

NUMBER BIRTHDAY CAKES BAKED = 5
MAX PROFIT = 12.00   AVERAGE PROFIT = 10.84
MIN PROFIT = 5.00   VARIANCE = 5.52

NUMBER BIRTHDAY CAKES BAKED = 6
MAX PROFIT = 14.40   AVERAGE PROFIT = 11.1
MIN PROFIT = 3.90   VARIANCE = 13.50

NUMBER BIRTHDAY CAKES BAKED = 7
MAX PROFIT = 16.80   AVERAGE PROFIT = 10.80
MIN PROFIT = 2.80   VARIANCE = 22.82

NUMBER BIRTHDAY CAKES BAKED = 8
MAX PROFIT = 19.20   AVERAGE PROFIT = 10.41
MIN PROFIT = 1.70   VARIANCE = 28.26

"That looks very good, Howie. What strategy do you recommend, based on your results?"

"I don't know," said Howie. "The highest average profit is $11.56 when the number of cakes baked is 6. But the variance is higher for baking 6 than for baking 5. My experience tells me that the baker doesn't like leftover cakes very much. I guess that means he doesn't like a high variance."

"That's a good point," responded Prof. Ovitt. "The final decision that should be made depends on exactly what the people involved care about. If the value of the highest average profit is what counts then one decision should be made, but if there are other factors to consider, like the variance of profits, then perhaps a different decision should be made."

"I think I have learned a few additional points about simulation studies today. I'm going to jot them down so that I won't forget them," said Howie.

He wrote on the back of his computer printout:

1. The model for the computer should correspond to the realities of the real problem.
2. The historical data available may not be exactly correct for the purposes of the model (e.g., the past sales of birthday cakes didn't reflect true demand because sometimes demand exceeded the available supply, and these data weren't recorded).
3. The simulation model may be run for different decisions to show their effects.
4. The final decision to be used should reflect the objectives of the people it affects.

"You know, Howie, if I had listed these statements on the board in class you probably would have fallen asleep. I guess the material doesn't always seem relevant until you start to use it. Right?"

Howie had fallen asleep.

Prof. Ovitt quietly left the room. He was leaving for a symposium on applications of simulation techniques. He had heard that there would be a good session concerning recent advances in the simulation of traffic in cities and the effects of synchronized traffic signals. The main speaker was Dr. Morris Brown, who had achieved quite a bit of recognition for his excellent suggestions for hospital management that were the results of his simulation work in that field.

Prof. Ovitt was riding to the seminar with his associate, Justin Case, who was doing research on the current models simulating the world.

"Exactly what is it you're doing on this project?" asked Phil.

"Well," started Justin, "as you know there are several books that discuss the future of the earth, based on results of simulation models. I have obtained a research grant to study these models and report on their assumptions and their conclusions. Furthermore, the goal of the study I'm doing is to see how the different models are affected by the policies of the United States."

"A model of the world. I wonder if the model predicted that I would stop for an ice cream cone now," said Phil jokingly.

"The models aren't quite that detailed yet," responded Justin. "I have a chart of the interactions of various key components of society that one model uses as its parameters," said Justin, pulling out a piece of paper from his briefcase. "The arrows show the effects of the parameters on each other."

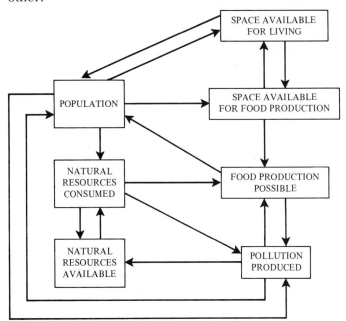

"The model specifies mathematically the anticipated way in which each parameter will interact with each other. Certainly this rather macroscopic chart cannot present the detail of the model. Each of those boxes represents complex systems themselves. The output from the model is quite interesting and quite controversial," said Justin.

"I know," replied Phil. "I read the book and I also read a couple of reviews of it in major newspapers. It should be a very interesting project."

The professors arrived at the conference and obtained a list of the different studies being presented. The list was as follows:

TOPICS FOR PRESENTATION AT SIMULATION CONFERENCE

1. The simulation of business systems with applications in inventory management, production, and pricing. ·
2. The simulation of biological systems. The ecology of a lake. Models of living organisms.
3. Models of the balance of payments of a country to show the effects of floating the exchange rate.
4. A program to simulate the path of a space vehicle.
5. The urban environment and the effects of city planning.
6. Application of simulation for the resolution of conflict.
7. Organizational behavior. Comparison of actual results with simulation results.
8. The use of simulation games as learning tools in management education.
9. Queueing systems with applications to traffic management.
10. The use of computer simulation languages.
    - (a) GPSS
    - (b) SIMSCRIPT
    - (c) DYNAMO
    - (d) Others

Prof. Ovitt was looking forward to the lectures. He particularly was interested in lecture 10 because he was in charge of a committee whose task it was to decide on a simulation language to be put on the computer at UGH.

Problems for Sec. 7.1

1. Program and run the simulation of Howie's bakery.
2. I have discovered a game that will keep my daughter, Jennifer, busy and happy while I watch football games on TV. The game is for her to try to build 10 houses in a row with cards. I have noticed that on the

average a card house will stand 40 percent of the time (regardless of whether the previous houses stood up or fell). If she builds card houses well, I reward her with an M & M. If she builds poorly (a lot fall down), she gets nothing. We play this game repeatedly for about 2 hours and 42 minutes on Saturday and Sunday.

(a) Write down a method for simulating, in the computer, the building of one card house.

(b) Write down a method for simulating, in the computer, the building of 10 card houses.

(c) Write and run a program that simulates the building of 10 houses 1000 times.

(d) What is the proportion of times that 0 houses stood? One house stood? Fill out a table like this:

No. of houses stood	Proportion of times
0	
1	
. . .	
10	

3. A single-server queueing model.

   Assume that patients arrive at a clinic to see the gastroenterologist at all times during a day. When a patient arrives, if the doctor is available he sees the patient immediately. If the doctor is busy, the patient waits to be seen. If several patients are waiting, they are seen in order of their arrival.

   Assume it takes exactly 0.4 hours for the doctor to treat any patient. Assume also that the time between the last patient's arrival and the next patient's arrival is a random number from the uniform distribution between 0 and 1 hours.

   Simulate the operation of the clinic for 10 hours. (Run the simulation several times to get average results, worst cases, best cases, variance.)

4. Assume in Problem 3 that the arrival process is from the uniform distribution between 0 and 1 hours, but the service process is from the uniform distribution from 0.2 to 0.6 hours. Simulate this queueing process.

7.2 POLITICS, SAMPLING, AND COMPUTERS

Howie was walking from his statistics class and talking to Clara. "You know, Clara, I don't see why we have to do these statistics problems, anyway. Look at this assignment." Howie handed the assignment paper to Clara.

There is an urn with 1000 marbles in it, some are red and some are green. In an experiment to obtain information about the fraction of the marbles that are red, a marble is selected at random from the urn. ("Selected at random" means that every marble is equally likely to be selected.) The color of the marble is recorded, and the marble is returned to the urn. Then another marble is selected from the urn, its color recorded, and it is returned. This is done repeatedly. In all, 20 marbles are selected, each being returned after its color is recorded. (This process is called *sampling with replacement*). When the experiment was over, there were 12 red marbles and 8 green ones selected. If the actual number of red marbles in the urn is 450, what is the probability that on a sampling of 20 marbles with replacement there would be a result of 12 or more red marbles selected? (Hint: Remember that the probability of a red marble on each selection is 0.45.)

"Looks like a good problem, Howie. After you figure it out with your statistics, you might simulate it on the computer to check your results. I'll see you later, I have to go vote."

The campus elections were being held today, and Rudy Mentry was so busy he seemed to be scurrying in all directions at once.

"What's your hurry, Rudy?" asked Howie.

"You know my sister Paula is running for Student Parliament and I'm going over to the computer center to see if she will win."

"Voting is taking place at the Student Union, not the computer center. And furthermore, voting doesn't end for another half hour," remarked Howie.

"I know, but I have a computer model that will predict the outcome based on sampling of the voters," said Rudy.

"Hey, I always wondered how those computers predict who will be President when only 1 percent or 2 percent of the votes have been counted. Can I tag along?"

"Sure. Of course, my model isn't nearly as elaborate as the big models used to predict national elections. But, I bet it'll give pretty good results."

"How does it work?" asked Howie as they walked toward the computer center.

"Since Paula is in the Academic Party and her opponent Jake Hands is in the Beer Party, I have divided the student body by party lines."

"I know," interjected Howie, "since you had the student body on party lines, you just called them up on the telephone."

"Not exactly, I considered in my model these parameters:

F_A = the fraction of people voting who are in the Academic Party
F_B = the fraction of people voting who are in the Beer Party
P_A = the fraction of voters who voted for Paula and are in the Academic Party

J_A = the fraction of voters who voted for Jake and are in the Academic Party

P_B = the fraction of voters who voted for Paula and are in the Beer Party

J_B = the fraction of voters who voted for Jake and are in the Beer Party

"Wow! That's a lot of parameters," exclaimed Howie.

"It's not so bad because all voting students are members of either the Academic Party or the Beer Party. This means $F_A + F_B = 1$. Also, since Jake and Paula are the only candidates in the election, we have these relations:

$$P_A + J_A = 1$$

$$P_B + J_B = 1$$

Hence, the only parameters I need to know are F_A, P_A, and P_B.

"What will they tell you?" asked Howie.

"Paula's fraction of the total vote will be $F_A P_A + F_B P_B$; if this is greater than 0.5, she will be elected."

"Yeah, but you won't know those numbers until after the vote is in. You'll know the results of the election by then."

"That's true, Howie," continued Rudy. "But I can estimate the parameters by sampling the voters. I had Juan P.M. go out at random times during the day and discuss their choices with the voters. Here are his results by 1 P.M.

SAMPLE OF 31 VOTERS BY JUAN P.M. BEFORE 1 P.M.

	Jake	Paula	Total
Academic Party	4	16	20
Beer Party	8	3	11
Total	12	19	

"Well, it's clear that Paula's going to win because she has 19 votes to only 12 for Jake. If that trend continues she'll win easily."

"I don't think it's quite that certain, Howie. The problem is that, while the campus is split about 50-50 on party registration before the election, only 11 of the 31 voters sampled by 1:00 P.M. were from the Beer Party. That may be because the Beer Party had a big beer party last night and most of their members were still asleep at 1 P.M."

"Well then how are you going to use the data?" asked Howie.

"I looked at the 1 P.M. sample taken in past years, and taking into account the late vote for the Beer Party I came to the conclusion that, for Paula to win, the real results should be that Paula have at least 68 percent of the Academic Party votes and 32 percent of the Beer Party votes. That way, if everyone votes, Paula will get 68 percent of half the student population (the Academic Party) and 32 percent of the other half (the Beer Party) and will get 50 percent of the total vote. There is even a little extra safety margin there because the Academic Party usually has a little better voter turnout than the Beer Party. But we'll assume $F_A = F_B = \frac{1}{2}$ to be on the safe side."

"Let me see that little table of sample votes," said Howie as he took a pocket calculator out of his shoe. "Sixteen divided by 20 is 0.75, so Paula has 75 percent of the Academic Party votes in the sample. Three divided by 11 is 0.273 so Paula has 27.3 percent of the Beer Party votes in the sample. It looks like Paula's a cinch to win. She almost beat both the requirements you set."

"I wish I could be so sure, Howie. The problem is that the sample data doesn't necessarily reveal the whole picture. The numbers I quoted you were percentages of the entire voting population, while the numbers you calculated were for the small sample. Now I have to run my program to see how well I think the sample represents the entire population."

Howie remembered his statistics assignment. "You mean something like this?" Howie said, as he produced the assignment he had just been showing Clara. "How are you going to test the data?"

"I think I'll first assume that the actual percent of all the voters in the Academic Party who chose Paula is 68 percent and that the percent of all the voters in the Beer Party who chose Paula is 32 percent," said Rudy. "Then I'm going to simulate the voting of 20 Academic Party voters and 11 Beer Party voters and see how many times in 1000 simulations that I get a total vote of 19 or more for Paula."

"I guess you'll have to write a program to perform the simulation," said Howie as they entered the computer room.

"I did that yesterday," answered Rudy. "Here's a flowchart for the program I saved in the computer (see page 357)."

Note: V is a 32-element list. V(I) records the number of simulations in which I votes (of the 31 votes) were for Paula. Thus if Paula received 25 votes on a particular simulation of the 31 votes, V(25) would be increased by 1. If total votes is 0, let V(32) be increased by 1 since V(0) may not be allowed. (No 0 subscripts.)

"That's not a very detailed flowchart," commented Howie.

"I guess you're right. Some of the blocks in the flowchart could have been written in much more detail. Here, I have my program accessed on this terminal."

Rudy typed in the input numbers, 20 and 11, and the computer soon typed out the V list.

"Look, Howie. In 29 percent of the simulations Paula received 19 or more votes," said Rudy, a little disappointedly.

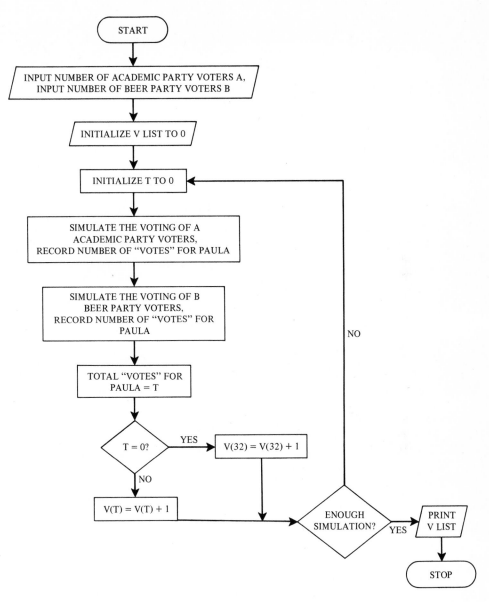

"What does that mean?" asked Howie.

"If the actual percent of the Academic Party voting for Paula were 68 percent, and the actual percent of the Beer Party voting for Paula were 32 percent and the number in each party were even, then there is about a 29 percent chance the sample would have come out with Paula getting 19 or more of the 31 votes. Thus, if the actual election is about even (Paula getting 68 percent of the votes of half the students and 32 percent of the votes of the other half), there is about a 29 percent chance that the sample would make Paula look way ahead (19 or more out of the sampled 31). I guess the election is still too close to tell with any reliability," said Rudy.

"But it sure doesn't look bad for Paula," said Howie.

"That's true," returned Rudy.

"Say, Rudy, do you think you could help me with this statistics problem?" asked Howie, producing his homework assignment. "I don't know why anyone would even want to know how to do problems like this anyway."

Problems for Sec. 7.2

1. Solve Howie's homework assignment by simulation. Simulate many times the drawing of 20 marbles when the probability of a red marble on each draw is 0.45. In what fraction of the simulations did the drawing of 20 marbles result in 12 or more red marbles? Check this result with the answers in a statistics book containing the binomial distribution.

2. See Problem 1. Instead of drawing 20 marbles on each simulation, you draw N number of marbles. You would like to determine what N should be to satisfy these two specifications:

   (a) You would like N to be as small as possible.

   (b) If there are 450 red marbles in the urn, you would like the probability of obtaining $0.6N$ or more red marbles to be 0.05 or less.

   Having solved this problem you have determined a test of the hypothesis that the number of red marbles R in the urn is 450, against the alternative that the number of red marbles is higher than that. In particular, if you decide to draw N marbles and reject the hypothesis that $R = 450$ if you get $0.6N$ or more red marbles, then the probability that you will reject the hypothesis when it is true is 0.05.

3. Continuing with Problem 2. Suppose the hypothesis you are testing is $R = 450$, and the alternative is $R = 700$. In Problem 2 an N was found such that the probability that the number of red marbles drawn would equal or exceed $0.6N$ was 0.05. If this number, N, of marbles were to be selected and if R were truly 700, what is the probability that the number of red marbles selected would be less than $0.6N$? This is the probability that the hypothesis, $R = 450$, will be accepted given that it is in fact false and the test of Problem 2 is used.

4. Write a program to perform Rudy's simulation of the campus election.

7.3 COMPUTERS IN EDUCATION

Howie was in the library working on a paper when his friend Rudy approached. "Hey, How, I just got a part-time job that I'm pretty excited about."

"That's great! Let's go outside and talk about it. I'm not getting anywhere in here anyway," said Howie. The two students walked outside.

"What's the job about?" asked Howie.

"I've been hired to tutor 20 third-grade children in arithmetic at Stella Kidd elementary school."

"But, Rudy, that's a lot of kids. The fact that they need tutoring indicates that the classroom approach to math education hasn't worked for them. If you try to give them individual instruction, then just 2 or 3 hours a week each will mean a full-time job for you."

"That's true," responded Rudy. "I have an idea, though. I'm going to write a computer program that will help the kids practice. I took a portable terminal over to the Kidd School today and the principal was enthusiastic enough to promise to get me a remote terminal so that the kids can use the computer the school system already has set up at the high school."

"What kind of computer program can you write to help the kids learn arithmetic?" asked Howie. "They certainly don't know computer programming."

"They don't have to know programming, just how to read, which they can do. The program will be an interactive one, used by one kid at a time, and asking the kid specific questions. The kid will respond and, depending on the answer, either a new question will be asked or the same question will be re-asked with some hints."

"I think I get the concept, but I don't see how you can do it, exactly," commented Howie.

"I'll draw you a flowchart of the instruction program," continued Rudy. He took a laundry slip out of his pocket and started writing on the back of it. (See page 360.)

Rudy continued, "A sample of the output of the program might look like this: (The characters following the question marks were typed by the student.)

```
HELLO, I HOPE YOU ARE HAVING A GOOD DAY,
PLEASE TYPE IN YOUR NAME.
?"DANNY"
THANK YOU DANNY.
PLEASE TRY TO ANSWER THIS QUESTION.
WHAT IS 2 + 2
? 4
GOOD, DANNY.
PLEASE TRY TO ANSWER THIS QUESTION.
WHAT IS 23 + 18
? 42
TOO BAD. YOUR ANSWER WAS A LITTLE TOO HIGH.
PLEASE TRY AGAIN.
? 41
THAT'S GOOD. HERE'S ANOTHER ONE.
WHAT IS 17 + 18
?
```

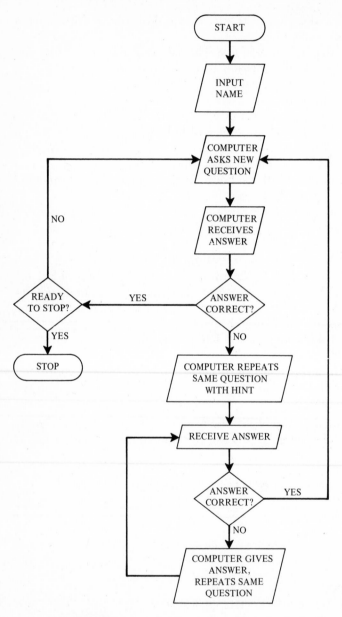

"What do you think, Howie?" asked Rudy, showing Howie the sample printout.

"36," said Howie.

"No, I meant what do you think of the whole idea?"

"It looks interesting," said Howie. "But what about the level of difficulty? All kids won't need practice with the same type of work. Some will still be in addition, while others may be working with multiplication or something else."

"Good point, Howie. A program that would take that into account might ask questions from several levels of difficulty. Then, as a student showed proficiency at a particular level, he could graduate to a higher level. A simplified flowchart for that system could be the following:

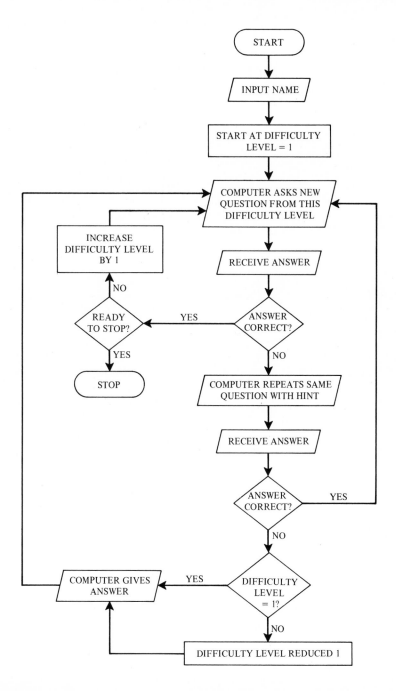

"I guess I can see how your system is technologically feasible. But will the kids like it? Don't people need to feel the warmth of another human?" asked Howie.

"Remember, this program is not to replace the teacher, but to augment the teaching methods. The students will be able to go to the computer room and practice during some free time. Systems like this have been tried already. In New York City a pilot project with nearly 200 terminals was run in 1971 for 6000 elementary school students with considerable success. The University of Illinois has developed a Computer Assisted Instruction (CAI) system called PLATO which has experimented with over 20 courses and over 100,000 student contact hours in work at all levels from elementary school through college. The response from the students using the CAI system has been very positive."

"Why do you think students would like it so well?" asked Howie.

"It allows them to go at their own pace and get immediate feedback at each step. Also, they may like the relative anonymity it gives them when they make mistakes. They can just learn the correct answers without feeling they have looked foolish to another person or kept someone waiting too long. Furthermore, working at remote typewriter terminals, some equipped with cathode-ray displays, the students become more totally involved with their work; it is fun to a lot of students."

"You say that this technique is used for levels from elementary school through college? I can't imagine giving someone, say in medical school, a CAI course on how to add numbers," remarked Howie.

"No, Howie. The medical school students would get a course in medical science. In fact, a class of 20 medical students took such a course on the PLATO system with no other teaching assistance and were able to perform as well on a national test as students who had had conventional classroom instruction. Actually the PLATO-taught students took only about one-half the student contact hours to learn the material and, when retested later, showed a greater retention than the other students."

"Sounds interesting, but I don't see how the computer could really help in such a course. Rudy, can't the computer only ask the specific questions you tell it to ask?"

"No, Howie. Computers are used in education in many different ways. For example, there is an interactive program in use at over 60 medical schools that is helpful for students learning about abdominal disorders. The instructor can have the computer simulate a human being with a particular disorder. Then the student asks the "programmed patient" questions about the symptoms, and the computer will answer as if it were a real patient. The program responds with results as if the tests were actually performed."

"Why doesn't the student just ask all the questions he can think of and do all the tests that might be at all relevant?" asked Howie.

"When the student is a doctor he simply won't have time to ask

Figure 7.1 Computer-aided instruction.

every possible question of every patient. Also, many lab tests are expensive and/or painful. The students need to know what questions to ask and what tests to request so that a correct diagnosis can be made. The program that is currently in use at the 60 medical schools can simulate many different cases of abdominal disorders and thousands of symptoms. Students can be judged on their efficiency, cost, and accuracy of diagnosis. The program has been tested with students and experienced doctors, with the more experienced doctors scoring well on efficiency and cost of examination required for a correct diagnosis."

"Are there any other examples of computer-assisted instruction?"

"Sure, Howie. Programs have been written to aid students in their ability to perform mathematical proofs. Here the computer can give feedback on the logic of each step of a proof and show the student any errors that may creep into a solution. Other programs have been written to analyze unexpected answers on complex problems and judge the answers according to some prescribed criteria of 'goodness.'"

"Why aren't these systems being widely used already?" asked Howie.

"The systems are expensive and the curriculum materials aren't really very extensively developed yet. Add to this the inertia in getting any new ideas adopted, plus the great amount of experimentation to be done before the systems are 'proven,' and you have a good idea why you haven't seen a CAI system yet. However, the University of Illinois group is planning an advanced model of the PLATO system called PLATO IV. If it operated only 10 hours a day, it could provide millions of student contact hours a year, for a cost of around 30 to 40 cents per student contact hour."

"Oh! It's getting late," said Howie, looking at his watch. "I better get back to the library. I'm doing a paper on the use of computers in education and I don't know where to start. I know that the administration at this university uses the computer to assign classrooms for courses, to perform payroll operations, and to keep records of students. However, those seem like administrative uses of the computer. Got any ideas?"

Rudy must have thought he heard a robber, because he threw up his hands and said, "I give up."

Problems for Sec. 7.3

1. Write an interactive program that could be used to give an elementary school child practice in addition. You may want to use a random-number generator to obtain the numbers to be added (see Section 7.1).
2. Draw a flowchart for an interactive program for practice in long division. The computer should not merely check the correctness of a student's answer; rather, it should check each step of the student's work and point out any errors as they occur.
3. Write a program for Problem 2.
4. Write an interactive program that can be used to give a student practice in addition and subtraction. If the student shows a proficiency in adding, he should go on to practice subtraction. If he has trouble with subtraction, the work should be explained to him in terms of addition of the numbers he has already used in the addition practice.

7.4 OPTICAL CHARACTER RECOGNITION

Howie had finished his homework, so he decided to visit his friend Tyrone, who had built a computer in his barn. When he arrived at Tyrone's barn, there appeared to be a party in progress.

"Hello, Tyrone. What's the occasion?" asked Howie.

"I just got OCHRE working. OCHRE stands for Optical CHaracter REcognition and is an attachment to my computer to read written documents, not documents prepared by a punched-card machine, but documents prepared by an ordinary typewriter."

"Hey, that's neat, Tyrone," said Howie, helping himself to a glass of champagne. "But how can you get information into the computer without having the material specifically prepared for a computer?"

"For my system I use two systems: an optical reading system and the computer system with a program designed to decode the input from the optical reading system. Suppose you wanted OCHRE to read a paper with some data on it. You would put the paper on this glass here . . ."

"You mean on that machine that looks like an electrostatic copier?" interrupted Howie.

"Yes. This machine projects the paper to be read onto a plate of photocells. A photocell can put out an electric current if light hits it, and no current if no light hits it. Thus the plate of photocells can convert the picture on the paper to be read into a collection of electric currents."

"I don't understand," said Howie.

"Well, suppose you had a plate with only four photocells, like this.

Column

		1	2
	1	photocell 1	photocell 2
Row	2	photocell 3	photocell 4

If light hit photocell 1, it would give off a unit of current, say the output of that photocell is then 1. If no light hit the other photocells, they would give no electric current output; call their output 0, 0, and 0 for the output of cell 2, cell 3, and cell 4, respectively. Thus we can represent the output of the photocell plate by four numbers, each representing the output of a photocell, and each number being a 0 or a 1."

"I think I follow you a bit," said Howie.

"Suppose," continued Tyrone, "the light hitting the photocell plate created a pattern like this:

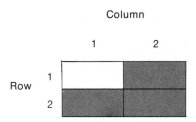

Column

What would be the output of the photocell plate where shaded areas are areas where no light hits the plate?"

"I guess 1, 0, 0, 0," said Howie.

"Right," responded Tyrone. "Let's say that the output from cell 1 is X_{11} (where X_{11} means row 1, column 1), the output from cell 2 is X_{12} (X_{12} means row 1, column 2), the output from cell 3 is X_{21}, and the output from cell 4 is X_{22}. What would the output be if the light hitting the photocell created this pattern?" Tyrone drew this pattern.

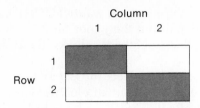

"$X_{11} = 0$, $X_{12} = 1$, $X_{21} = 1$, and $X_{22} = 0$," answered Howie.

"That's right again, Howie. You get the idea of how a black-and-white image can be converted into a sequence of coded numbers."

"Well, if I ever need to read a lot of pages with black-and-white squares, I know where to come," said Howie, not realizing the importance of the concept.

"That's not all OCHRE can do," defended Tyrone. "First of all, OCHRE has a 100-photocell grid. That means the page is divided into a grid that is 10×10, like this one:

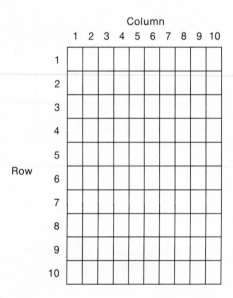

Now the pattern of light hitting the photocell plate is represented by a series of 100 numbers, each 0 or 1, depending on whether or not the cell is dark or light."

"So you can read a big checkerboard. That plus 25 cents will buy you a can of soda," continued Howie.

"That's true," said Tyrone, wondering why he was bothering with this explanation. "But some of these checkerboard configurations can begin to look familiar."

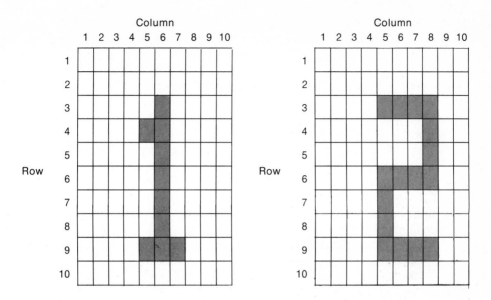

"Howie, could you draw a flowchart to read a page to see if the page had a '1' on it exactly like the '1' I drew?" asked Tyrone.

"I suppose so," said Howie. "Let's see, let X_{11} = the output from the photocell in row 1, column 1. Let X_{12} be the input from the photocell in row 1, column 2. In general, let X_{ij} be the input from the photocell in row i, column j (where i and j stand for numbers). Now your '1' produces a pattern of lighted photocells everywhere but where the character '1' is. Those shaded photocells produce an input of zero, so X_{36}, X_{45}, X_{46}, X_{56}, X_{66}, X_{76}, X_{86}, X_{95}, X_{96}, and X_{97} are all equal to zero. The other X_{ij}'s are all equal to 1. You want to test the input from a different page and see if it produces an input exactly the same as the input from your '1.' Then, I think this would work:

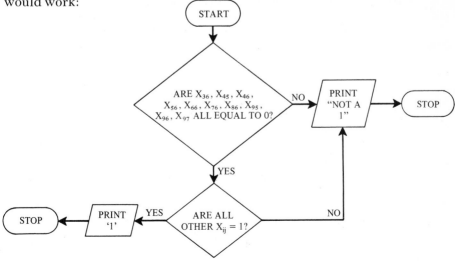

"Would that be hard to program?" asked Howie.

"No, Howie," replied Tyrone. "Notice that the first question can be answered by answering a similar question, namely, does $X_{36} + X_{45} + X_{46} + X_{56} + X_{66} + X_{76} + X_{86} + X_{95} + X_{96} + X_{97} = 0$? We know that the photocell grid has 100 photocells, each of which could produce a value of 0 or 1. The first requirement that $X_{36} + X_{45} + X_{46} + X_{56} + X_{66} + X_{76} + X_{86} + X_{95} + X_{96} + X_{97} = 0$ means that there are 90 other photocells, each of which must be equal to 1 if the page contains a '1.' Thus, the second question on your flowchart can be answered easily by seeing if the sum of all the X_{ij}'s is 90, since that's just the number of lighted photocells on the photocell plate."

"That's really clever, Tyrone," rejoined Howie. "But you said that OCHRE would read pages not prepared specifically for computers. Not everyone is going to write a '1' just the same way and in just the same spot on the page."

"You're not as dumb as you pretend to be, Howie. You're right about that. I guess I'll let you in on my technique of comparing a '1' with a '2.' Even though everyone doesn't write a '1' the same, they all use a vertical line that is longer than any other line in the number when they make a '1.' When they make a '2' this is not the case; there are probably some vertical lines, but each vertical line is short compared to the whole letter size. What my program really does is decide how big the number is. Then it finds the longest vertical line. If this line is about as big as the letter, the program calls the number a '1,' otherwise it calls it a '2.' Thus the program can read pages and differentiate between the handwritten numbers that look like

$$1 \quad \text{or} \quad | \quad \text{or} \quad 1 \quad \text{and} \quad 2 \quad \text{or} \quad 2$$

"Fantastic, Tyrone. Pass the champagne," shouted Howie. "But where is this going to lead you?"

"When I can get the money together, I want to build a photocell plate with many more, smaller photocells on it. Then I'll be able to write a program that can read a whole page of letters and numbers. I know that established companies have built Optical Character Reading (OCR) machines capable of reading thousands of characters per second, but I figure if I keep messing around with this, I may get some ideas they haven't thought of. It's a lot of fun also.

"People are already starting to use the OCR systems. A system going into use in New York is designed to handle 86,000 pieces of mail an hour."

"How about the banks? Don't they use these machines to read checks?" asked Howie.

"Yes, Howie. The banks use Optical Character Recognition equipment. They also use equipment that reads special magnetic ink numbers printed on checks at the rate of 2400 documents per minute. These tech-

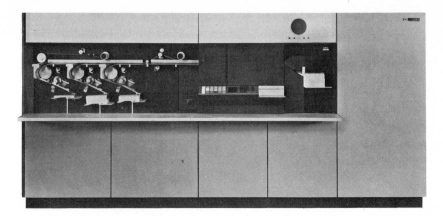

Figure 7.2 An Optical Character Reader.

niques and others, like the hand-held wand that reads magnetic ink characters, are all input devices for use with a computer system.

Problems for Sec. 7.4

1. Write a program that inputs a 10×10 matrix of values (each entry is 0 or 1) and tests to see if the matrix corresponds to a '1.'
2. Write a program that inputs a 10×10 matrix of values (each entry is 0 or 1) and tests to see if the matrix corresponds to a '2.'
3. Write a program that inputs a 10×10 matrix of values (each entry is 0 or 1). Assume that the entries that have the value '0' are contiguous and form a single integer. The program should measure the height of the integer and the width of the integer. Then check to see if the input integer is a '1' or a '2.' (Assume these are the only possibilities.) In this problem the integer may be anywhere on the input grid and should still be correctly identified.
4. Extend the work of Problem 3 to consider the possibility of the input integer being a '1,' a '2,' or a '9.'

7.5 APPLICATIONS IN MATHEMATICS

This section presents two applications of the computer in solving applied mathematics problems.

7.5.1 FINDING THE ROOT OF AN EQUATION

Howie was walking one day and ran into his friend, Al Geebra, the math whiz.

"Howie!" exclaimed Al. "I've almost finished solving that problem I've been working on. You know, the problem to find the optimal amount of water to give a 22-inch rhododendron each day to achieve a maximum flower bloom on Mother's Day."

"Fantastic!" said Howie, stifling a yawn.

"You see, if I let X be the amount of water (in pints) I give the plant each day, the optimal amount X is the value which makes $F(x) = -3.079 + X^5 + 2.1^X + X^4$ equal to zero. I just have to solve that."

"I don't know anything about that stuff," said Howie. "But, good luck. I have to go to the computer center to test out a program Rudy wrote to find the root of an equation."

"What," jumped Al. "You have a program to find a root of an equation? Let's see!"

"There's a program and a flowchart here. What would you like?" asked Howie.

"First the flowchart," answered Al. Howie showed Al the following flowchart.

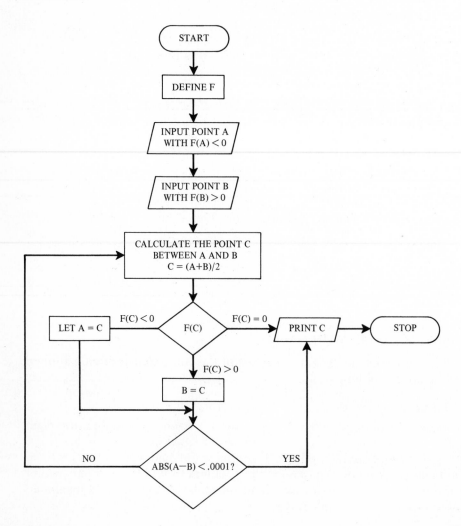

Flowchart for finding the root of a continuous function F when it is known that F evaluated at point A is negative and F evaluated at point B is positive (implying that there is at least one root between A and B). Algorithm uses the method of bisected intervals. Look at midpoint C of interval; if $F(C) < 0$ then A is replaced by C. If $F(C) > 0$ then B is replaced by C. Since it may not be possible to find the exact root (it may not be expressible as a decimal number), this algorithm finds a number whose absolute difference from the value of the root is less than 0.0001.

"Hey, Howie," said Al. "This program is just what I need."

"I should have realized that," said Howie, "since the water does go to the roots of the rhododendron."

"Let's go run the program," urged Al. "I'll start with $A = 0$ (since $F(x)$ is -3.079 for $x = 0$), and $B = 1$ (since $F(x) = 1.021$ for $x = 1$). I'll have this problem solved in no time.

7.5.2 SOLUTION OF SIMULTANEOUS EQUATIONS

Howie and Rudy were visiting their friend Brandon Cattle when someone walked into the room. It was Brandon's brother Russell.

"Hi," said Russell. "Say, Brandon, I've been having trouble with my high school algebra. Could you give me a hand?"

"I'm kind of busy ironing," said Brandon, who was pressing his monogrammed shirts. "Maybe Rudy and Howie can help you."

"Let's take a look," said Howie.

"Here's the problem," answered Russell.

ALGEBRA PROBLEM

Tom's age plus twice Bill's age is equal to Mary's age plus 2. In one year Mary will be three times as old as Tom. The sum of their ages now is 9. How old is each?

"I think I can express it in these terms," continued Russell. "Let

$$x_1 = \text{Tom's age}$$

$$x_2 = \text{Bill's age}$$

$$x_3 = \text{Mary's age}$$

This gives you these equations:

$$x_1 + 2x_2 = x_3 + 2$$

$$3(x_1 + 1) = (x_3 + 1)$$

$$x_1 + x_2 + x_3 = 9$$

Now what?"

"Let's rearrange the equations like this," suggested Rudy. He wrote on the back of a candy wrapper.

$$x_1 + 2x_2 - x_3 = 2$$

$$3x_1 - x_3 = -2$$

$$x_1 + x_2 + x_3 = 9$$

"How would you solve this?" asked Russell.

"Well," said Rudy. "You can look at this in matrix form. Consider that the equations are of the form" (Rudy wrote down the following):

$$Ax = b \qquad \text{where } A = \begin{bmatrix} 1 & 2 & -1 \\ 3 & 0 & -1 \\ 1 & 1 & 1 \end{bmatrix}$$

$$x = \begin{bmatrix} x_1 \\ x_2 \\ x_3 \end{bmatrix} \qquad b = \begin{bmatrix} 2 \\ -2 \\ 9 \end{bmatrix}$$

"Then the solution is $x = A^{-1}b$, where A^{-1} is the inverse of the matrix A. Computer subroutines that will invert matrices and multiply matrices are available for almost every computer system. The equations can be solved very easily."

Problems for Sec. 7.5

1. Program the algorithm presented in Section 7.5.1.
2. If there are two points A and B, such that $F(A) > 0$, $F(B) > 0$, and there is at least one root between A and B, then there must be at least two roots between A and B. Flowchart and program an algorithm that will find two roots of the equation $F(x) = 0$. Test your algorithm on $F(x) = x^2 - 2x - 8 = 0$ by starting with $A = -10$, $B = 10$.
3. Using built-in computer subroutines, solve the problem for Russell Cattle in Section 7.5.2.

7.6 MODELS IN FINANCE

Ray Tereturn, a classmate of Howie's, had a part time job at a company that manufactured Ators (Ators are a component in refrigerators). One day Ray noticed his computer science professor, Phil Ovitt, at the plant.

"Hello, Professor," said Ray. "What brings you here?"

"I'm helping Mr. Radee, owner of the company, decide which computer to use for his business. He's planning to use the computer to automate his billing, ordering, and inventory systems. He wanted some consultation on which machine would be the best for him. We've been working on this decision for a while now."

"What have you come up with?" asked Ray.

"We've decided on an Abacus-15362. Now, Mr. Radee has to decide whether to buy the machine or lease it. I have all the data on the costs of each option. Say, Ray, you're a finance major, maybe you'd like to work on that part of the project."

"Sure would!" responded Ray.

"Come by my office tomorrow morning, and we can get started," encouraged Prof. Ovitt.

When Ray arrived the next morning, Prof. Ovitt spread several pages of data out on the desk. "These are the figures for the two plans."

PLAN A: PURCHASE THE COMPUTER

Cost to purchase machine: $120,000

Expected average maintenance cost	Year
$300/month	1
$250/month	2
$300/month	3
$350/month	4
$350/month	5

Plan to sell the machine in 5 years to buy a larger computer. Expected sale value in 5 years is $40,000.

PLAN B: LEASE THE COMPUTER FOR 5 YEARS

Monthly payments (at beginning of the month) of $2400. Payments include all maintenance costs.

"What do you think, Ray? Interested in working on this?" asked Phil.

"Sure, let me jot down those figures and see what I come up with."

Ray went back to his room and started figuring. He said to himself, "I know the Radee Ator Manufacturing Company has some debt with the banks on which it pays an interest rate of three-fourth percent per month. From my studies in finance, I know that future cash flows of money are discounted to reflect the time value of money. That is, since $1 invested at three-fourth percent per month would be worth $1.0075 in one month, the converse applies; namely, $1.0075 in one month is worth $1 now.

"In a more general sense, any amount of money X in one month would be worth $X/1.0075$ dollars today if the interest rate was three-fourth percent per month. That is, the present value of that 'future amount' X is $X/1.0075$.

"If I invested $X now for 2 months at an interest rate of three-fourth percent per month, in 2 months my total would be

$$[(X)(1.0075)] \cdot (1.0075) \qquad \text{or} \qquad (X)(1.0075)^2$$

$\underbrace{\qquad\qquad\qquad}$
Value at end
of first month

$\underbrace{\qquad\qquad\qquad\qquad\qquad\qquad}$
Value at end of 2 months

"Again, the converse is true. That is, the present value of an amount Y in 2 months must be

$$Y/(1.0075)^2$$

"In the Radee Ator Company problem, I would like to know the present value of the cash flow from each investment plan." Ray wrote down an equation in his notebook to cover the 60 months of plan A. Since the cash flow consists of both income and payment, the present value of plan A (PVA) must be the following.

$$PVA = -120,000 - 300 * \left(\frac{1}{1.0075}\right) - 300 * \left(\frac{1}{1.0075}\right)^2 - 300 *$$

$$\left(\frac{1}{1.0075}\right)^3 - \cdots - 350\left(\frac{1}{1.0075}\right)^{60} + 40,000\left(\frac{1}{1.0075}\right)^{60}$$

"Wow! I could use a computer to calculate that equation. It has 62 terms in it! I'll move on to the present value of plan B." Ray wrote this equation down:

$$PVB = -2400 - 2400\left(\frac{1}{1.0075}\right) - 2400\left(\frac{1}{1.0075}\right)^2 - \cdots - 2400\left(\frac{1}{1.0075}\right)^{59}$$

Ray went to the computer room and quickly programmed the. problem. The results were:

PRESENT VALUE OF COSTS OF PLAN A $= -109,215$

PRESENT VALUE OF COSTS OF PLAN B $= -116,483$

He returned to Prof. Ovitt's office with the results, and together they went to see Mr. Radee at the manufacturing company.

After Ray had explained his results, Mr. Radee started talking. "That's a good start, Ray. Actually, we use the rate of return concept when we analyze an investment."

Ray Tereturn remembered about rate of return. The rate of return of an investment is the rate of interest that makes the discounted cash incomes equal the discounted cash outlays. "When you are comparing two methods of handling a purchase, how would you figure the cash inflow?" asked Ray.

"Since the cash savings from using the computer are the same regardless of the way we acquire the computer, we could just determine the rates of return for which plan A is better and the rates for which plan B is better. By the way, I think you should build into your model the tax savings that we get in both cases. And, don't forget that if we buy the computer, we can depreciate it 20 percent a year and save taxes from that also. Figure our tax rate at 50 percent of profits. Why don't you use those numbers and see what you come up with?"

Ray went back to his room realizing that the problem was a bit more complex than he had thought. He began to work on it by first reviewing his books on rates of return. He came across a problem he had worked:

PROBLEM 936

An investment requires $400 and yields $180 a year for 3 years. What is the rate of return?

SOLUTION

Find the interest rate r such that present value of the cash flow is 0. The present value of the cash flow is

$$-400 + 180\left(\frac{1}{1+r}\right) + 180\left(\frac{1}{1+r}\right)^2 + 180\left(\frac{1}{1+r}\right)^3$$

and the rate of return is the value of r that makes the above equal to 0. That value of r is about 0.1665, which is most easily found using a computer search. (See Section 7.5.1.)

When Ray saw this simple problem that he had already solved, he knew he would be able to solve the computer investment problem. All he would have to do is carefully figure the cash flow in each month. Then he would discount the cash flows by the rate of return r. He could then sketch a graph of the discounted cash flows for plan A minus the discounted cash flows for plan B plotted versus r, the rate of return. "The plot might look something like this," thought Ray.

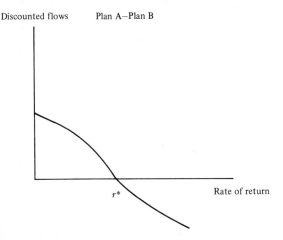

Discounted flows   Plan A–Plan B

r^* Rate of return

"Then for rates of return r less than r^*, plan A is better; and for rates of return higher than r^*, plan B is better."

7.7 INVENTORY MANAGEMENT AND PRODUCTION

Today Prof. Ovitt had invited a guest lecturer, Orson Buggy, president of Orson Buggy Auto Parts.

"Hello, I'm Orson Buggy. I am pleased to be here with you. Prof. Ovitt asked me to come today to discuss our computerized inventory system at the plant. We stock about 80,000 different types of replacement parts for automobiles. These parts are kept in a large warehouse in bins measuring about 2 feet on each side and are stacked on 900 shelves 12 feet high and 30 feet long. When we get orders from auto repair shops and car manufacturers for parts, a person goes to the appropriate bins and picks the parts to bill the order. When the order is picked, the inventory parts manager records which parts were shipped for the order. This record is then sent to the computer facility in the same building, where the information is entered into the computer file of inventory parts."

"What does the computer do for you?" asked Howie.

"The computer keeps a record of what we have in inventory, what we have on order, plus a record of the order numbers for which parts must be backordered. Here, let me explain our inventory control system a little more thoroughly. Consider a single part, say, the nuts that hold the steering wheel of a 1971 Stallion. Those parts have a somewhat irregular demand, so we didn't know exactly how many parts we should keep on hand. It costs money to keep a parts inventory, so we don't want the inventory to be too large. However, we don't want to run out of parts frequently, and we don't want to have to produce more parts too often. See, we produce more parts when the level of parts gets low, and each time we start production of a part we incur a not inconsequential setup cost. Thus, a history of the inventory over a year might look like this." Orson drew on the blackboard.

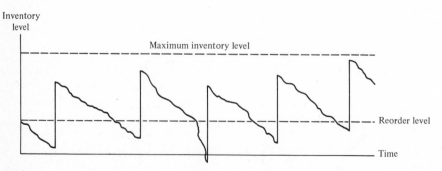

"How can you have negative inventory, as in your graph?" asked Phyllis.

"That would indicate that parts have been backordered," answered Mr. Buggy. "When a batch of parts is produced and delivered to inventory, the inventory graph spikes up. We have had our inventory requirements analyzed by an operations research consulting group, which suggested that we should have the following production policy:

"When the level of inventory of parts of type I falls below a certain number, we should plan to produce enough to get the level back up to beyond a higher number that represents a safer level. Both these numbers, or levels, can be quantitatively determined for each part. It is often referred to in inventory control theory as an rR policy where little r is the reorder point and big R is the maximum desirable inventory level."

"Does each part have a number?" asked Clara.

"Yes," Orson replied. "For example, the nuts I was mentioning before, part #4283, have a reorder point $r(4283)$ and a maximum level $R(4283)$. Perhaps you are beginning to see the way in which we might computerize our records. Let's carry this example further. Suppose that the reorder point for the steering wheel nuts is 27, thus $r(4283) = 27$ and further, let's suppose that the maximum level desired for this part is $R(4283) = 850$

"Here is how our computer system is set up. We have stored all the inventory records on a disk pack. Each record contains

1. The part number
2. How many are currently in inventory
3. The reorder point for that part
4. The maximum level desired for that part
5. An indicator as to whether parts are being produced

"Each evening, a program is run that directs the machine to search the inventory file to see which parts may have gone to or below their reorder point. The computer then prints a report indicating which parts have to be produced and the amount of each part that will be needed to bring its inventory level back up to the desired level. Furthermore, the program then uses this data to prepare the next day's schedule for those machines that produce the required parts. It has been working rather well."

"Have you considered using the computer to do other things?" asked Brandon.

"Well, if you mean play a game of chess, then I guess I'd have to say no," replied Orson. "But we do use it for other studies of our inventory. We have written programs to give us a statistical breakdown of the high turnover items in our inventory. Our analysts have been using our historical inventory data to forecast future sales. There are stockout reports, machine schedules, optimal delivery routes for our parts vans, raw material requirements lists, and a variety of other reports prepared for management's use."

"Do you prepare a payroll there also?" asked Brandon.

"Yes, we do," responded Buggy. "It's a very busy place. Perhaps some of you will be working with us one day."

"We'd like to," called Seymour, "but I think we're below the re-order point for passing grades in this course, and there is no rR policy here."

Prof. Ovitt interjected. "Don't worry, Seymour, in your case the carrying costs are too high. You'll pass the course with ease."

"No, sir, you've got to get at least a D at this school to pass," reminded Seymour.

Prof. Ovitt took his Orson Buggy to lunch.

chapter
8

Computers and the future

This chapter discusses possibilities for future developments in the application and design of computers. Such discussion is subject to opinion and speculation and should be read in that light. The chapter is divided into two sections which could be approximately categorized as implications for society and limits of machines.

8.1 COMPUTERS AND SOCIETY

Howie, Clara, Rudy, Phyllis, Tyrone, and Cole were sitting in the student lounge one evening having a discussion about their courses—their computer course in particular.

"What do you think we've accomplished in the course so far?" asked Howie.

"Well," said Rudy, "we've learned a lot about organizing problems through flowcharting, about obtaining solutions to problems with algorithms, and how the computer actually works."

"Mostly," interrupted Seymour, "I learned how a computer doesn't work."

"What about their actual applications?" asked Phyllis. "Prof. Ovitt hasn't taught much about them. Do you think it's because he doesn't really know about them?"

"No," answered Rudy. "I think it is more likely that he felt that if we knew how computers worked and how to set up small systems to accomplish particular jobs, we would recognize how computers could be used. I'm sure he realizes that we've all seen computers and know about computer systems for processing information. The newspapers and books are full of applications of computers for management problems and discussions of computer models of systems, including models of the world. We all know, for example, about the use of computers by the Internal Revenue Service to keep track of people's earnings and to process their income tax forms and the use of computers by airlines to maintain airplane reservation lists so that the airlines can instantly answer questions about flight availability."

"What do you think the future applications of computers might be?" asked Howie. "I mean, in a few years, say 10 to 20, what can we expect computers to be doing?"

8.1.1 A CASHLESS AND CHECKLESS SOCIETY.
HEY BUDDY, CAN YOU SPARE TWO BITS?

"I was just reading a book about that," interjected Clara. "One thing mentioned in the book was that there may be no need for the use of money, or even checks, in the future. Every person will have a secret identification number and card which will allow him to access directly his own bank account by computer. Then when a person goes to a store and buys something, instead of paying money or writing a check, the person can use his secret account number and personal card to transfer money directly from his account to the account of the store."

"Wow," said Seymour, "but I wonder how I would borrow 12 cents from Howie when I'm a little short and want to go to a movie. Would we have to go to a store together so Howie could put his card in a 'card register' to transfer 12 cents from his account to mine? And how's a kid going to get a 1-cent gumball from a machine; will he need his parents' card?"

"Good questions, Seymour," answered Rudy. "I guess the details of those everyday small-money transactions would have to be worked out."

"What other applications are mentioned in that book?" asked Phyllis In.

8.1.2 COMPUTERS AS TEACHERS

"Well, there's a lot of discussion," continued Clara, "on the use of computers in education. We already know something about that because of the example Rudy brought into class last week and the discussion that he gave on the development work already proceeding in computer-assisted instruction."[1]

"I'm still afraid that kind of system will be very impersonal," said Cole Shoulder. "I just don't think I would respond very well to a machine all day."

"But that's not really how it will be used, Cole," responded Rudy. "The computer won't be replacing the teacher completely. Think of it as an addition to the teaching methods available. This field is certainly still in its infancy. I think some ideas and techniques will be developed that are quite different from what most people conceive of now as the computer's role. But I don't want to repeat what I've said in class already. After all, how much sleep does Howie need?"

8.1.3 CREATIVE COMPUTERS

"How about applications in the arts?" asked Seymour jokingly.

"Actually," said Clara, "people are really talking about using the computer to make pictures, to produce music, and even write poetry."

"I have seen some pretty good pictures drawn by computers," said Phyllis. "And, furthermore, music really is very mathematical, so it seems possible that a computer will generate some ideas for some good music. Certainly this will be subject to the same criticisms that Cole voiced a few minutes ago when we discussed computers in education. In fact, the criticism may be much more justified in this area. But we mustn't be too hasty. We will have to wait and see what is produced before we can evaluate it."

"You know the mechanical production of artistic work certainly isn't new; it's intrigued people for quite a number of years," interjected Clara. "Henry-Louis Jaquet-Droz and Jean-Frederic Leschot built mechanical dolls, one that drew pictures and one that wrote in script, back in the 1770s. And we've all seen or at least heard of player pianos and music boxes. These are mechanical objects that produce art and music, albeit not original art and music. The next step, of course, would be for the computer to provide the ideas."

8.1.4 TRANSPORTATION—FULL-SPEED AHEAD

"How about some more everyday kinds of things?" asked Howie. "How will the computer change our everyday life?"

Rudy answered, "Well, certainly transportation systems will be markedly changed. The cars in the subways can be monitored by computer systems. Information about their location and speed, and even the number of passengers in them, will be sent to the central control unit which can evaluate the performance of the subway system. The central control unit can then add cars to the lines that are busy, reduce the service on the lines

[1]See Section 7.3.

that are not busy, and control the speed of the cars to ensure greater efficiency and also greater safety."

"I saw in a movie," said Seymour, "that they are already using a computer to do a lot of that on the Bay Area Rapid Transit (BART) in the San Francisco area. So, those applications aren't very far away from being a reality."

"What about car traffic?" asked Howie.

"Already computers are being used to plan the timing of traffic lights for urban areas," continued Clara. "Models have been run suggesting timing schedules to improve traffic flow in cities. A study was run on the Holland Tunnel in New York which gave the tunnel officials some real insights into the traffic flow patterns in that tunnel. The simulation revealed the somewhat surprising result that traffic flow through the tunnel could be increased if tollbooth collectors would occasionally hold up the rate at which they allowed cars to enter the tunnel. In other words, at certain times the tollbooth collectors should actually slow the rate at which they allow cars to enter the tunnel in order to increase the total number of cars that could flow through the tunnel. This, incidently, is an example of another one of the computer's important features—a complicated system can be simulated on the computer, and the model frequently will give results that are counterintuitive. The insights thus gained, while being far from obvious, have been applied. in many cases and have proven to be quite useful."

"Yeah, but are there examples of other things that are going on now?" asked Howie.

"Well," answered Rudy, "computers are already used to prepare synchronized light systems, and they also are already being used to monitor systems like the rapid transit Seymour mentioned. Computers also are monitoring car traffic. Electronic devices sense traffic patterns and relay this information to a central computer which continuously evaluates the traffic lights in the city and retimes them to alleviate congestion before it builds up. The lights then automatically compensate for such irregularities as accidents or delays on the road by retiming the signals to allow traffic faster travel on alternate routes."

"Do you think we'll ever really see cars with computers in them, so that you could tell the computer where you are and where you want to go, and the car would drive itself?" asked Clara. "I mean, could a computer sense the road and the other cars to enable the car to drive itself safely and quickly to the desired destination?"

"That's a good one to speculate on, Clara," entered Tyrone. "Of course large airplanes are equipped with automatic pilots which can perform a role similar to the one you mentioned. But do you think people would want the computer to drive their cars? Maybe they like to drive the cars themselves. Besides, when computers are cheap enough and sophisticated enough to do those things in a car, we may be using a very different transportation system altogether."

"That's true," said Rudy. "In fact, not only the transportation systems may change; the entire character of the cities may change."

8.1.5 The Impact on Cities

"Cities are used as centers for manufacturing, commerce, entertainment, and communication. Because of the technological improvements in transportation, manufacturing activities have been moving out of the cities. The importance of the city as a center of commerce could also decrease in the future. If buyers and sellers of merchandise each had video and audio communication facilities, the transactions could be performed across long distances. Items could be viewed and discussed via the communications facilities, and orders could be typed into a computer by the buyer and received almost instantly by the seller. It's the idea of catalog purchasing from a mail-order business, only made technologically more sophisticated. Thus, the need to be physically present to complete a sale would be greatly diminished."

"What you are saying, Rudy," interjected Clara, "is that cities may be less important. But what about the big office buildings you see today. The activities that are being carried on in those buildings aren't buying and selling, but rather data handling and communication—billing, receiving of payments, and maintaining of records."

"I think that some of that work will become more automated," answered Rudy, "as with the checkless payments we already discussed. Also, if there were better communication channels, there would be no need to have all these data-handling operations under one roof. Data could be transmitted long distances instantaneously; even 'personal' meetings could occur by audiovisual long-distance communication."

"So you think that cities may not continue to grow," commented Phyllis.

"Well, it's possible," answered Rudy.

8.1.6 Computers and People

"Rudy, the systems that you have mentioned sound very complicated," started Lynn Olium as she got up from the floor. "The trouble with systems that get complicated is that when they get messed up, they're so hard to get straightened out. About 2 months ago I got a bill from the clothing store, Suit Yourself, that has gone to a computerized system. The bill said I owe $80,012.19 for the sweater I bought that cost $12.19. You know, I've called them a dozen times, and they can't get it straight. The trouble is that the person you talk to can't run the computer, and you can't talk to the person who does run the computer. I wonder who set up their new system anyway?"

"I'm sure they'll work it out soon," said Clara.

"I hope not. I bought a new suit there and never got billed," said Scott Free.

"I guess complicated systems will cause some problems," interjected Rudy. "And sometimes they can be quite annoying."

"What about the people who are put out of work because of a computer? That's a problem that is more than just quite annoying. How severe will that problem be in the future?" asked Cole.

"If you look at it from a macroscopic point of view," began Tyrone, "it doesn't appear as though it should be too severe."

"What do you mean?" asked Phyllis.

"Well," Tyrone continued, "if the computer, or automated machine, is doing the work previously performed by a human being, then the work is still getting done. Presumably, the only reason to bring in automation is to have the work done more cheaply or efficiently, freeing people to do other kinds of work. Thus the total amount of work done by all of society does not decrease because of automation but should increase. In other words, the total output from society should increase. Thus there should be at least as much 'societal product' for everyone to share after automation as before."

"Try telling that to a billing clerk or a machine operator who has lost his job because of automation," interjected Cole.

"You're right about that, Cole," answered Tyrone. "That to me pinpoints the problem. There will have to be some equitable sharing of the production of society. Otherwise automation will cause hardships for the average person. The jobs created will be highly technical, like designing, installing, and maintaining the new equipment. But on the less technical level, there could be a gradual elimination of the jobs that people find interesting, jobs in which these people perform a variety of tasks, including interacting with other people."

"But this isn't a problem that will be totally new in the future," said Rudy. "There was an industrial revolution in the eighteenth and nineteenth centuries. There were certainly dislocations then, but in terms of production, working hours, leisure opportunities, and health, society eventually became much better off."

"But in that revolution the physical labor of people was taken over by machines. Now we're talking about something a little different," said Phyllis.

"Okay," answered Rudy. "But we can look at what has occurred already in this area to see if we can draw any conclusions. Have people been replaced by computers?"

"Certainly they have in some areas," began Clara. "The real questions are 'Have more interesting opportunities become available because of computers?' and 'Did the people who were replaced have a chance to utilize these opportunities?'"

"I was doing a report on the telephone industry for my communications course," said Howie, "and during the 1950s, the decade of early automation in that industry, the total employment of the industry rose by about 100,000 people, or about 15 percent. So the automation didn't replace everyone. But these aggregate figures don't answer Clara's two questions."

"What about all the exciting possibilities that get opened up when a society can produce its needs on less than its total energies," interceded Tyrone. "When people no longer had to spend all their time to grow food and find shelter, they began to make contributions in science and medicine. So many diseases have been conquered; now people will be able to spend sufficient time to research the remaining ones. Continued scientific exploration will produce results not yet conceived of."

"Like nuclear bombs?" asked Phyllis.

"And besides," said Seymour, "that exciting scientific exploration stuff is for people like you, Tyrone, people who can build their own computers. What about people like me? My Dad runs a lathe at a machine shop, and he likes his work. He does some routine jobs repetitively, but sometimes he has a real challenging piece to make and he enjoys that. He likes the guys he works with; he makes a decent living, and he has a nice family. I wouldn't mind a job like his some day. Now I hear that those jobs may be automated. What am I going to do, sweep the floor once a day when the automated machine is finished?"

"That's a tough question, Seymour," said Clara. "Maybe you will become a skilled artisan, producing individualized items."

"How many people does the world need to make artistic candles and belts?" someone called.

"Not just candles and belts, maybe furniture or special tools," explained Clara Fy.

"The irony! The automation revolution will enable people to perform work that they were freed from by the industrial revolution," commented Rudy.

"Maybe Seymour will make movies," suggested Howie. "People should have more leisure time and will want to see more movies."

"Many people really will have a lot more leisure time," said Phyllis. "Some people seem to know how to use their leisure time constructively and enjoy it. They have hobbies, read, socialize, or just enjoy doing nothing. But some people really find leisure time a burden and get quite confused by a lack of regimen."

"Yeah," interjected Howie, "and when they don't have anything else to do, they start getting into other people's business."

8.1.7 COMPUTERS AND PRIVACY

"Speaking of getting into other people's business," began Rudy. "What about the influence of the computer on a person's privacy? I mean, with everything getting computerized, pretty soon everybody will know everything about everybody else."

"Why do you say that?" asked Seymour.

Tyrone responded, "Well, when a person has a bank account, he is on a computer list with information about him. Then the IRS has the person on another list with his income and taxes and other records of the person's finances. And the police have a record of anyone who's ever been arrested, and the highway departments have lists of all drivers, and credit companies keep lists, and so on. With all this information on computer records, and with the ease with which one computer's record can be copied by another computer, pretty soon lots of people will have all the information about a person."

"I guess a person's record could follow him everywhere he goes," said Clara. "Someone who made a mistake early in life might never be able to shake the stigma that becomes attached to his information file. Prospective employers might be able to have the whole record of the person. So would credit agencies, banks, and even neighbors, who might work for any of the agencies that can access the computerized file."

"That might be a problem for some," said Howie. "But I've got nothing to hide."

"Maybe that's true. But why should everyone who has a *computer file access clearance* be able to look up all your school and medical records. People shouldn't have to bare themselves to the public," said Phyllis, trying to rectify her image as the school gossip.

"Furthermore," entered Tyrone. "Problems can arise in other ways. Let me give you an example: the FBIs National Crime Information Center (NCIC).[1] This is a computerized clearinghouse of information about people who have been arrested or items that have been stolen. The purpose of the center is to provide prompt information by computer access to criminal justice agencies throughout the United States. Sounds like a reasonable idea. A policeman in Los Angeles arrests a person and by telecommunications can find out in seconds if the person has a criminal record, if the car he was driving was stolen, or whatever. But consider this. Suppose a person is arrested, and a record of this arrest is put on the NCIC data files. The person is eventually cleared and released, but the arresting agency forgets to input that information to the NCIC. Then someone has an arrest record following him around, although he was found legally innocent. How is that going to affect his chances of getting the bank to finance his buying a house, or his chances for a new job?"

"I can see your point," responded Rudy. "What if only records of convictions are used?"

[1]*Records, Computers and the Rights of Citizens*, U.S. Dept. of Health, Education and Welfare, July 1973, DHEW Publication (OS) 73-94.

"There could still be plenty of problems," continued Tyrone. "For example, the problem of mistaken identity is always a possibility. This could be alleviated somewhat by adding fingerprints as part of the required description."

"I did a report on this for my law course," remembered Cole. "There have been several cases in which hapless victims of computerized information searches have been unfairly treated because of mistakes. In some cases, the problems have been things like the local authorities not reporting the return of a vehicle previously reported as having been stolen. Then later a person who is rightfully driving that vehicle is arrested. Or a warrant for an arrest is cancelled, but that cancellation is not correctly reported to the information file. Some of the local information centers that are doing the type of thing the NCIC wants to do have been sued because of the mistakes they have made."[1]

"Some of these problems could be cleared up if each person periodically reviewed his own record to check it for accuracy," said Howie.

"That brings up another one of the big problem areas," remarked Tyrone. "People frequently don't know they are on a data file; they may not even know that those data files exist. Also, people usually are not allowed to see their own records on these files. Thus, great injustices can arise because incorrect data on a person will not be corrected, mainly because no one who knows the facts will ever see the data file."

"Gee, sounds like large computerized data files may be a big can of worms," surmised Howie.

"Yes," answered Rudy, "while the information would be very useful to various governmental agencies, including law enforcement agencies, there must be some real thought given to the appropriate steps to be taken to ensure individual rights and the correctness of the data involved."

"Fortunately, there is time to consider the questions," entered Phyllis.

"Actually," joined Clara, "the collection of personal data records has been a big effort already. According to a *New York Times* article,[2] in the 1960s the Army had more than 1500 plainclothesmen whose responsibility it was to report on individuals to data banks. Between 1968 and 1972, federal and state governments wiretapped 1,623,000 conversations involving 120,000 people. Some authors have suggested that the federal agencies in this country have more than 20,000 investigators to provide information."

"Wow!" exclaimed Howie. "What types of guidelines do you think should be adopted by data bank centers?"

Tyrone answered, "In a report on just this issue, an advisory group

[1]For example see, "S.F.'s Forgetful Computer," *San Francisco Examiner*, May 9, 1973, p. 3; and "Coast Police Sued as Computer Errs," *New York Times*, May 5, 1973, p. 23.
[2]*New York Times*, December 10, 1973.

to the Secretary of HEW reported some recommendations in July 1973.[1]

"The recommendations detail the precautions that might be taken to limit the availability of personal data to appropriate groups, to ensure that people know what data banks their records were in, and to permit people to check the authenticity of their records."

8.2 CAN COMPUTERS SIMULATE HUMAN ACTIVITIES?

The conversation in the lounge continued with Cole talking, "You know, with the insecurities that can arise from people wondering what's in their records in the data banks and with people losing jobs or at least being shifted in jobs due to continued automation, there should be plenty of work for psychiatrists."

8.2.1 TALKING WITH COMPUTERS

"That," Clara began, "reminds me of something I read last week. Some computer scientists doing research at MIT developed a program called ELIZA with which the computer carries on dialog, in English, with someone. When ELIZA is given a script called DOCTOR, the computer simulates a psychiatrist."[2]

"That would never fool anyone," said Lynn.

"Wait, let me show you a sample of the output from the program. I have a copy that I made." Clara produced this copy and said, "The computer's responses are written in capital letters."

> Men are all alike.
> IN WHAT WAY
> They're always bugging us about something or other.
> CAN YOU THINK OF A SPECIFIC EXAMPLE
> Well, my boyfriend made me come here.
> YOUR BOYFRIEND MADE YOU COME HERE
> He says I'm depressed much of the time.
> I AM SORRY TO HEAR YOU ARE DEPRESSED
> It's true. I am unhappy.
> DO YOU THINK COMING HERE WILL HELP YOU NOT TO BE
> UNHAPPY
> I need some help, that much seems certain.
> WHAT WOULD IT MEAN TO YOU IF YOU GOT SOME HELP
> Perhaps I could learn to get along with my mother.
> TELL ME MORE ABOUT YOUR FAMILY
> My mother takes care of me.

[1]*Records, Computers and the Rights of Citizens,* U.S. Dept. of Health, Education and Welfare, July 1973, DHEW Publication (OS) 73-94.

[2]J. Nievergelt and J. C. Farrar, "What Machines Can and Cannot Do," *Computing Surveys, Journal of Association of Computing Machinery,* 4 (2): June 1972, p. 84.

WHO ELSE IN YOUR FAMILY TAKES CARE OF YOU
My father.
YOUR FATHER.
You are like my father in some ways.
WHAT RESEMBLANCE DO YOU SEE
You are not very aggressive but I think you don't want me to notice that.
WHAT MAKES YOU THINK I AM NOT VERY AGGRESSIVE
You don't argue with me.
WHY DO YOU THINK I DON'T ARGUE WITH YOU
You are afraid of me.
DOES IT PLEASE YOU TO BELIEVE I AM AFRAID OF YOU
My father is afraid of everybody.
WHAT ELSE COMES TO MIND WHEN YOU THINK OF YOUR
FATHER
Bullies.
DOES THAT HAVE ANYTHING TO DO WITH THE FACT THAT
YOUR BOYFRIEND MADE YOU COME HERE

"Say, that's very interesting," concluded Howie. "How does it work?"

"Actually," Clara answered, "this is an example of a conversation with little understanding. True, the computer is responding to a question or statement with a response that seems plausible. But the computer, in this instance, is not really evaluating the severity of the patient's problems. Are you with me?"

"So far so good. The computer is not really evaluating the severity of the patient's problems," said Howie.

"The program," continued Clara, "works by looking for key phrases and responding in a predetermined way to these key phrases."

"The program picks up key phrases," nodded Howie.

"Yes," said Clara. "If the patient inputs 'I am ABC' the computer may respond "How long have you been ABC?' or 'Do you want to be ABC?' In other words, the program decomposes a sentence input into sections involving those key phrases it has been looking for, and rephrases the input as output. To do this the program adds some standard phrases like 'What makes you think _____' or 'Tell me about _____.'"

"The program decomposes a sentence, then adds standard phrases. I see," nodded Howie again.

"If the computer doesn't recognize any key phrases in the input, it just rephrases the output as a question, or says something noncommittal like 'Can you be more specific?'" continued Clara.

"I see. It can rephrase the input as output," followed Howie. "But the program is not really evaluating the severity of the patient's problems."

"Right. And the computer will remember particular input words to use later to get the patient to tie everything together, and to make the dialog more believable."

"Yes, the computer makes the dialog more believable," agreed Howie.

Clara continued. "You know the whole idea seems quite sophisticated, and yet the script for DOCTOR consists of about a page and a half of decomposition and reassembly rules. These rules help the program disguise its lack of understanding."

"The computer can disguise its lack of understanding," followed Howie.

"Yep, and yet it really understands as little as Howie does," answered Clara.

"It understands as little as Howie does," repeated Howie. "Hey, that's not very nice!"

Everyone laughed at Howie's joke.

"That's really a great example of a computer dialog in English. But you said that it was conversation with little understanding. Are there any examples of programs that give the computer the ability to understand?" asked Phyllis.

Clara answered, "In the same article,[1] a program called STUDENT is discussed. That program can accept as input many problems from algebra and print out the solutions. For example, look at the following problem:

'Mary is twice as old as Ann was when Mary was as old as Ann is now. If Mary is 24 years old, how old is Ann?'

If that problem were input for the program STUDENT, the output would be

ANN'S AGE IS 18

"How does that program work?" asked Howie.

"The program tries to convert the relations in the English sentence into algebraic relations and solve for the variables asked for," answered Clara. "The words that aren't relational operations or numbers are considered the variables (or maybe substitutes for the variables). The program doesn't care if you are asking about Mary's age or the weight of a bridge, as long as it can define the variables and the relations."

"Does that program understand what it is doing?" asked Seymour.

"It can solve the well-defined problem I showed you. It could not solve the problem if it were rewritten in the following form:

'Mary is twice as old as Ann was when Mary was as old as Ann is now. If Mary is 24 years old, how many years have elapsed since Ann's birth?'

The program thus does not understand much about the problem except what is explicitly written in the problem."

---

[1] *Ibid.*

"How about if it had a dictionary on disk; could it translate better then?" continued Seymour.

8.2.2 WILL COMPUTERS THINK?

"You know," Howie addressed the group, "we've seen examples of a program that can carry on dialog, a program that can solve algebra problems that are stated in words. We know that a computer can calculate very fast, can simulate realistic systems to obtain recommendations on actions for these systems, and can store in memory the results of previous calculations. What about the big question? Will computers ever be able to think like I can?"

"We all hope not," said everyone in unison.

"Very funny," said Howie. "But really, do you think computers will ever be able to think?"

"People have been wondering about that same question for quite a while," said Clara. "The hardest part of the question may be deciding what it really means when you say something thinks."

"Yes," said Rudy. "The philosopher Turing worried about this same question even before computers were very advanced. To circumvent the problems inherent in the word 'think,' he devised what is now known as a 'Turing Test.'[1] Here is a model of the Turing Test. Consider a computer in a closed room with a person P. The computer does not interact with this person. Both the computer and the person are connected by teletypewriter to another person I, an interrogator, in a different room. The interrogator thus has two teletypewriters himself, one connected to the computer and one connected to the person in the room with the computer. The interrogator's job is to determine which of his teletypewriters is connected to the computer, by asking questions over the teletypewriters and analyzing the answers. The computer should have the task of fooling the interrogator, while P's job is to help I make a correct analysis. Now, instead of asking, 'Can machines think?' the question could be, 'Are there machines that could do well in this test?'[2]

"In 1950, Turing expressed the opinion that by the end of the century machines would be able to fool interrogators at least 30 percent of the time after 5 minutes of questioning."

"After looking at the output from the program ELIZA and considering the program STUDENT, it seems like Turing may have been conservative in his estimate of the time horizon for the machine to do well," said Phyllis.

"That seems to be a possibility," joined Rudy. "But would that be an indication that the machine was thinking? I guess that would take us back to the definition of thinking. Or alternatively, is there some type of

---

[1]A. M. Turing, "Computing Machinery and Intelligence," *MIND*, 9, 1950, pp. 433–460.
[2]Nievergelt and Farrar, *op. cit.*

reasoning process, or creativity, a machine will not be able to do, but that humans can do?"

Tyrone began, "In an article[1] I read, Prof. Philip Morrison of MIT expressed the idea that a key mental process is that of asking the right questions and raising new problems. He said that to simulate human mental life a machine would have to do that. I think that is an interesting possibility to explore."

"That question and the discussion we had about original works of art by a computer seem to be very similar," said Seymour. "It seems to me that nothing can come out of a machine that has not been programmed into the machine. Therefore, I don't see how a machine can show originality in its output."

"I don't want to sound like I'm showing off," said Clara, "but I seem to remember reading an article[2] on that subject by Norbert Wiener. I don't think he really agreed with your conclusions, Seymour."

"Who's Norbert Wiener?" asked Cole.

"He was a great mathematician who died in the late 1960s. He wrote several books on the impact of automation on society, one called *Cybernetics*," answered Tyrone.

"I think I read that article Clara read," joined in Rudy. "Wiener expressed the opinion that machines can transcend the limits of their designers."

"What do you mean?" asked Howie.

"For example, computers can play games against the people who programmed them, and the computer can win."

"Yeah," said Howie, "the computer beat me in Tic Tac Toe. But that's not because it thought; it's because it could evaluate the strategies and determine the best strategy. That's not originality there; it plays the same predictable way every time it faces the same situation."

"Right, Howie," began Rudy. "But the computer can play chess and checkers also, and there are too many possibilities in those games for the computer to evaluate every strategy."

Tyrone started speaking, "I can see how the computer would play those games. It puts values on pieces, and values on locations of those pieces; then it can calculate at each play the move that will most increase its value over its opponent's. It could even look forward to see the best move for its opponent, contingent on the computer's move. In this way the computer can plan ahead several moves."

"That is one way that computers play those complicated games," said Rudy.

"But there's no originality in that play," countered Howie. "It

[1]"The Mind of the Machine," *Technology Review*, **75** (3): January 1973.
[2]Norbert Wiener, "Some Moral and Technical Consequences of Automation," *Science*, **131**: May 6, 1960.

seems that the computer will pick the same play each time it plays a game with the same setup as a previous game."

"Yes, Howie, that would be a rigid type of play, all based on the values the computer had placed on the pieces and locations of those pieces," answered Rudy. "But programs have been written, as early as 1960, that will 'remember' the plays of previous games against an opponent in checkers. Thus the computer will learn which moves were unsuccessful in earlier games and, using this information, will change the value factors used for pieces and situations of those pieces. Thus, a trick that fooled the computer in an early game will no longer work in later games. The computers playing checkers show a marked superiority to the person who programmed them after 10 to 20 hours of play."

"If they beat the person who programmed them, then the computers are no longer under the 'control' of the programmer, at least in this situation," interjected Cole.

"That's right, Cole," continued Rudy. "The people who have played against the computers say that the computers show originality in their tactics. Well, if this is true, it's not very different conceptually to anticipate the computer showing originality in other ways."

"Maybe," said Clara. "And if the computer can make better decisions in checkers, isn't it reasonable to conclude that a machine may be able to make better decisions than people in a very wide variety of activities? Some might even say that this means the computer will be smarter than people."

"Wow! What if computers could reproduce themselves?" said Howie jokingly.

"Actually, Howie, that's a question a lot of people have given serious thought to. A famous mathematician, Von Neumann, wrote extensively on the theory of such self-reproduction of nonliving machines.[1] We know that there are factories that are controlled by computers. Also, we've all seen models of artificial limbs that can be attached to machines to pick up objects and use special tools, say, for handling radioactive material. Well, it's not hard to conceive of a machine, on wheels, that could roll around a room, pick up pieces, and put these pieces together."

"Yeah, but the pieces have to go together in a particular way," said Howie.

"True, but the constructing machine could have a set of instructions on how to put the pieces together. Think of the machine as several parts—a constructor to do the building, a tape which contains the plan of construction, a computer to read the tape and control the construction, and a tape duplicator to produce a copy of the tape for the new machine. Then, if it had the parts it needed, the machine could build an identical

[1] J. Von Neumann, *Theory of Self-Reproducing Automata,* Arthur W. Burks, Ed., University of Illinois Press, Urbana, Ill., 1966.

copy of itself, which could build, in turn, a copy of itself, and on and on."

Howie answered, "I guess it won't be too long before computers will be sitting around a 'Computers Only' lounge trying to define what people are. Imagine one computer saying to the rest, 'People are the slaves who get us paper when we are too tired to get it ourselves.'"

Just then the janitor flicked the lights to indicate that the student lounge was closing for the evening. The group broke up and headed off to their rooms, ending another typical evening bull session at the college.

Exercises

1. Prepare for a debate on the subject: There is some characteristic of "originality" which people can possess, but that computers can never possess.
   (*a*) Prepare the affirmative argument.
   (*b*) Prepare the negative argument.
2. Write a diary of a day in your life in 30 years, in which you show the effects computers will have on your activities.
3. Can computers think?
4. Can Howie think?
5. What activities do computers do now that society would be better off if people did?
6. If a computer is programmed to make decisions, will the value judgments of the computer programmer be evident? Can a computer be unbiased? (Imagine a Republican computer and a Democrat computer.)
7. Could a computer serve on the jury in a criminal trial? (Imagine a person being convicted by a vote of 7 out of 12 computers.)
8. Will computers form emotional attachments to other computers? To their programmers?
9. Will a computer have a sense of humor?
10. What will people do if computers and automata start performing most of society's work? Who will benefit most? Who will benefit least?

appendix A

Using a keypunch

The purpose of this appendix is to provide instructions for the elementary use of a card punch machine for the preparation of cards for use as input into a computer. The instructions will be given for the use of the popular IBM Model 029 keypunch machine used for the preparation of 80-column cards.

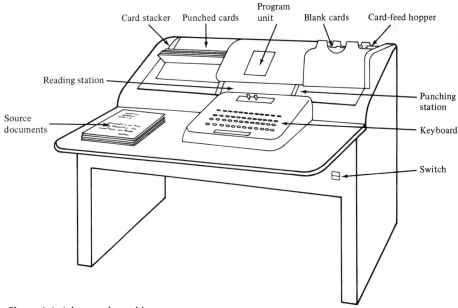

Figure A.1 A keypunch machine.

The keypunch machine consists of the following functional areas:

1. The card-feed hopper, which holds and feeds blank cards to be keypunched
2. The punching station, where holes are punched into the cards to code the information desired as input
3. The reading station, where the person operating the keypunch can read the last card punched and check it for errors
4. The card stacker, where punched cards are stacked after they have been keypunched
5. The program unit, which is a section between the card-feed hopper and the card stacker that can be used for the automatic control of the keypunch machine
6. The keyboard, where the character keys and functional keys used to operate the keypunch are located
7. The switch that turns the machine on and off, which is located to the right underneath the keyboard

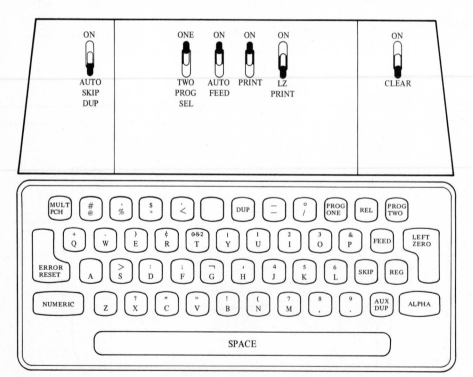

Figure A.2 Keyboard of the 029 keypunch.

The following is a list of steps used to operate the IBM Model 029 keypunch machine for elementary card punching (not utilizing the programming unit for automatic card alignment):

1. Turn on the machine and the PRINT and AUTO FEED switches which are located on the keyboard. The PRINT switch causes the characters that are punched on the card to be printed at the top of the card. This is useful for the reading of the card by the keypuncher. The AUTO FEED causes cards to be automatically fed from the card hopper to the keypunching station. Cards already punched will automatically be moved to their next station.

2. Make sure the cards in the card hopper have not been previously punched. If the card hopper is empty or you desire different cards, place your cards in the hopper facing forward with the 9 edge down.

3. Depress REL button twice. This action will prepare your initial card for keypunching.

4. Keypunch the desired input, using a depressed NUMERIC button to type upper case from the keyboard (this includes numbers and symbols).

5. Press the REL key to position a new card.

6. After you have punched your last card, lift the CLEAR switch to remove the last card from the read and punch station.

To duplicate a card, position it in the read station (this can be done manually or through automatic feeding) and a blank card in the punch station; depress the DUP key until all the desired columns have been reproduced on the previously blank card. Remove the cards with either the CLEAR switch or the REL key.

appendix
B

IBM FORTRAN functions[1]

[1]Reprinted from: IBM System/360 and System/370 Fortran IV Language.

General Function	Entry Name	Definition	No.	Type	Range	Type	Range[3]
					Argument(s)		Function Value Returned
Natural and common logarithm	ALOG DLOG QLOG	$y = \log_e x$ or $y = \ln x$	1 1 1	REAL *4 REAL *8 REAL *16	$x > 0$	REAL *4 REAL *8 REAL *16	$-180.218 \leq y \leq 174.673$
	CLOG CDLOG CQLOG	$y = PV \log_e z$ PV = Principal Value. See Note 1	1 1 1	COMPLEX *8 COMPLEX *16 COMPLEX *32	$z \neq 0 + 0i$	COMPLEX *8 COMPLEX *16 COMPLEX *32	$-180.218 \leq y \leq 175.021$ $-\pi \leq y_2 \leq \pi$
	ALOG10 DLOG10 QLOG10	$y = \log_{10} x$	1 1 1	REAL *4 REAL *8 REAL *16	$x > 0$	REAL *4 REAL *8 REAL *16	$-78.268 \leq y \leq 75.859$
Exponential	EXP DEXP QEXP	$y = e^x$	1 1 1	REAL *4 REAL *8 REAL *16	$-180.218 \leq x \leq 174.673$	REAL *4 REAL *8 REAL *16	$0 \leq y \leq \gamma$
	CEXP	$y = e^x$ See Note 2.	1	COMPLEX *8	$x_1 \leq 174.673$ $|x_2| < (2^{18} \cdot \pi)$	COMPLEX *8	$-\gamma \leq y_1, y_2 \leq \gamma$
	CDEXP		1	COMPLEX *16	$x_1 \leq 174.673$ $|x_2| < (2^{50} \cdot \pi)$	COMPLEX *16	
	CQEXP		1	COMPLEX *32	$x_1 \leq 174.673$ $|x_2| < (2^{100})$	COMPLEX *32	
Square root	SQRT DSQRT QSQRT	$y = \sqrt{x}$ or $y = x^{1/2}$	1 1 1	REAL *4 REAL *8 REAL *16	$x \geq 0$	REAL *4 REAL *8 REAL *16	$0 \leq y \leq y^{1/2}$
	CSQRT CDSQRT CQSQRT	$y = PV \sqrt{z}$ or $y = PV\, z^{1/2}$ PV = Principal Value. See Note 1	1 1 1	COMPLEX *8 COMPLEX *16 COMPLEX *32	Any COMPLEX argument	COMPLEX *8 COMPLEX *16 COMPLEX *32	$0 \leq y_1,$ $1.0987 \cdot (y^{1/2})$ $|y_2| \leq$ $1.0987 \cdot (y^{1/2})$
Arcsine and arccosine	ARSIN DARSIN QARSIN	$y = \arcsin x$	1 1 1	REAL *4 REAL *8 REAL *16	$|x| \leq 1$	REAL *4 (in radians) REAL *8 (in radians) REAL *16 (in radians)	$-\dfrac{\pi}{2} \leq y \leq \dfrac{\pi}{2}$
	ARCOS DARCOS QARCOS	$y = \arccos x$	1 1 1	REAL *4 REAL *8 REAL *16		REAL *4 (in radians) REAL *8 (in radians) REAL *16 (in radians)	$0 \leq y \leq \pi$

1. The answer given $(y_1 + y_2 i)$ is that one whose imaginary part (y_2) lies between $-\pi$ and π: $-\pi \leq y_2 \leq \pi$.
2. z is a complex number of the form $x_1 + x_2 i$.
3. $\gamma = 16^{63} \cdot (1 - 16^{-6})$ for single precision, $16^{63} \cdot (1 - 16^{-14})$ for double precision, and $16^{63} \cdot (1 - 16^{-28})$ for extended precision routines.

General Function	Entry Name	Definition	Argument(s)			Function Value Returned	
			No.	Type	Range	Type	Range[2]
Arctangent	ATAN	$y = \arctan x$	1	REAL *4	Any REAL Argument	REAL *4 (in radians)	$-\dfrac{\pi}{2} \leqq y \leqq \dfrac{\pi}{2}$
	DATAN		1	REAL *8		REAL *8 (in radians)	
	QATAN		1	REAL *16		REAL *16 (in radians)	
	ATAN2	$y = \arctan \dfrac{x_1}{x_2}$	2	REAL *4	Any REAL Arguments except (0, 0)	REAL *4 (in radians)	$-\pi \leqq y \leqq \pi$
	DATAN2		2	REAL *8		REAL *8 (in radians)	
	QATAN2		2	REAL *16		REAL *16 (in radians)	
Sine and cosine	SIN	$y = \sin x$	1	REAL *4 (in radians)	$\|x\| < (2^{18} \cdot \pi)$	REAL *4	$-1 \leqq y \leqq 1$
	DSIN		1	REAL *8 (in radians)	$\|x\| < (2^{50} \cdot \pi)$	REAL *8	
	QSIN		1	REAL *16 (in radians)	$\|x\| < (2^{100})$	REAL *16	
	COS	$y = \cos x$	1	REAL *4 (in radians)	$\|x\| < (2^{18} \cdot \pi)$	REAL *4	$-1 \leqq y \leqq 1$
	DCOS		1	REAL *8 (in radians)	$\|x\| < (2^{50} \cdot \pi)$	REAL *8	
	QCOS		1	REAL *16 (in radians)	$\|x\| < (2^{100})$	REAL *16	
	CSIN	$y = \sin z$ See Note 1	1 *	COMPLEX *8 (in radians)	$\|x_1\| < (2^{18} \cdot \pi)$ $\|x_2\| \leqq 174.673$	COMPLEX *8	$-\gamma \leqq y_1, y_2 \leqq \gamma$
	CDSIN		1	COMPLEX *16 (in radians)	$\|x_1\| < (2^{50} \cdot \pi)$ $\|x_2\| \leqq 174.673$	COMPLEX *16	
	CQSIN		1	COMPLEX *32 (in radians)	$\|x_1\| < (2^{100})$ $\|x_2\| \leqq 174.673$	COMPLEX *32	
	CCOS	$y = \cos z$ See Note 1	1	COMPLEX *8 (in radians)	$\|x_1\| < (2^{18} \cdot \pi)$ $\|x_2\| \leqq 174.673$	COMPLEX *8	$-\gamma \leqq y_1, y_2 \leqq \gamma$
	CDCOS		1	COMPLEX *16 (in radians)	$\|x_1\| < (2^{50} \cdot \pi)$ $\|x_2\| \leqq 174.673$	COMPLEX *16	
	CQCOS		1	COMPLEX *32 (in radians)	$\|x_1\| < (2^{100})$ $\|x_2\| \leqq 174.673$	COMPLEX *32	

1. z is a complex number of the form $x_1 + x_2 i$.
2. $\gamma = 16^{63} \cdot (1 - 16^{-6})$ for single precision, $16^{63} \cdot (1 - 16^{-14})$ for double precision, and $16^{63} \cdot (1 - 16^{-28})$ for extended precision routines.

General Function	Entry Name	Definition	Argument(s) No.	Argument(s) Type	Argument(s) Range	Function Value Returned Type	Function Value Returned Range[4]
Tangent and cotangent	TAN	$y = \tan x$	1	REAL *4 (in radians)	$\lvert x \rvert < (2^{18} \cdot \pi)$ See Note 2	REAL *4	$-\gamma \leq y \leq \gamma$
	DTAN		1	REAL *8 (in radians)	$\lvert x \rvert < (2^{50} \cdot \pi)$ See Note 1	REAL *8	
	QTAN		1	REAL *16 (in radians)	$\lvert x \rvert < (2^{100})$ See Note 1	REAL *16	
	COTAN	$y = \cotan x$	1	REAL *4 (in radians)	$\lvert x \rvert < (2^{18} \cdot \pi)$ See Note 2	REAL *4	$-\gamma \leq y \leq \gamma$
	DCOTAN		1	REAL *8 (in radians)	$\lvert x \rvert < (2^{50} \cdot \pi)$ See Note 2	REAL *8	
	QCOTAN		1	REAL *16 (in radians)	$\lvert x \rvert < (2^{100})$ See Note 2	REAL *16	
Hyperbolic sine and cosine	SINH DSINH QSINH	$y = \dfrac{e^x - e^{-x}}{2}$	1 1 1	REAL *4 REAL *8 REAL *16	$\lvert x \rvert < 175.366$	REAL *4 REAL *8 REAL *16	$-\gamma \leq y \leq \gamma$
	COSH DCOSH QCOSH	$y = \dfrac{e^x + e^{-x}}{2}$	1 1 1	REAL *4 REAL *8 REAL *16		REAL *4 REAL *8 REAL *16	$1 \leq y \leq \gamma$
Hyperbolic tangent	TANH DTANH QTANH	$y = \dfrac{e^x - e^{-2}}{e^x + e^{-x}}$	1 1 1	REAL *4 REAL *8 REAL *16	Any REAL argument	REAL *4 REAL *8 REAL *16	$-1 \leq y \leq 1$
Absolute value	IABS*	$y = \lvert x \rvert$	1	INTEGER *4	Any INTEGER argument	INTEGER *4	
	ABS* DABS* QABS		1 1 1	REAL *4 REAL *8 REAL *16	Any REAL argument	REAL *4 REAL *8 REAL *16	
	CABS CDABS CQABS	$y = \lvert z \rvert = (x_1{}^2 + x_2{}^2)^{1/2}$	1 1 1	COMPLEX *8 COMPLEX *16 COMPLEX *32	Any COMPLEX argument See Note 3	REAL *4 REAL *8 REAL *16	$0 \leq y, \leq \gamma$ $y_2 = 0$
Error function	ERF DERF QERF	$y = \dfrac{2}{\sqrt{\pi}} \displaystyle\int_0^x e^{-u^2}\, du$	1 1 1	REAL *4 REAL *8 REAL *16	Any REAL argument	REAL *4 REAL *8 REAL *16	$-1 \leq y \leq 1$
	ERFC DERFC QERFC	$y = \dfrac{2}{\sqrt{\pi}} \displaystyle\int_x^\infty e^{-u^2}\, du$ $y = 1 - \mathrm{erf}\, x$	1 1 1	REAL *4 REAL *8 REAL *16		REAL *4 REAL *8 REAL *16	$0 \leq y \leq 2$

1. The argument of the tangent functions may not approach an odd multiple of $\pi/2$.
2. The argument of the cotangent functions may not approach a multiple of π.
3. Floating-point overflow can occur.
4. $\gamma = 16^{63} \cdot (1 - 16^{-6})$ for single precision, $16^{63} \cdot (1 - 16^{-14})$ for double precision, and $16^{63} \cdot (1 - 16^{-28})$ for extended precision routines.
* ANS FORTRAN Intrinsic Function

General Function	Entry Name	Definition	Argument(s) No.	Argument(s) Type	Argument(s) Range	Function Value Returned Type	Function Value Returned Range[3]
Gamma and log-gamma	GAMMA DGAMMA	$y = \int_0^\infty u^{x-1} e^{-u}\, du$	1 1	REAL*4 REAL*8	$2^{-252} \leq$ $x < 257.5744$	REAL*4 REAL*8	$0.88560 \leq y \leq \gamma$
	ALGAMA DLGAMA	$y = \log_e \Gamma(x)$ or $y = \log_e \int_0^\infty u^{x-1} e^{-u}\, du$	1 1	REAL*4 REAL*8	$0 < x$ and $< 4.2913 \cdot 10^{73}$	REAL*4 REAL*8	$-0.12149 \leq y \leq \gamma$
Maximum and minimum values	MAX0* AMAX0* MAX1* AMAX1* DMAX1* QMAX1	$y = \max(x_1, \ldots, x_n)$	≧2 ≧2 ≧2 ≧2 ≧2 ≧2	INTEGER*4 INTEGER*4 REAL*4 REAL*8 REAL*16	Any INTEGER argument Any REAL argument	INTEGER*4 REAL*4 INTEGER*4 REAL*4 REAL*8 REAL*16	
	MIN0* AMIN0* MIN1* AMIN1* DMIN1* QMIN1	$y = \min(x_1, \ldots, x_n)$	≧2 ≧2 ≧2 ≧2 ≧2 ≧2	INTEGER*4 INTEGER*4 REAL*4 REAL*8 REAL*16	Any INTEGER argument Any REAL argument	INTEGER*4 REAL*4 INTEGER*4 REAL*4 REAL*8 REAL*16	
Modular arithmetic	MOD* AMOD* DMOD QMOD	$y = $ remainder $\left(\dfrac{x_1}{x_2}\right)$, i.e., $y = x_1 (\text{modulo } x_2)$ See Note 1.	2 2 2 2	INTEGER*4 REAL*4 REAL*8 REAL*16	$x_2 \neq 0$ See Note 2.	INTEGER*4 REAL*4 REAL*8 REAL*16	
Truncation	AINT* DINT QINT INT* IDINT* IQINT	$y = (\text{sign } x) \cdot n$ where n is the largest integer $\leq |x|$	1 1 1 1 1 1	REAL*4 REAL*8 REAL*16 REAL*4 REAL*8 REAL*16	Any REAL argument	REAL*4 REAL*8 REAL*16 INTEGER*4 INTEGER*4 INTEGER*4	

1. x_1 (modulo x_2) is defined as $x_1 - \left[\dfrac{x_1}{x_2}\right] \cdot x_2$, where the brackets indicate that the largest integer whose magnitude does not exceed the magnitude of $\dfrac{x_1}{x_2}$ is used. The sign of the integer is the same as the sign of $\dfrac{x_1}{x_2}$.

2. If $x_2 = 0$, then the modulus function is mathematically undefined.

3. $\gamma = 16^{63} \cdot (1 - 16^{-6})$ for single precision, $16^{63} \cdot (1 - 16^{-14})$ for double precision, and $16^{63} \cdot (1 - 16^{-28})$ for extended precision routines.

*ANS FORTRAN Intrinsic Function

General Function	Entry Name	Definition	Argument(s) No.	Type	Range	Function Value Returned Type	Range
Float	FLOAT* DFLOAT QFLOAT	Convert from INTEGER to REAL	1 1 1	INTEGER *4 INTEGER *4 INTEGER *4	Any INTEGER argument	REAL *4 REAL *8 REAL *16	
Fix	IFIX* HFIX	Convert from REAL to INTEGER	1 1	REAL *4 REAL *4	Any REAL argument	INTEGER *4 INTEGER *2	
Transfer of sign	ISIGN*	$y = (\text{sign } x_2) \cdot x_1$, $x_1 \neq 0$	2	INTEGER *	Any INTEGER argument	INTEGER *4	
	SIGN* DSIGN* QSIGN		2 2 2	REAL *4 REAL *8 REAL *16	Any REAL argument	REAL *4 REAL *8 REAL *16	
Positive difference	IDIM*	$y = x_1 - \min(x_1, x_2)$	2	INTEGER *4	Any INTEGER argument	INTEGER *4	
	DIM* DDIM QDIM		2 2 2	REAL *4 REAL *8 REAL *16	Any REAL argument	REAL *4 REAL *8 REAL *16	
Obtain most significant part of a REAL argument	SNGL* SNGLQ DBLEQ		1 1 1	REAL *8 REAL *16 REAL *16	Any REAL argument	REAL *4 REAL *4 REAL *8	
Obtain real part of a COMPLEX argument	REAL*		1	COMPLEX *8	Any COMPLEX argument	REAL *4	
	DREAL		1	COMPLEX *16		REAL *8	
	QREAL		1	COMPLEX *32		REAL *16	
Obtain imaginary part of a COMPLEX argument	AIMAG* DIMAG QIMAG		1 1 1	COMPLEX *8 COMPLEX *16 COMPLEX *32	Any COMPLEX argument	REAL *4 REAL *8 REAL *16	

*ANS FORTRAN Intrinsic Function

General Function	Entry Name	Definition	Argument(s)			Function Value Returned	
			No.	Type	Range	Type	Range
Precision increase	DBLE* QEXT QEXTD		1 1 1	REAL *4 REAL *4 REAL *8	Any REAL argument	REAL *8 REAL *16 REAL *16	
Express two REAL arguments in complex form	CMPLX* DCMPLX QCMPLX	$y = x_1 + x_2 i$	2 2 2	REAL *4 REAL *8 REAL *16	Any REAL argument	COMPLEX *8 COMPLEX *16 COMPLEX *32	
Obtain conjugate of a COMPLEX argument	CONJG* DCONJG QCONJG	$y = x_1 - x_2 i$ for $arg = x_1 + x_2 i$	1 1 1	COMPLEX *8 COMPLEX *16 COMPLEX *32	Any COMPLEX argument	COMPLEX *8 COMPLEX *16 COMPLEX *32	

*ANS FORTRAN Intrinsic Function

appendix
C

The following pages present some of the key features of BASIC[1] and may be used as a reference once the language has been learned. The arrangement of this Appendix is as follows:

BASIC character set
Variables
Arithmetic operations
Hierarchy of operations
Relational symbols
BASIC program statements (examples and comments)
Array operations
Functions in BASIC
Sample system commands using a time sharing system

---

[1]Each implementation of BASIC may differ slightly from system to system. For a detailed description of the version on your system, see the user's guide available at your facility.

CHARACTERS

A BASIC program is written using these characters:

1. Alphabetic characters:
    The letters A to Z
    The alphabetic extenders @, #, $.
2. Digits:
    0, 1, 2, 3, 4, 5, 6, 7, 8, 9
3. Special characters:
    $- + * / = ( ) . , ; : \quad " ' \uparrow < >$
    $\uparrow$
    (BLANK)

VARIABLES

SIMPLE VARIABLES

An *arithmetic variable* is named by a single character (A, B, C, etc.) or an alphabetic character followed by a single digit (A1, A9, C5, etc.).

A *character variable* is an alphabetic character followed by the dollar sign character (A$, B$, etc.). The length of simple character variables can, at most, be 18 characters long.

ARRAY VARIABLES

An *arithmetic array* is named by a single alphabetic character. An arithmetic array may be declared to have one dimension (e.g., DIM A(5)) or two dimensions (e.g., DIM B(3,5)). In the two-dimensional example, the 3 stands for the number of rows and the 5 for the number of columns.

A *character array* is named by an alphabetic character followed by a dollar sign character. A character array may have only one dimension, and each member of the array can be, at most, 18 characters long.

Example: DIM A$(10), DIM C$(4), DIM S$(12)

Some versions of BASIC do not permit character arrays. In these systems, the DIM statement usually specifies the character length of a character variable. For example, DIM A$(25) in such a system would indicate that variable A$ could hold a character string of up to 25 characters.

ARITHMETIC OPERATIONS

$\uparrow$ or **	Exponentiation
*	Multiplication
/	Division
+	Addition
−	Subtraction

HIERARCHY OF OPERATIONS

1. Perform operations in parentheses
2. Exponentiation
3. Multiplication and division
4. Addition and subtraction

Operations of the same priority are usually performed from left to right.

RELATIONAL SYMBOLS

$=$	Equal to
$<>$	Not equal to
$>$	Greater than
$<$	Less than
$>=$	Greater than or equal to
$<=$	Less than or equal to

PROGRAM STATEMENTS

CLOSE   105   CLOSE 'DC', 'XYZ'

105 is the statement number. 'DC' and 'XYZ' are the names of files. These names can be up to three characters long.

DATA   10   DATA 50, 37.4, 'ABC'
                    27   DATA 24.7, 33E−51

10 and 27 are statement numbers. The DATA statement is used to supply values for variables named in READ statements.

DEF   144   DEF FNA(B) = C

144 is the statement number. 'A' can be any letter of the alphabet, 'B' is an unsubscripted variable, and 'C' is an expression that uses the variable B.

100   DEF FNA(B) = SQR(B**4)
200   LET R = FNA(3) + 10

This would cause three to be assigned to B, then compute the square root of the fourth power: $\sqrt{3^4} = \sqrt{81} = 9$. Then add 10 and finally assign the value 19 to the variable R.

DIM   10   DIM Z(5), A$(7), B(15,25)

10 is the statement number. Z, A$, B are array names. Z is a one-dimensional arithmetic array with five members. A$ is a one-dimensional char-

acter array with seven members. B is a two-dimensional arithmetic array with 15 rows and 25 columns of data or 375 total members.

END   99   END

The end statement is used simply to indicate the logical end of a program.

FOR   75   FOR A = B TO C STEP D

75 is the statement number, 'A' is any alphabetic letter, 'B' and 'C' are bounds to the value of 'A' and can be either variable names or numerals. 'D' is the amount the value changes each time through the loop.

$$20 \quad \text{FOR X} = 1 \text{ TO } 25 \text{ STEP } 2$$
$$\text{or } 20 \quad \text{FOR X} = \text{I TO J STEP } 2$$

GET   20   GET 'ABC', X, Y, Z(2)
                 30   GET 'DE', S, T, V(5)

20 and 30 are statement numbers. 'ABC' and 'DE' are file names and can be up to three characters long. X, Y, S, and T are simple variables and Z(2) and V(5) are subscripted references to arrays. The GET statement causes values to be read from the specified input file, beginning at the current file position, and assigned to the variable references specified in the GET statement.

GOSUB   50   GOSUB 100

50 is the statement number. 100 is the number of a statement to which control is transferred.

COMPUTED GO TO   110   GO TO 10, 20, 30 ON S

110 is the statement number. Control is transferred to one of the statement numbers 10, 20, or 30, depending on the value of S. If S = 1, the branch will GO TO statement number 10; if S = 2, it will branch to statement 20; and if S = 3, it will branch to statement 30. S does not have to be a single variable. That position can be occupied by an entire arithmetic expression.

SIMPLE GO TO   37   GO TO 50

37 is that statement number. Control is unconditionally transferred to statement 50.

IF   670   IF A + B > C THEN 71
                 34   IF S1 <= 37.2 GO TO 100

The IF statement tests a relational expression, and if the relation is true, control is transferred to the specified statement number; if the relation is false, the next logically executable statement is executed. 670 and 34 are statement numbers. A + B > C and S1 <= 37.2 are the relations tested. Either THEN or GO TO can be used to signify which statements will be branched to.

IMAGE   30   :THE ANSWER IS ####
        40   :THE BALANCE FOR #### IS $#####.##

The IMAGE statement is used in conjunction with the PRINT USING statement and specifies the format that the print line will have. 30 and 40 are line numbers followed by a blank and then a colon. Immediately following can be either alphabetic characters to form words or # to designate places for defined output.

INPUT   10   INPUT X, Y, Z(4)

The INPUT statement allows the user to assign values to variables from the terminal during execution. 10 is the statement number. X, Y are simple variables and Z(4) is a subscripted array variable.

LET   10   LET X(3), Y, Z = 105
      20   LET B = A(5)/16.5
      30   LET D$, B$ = J$

The LET statement evaluates an expression and assigns it to one or more variables. The word LET can often be omitted depending upon the system in use.

NEXT   30   FOR I = 1 TO 5 STEP 1
       40   NEXT I

The NEXT statement marks the physical end for a FOR-NEXT loop. The variable which appears in the NEXT statement must be the same as that in the FOR statement, in this example I.

PAUSE   80   PAUSE

The PAUSE statement causes program execution to halt and the following message to be printed at the terminal: "PAUSE AT LINE 80"

PRINT   10   PRINT 'GO HOME'; A$
        36   PRINT A, B$; D(3,4), B(6)
        80   PRINT A$(4), C5

The PRINT statement causes the values of the specified arithmetic and character expressions to be printed at the terminal. 10, 36, 80 are line numbers. 'GO HOME' is an alphabetic label. A and C5 are simple arithmetic variables. D(3,4) and B(6) are elements of arithmetic arrays. A$ and B$ are character variables, and A$(4) is an element of a character array.

PRINT USING   30   PRINT USING 31, A, B
                  31   :NUMBER ## WEIGHS ### POUNDS

The PRINT USING statement is used in conjunction with an IMAGE statement to print values. 31 in the PRINT USING statement refers to the number of the IMAGE statement; 'A' will be printed according to ## following the word NUMBER and 'B' will be printed according to ### following the word WEIGHS in the IMAGE statement.

PUT   PUT 'ABC', X, Y, Z

The PUT statement causes values to be put in a specified file. 'ABC' is a file name and the values of variables X, Y, and Z are to be written there.

READ   10   READ A, B, C, B$
                  15   READ X(4), C1, Z9

The READ statement specifies variables which are supplied with values in data statements. A, B, C, X(4), C1, and Z9 will be assigned alphabetic characters.

REM   10   REM THIS IS PROBLEM #20.

The REM statement adds a comment to a program listing and in no way affects program execution.

RESET   60   RESET 'ABC'

The RESET statement causes the specified file or files to be repositioned to the beginning. A subsequent GET or PUT statement will refer to the first item in the file.

RESTORE   20   RESTORE

The RESTORE statement causes the next READ statement to begin reading at the first item in the first data statement in the program.

RETURN   50   RETURN

The RETURN statement is used in conjunction with the GOSUB statement. It causes control to be transferred to the next logically executable statement following the last active GOSUB statement.

STOP   325   STOP

The STOP statement terminates program execution.

ARRAY OPERATIONS

| SIMPLE MAT ASSIGNMENT | 10   DIM B(15), A(15) |
| | 20   MAT A = B |

This statement assigns the members of one array to another array. The two arrays must have the same dimensions.

| MATRIX ADDITION | 10   DIM A(5,5), B(5,5),C(5,5) |
| | 45   MAT C = A + B |

This statement assigns the sum of the members of two arrays to the members of a third array. The specified arrays must have identical dimensions.

| MATRIX SUBTRACTION | 10   DIM X(3,3), Y(3,3),Z(3,3) |
| | 26   MAT X = Y − Z |

This statement assigns the difference of the members of two arrays to the members of a third array. The specified arrays must have identical dimensions.

| MATRIX MULTIPLICATION | 10   DIM A(2,3), B(3,4), C(2,4) |
| | 15   MAT C = A * B |

This statement multiplies two arrays and assigns the product to a third. Note: The number of rows in matrix C equals the number of rows in matrix A, and the number of columns in matrix C equals the number of rows in matrix B.

| SCALAR-MATRIX MULTIPLICATION | 10   DIM A(2,2), B(2,2) |
| | 30   MAT B = (4) * A |

This statement causes one array to be multiplied by an expression and then assigns the result to the corresponding members of a second array. In this example, the members of B are simply equal to the members of A multiplied by 4.

| MAT PUT | 80   MAT PUT 'ABC', X, Y, Z |

This statement causes the specified array to be written on the output file without referring to each member individually, 'ABC' is the file name and X, Y, Z are names of arrays.

| MAT READ | 10   DIM S(10), T(3,5) |
| | 50   MAT READ S, T(3,3) |

This statement is used in conjunction with the DATA statement. It causes arithmetic data to be read into specified arrays without referring to each member individually. If an array name is followed by dimension specifications in a MAT READ statement the matrix is redimensioned. Here T(3,3) redimensions T to a 3 by 3 matrix from a 3 by 5 matrix in line 10.

ZER function   10   DIM X(2,2)
                                20   MAT X = ZER(3,3)

This statement assigns the value zero to all members of the specified array. The specified array can be redimensioned in the ZER statement. Here, it is redimensioned to a 3 by 3 matrix.

MAT GET   40   MAT GET 'ABC', A(10), Z(2,2)

This statement allows arithmetic data to be read into specific arrays from specific files without referring to each member individually. 'ABC' is the file name, and A(10), Z(2,2) are array names and dimensions.

MAT INPUT   10   DIM A(2,2), B(2,2), C(2,2), D(5,5)
                         20   MAT INPUT A, B, C5, D(2,2)

This statement allows the user to assign values to an array during execution without referring to each array member individually. A matrix can be redimensioned in the input statement as D is here.

MAT PRINT   60   MAT PRINT A, B, X

This statement causes each member of the specified array to be printed at the terminal.

MAT PRINT USING   10   DIM A (4,3)
                         20   : ### ##.# ##.#
                         30   MAT PRINT USING 20, A

This statement and its associated IMAGE statement allow the user to have the values of all the members of the array printed in a format of his own choosing, without having to specify each member individually. Here, each row of A is printed according to the format set in line 20.

CON function   20   DIM A(2,2)
                         25   MAT A = CON(3,3)

This statement assigns the value 1 to all members of the specified array. The dimensions following CON, here (3,3), if present, specify redimensioning. Now A is redimensioned as a 3 by 3 matrix.

IDN function   10   DIM X(3,3)
                         20   MAT X = IDN(4,4)

This statement causes the specified array to assume the form of an identity matrix; it will contain ones along the diagonal and zeros elsewhere. The array must be square and if IDN is followed by different dimension specifications, the matrix will be redimensioned.

MATRIX INVERSION   10   DIM A(3,3), B(3,3)
                                    20   MAT B = INV(A)

This statement causes an array to be assigned the mathematical inverse of another array. The arrays must be square and have equal dimensions. Multiplication of a matrix and its inverse will always equal an identity matrix.

TRANSPOSE OF A MATRIX   10   DIM X(2,3), Y(3,2)
                                    20   MAT Y = TRN(X)

This statement causes one array to be replaced by the matrix TRANSPOSE of another array. Note: The number of rows in X equals the number of columns in Y and the number of columns in X equals the number of rows in Y.

FUNCTIONS IN BASIC

FUNCTION	RESULT
ABS(x)	Absolute value of x
ACS(x)	Arccosine (in radians) of x
ASN(x)	Arcsine (in radians) of x
ATN(x)	Arctangent (in radians) of x
COS(x)	Cosine of x radians
COT(x)	Cotangent of x radians
CSC(x)	Cosecant of x radians
DEG(x)	Number of degrees in x radians
DET(x)	Determinant of an arithmetic array x (x must be a square array)
EXP(x)	Natural exponential of x
HCS(x)	Hyperbolic cosine of x radians
HSN(x)	Hyperbolic sine of x radians
HTN(x)	Hyperbolic tangent of x radians
INT(x)	Integer part of x
LGT(x)	Logarithm of x to the base 10
LOG(x)	Logarithm of x to the base e
LTW(x)	Logarithm of x to the base 2
RAD(x)	Number of radians in x degrees
RND [(x)]	Random number between 0 and 1
SEC(x)	Secant of x radians
SGN(x)	Sign of x (−1, 0, or 1)
SIN(x)	Sine of x radians
SQR(x)	Square root of x
TAN(x)	Tangent of x radians

SAMPLE SYSTEM COMMANDS USING A TIME SHARING SYSTEM[1]

COMMAND	FUNCTION
DELETE	Used to delete a library member; used to delete one or more lines from the current program or text collection.
EDIT	Used for the creation or modification of programs or text collection.
LIST	Used to display the contents of the current collection; used in the test sub-mode to display one or more variables and their values.
LISTCAT	Lists the name of each member of your library.
LOGOFF	Ends a terminal session.
LOGON	Initiates a terminal session. It must be the first command you use. There is no mode in effect when you use it.
MERGE	Inserts one or more lines obtained from a collection in your library into the current collection.
RENAME	Renames a library member.
RENUM	Renumbers all or part of the current program or text collection.
RUN	Executes the current program in short- or long-form arithmetic; if TEST is specified, it initiates the test submode.
SAVE	Saves the current program or text collection.
TRACE	Establishes traces for variables, branch points, files, and intrinsic functions, so that you will be aware of program changes when they occur.

[1]Remember: These are only examples of system commands. Look up the commands for your system in your systems manual.

appendix
D

A
short
history
of
computers

Devices for storing numbers and calculating sums were logical predecessors of the modern computer. Even before mechanical systems were in use, it was necessary to keep records. For example, herdsmen needed to know how many sheep they had out in the pasture. When a herdsman let his sheep out of a pen for the day, he would put one stone on a board for each sheep leaving the pen. Then, at the end of the day, when the sheep were returned to the pen, as each sheep entered the pen, a stone would be removed from the board. Thus, when all the stones were removed from the counter board, the herdsman would know that all the sheep were back in the pen. The word calculate comes from the latin word calculus, meaning a stone.

Figure D.1.

An early mechanical device for counting and calculating is the abacus. Developed in Asia about 2000 years ago, and used by Greeks and Romans, it is still widely used in the Orient today. The abacus consists of beads strung on parallel wires. The beads are moved manually to perform addition and subtraction on numbers as large as 999,999.

In the early 1600s, John Napier invented the logarithm, which allows multiplication to be performed by addition. This development, refined by Edmund Gunter, led to the development in 1654 of the first slide rule by Robert Bissaker. This mechanical calculating aid is still quite popular with engineers.

During the mid-seventeenth century, the French mathematician Blaise Pascal invented a mechanical wheel calculator for adding coins. The calculator had wheels, each with 10 positions, each position representing a digit from 0 to 9. Numbers were added by rotating the wheels the appropriate number of positions. There were gears inside the box so that when a wheel was rotated from 9 to 0, the wheel to its left would be increased by 1. Near the end of the seventeenth century Leibnitz advanced Pascal's rotary wheel concept and built a calculator that could multiply and divide directly, as well as add and subtract. The machine was based on the principle of repeated addition. For example, by adding 18 five times, the product of 18 times 5 was achieved. Unfortunately, the construction of Leibnitz's machine left something to be desired, and thus the accuracy of the machine was not always reliable.

In the early 1800s, a Frenchman named Joseph Jacquard developed a method of storing on punched cards designs for intricate fabrics. The punched cards were arranged in order and formed a program for a loom to weave a pattern. Thus, a stack of program cards could be fed through a loom, and the pattern of punches on the cards could mechanically control the pattern of weaving on the fabric. The punched card became an appealing way to store information.

At about the same time a mathematics professor in Cambridge, England, Charles Babbage, developed a machine he called a Difference Engine. The machine was to use rotating gears to perform arithmetic operations without human intervention. The Difference Engine was designed to evaluate polynomials. A refinement of the Difference Engine, called the Analytical Engine, was designed to calculate arithmetic operations, store results, and then perform other calculations. To the great frustration of Babbage, the Analytic Engine could not be built because of engineering difficulties.

While working for the U.S. Census Bureau during the 1880s, Dr. Herman Hollerith was dismayed by the fact that it took eight years to process the data from the 1880 census. If techniques of processing the data

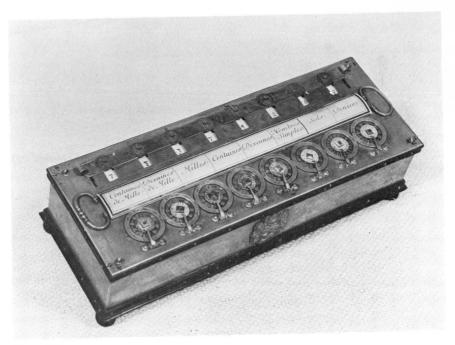

Figure D.2.

Figure D.3.

were not changed, the data from the 1890 census would probably not be compiled before the 1900 census began. Therefore Dr. Hollerith decided to mechanize the process. He had the data put on punched cards and developed a mechanical tabulating machine that could read the cards and sort them. With the use of Hollerith's tabulating machine, the results of the 1890 census were available in less than three years. Dr. Hollerith then left the Census Bureau to start his own company, the Tabulating Machine Company. This company became part of International Business Machines.

John Powers succeeded Hollerith at the Census Bureau, where he refined the tabulating machine. Then in 1911, Powers left to form Powers Accounting Machines which later became part of Sperry Rand Corporation, another large computer maker.

In 1937, Howard Aiken at Harvard University was extending the work on mechanical calculators and controlled sequences of mathematical operations. Dr. Aiken obtained support from International Business Machines (IBM) and Harvard University and constructed the first computer, completed in 1944. The computer, called Mark I, was electrically powered,

Figure D.4.

Figure D.5.

and while large in size, it was slow and limited compared to modern computers. Because it was not fully electronic, it took Mark I about three seconds to multiply two 10-digit numbers. Nevertheless, it was a real breakthrough in computing machinery.

The first fully electronic computer was built at the University of Pennsylvania by Prof. John Eckert and graduate student J. Presper Mauchly. The machine, called ENIAC (Electronic Numerical Integrator And Computer), was operational in 1945 and was 1000 times faster than the Mark I.

The great mathematician John von Neumann introduced the storage of instructions in the computer in numerical form. Previously, instructions were coded externally and modified only by external operations. Von Neumann also introduced the idea of flowcharting instructions and promoted the use of binary arithmetic in computers.

The first computer to apply the numerically stored program concept fully was the EDSAC, built at Cambridge University in 1949. In 1950, Remington Rand bought the Eckert-Mauchly Computer Corporation, which was already constructing a large computer. This computer, known as UNIVAC-I, became the first commercially marketed computer in 1954. UNIVAC-I was a stored-program computer with about 5000 vacuum tubes. Forty-eight UNIVAC-I machines were built, with the first one going, appropriately, to the Census Bureau.

IBM developed many machines in the mid-1950s, starting with the IBM-701 for the military in 1953, then the commercially available IBM-650 and IBM-704 in 1955.

In 1959, IBM and RCA independently introduced the second-generation computers—using transistors or solid state technology, which had been invented in 1948. The second-generation computers were batch oriented, with tape as the auxiliary storage medium.

With the development of monolithic integrated circuits, or silicon chips, entire circuits could be made smaller than a paper clip. In 1964 IBM introduced System 360, which used this new technology for more powerful, faster computers that became part of the third generation of computers. These computers could utilize time sharing and could process several jobs simultaneously.

The IBM-370 series may be a representative of the fourth generation of computers, depending on your definitions. The technology is more advanced, with large-scale integrated circuits and much greater flexibility in computer usage. Greater speed, lower costs, and more computing power are available. The changes in the industry in the 1970s have come so quickly, however, it is not easy to identify each new generation of computers.

Index

Index